Tariq Rahman

Interpretations of Jihad in South Asia

Tariq Rahman

Interpretations of Jihad in South Asia

An Intellectual History

2nd, revised edition

DE GRUYTER

ISBN 978-3-11-055039-9
e-ISBN (PDF) 978-3-11-071698-6
e-ISBN (EPUB) 978-3-11-071700-6

Library of Congress Control Number: 2020913935

Bibliographic Information published by the Deutsche Nationalbibliothek
The Deutsche Nationalbibliothek lists this publication in the Deutsche Nationalbibliografie; Detailed bibliographic data are available in the Internet at http://dnb.dnb.de.

Cover image: Intérieur de la mosquée Wazir Khan à Lahore (vallée du Pendjab, Pakistan), vers 1875, bpk / Coll. Gérard Lévy / adoc-photos
Printing and binding: CPI books GmbH, Leck

www.degruyter.com

To the Bodleian and other libraries of the University of Oxford
where this book was researched
and my wife Hana who encouraged me to write it.

Contents

Preface and Acknowledgements — IX

Abbreviations — XV

Translation and Transliteration — XVII

1 Introduction — 1

2 Interpretation of the Qur'an and the Hadith — 25
- Lexis and Semantics — **32**
- Abrogation as an Interpretive Device — **40**
- Explanation by Citing Occasions of Revelation — **44**
- Specification — **45**
- Privileging Principles over Particulars — **47**
- The Interpretation of Hadith — **49**

3 Jihad in Transition — 62
- Hadith Literature — **69**
- Jihad in the Collections of Hadith — **73**
- Exegeses of the Qur'an — **76**
- Books on Jihad — **83**

4 Jihad and the Family of Shāh Walīullāh — 89

5 Colonial Modernists — 112

6 Jihad as Anti-Colonial Resistance: Emerging Trends — 134

7 The Age of Mawdūdī — 167

8 Radical Imports — 193

9 Pakistani Radicals — 211

10 Refuting the Radicals — 232

11 Conclusion — 248

Annexure A: War–related Verses in the Qur'an — 264

Annexure B — 278
Al-Baqarah 2 (The Cow) — **278**
Al-Anfāl 8 (Spoils of War) — **278**
Al-Tawbah 9 — **278**
Al-Mumtaḥina 60 (She that is to be examined) — **279**

Annexure C — 280
Aḥādīth — **280**

Glossary — 282

Bibliography — 283
1 Primary Sources — **283**
1.1. The Qur'an and its Exegeses — **283**
1.2 The Hadith — **284**
1.3 Edicts (fatāwā) — **285**
1.4 Manuscripts and Recordings (all these sources are from the Oriental and India Office Collection, the British Library, unless otherwise indicated) — **286**
2 Other Sources — **286**

Index — 307

Preface and Acknowledgements

It was a hot and humid summer day in July 2007 and I was in Islamabad attending a seminar at a hotel. Soon after I left I heard the news that there had been an explosion on the very road I always travelled by. Fifty lay dead and at least a hundred, groaning with pain and covered with blood, desperately pleaded for beds in hospitals. The militants who claimed responsibility for it said it was in revenge for the attack on the Red Mosque (Lal Masjid) near the hotel. Then, in the same summer, my daughter Tania used the main Mall Road of Rawalpindi minutes before the Surgeon-General of the army was killed on it by a suicide bomber. Meanwhile ordinary Pakistani-Americans—people who had thought themselves to be Americans earlier—were picked up as 'Moozlims' (Muslims) and assaulted verbally in the United States of which I and my family had lovely, nostalgic memories from our stay on a senior Fulbright fellowship at the University of Texas at Austin and again as the first incumbent of the Pakistan chair at the University of California, Berkeley. Bad news was also coming from my daughter's adopted country after marriage, the country she was born in, Britain. It was my own favourite country too since my student days in the eighties. What was happening to the world while I wrote on the history of languages? At last, in early 2014 I decided that I would use the historian's tools to find out about Islamic militancy, i.e militancy using the name of Islam, in Pakistan.

But after reading the secondary sources I discovered that there was little I could say about it which had not been covered. The only original contribution I could think of was a profile of the militants but they were in military custody and access to them was impossible. Meanwhile, I had already written a research proposal and sent it to the Oxford Centre for Islamic Studies in November of that year. I did not expect it to be accepted for an award of a paid fellowship but, much to my surprise, it was. Now I would have to go but, instead of working on this book, I would work on an alternative history of Pakistan of which militancy would be a chapter. I told my wife Hana that we would have a holiday in Oxford this time since I had no serious plan of research.

> 'This you have never done in all your life. You will find something which will keep you in the Bodleian like the last time'.
>
> 'The last time I was doing serious work. Trust me, it will be a holiday with some pleasure reading this time'.
>
> 'We will see. I bet the pleasure reading will lead to obsession like it always has'.
>
> 'We will see', I riposted.

https://doi.org/10.1515/9783110716986-001

In the spring of 2015 we went for a walk in one of Lahore's lovely parks and Hana made me listen to a TEDTalk of a scholar who had studied some aspect of Islam by placing four translations of the Qur'an in front and reading every verse with its meanings. That gave me an idea—why could I not do the same for the concept of jihad? I came home all atremble with excitement and so began a phase of intensive study of jihad. Luckily, just at that time, a lawyer with great interest in Persian and Arabic, Tausif ul Hasnain, volunteered to teach me Arabic. And so the hot gruelling summer of 2015 was spent in memorizing Arabic verb forms and reading the Qur'an and the hadith. Of course, Hana won the bet about Oxford. The Michaelmas term of 2015, in which we had Professor Barbara Harriss-White's lovely house in Summer Town at our disposal, was spent in the Bodleian. So were the summers of 2016 and 2017 when I was a visiting fellow of Wolfson College, Oxford, thanks again to Barbara and Dr. Matthew McCartney, also a fellow of Wolfson's, who had recommended my name for the honour. In between I worked as hard as any diligent Ph.D. student to acquaint myself with a new subject. By the September of 2017, the first draft of the book was ready.

My debt is to so many people who made the book possible that it would be invidious to think that a few words of thanks will do. They will not– but words are all I have, so let me begin. First, to my wife and companion Hana who encouraged me to write and continue writing when I was in despair because of some disturbing writings I had to read, and who never grudged me the money I needed for the research material and two trips to Oxford (2016 and 2017). These, after all, were years of financial constraints since our son, Fahad, was being supported by us financially in his studies at Oxford University.

Let me also thank other members of my family, my son-in-law Atif Kaudri (Tania's husband) and his family, who very generously offered me hospitality at their home in Chesham during our trips. Our 2017 stay is especially memorable since we stayed first in Wolfson College and enjoyed the therapeutic view of the pond and the geese waddling all over the lawns. And then we stayed in Atif and Tania's flat in Headington, Oxford, which was a rare pleasure. I also take this opportunity to thank our son Fahad Rahman not only for his patience in getting books scanned for me and lodging us in his room at Wolfson overlooking the lovely pond, but also encouraging me from time to time and giving laconic yet insightful comments about progressive Muslims. I would also like to thank my nephew Umair Jaffar for having helped me with the final editing. But for him the computers would have stumped me. I would also like to thank Yasser Khan, a doctoral student at Oxford, who helped me in making the index in July 2018.

I have mentioned Barbara above but I would like to thank her again for her various kindnesses: first, for giving us her house to live in; then for recommending me for fellowships and, above all, for unfailing courtesy and support throughout my work. I could hardly have benefited from the invaluable resources in the Bodleian but for the Islamic Centre and her. I also thank my friend, Dr. Chandramohan, who was always there to offer company and hospitality during all my visits.

I would also like to thank Dr Farhan Nizami and the fellows of the Oxford Centre for Islamic Studies, especially Dr Adeel Malik and Dr Muhammad Talib, for always being kind to me and giving me access to their library. The Centre also enabled me to attend a basic course in Arabic which was of immense benefit. The library staff at the Oriental Institute, where I used to be part of the furniture during my visits, deserves my thanks for their help as do the librarians of the British Library who must have wondered at my lack of skill in handling computers and other gadgets. While on the subject of libraries, let me thank Muhammad Naeem, Librarian of the Government College University Library in Lahore, for having provided research material even if he had to buy it from the market. I also thank the vice chancellor of GCU, Dr Hassan Shah, who kindly allowed me to use this library. Likewise, the library of the Lahore University of Management Sciences (LUMS) also had some rare material which I was able to use thanks to the librarian and my friends Dr Mohammad Waseem, Dr Yunas Samad, and Ateeb Gul. My special thanks go to Ateeb because had he not drawn my attention to Shahab Ahmed's book called *What is Islam?* (2016) I would have missed an important study about Islam. Our own library at the Beaconhouse National University did not initially have any of the books I required but I am grateful to the vice chancellor, Shahid Hafeez Kardar, for having purchased some especially for me. Our library staff, especially Awais Nawaz, also deserves my gratitude for having procured books from other libraries as a personal favour. My friends, Drs Tahir Kamran and Mohammad Waseem, also gave me whatever material I asked for and I thank them for it. I am very grateful to another friend, a well-known German professor of Islamic Studies, Professor Jamal Malik, who very kindly sent me digital copies of his works. Here I also want to express my gratitude to my brother, Ahmad Sami, and sister, Tayyaba Azam, for having lent me some exegeses of the Qur'an in their possession. I especially want to thank Dr Ayesha Siddiqa for first bringing to my notice and then lending me Samina Yasmeen's and Christine Fair's studies about the publications of the Lashkar-e-Tayyaba (LeT) later renamed Jama 'at ud Dawa (JUD). These were really invaluable. I also want to thank Afzal Khan whose Ph.D.thesis on two Pakistani militant scholars, which was supervised by Dr Jamal Malik at the University of Erfurt, was very useful for me.

One of the important things for venturing into a field not your own by training is that one should have academic guidance. I was very lucky to have been helped by two excellent scholars of Islamic studies, Dr Ali Usman Qasmi and Asif Iftikhar, both members of the faculty at LUMS. They guided me into the discipline of Islamic studies, pointed out the sources to consult and even gave me research material. Ali began by giving me Sir Sayyid's exegesis and Asif Iftikhar let me use his copy of the *Fatāwā-e-'Alamgīrī*. The latter proved to be such an encyclopedia of the Qur'an that he sometimes gave me the name of the chapter and verse even if all I could offer him was a few words from it. Indeed, they acted as a good supervisor should towards a doctoral student. I can hardly thank them in words for their help and kindness. I especially derived much guidance from Asif Iftikhar's deep knowledge of Arabic for which I am really indebted to him.

I have already mentioned one of my sources for funding, the Oxford Centre for Islamic Studies, which gave me a research fellowship worth GBP 4,000 in the Michaelmas term of 2015. The other one is Ameena Sayyid, Managing Director of the Oxford University Press (OUP) in Pakistan, whom I mention since publishers typically do not fund authors, especially when the author intends to publish with another publisher. I met her at a dinner in Lahore and asked her if she could help with accommodation in Oxford. She could not, but she volunteered a sum of PKR 400,000 (GBP 1= Rs 137 in 2016) to defray part of my expenses for travel and stay. Thereupon I told her that I was negotiating with a European publisher and was not even sure if the rights for Pakistan would be given to OUP. She told me to take the money and give her some other book (I had two in mind) at some uncertain time in the future. To this I agreed and the money, ostensibly for other books, was very helpful for me. The rest of the money for this project came from our savings for which, as always, I thank my wife.

My negotiations with my European publisher, Walter de Gruyter, were successful, and they very kindly even gave the rights for publication in Pakistan to OUP Pakistan. I thank Dr Sophie Wagenhofer who oversaw the whole project. I am much impressed by the de Gruyter team, especially with Dr Eva Frantz, who made much effort to improve the book in every respect and showed excellent taste in selecting the picture on its cover. I also thank Katrin Mittman for her efforts to promote the book and Sabina Dabrowski and her colleagues in the production department for their proofreading and other work. Also, I take this opportunity to thank all those who performed the thousand and one little tasks to bring this finished product in your hands. In Pakistan I was helped in various ways—proofreading, making the bibliography, and charts etc.—by my research assistants and secretaries, Fatima Hasan and Iram Farooq. Iram also helped with preparing the index and the glossary and I am really grateful to her for actually reading this book from cover to cover. I also thank our IT experts, Bilal and Umar Shahid, for dealing with the erratic computers. The book was proofread by a professional editor, Ateeb Gul, who has worked for the Oxford University Press (Pakistan) and now serves as an editor and faculty member at LUMS. With his expertise in editing, academic English and transliteration from Arabic and

Urdu, he was the most suitable editor I could wish for. But for him the book would offend the perfectionist beyond measure. If mistakes still remain, and I am sure they do, I take full responsibility for them.

Tariq Rahman Lahore, Pakistan.
March 2018

Abbreviations

Quotations from the Qur'an will be according to convention, i.e the number of the chapter (*surah*) followed by the number of the verse (*aya*) as given in annexures A and B.

Other abbreviations (and simplified spellings) include:

BL	British Library, London.
ISI	Inter Services Intelligence Directorate (Pakistan).
ISIS	Islamic State of Iraq and Syria. Also known as IS or Daesh.
Jamat	Abbreviated form of *Jamā'at-e-Islāmī.*
Jamiat	Abbreviated form of *Jam'īyyat-e-Ṭulabā'* (the association of Students which is a student wing of the Jamat).
JUD	*Jamā'at ud Dā'wah* (normally written Jamat ut Dawa).
KP	Khyber Pakhtūnkhwa. New name for the North-West Frontier Province (NWFP).
LeJ	*Lashkar-e-Jhangwī.*
LeT	*Lashkar-e-Ṭayyabah* (normally written as Tayyaba). Also, LT.
Mss. Eur	Manuscript European followed by numbers and shelf marks of documents in the OIOC (see below).
NWFP	North-West Frontier Province (of Pakistan). Now called Khyber Pakhtūnkhwa.
OIOC	Oriental and India Office Collections, British Library, London.
PBUH	Peace Be Upon Him (used by Muslims after the name of the Prophet of Islam. Such usage is assumed in keeping with Muslim norms wherever he is mentioned).
SP	*Sipāh-e-Ṣaḥābah* (it also stands for Superintendent of the Police, as the context will clarify).

https://doi.org/10.1515/9783110716986-002

Translation and Transliteration

Translation of Arabic and Persian texts in English is from standard works the authors of which have been identified. All translations from Urdu and Persian are by the present writer unless otherwise indicated.

Texts from Near Eastern and South Asian languages—Arabic, Persian, and Urdu—have been transliterated using the symbols given below. *Hamzah*, however, has not generally been transliterated.

Names of contemporary writers who write in English are used as they spell them. Other South Asian names have, however, been transliterated. To avoid unnecessary complication, familiar words and names of people and places in South Asia as well as Arabic names which are often used in the press have been written as they normally appear in books on South Asian studies in the notes and the bibliography. This facilitates referring to them in the literature and library catalogues. To facilitate the reader, names of important people and concepts have been transliterated in the index. Certain words in Arabic and other languages ordinarily used in English and found in dictionaries have not been transliterated. For instance, jihad (*jihād*), hadith (*ḥadīth*), madrasah (*madrasah*), and Qur'an (Qur'ān). Words in direct quotations are written as originally spelled.

Symbols Used for Arabic

Letter	Name	IPA	Modified ALA-LC (American Library Association and the Library of Congress) Arabic	
ء	Hamzah	ʔ	'	
ب	bā'	b	B	b
ت	tā'	t	T	
ث	thā'	θ	Th	
ج	jīm	d͡ʒ~g~ʒ	J	
ح	ḥā'	ħ	Ḥ	ḥ
خ	khā'	x	Kh	kh
د	Dāl	d	D	d
ذ	dhāl	ð	Dh	dh
ر	rā'	r	R	r

https://doi.org/10.1515/9783110716986-003

Symbols Used for Arabic *(Continued)*

Letter	Name	IPA	Modified ALA-LC (American Library Association and the Library of Congress) Arabic	
ز	zāy	z	Z	z
س	sīn	s	S	s
ش	shīn	ʃ	Sh	sh
ص	ṣuād	sˤ	Ṣ	ṣ
ض	ḍuād	dˤ	Ḍ	ḍ
ط	ṭā’	tˤ	Ṭ	ṭ
ظ	ẓā’	ðˤ~zˤ	Ẓ	ẓ
ع	‘ayn	ʕ	‘	
غ	ghayn	ɣ	Gh	gh
ف	fā’	f	F	f
ق	qāf	q	Q	q
ك	kāf	k	K	k
ل	lām	l	L	l
م	mīm	m	M	m
ن	nūn	n	N	n
ه	hā’	h	H	h
و	wāw	w, uː	W;Ū	w; ū
ي	yā’	j, iː	Y;Ī	y; ī
آ	alif mad-dah	ʔaː	Ā	ā
ال	alif lām	Nil	Al-	al-

Symbols used for Persian

Same as Arabic except the following graphemes in Persian not shared with Arabic.

Persian Letter	IPA	Modified ALA-LC (American Library Association and the Library of Congress) Persian	
پ	/p/	P	p
چ	/tʃ/	Ch	ch
ژ	/ʒ/	Zh	zh

Symbols used for Urdu

ڑ	ɽ	Ṛ	ṛ
ڑھ	ɽh	Ṛh	ṛh
ڈ	ḓ	Ḓ	ḓ
ڈھ	ḓh	Ḓh	ḓh
ٹ	ṱ	Ṱ	ṱ
ٹھ	ṱh	Ṱh	ṱh
تھ	<u>th</u>	<u>Th</u>	

/ē /as in Urdu/pēt/=stomach or /lōg/ = people.
/ẽ/ nasalised).

1 Introduction

Since the attacks of September 11, 2011 (popularly referred to as 9/11), the term 'jihad' has become a household word. After every attack on targets in the Western world, be it the underground of London, Madrid, or Paris, or the 2016 March attacks in Brussels, Muslims, as well as people in the West who want good relations with them, insist that jihad means the quest for moral improvement and that, if one kind of jihad (the lesser one) does mean fighting, it is only in self-defence which is an internationally recognised right of all nations and peoples. Their antagonists dismiss these claims, arguing that jihad in practice as well as theory actually refers to aggressive warfare against non-Muslims. Among Muslims too, in an ironic twist, there are supporters of that argument. Indeed, Islamist militants have written tracts calling for unending war against the West (whom they call 'crusaders') and their supporters, i.e. rulers of Muslim countries. These are no mere theoretical concerns; these are matters of life and death. Hence, not only out of intellectual curiosity but also for practical reasons of policy-making, it is imperative that the interpretations of jihad should be understood for the world as a whole and, particularly, for flashpoints in it. And one of these flashpoints, incidentally one in which the author happens to live, is Pakistan. Pakistan has been at the centre of violent *jihādī* activities for more than a decade. Afghanistan has been fighting a series of wars, which have been called jihad, for thirty years, and India has been the brunt of attacks by groups claiming to be *jihādī* in the last few years.

Giving precise definitions of the various interpretations of Islam is a difficult undertaking. However, some guidelines for the usage of terms which will appear in this work are necessary. Here the term *radical Islamists* is used for people or groups who believe it is justified to use violence to create an Islamic state or fight 'Western' powers which, in their perception, exploit Muslims or prevent Islam from gaining political ascendancy over the world. The terms *jihādī*s and *Islamist militants* are used interchangeably for groups actually using violent means as opposed to merely approving of such use. Other studies, generally by political scientists, often use the term, Islamism, for the terms given above. Islamism is defined by Volpi in his introduction to 'political Islam' as 'the political dynamics generated by the activities of those people who believe that Islam as a body of faith has something crucial to say about how society should be organized, and who seek to implement this idea as a matter of priority'.[1] Political Islam may not always lead to violence but sometimes it does. Hence the need for pre-

1 Volpi 2011 a: 1.

https://doi.org/10.1515/9783110716986-004

cise terms such as the ones used above for groups choosing to apply their ideas to change the world by violence in the name of Islam. Other terms used at places in this study are *salafism* and Wahhābism (or Wahabism as it is called in the popular press). The first is based on following the way of life of the pious early Muslims. The second is based on the thought of the 18th century religious reformer Muḥammad Ibn 'Abd al-Wahhāb (1703–91) who preached a return to 'original' Islam since innovations– like mysticism and asking for the intercession of saints or worshipping at their tombs– he said, were akin to idolatry. Those who interpret the canonical sources literally are often labelled in the press as *fundamentalists* but this usage is disputed by Muslims. Labels like *neo-fundamentalists* and *moderate Islamists* are also used in the literature but remain imprecise and will, therefore, be avoided in this study. It is, however, wise to remember that these categories are neither immutable nor hermetic.[2] Not only strict practitioners of the faith and radical Islamists shade into one another, but, in fact, all groups do. Indeed, it is true to say that 'actual Islamist groups do not necessarily fall neatly into either of these ideal-type categories'. Moreover, 'movements frequently change their identity over time, becoming more radicalized or more "mainstream"'.[3] But our interest is in the ideas of those who believe in initiating wars, attacks, and armed insurrections with reference to 'Islamic referents—terms, symbols and events taken from the Islamic tradition'.[4] And this is because some of this kind of thought has influenced Pakistan in recent years. While we are not concerned with finding the causes or cures of radical Islamist thought or militancy, we are interested in tracing out the intellectual history of this interpretation in South Asia. For the purposes of this study, the term South Asia refers primarily to the Urdu-using part of what used to be British

2 The following categorisation of Muslim ideological groups is based on a number of sources. William E. Shepard, in his note 1 to his article on 'Islam and Ideology: Towards a Typology' (1987) gives a review of scholarly efforts to identify Weberian 'ideal types' or analytical constructs in order to discuss ideological orientations among Muslims. He himself uses the terms secularism, Islamic modernism, radical modernism, traditionalism, and neo-traditionalism. The first three are 'very high on the scale of "modernity"' and the last two 'vary from them primarily on the scale of "modernity"' (Shepard 1987: 307). Contemporary intellectual successors of classical modernists but different from them are Progressive Muslims who use a 'systematic, thematicoholistic and corroborative, inductive approach to interpretation of Qur'anic content' (Duderija 2011: 148). Other terms which are used are salafism and Wahhābīsm. Still another term used for such interpreters of Islam is Neo-traditional Salafism (NTS) (Duderija 2011: 47). Islamism is a term coined by political scientists for those who use the Islamic idiom to gain political power.

3 Denoeux 2011: 70.

4 Ibid 60.

India and is also called the Subcontinent. Urdu is used for formal writing of the works, mainly exegeses of the Qur'an that we shall be dealing with from the Khyber Pass in present-day Pakistan up to the urban areas of Bengal as well as in the former states of Hyderabad, Rampur, and Bhopal. However, while we shall touch in passing upon the last three areas, our focus will be on the Muslim societies of north India and Pakistan. Essentially it boils down to the question of how jihad came to be interpreted in this manner. This is the central question of this book. But before answering this question let us give a brief introduction to what is available in the canonical sources, the Qur'an and the hadith (pl. *aḥadīth*), about war. Our major objective is to highlight interpretations of texts which are used by radical Islamists to justify their actions.

There are references to war and fighting in 183 verses of the Qur'an. The ones used for analysis in this book (given in Table 1) are given in English translation in Annexure B. The relevant gist of the other Quranic verses mentioned in the text is given parenthetically in the form of brief abstracts. The number given above varies in other counts because some verses which seem to describe historical events dealing with war or conflict are added by some while not by others. The word which is mostly used for warfare is *qitāl* (78 occurrences). It is derived from the root -*q.t.l*- which is translated both as fighting and killing. This number is disputed by others since, for instance, Asma Afsaruddin counts fifty-four 'lexemes from the third verbal form of the root *qtl* '.[5] The *Encyclopaedia of the Qur'an*, however, counts only forty-four occurrences from the -*qtl*-root.[6] This is mainly because one can count only lexemes relating to war as it relates to Islam and Muslims or to anyone. Moreover, one can count the occurrences of the lexemes in verses relating to fighting or all verses. I count words derived from the root -*q.t.l*- referring to all meanings of it: you fight/kill; you are fought with/killed; killing/fighting, and so on. However, words used from the same root in verses not relating to fighting have not been counted. The word jihad, from the root -*j.h.d*- which is translated as effort and endeavour[7] (27 occurrences), does not necessarily refer to fighting. Indeed, five occurrences of the word refer to oaths, leaving us with thirty-six. 'Only ten out of the thirty-six' references to jihad signify or are 'unequivocally interpreted as signifying warfare'.[8] Thus, there are instances when the term Jihad has been used for peaceful struggle in the Qur'an (see Annexure A). For instance, the following verse of *Sūrah al-Furqān* (Q. 25) mentions only struggle (jihad) but not fighting (*qitāl*).

---

5 Afsaruddin 2013: 34.
6 Landa-Tassecron 2003: 38.
7 Ibid 35.
8 Ibid 36.

> So do not believe in the infidels but 'undertake a Great Struggle against them' (*jāhidhum bihī jihādan kabīrā*) (25: 52).

Here the imperative–as explained by most exegetes–is to struggle against the infidels with the Qur'an, which is called the 'great struggle' here.

However, at places it is clear that this struggle will involve the loss of both wealth and life. In such cases the words used are '*wa jahadū bi amwālihim wa anfusihim*' which means 'struggle with your wealth and selves' (9 instances). This has generally been interpreted traditionally as the kind of effort which involves donating one's wealth and enrolling among the fighters. Some of the verses using this word are obviously from a context of ongoing warfare. For instance, *al-Ṣaff* (Q. 61) instructs Muslims to 'strive for God with their wealth and lives' (61: 11); *al-Tawbah* (Q.9), which is about the war of Tabuk, mentions God's appreciation of those who leave their homes and 'struggle with their lives and wealth' (9: 20). And 9: 41, about the same war, begins with 'go forth heavy or light' (*infirū khifāfan wa thiqālan*), and goes on to advocate striving with lives and property (see Annexure A). Fazlur Rahman (1919–1988), an American academic scholar of Islam of Pakistani origin, points out that the term jihad changes meaning from Mecca to Medina. In the former it refers to 'a strong-willed resistance to the pressures of *fitnah* and retaliation in case of violence'. In Medina, however, 'it is often equivalent to *qitāl* or to active war'.[9] Besides, as Michael Bonner brings out, the words *ribāt, ghazwā*, and *ḥarb* have also been used. *Ribāt* refers to the 'pious activity, often related to warfare' as well as a fortified garrison in the face of the enemy. '*Ghazw, ghazwa* and *ghaza*' come from offensive warfare or raids on the enemy; *ḥarb* simply means war and not necessarily one fought for religious reasons.[10] So, out of the terms used for sacred war, the one normally used is that of jihad while it might more appropriately be *qitāl*. After all, as Patricia Crone points out, all classical schools of law do identify such war with reference to *al-Baqarah* (Q. 2)–'prescribed for you is fighting, though it be hateful to you' (2: 216). Here the word used is *qitāl*, not jihad. Indeed, she continues, 'it is a bit of a mystery that jihad came to be the technical term for holy war'.[11]

Besides establishing the frequency of occurrence of derivatives of jihad and *qitāl*, the verses referring to war have been placed in separate categories in a chart given in Annexure A. These are: orders (for war as well as peace, exemption from war and so on); values (praise for the fighters), regulations (for distri-

9 Rahman, F 1980: 110.
10 Bonner 2006: 2.
11 Crone 2004: 363.

bution of booty etc), history (the wars of the Jews under Moses, the battles of the Muslims with the Quraish), and prognostication (that of the domination of Muslims subject to their piety).[12]

The Islamist militants who are fighting today in Pakistan and parts of Afghanistan and India are Sunnis, not Shī'as (Shīites). Thus, we need to be concerned only with the Sunni interpretations of jihad for the purposes of this study. Although all Muslims consider the Qur'an and the hadith as the canonical sources of Islam, both are interpreted to yield discrepant meanings through hermeneutical methods which will be described in the following chapter.

Based on the two foundational sources mentioned above, there are books of jurisprudence which lay down recommended practices towards the treatment of prisoners of war, collection of poll tax (*jizyah*) from non-Muslims vanquished in war, and so on.[13] For instance, 'Ali ibn Ṭāhir al-Sulamī al-Naḥwī's *Kitāb aljihād* is meant to incite his listeners to undertake jihad as this was the period of the Crusades.[14] These traditional sources of law pertaining to jihad, and most importantly, treatises written on the subject in India, will be dealt with in detail in chapter 3.

Let us now turn to how jihad is understood in scholarly literature at present. Books upon books and articles upon articles have been written on this issue.[15] Having already referred to Bonner's comprehensive history of the evolution of jihad in history, let us look at another book of the same kind, namely Richard Bonney's comprehensive historical introduction to it. This book traces out how events called 'jihad' played out in modern history all over the world. The last section presents secondary sources aiming at rehabilitating Islam as a religion which can coexist with other belief-systems.[16] Reuven Firestone makes the point that there were several passages from the foundational texts which a given faction 'would refer to' for 'support of its views'. But then the transition from a pre-Islamic (tribal) worldview to an Islamic one occurred and ideological, rather than kinship-based, fighting emerged as the desiderated norm for sacred

---

12 These categories are flexible and other scholars might change them. Moreover, the category 'orders' are not only about fighting but also refer to other instructions regarding the conduct of war and peace.These categories are different from Rosalind Ward Gwynne's thirty forms of reasoning which she subsumes under ten broad categories: commands, rules, legal arguments, comparisons, contrasts, categorical syllogisms, conditional syllogisms, and disjunctive syllogism (Gwynne 2016).

13 Ṭabarī c. 10 C a.

14 Sulamī c. 12 C in Christie 2015

15 Bonner 2006; Bonney 2004; Firestone 1999; Lewis 2003; Cook 2005; Crone 2004; Kepel 2000; Roy 1999; Kelsay 2007.

16 Bonney 2004.

war.[17] Lewis blames the 'failure of modernity', by which he means bad living standards in the Muslim world, for the rise of radical Islamist thought. He then goes on to pin the blame on the Saudi 'Wahabi' ideology which 'offers a set of themes, slogans, and symbols that are profoundly familiar and therefore effective in mobilizing support and in formulating a critique of what is wrong and a program for putting it right'.[18] Cook explains the concept of jihad in the canonical sources of Islam—Qur'an, hadith, and *Fiqh* (body of law derived from the canonical sources of Islam. Jurisprudence)—concluding that during the first several centuries of Islam 'the interpretation of Jihad was unabashedly aggressive and expansive'.[19] Patricia Crone, in her magisterial work on political thought in medieval Islam, also points out that, among Sunnis at least, 'Muslims were legally obliged to wage holy war against *dār al ḥarb* [the land of war] until it ceased to exist or the world came to an end'.[20] However, she also adds that Muslims were, in theory, supposed to fight only for faith and not for conquest or material gain. This, of course, did not really happen since the conquered people were not forced to convert to Islam. In other words, according to her, it was imperialism after all but one 'linked to a religious *mission civilisatrice* rather than the satisfaction of Arab chauvinism'.[21] This, she adds, was more like British and French 'white man's burden' theory rather than Charlemagne's 'forced conversion of the Saxons'.[22] But Crone's basic hypothesis is that, like other Near Eastern people, the Arabs 'understood their religion in a particularist vein' hence Arab imperialism came to be clothed in terms of ideological universalism. But this conclusion would be contested by Muslims as well as 'apologist' Western scholars.[23]

Kepel presents a history of modern Islam in the broad context of international relations and the rise and ultimate failure of fundamentalist Islam. His main argument is that terrorism is more a consequence of the failure of Islamists to take over any major state and establish their rule there. In short, it is a sign of defeat rather than triumph.[24] This is also Olivier Roy's argument, i.e. that political Islam 'has lost its original impetus'.[25] Others explain militant actions by in-

17 Firestone 1999.
18 Lewis 2003: 102.
19 Cook 2005: 30.
20 Crone 2004: 362.
21 Ibid 369.
22 Ibid 372.
23 Ibid 367.
24 Kepel 2000.
25 Roy 1999: ix.

dividual leaders such as Osama bin Laden (1957–2011), or groups and organisations such as al-Qaeda or ISIS as political Islam, Islamism or Jihadism[26]. One of the early attempts at this kind of explanations is Jason Burke's *Al-Qaeda.*[27] His main argument is that there is a narrative about the sufferings of Muslims as a group from the aggressive and exploitative policies of the 'West', again taken as a hegemonic whole, which is supported by the rulers of Muslim countries who are stooges of the 'West'. Using religious vocabulary promoted by militant intellectuals, the 'West' is called the Crusader and the Muslim rulers who support Western policies are perceived as infidel oppressors for whom the word *tāghūt*—which has several meanings but which is normally used for a tyrant who rebels against God's laws—is used. Angry young rebels seeking an explanation for their own frustrations, resenting the lifestyle of their rulers, or exposed to the images of Muslims facing violence in Chechnya, Bosnia, Palestine, Kashmir, and Myanmar, find bin Laden's idea of a conspiracy against Muslims very convincing. Burke gives examples of Dīdār, a Kurdish would-be suicide bomber, who read 'Abdullāh Yūsuf 'Azzām's (1941–1989) works in a local mosque which made him feel that he should die for the cause of Islam.[28] Likewise, Al-Owhālī, a young Saudi, had also read 'Azzām and the militant magazine *al-Jihād*, before he decided to offer his services to al-Qaeda in Afghanistan. Moreover, when in a training camp there, he kept on receiving *fatwās* (religious edicts: pl. *fatāwā*) which called for violence.[29] Siddique Khan, the British man of Pakistani origin who planned and carried out the London bombings, explained his violent actions with reference to a global war between Islam and the West in which 'violent resistance' is 'an obligation on all believers and "collateral damage" in the form of death of innocents is thus acceptable.'[30] This, as we shall see, is one of the major interpretations of jihad by Islamist militants. Bergen goes into details of al-Qaeda and its founder, Osama bin Laden, providing much useful data from his statements. And the historian Faisal Devji, again referring to international jihad, provides insights into the way ideas of jihad interact with the actions of organizations and individuals. John Kelsay's book, *Arguing the Just War in Islam*[31], in keeping with its title, gives a history of what has been the intellectual pedigree of the 'just war' beginning with medieval jurists but giving most space to the Islamists and modern scholars, both Sunni and Shī'a, who argue

26 Bergen 2001, 2006; Burke 2003; Devji 2005.
27 Burke 2003.
28 Ibid 298.
29 Ibid 169–70.
30 Ibid 289.
31 Kelsay 2007.

that a legitimate response to the 'West' is the kind of asymmetrical war which the world is witnessing.[32]

Among modern Muslim authors there is, for instance, Yūsuf al-Qaraḍāwī (b. 1926) whose treatise on jihad in Arabic, *Fiqh al-jihād*, published in 2009, has been ably summarised in English in a book edited by the Tunisian scholar, Raschid al-Ghannoushi (Rāshid al-Ghannūshī) (b. 1941). Qaraḍāwī's book is important because of its wide circulation in the Muslim world. It is best summarised here in the form of the author's counter-arguments against the pro-jihad arguments of the radical Islamists. The latter use nine pro-jihad arguments summed up under five heads: (a) verses of the Qur'an from *al-Baqarah* (Q. 2) and *al-Anfal* (Q. 8),i.e. (2: 193; 8: 39) and, above all, the 'sword verse' (9: 5)(the first two command Muslims to keep fighting till *fitnah* comes to an end and Islam is established, while the last one tells Muslims to kill the 'polytheists' wherever found (see Annexure B for texts)); (b) Hadith reports according to which the Prophet was sent with a sword and that he was to keep fighting till everyone converted to Islam (see Annexure C for texts); (c) that the wars of the Prophet and his Companions were offensive ones and not defensive ones; (d) that disbelief is sufficient reason for aggression; (e) that all political systems must be subjugated by Muslims to enable people to choose Islam freely.

Qaraḍāwī's counter-arguments are: (a) that *fitnah* is 'turning Muslims back from their religion', not 'disbelief', which is the reason for war, so that the first two verses restrict fighting once Muslims are no longer persecuted,while for 9: 5, it does not abrogate the peaceful verses but is itself specific to the Arab polytheists who no longer exist; (b) that the *aḥadīth* in question are weak and in conflict with the Qur'an;(c) that the Prophet never initiated hostitilites against those who had entered into treaties with him (as for the Companions, they fought to protect the embryonic Islamic state through preemptive attacks or attacked tyrants to liberate their oppressed people) (d) notwithstanding the views of some medieval exegetes, there are many reasons for suggesting that disbelief is not the reason for war (e. g., the conquered people are allowed to retain their beliefs); (e) such views are only held by the Egyptian radical Islamist thinker Sayyid Quṭb (1906 – 1966) and the Pakistani revivalist scholar Abū'l A'lā Mawdūdī (1903 – 1979) but are obviously erroneous. As such arguments and counter-arguments are much in evidence in South Asia also, Qaraḍāwī is as relevant here as he is to the rest of the Muslim world.[33]

32 Ibid 142 – 144.
33 Qaraḍāwī 2009.

Qaraḍāwī distinguishes between a defensive jihad and one of choice (*jihād al-ṭalab*). In contrast to medieval jurists, he argues that the latter is not an obligation. Among other things, he offers a critique of the hermeneutical device of abrogation which allows the radical Islamists to write off the peaceful verses.[34] Among other things, Muhammad Qasim Zaman, an American Islamic scholar of Pakistani origin, points out that Qaraḍāwī takes the support of the medieval Islamic scholar Taqī al-Dīn Aḥmad ibn Taymiyyah's (1263–1328) work called *Qā'idah mukhtaṣarah* which asserts that unbelievers are not to be fought with because of their beliefs but because they could be a danger to Muslims. This is significant since Ibn Taymiyyah is normally used by radical Islamists to argue just the opposite.[35]

Another author whose book on jihad is taken seriously is the Iraqi born American academic, Majīd Khaddūrī (1909–2007). Khaddūrī agrees with the classical theory that 'inherent in the state's action in waging a jihad is the establishment of Muslim sovereignty, since the supremacy of God's word carries necessarily with it God's political authority'.[36] In this he agrees with contemporary Islamist radicals but also differs from them in that he does not allow individuals to assume leadership in a holy war. This remains a function of the state and that too only for religious purposes. Moreover, while he believes that jihad is perpetual since there will always be unbelievers, this does not mean that there should be 'continuous fighting'. Indeed, when Muslim power declined, jihad was 'no longer compatible with Muslim interests' and so peace agreements were entered into and honoured.[37]

Muslims also write what may be called apologia about jihad. For instance, Mahmoud (Maḥmūd) Shaltūt (1893–1963), the rector of Al-Azhar, tried to prove that the early wars of Islam were basically defensive as the small Muslim community was transgressed against.[38] Another collection of articles emphasising peace and interpreting the apparently aggressive verses differently is *War and Peace in Islam*.[39] In Pakistan there are very few such studies by academics trained on Western lines—Iftikhar Malik's introduction to jihad being one of them–but there are some by traditionally-trained Islamic scholars (*'ulamā*): Mawdūdī, Ghulām Aḥmad Parwēz (1903–1985), Mawlānā Waḥīduddīn Khān

---

34 Jackson 2015: 312–333.
35 Zaman 2012: 265.
36 Khaddūrī 1955. Quoted from Bostom 2005: 309.
37 Ibid, 311.
38 Shaltūt 1948.
39 Muhammad et. al. 2013.

(b.1925), to name a few.[40] One study in particular needs to be highlighted. It is a monograph by 'Ammār Khān Nāṣir (b.1975), a contemporary Pakistani scholar of Islam, who argues that: (a) the classical jurists considered jihad a part of 'doing good and stopping evil' (*al-amr bi 'l mā'rūf wa 'l nahī 'an al-munkar*). The aim was to invite people to Islam and, if they do not accept the faith, to fight and subjugate them; (b) modernist scholars have interpreted jihad as merely a defensive war necessitated by the aggression directed by the Arab polytheists towards the early Muslim community; (c) the conquests of foreign lands was not meant to go on but was restricted to the Persian Empire and parts of the Byzantine Empire. Indeed, Muslims were supposed to avoid fighting the Turks and the Africans. For (a), the author presents opinions, both for and against, from the classical and later sources. The majority opinion seems to be that this order was only for the Arab polytheists and applied to no other group. However, he does criticise opinions previously held on issues related to such a reading which will be examined in the relevant chapters.[41]

In short, interpretations of jihad range between the desire to live in peace and harmony with the world as well as perpetual strife. The latter can act as the spark which sends young men to missions of death and destruction in the contemporary world. This, ironically, is the kind of action which makes headlines though there are others which, by their very nature of seeking peace, remain unnoticed. Hence, it is necessary to understand how jihad has been interpreted in the modern world. This study, however, confines itself only to South Asia.

The most relevant study for this book is the American academic Asma Afsaruddin's book, *Striving in the Path of God*, appropriately sub-titled 'Jihād and Martyrdom in Islamic Thought'.[42] Afsaruddin's study tries to understand the changing meanings of jihad through the medieval exegeses of the Qur'an, the hadith, and studies on the subject. She concludes, after an impressive study of the original sources, that the literature about jihad suggests that it has been variously interpreted and that political circumstances—ongoing battles against the Iranian and Byzantine Empires followed by the crusades—privileged the combative aspects over other connotations. She also refutes the militant interpretations of present-day Islamist radical theoreticians who construe jihad as permanent war against non-Muslims as well as secular Muslim rulers. Her conclusion is

---

40 Iftikhar Malik provides an introduction to the concept of jihad linking it to the Taliban movement (2005: 40–82). For studies by religious scholars, see Mawdūdī 1930, Matālib1975–1991, Khān, W Tazkīr 1985.

41 Nāṣir 2012: 111–300.

42 Afsaruddin 2013.

that the Qur'an 'advocates only limited, defensive fighting when peaceful overtures and stoic, non-violent resistance have failed and the adversary attacks first. The religious affiliation of the adversary in itself is irrelevant'.[43] The fact that her book is an intellectual history of the evolution of the idea of jihad makes it a model to be followed in the present study.

Scholars of South Asia have, however, written about manifestations of movements which call themselves jihad in their part of the world. Perhaps the work which will appear at first sight to be very close to the present author's endeavour is the Pakistani-American historian Ayesha Jalal's book, *Partisans of Allah.*[44] It starts with the following objective:

> This book ... focuses on the development of the idea and practice of Jihad over several centuries and across the space that connects West Asia to South Asia.[45]

This is very close to the objective of providing a history of the idea of jihad in South Asia in this book. However, there are so many differences in the way Jalal has argued her case and the way it has been done in the following pages that these are two very different projects.

First, Jalal has given her preferred interpretation of jihad in the beginning of the book and comes back to it in the end. She says that 'the Qur'an does not lend itself well to the notion of jihad as holy war, and far less to the idea of continuous warfare against infidels, how did this discrepancy between the text and the later, legally based interpretations of the concept arise?'.[46] This study, on the other hand, studies the way scholars of Islam give interpretations of jihad without attempting to start with one. Second, Jalal has not given any account of the hermeneutical devices used to interpret the Qur'an and the hadith which is the main focus of this study. Thirdly, while Jalal has looked at the history of the concept of jihad in the works of Sayyid Aḥmad Khān (1817–1898), Chirāgh 'Alī (1844–1895), Abū'l Kalām Āzād (1888–1958), Mawdūdī, Ḥāfiẓ Sa'īd (spelled as Hafiz Saeed in English sources) (b. 1948), and so on with reference to sources other than exegeses, this study gives primary importance to Quranic exegeses by these writers. However, Jalal's work is valuable and its historical narrative about events understood as jihad leaves little room for duplication in that direction. Thus, chronological description of such events is reduced to a minimum

43 Ibid 297.
44 Jalal 2008.
45 Ibid 6.
46 Ibid 7.

and often relegated to notes so as to avoid duplicating her work and other similar studies.

Another study which partly overlaps with this one, is Samina Yasmeen's *Jihad and Dawah.*[47] The author carries out a longitudinal analysis of the narratives of Lashkar-e-Tayyabah and Jamat ud Dawah, both under the general leadership and guidance of Ḥāfiẓ Sa'īd, who has interpreted verses of the Qur'an in order to inspire Pakistanis to fight India for Kashmir. Yasmeen has analysed not only Sa'īd's *Tafsīr Sūrah Tawbah*, which has also been done in this book (chapter 9), but also other narratives: pamphlets, magazines, messages, etc. Among other things she points out how narratives evolve in response to historical, social, and other pressures and how they are used to promote jihad. Despite the overlap with a part of one chapter, Yasmeen's work is very different from this study. First, it pays close attention to the printed works of Ḥāfiẓ Sa'īd's organisations, but does not touch upon those by other Pakistani Islamists. Secondly, it tells us how these narratives evolve from promoting jihad to creating a wider space in Pakistani society by emphasizing patience (*ṣabr*), social service, and piety under international and domestic pressures. The present study, however, mostly analyses Ḥāfiẓ Sa'īd's exegeses with a view to finding out as to what hermeneutical devices he uses to arrive at militant meanings of verses. Lastly, Yasmeen's work is a study of narratives and their role in society whereas this book is a history of the idea of jihad for the last three hundred years with focus on the Quranic exegeses though not to the exclusion of other interpretations of the concept of jihad in South Asia.

Likewise Christine Fair's book, sub-titled 'Understanding the *Lashkar-e-Tayyaba*'[48]is what it says—a history of Ḥāfiẓ Sa'īd's organisation with a view to proving that it is supported by the ISI to inflict such punishment on India as would bring it to negotiate on Kashmir. Its title, *In Their Own Words*, refers to some of the publications of Ḥāfiẓ Sa'īd's organisations—books or pamphlets rather than the magazines and other works used by Yasmeen—which refer to reasons for fighting in Kashmir and the imperative not to fight the Pakistani state nor to declare Muslims as heretics (*takfīr*). Fair does not refer to the exegeses of Sa'īd or Mas'ūd Aẓhar (spelled as Masood Azhar in the literature)(b. 1968), the head of the UN-designated terrorist group Jaish-e-Muhammad, which are important concerns of the present study. While the archive which Christine Fair has assembled for this study, especially the biographies of LeT/JUD fighters, is impressive, her tone towards Pakistan is acerbic rather than neutral and the last

47 Yasmeen 2017.
48 Fair 2018.

chapter, contemplating the punishment to be given to Pakistan for using non-state actors in Kashmir (even hinting at nuclear war), is disturbing for anyone who desires peace in South Asia.

Yet another study of some of the narratives of the Taliban, especially relevant for Pakistan and Afghanistan, is a Pakistani academic Afzal Khan's doctoral dissertation submitted to the University of Erfurt in 2016. Khan chooses three texts: Mawdūdī's *Al-jihād fī al-Islām*; Nūr (spelled Noor) Muḥammad's *Jihād-i afghānistān*, and Faḍal Muḥammad Yusufzaī's *Dā'wat-i jihād* for analysis. He argues that Mawdūdī places jihad in the tradition of 'commanding right and forbidding wrong' (*al-amr bi 'l mā'rūf wa 'l nahī 'an al-munkar*). This is explained by Nūr Muḥammad Yusufzaī in moral terms of right and wrong so that, in the words of Afzal Khan, the moral vision of the Taliban is a kind of 'man standing-guard-over-the-morals' but the tactics to achieve this became anarchic. Afzal Khan's approach is philosophical and he uses lexicology and 'anthropology'—basically interviewing and observation—in his research. His work does not overlap with the concerns of this study though it offers some useful insights into the phenomenon of jihad.[49] Another recent book-length work, Tariq Hasan's *Colonialism and the Call to Jihād in British India*,[50] purporting to cover some of the areas already covered by Jalal, is based on selective secondary sources and is mostly tendentious and journalistic.

Apart from these studies of jihad movements in South Asia as a whole, there are also scholarly studies of iconic militant (*jihādī*) figures. Foremost among them is Sayyid Aḥmad Barēlwī (i.e., of the city of Rae Bareilly. The name is also written a Barelvi's) (1786–1831). Though much has been written about him in the hagiographic mode, there was a lack of objective and rigorous writing.[51] This gap has been filled by Altaf Qadir, a Pakistani academic, who looks at this movement from the point of view of the local people of Khyber Pakhtunkhwa and provides a detailed and accurate sketch of events.[52] Among the most notable of the scholarly studies on the religious figures of KP—the *mullāhs*, *faqīrs*, and others—who used the concept of jihad to evoke hostility among the tribesmen against the British, is a book by Sana Haroon.[53] Studies on iconic figures such as Ubaydullah Sindhī (1872–1944), the Faqīr of Ipī (1897–1960),[54] the

49 Khan, A 2016.
50 Hasan 2015.
51 Khan n.d, Mahar 1952, Nadwī, A 1939 & 1969.
52 Qadir 2015.
53 Haroon 2007
54 Shaikh 1986; Laghari 1980; Warren 2000; Hauner 1981.

Ḥājjī of Turangzaī (1858–1937),[55] and others also deserve attention. Although the aim of this study is not to describe the causes or the historical events which go by the name of jihad, they will, nevertheless, be inevitably sketched out in order to understand how the concept itself was interpreted.

Having said that, the idea and practice of interpretation is so central to this book that it has been given a separate chapter to itself which focuses on the hermeneutics of the canonical sources of Islam—the Qur'an and the hadith. However, since the book is sub-titled 'An Intellectual History', this latter concept may be explained here. This is meant to distinguish this study from theology and place it within the discipline of the history of ideas.[56] Whereas a theologian is expected to give an essentially theological interpretation of what jihad is, a historian of this idea may trace out what theologians and other intellectuals have said about it and place it in the context of such larger intellectual frameworks as the impact of modernity, the interaction of political forces, and cultural trends. Such a history deals with the formation of an idea and its evolution over time and relates it to the forces which play upon it to give it the meanings and implications it imbibes over time.

Such a history has its own problems. First, as an author of an intellectual history of Islam in the Ottoman Empire and the Maghreb points out, it 'has itself been under something of a cloud in recent years' because of the impression that it focuses 'on the intellectual elite' and does not take cognizance of 'social and political realities'.[57] Secondly, as Quentin Skinner has pointed out, its very source material—written texts—needs to be interpreted which is by no means a transparent undertaking. As the next chapter will focus in more detail on what Skinner has written about—that texts are interpreted with reference to both the intention to be understood and 'the intention that this intention be understood'—we need not go into detail about this process here.[58]

Thus, the history of ideas as they occur in texts is the history of what they were meant to communicate to audiences which were themselves products of historical forces. It may be, as Skinner warns us, that the history of thought cannot solve our immediate problems,[59] but it can help us in understanding how a term is interpreted and what practical effects this can have on the world. Thus, our different understandings of jihad can help explain the forces which drive

55 Qadir 2006, 2008.
56 Kelly 2002.
57 El-Rouayheb 2015: 3.
58 Skinner 1969: 48.
59 Ibid, 53.

human beings into adopting courses of action (such as suicide bombing) which appear inexplicable to observers outside of those webs of meanings.

Generally, the sub-genre of the history of ideas is used for the history of philosophical and scientific ideas—the idea of zero, the idea of numbers, the idea of democracy, the idea of freedom, etc. There are also books like Mikkel Thorup's *An Intellectual History of Terror*[60] which is relevant for the theme of this study. Thorup calls his work as 'the first attempt at an *intellectual history* of terror, or rather of our legitimizations and delegitimizations of political violence' carried out by the state (emphasis in the original).[61] He uses ideas such as Michel Foucault's 'geneological history', Quentin Skinner's 'intellectual history', and Reinhart Koselleck's 'conceptual history' in order to understand how ideas which legitimise certain forms of political violence evolve.[62] Similarly, there is an intellectual study of the idea of gratitude. The author contends that his study 'is a history of *persons* responding to social and political circumstances with the intellectual resources at their disposal'.[63]

In the field of Islamic studies, much has been written on the history of thought, so much so that making a list of important works alone will require volumes. There is, for example, Montgomery Watt's history of the formative period of Islamic thought.[64] Daniel Brown's *Rethinking Tradition in Modern Islamic thought*[65] is another example. It is a history of the idea of Prophetic authority (*sunnāh* and hadith) in modern Muslim societies. Brown defines it as a 'history of ideas' and places it in the tradition of 'intellectual history' on the grounds that his focus is the 'current of thought that would seem to be new, innovative, holding promise for change'. To do this, he argues, one can 'emphasize individuals, trends, or schools of thought'. He chooses the second alternative since he is concerned 'with the *influence* of ideas and not just with the ideas themselves'.[66] And, finally, one may look as an example of a paradigmatic work in this field at Qasim Zaman's book called *Islamic Thought in a Radical Age*.[67] The book raises important points such as the intellectual history of internal criticism in the Islamic tradition and how, with the dilution of traditional authority, the Islamists 'share much with the modernists in their intellectual backgrounds and the nov-

---

60 Thorup 2010.
61 Ibid 4.
62 Ibid, 5. See also Koselleck 2002.
63 Leithart 2014: 3.
64 Watt 2006.
65 Brown 1996.
66 Ibid 4.
67 Zaman 2012.

elty of many of the positions they advocate'.[68] This is an important point, touching as it does on the question of the dispersal of authority in modern Islam which is relevant for understanding which activities are called jihad, how they are justified, and by whom—questions which constitute important parts of the present study.

This does not mean that the present work gets reduced to a history of people; even their intellectual beings. Rather, it focuses on the idea of jihad as interpreted by people in order to understand how the idea has evolved in South Asia. The idea is an important one as it affected society, creating anti-colonial aspirations using the idiom of jihad, militant movements, and, in the contemporary context, Islamist militancy. As Fazlur Rahman noted, 'the Islamic concept of Jihād was heavily relied upon to arouse the sentiments of the general public against foreign rulers'.[69] But, as we shall see, it could also be used to suppress dissent, create a theocracy, and augment the power of its practitioners.

This study seeks to answer the following questions:

1. What are the major interpretations of jihad in the colonial and contemporary periods in South Asia?
2. In what ways have the concepts of jihad and terms associated with it (Islamic state, *Dārul Ḥarb* (land of war), *Dārul Islām* (land of peace), *fitnah* (evil, persecution, oppression), *fasād* (disorder, mischief), *tāghūt* (forces or systems rebelling against God; idol; evil forces), *jizyah* (poll-tax), etc.) been used by exegetes in particular and others in general to pursue their ideological, political, and other objectives?
3. In what way are the traditional Sunni notions of jihad different from those of the modernists (apologists, progressives) as well as radical Islamists?
4. And, finally, what interpretations of jihad are appealed to by the theoreticians of militant movements (especially the Al-Qaeda and Pakistani Taliban including the Punjabi Islamist militant groups)? This final question, in fact, is the *raison d'être* of this study.

If militant interpretations have been influenced, partly or fully, by the modern theoreticians of Islamist militancy—Ḥassan al-Bannāh (1906–1949), Mawdūdī, Quṭb, 'Abdullāh Azzām, Muḥammad 'Abd al-Salām Farāj (1954–1982), Ayman al-Ẓawāhirī (b. 1951), etc.—how have they justified militancy? The answers to these questions constitute an intellectual history of the way the concept of jihad has been interpreted in South Asia and elsewhere.

68 Ibid 2.
69 Rahman 1982: 55.

But before answering these questions it should be remembered that in some ways present-day Islamic militancy has precedents in history. These were the wars of the Kharijites, whose ideas as well as practices have been described by scholars,[70] and whose history is given by the famous historian, exegete, and scholar Abū Jā'far Muḥammad ibn Jarīr al-Ṭabarī (224/839–310/923).[71] The other precedent which comes to the mind is the assassination of establishment figures during Abbaside rule carried out by the followers of Ḥasan ibn Sabbāh (1050s-1154), to which the Persian historian 'Ala al-Dīn 'Aṭā Allāh Malik Juwainī (1226–1283) bears witness[72] and which has been discussed by contemporary scholars.[73] Since there are some parallels between these militant phenomena and present-day events in the Muslim world, these will be touched upon briefly. However, the contemporary militant movements called jihad are a modern phenomena created, in great part, by the reaction to modernity in general and the international situation in the world as perceived by many Muslims in particular. This is true in the obvious sense that modern conditions—rapid change, disloca-

70 Salem 1956, Crone and Zimmermann 2001, Kenny 2006.

71 The Kharijites was a group which separated from the caliph 'Alī ibn Abī Ṭālib (23 /600–40/ 661) when he was forced to agree to arbitration with Mu'āwiyyah after the battle of Siffīn (Ṭabarī c. 10 C b. Vol. 3: 288–391). The Kharijites often fought with desperate courage risking life and limb in their wars against the Ummayads and the Abbasides.This could be equated with suicide attacks which is a battle tactic used by modern-day militants. The original sources (such as Ṭabarī) describe a number of practices of the Kharijites which parallel those of the present-day Islamist militants (Taliban, al-Qaeda, IS, Boko Haram, etc.). First, both believe in *takfīr*, i.e. they excommunicate other Muslims and permit their assassination by non-state actors, the confiscation of their property and the enslavement of their women and children. Secondly, they believe it is permissible to revolt against Muslim rulers on the grounds that they do not govern according to the Sharī'ah or do not practise Islam in their personal lives. Thirdly, they believe that it is necessary to use force to create an Islamic state which will ensure that governance is carried out according to God's laws. Other parallels, such as the cruel methods of execution and the killing of women and children, are also pointed out.

72 Boyle 1958.

73 Hodgson 1955; Daftary 1994. The nearest parallel to the suicide attacks used by radical militants and called 'attacks of self-sacrificers' (*fidāyīn*) are similar attacks by the followers of Ḥasan ibn Sabbāh, the pioneer of the Isma'īlī Nizārī sect (al Nizāriyyūn), who established himself in a castle at Alamut and sent young men (known in Western sources as the Assassins) to kill individual functionaries of the establishment at the cost of their own lives. Juvainī, a contemporary historian, describes how rulers were assassinated and received threats. For instance, Ibn Sabbāh got a dagger planted near Sultān Sanjar's bed and the Sultan 'took fright and from then on inclined towards peace' with the Assassins. Another ruler, Al-Rāshid Billah reached Isfahan while sick and 'suddenly some vile fida'is entered his audience-chamber and stabbed him to death' (Juvainī in Boyle 1958: 682 and 686). Thus, it appeared as if nobody was safe. The fear this induced is familiar in today's world where terrorists can strike almost anywhere.

tion, access to news sharpening grievances against the USA and Israel, a sense of community created by the idiom of a Muslim group spread internationally, the use of technology—did not exist earlier. But whether it is also true in the deeper philosophical sense of reacting to modernity with its grand narratives and a sense of the triumphant, rational West is yet to be established. Similarly, it is also questionable whether the doubt created by post-modern ways of thinking and the fragmentation of the self can be used to explain conservative, Wahhābī and Islamist interpretations as the quest for certainties. It is best that the theory should emerge out of the evidence and not vice versa. Yet, it is tempting to give a brief account of modernity since we will refer to it frequently.

Modernity as a way of thinking entails faith in reason, emphasis upon the natural with epistemology based upon empiricism, belief in progress, and rejection of authority (religious, social, ancestral, etc.). It has been associated with rapid social change involving the use of Western categories of thinking, categorisation and behaviour in non-Western countries especially those which experienced colonisation.[74] It is argued that, instead of modernity, the concept of multiple modernities should be used as it allows us to move away from 'the homogenic and hegemonic vision of modernity imagined in the 1950s'.[75] This is a useful insight only in so far as it is not allowed to relativise the concept of modernity till it loses its value as an analytical concept. Thus, one could concede that the modernities of Britain as well as India were influenced by each other.[76] However, when Appadurai and Brekenridge contend that Indian modernity is 'as varied as magic, marriage, or madness', they are manifestly wrong.[77] At the most we can talk of a 'fractured modernity' in India as Sanjay Joshi does in his study of the making of the middle class in north India (Lucknow).[78] This means that some pre-modern elements—Joshi's example is hierarchy masquerading as education—might mix in with modernity. However, when Partha Chatterjee says that our modernity 'is the modernity of the once-colonized',[79] this only explains the ambivalence many South Asians have for Western values, artifacts, institutions, and attitudes. This can explain why Islamists can accept gadgets which empower them: machines, computers, weapons, and means of communication and travel etc., while hating the freedom of people to date each other or, for women, to wear revealing clothes. But, unless we are talking

74 For a history see Bayly 2004.
75 Eisenstadt 1999: 294; also see Eisenstadt 2000.
76 Veer 2001; Therborn 2003.
77 Brekenridge and Appadurai 1996: 1.
78 Joshi 2001.
79 Chatterjee 1997: 20.

of the ideological change, the worldview, the belief-system, we are not talking of people who have converted to modernity. I would contend that, despite being different in certain peripheral ways, modernity is ontologically the same all over the world. And one of its core values, as Talal Asad (b. 1932) concedes but critiques, is the privatisation of religion.[80] So, modern India and (to a lesser degree) Pakistan, at least in their constitutions, uphold this core value and appeal to rationality in their education systems. Of course, the political promise is often compromised and informal education still emphasises the magical—modernity is fractured and mistrusted—but where it exists as an aspiration or in partial reality, it is essentially different from movements militating against it.

Among the movements which militate against it and react to it are those which fall back upon things to which they ascribe iconic value to mark their 'differences' from what they see as the homogenising Western imposition of modernity. As Talal Asad argues, there is no escaping the intellectual, aesthetic, and cultural domination of secularism which is the byproduct of modernity (the same would be true if religion were dominant in a society).[81] Thus, the argument is that people assert their difference through the symbol of religion. However, it is simplistic to accept the secularisation thesis—modernity having secularised the West *in toto* while South Asia remains 'spiritual'—as Peter van der Veer reminds us. Indeed, modernity also produced evangelical movements in England as it did what Kenneth Jones calls 'socio-religious reform movements' in South Asia.[82] In South Asia, at least, the resurgence of high Islam, as well as other religions, such as Sikhism and Hinduism, suggests that the classical claim of early modernity that the process entails secularisation as it did in Western societies needs rethinking.[83] According to Khalid Masud (b. 1939), a Pakistani scholar of Islam, 'Muslim modern trends range from reform to total rejection of either tradition or modernity'.[84] The 'Western modernists' reject the Islamic tradition while the 'Islamic modernists' range from calling for revivalism to reinterpreting Islam so that it conforms to certain humanist values.[85] In a sense, fundamentalism, Islamist radicalism, and militancy too are reactions to the totalising experience of modernity but are not a form of modernity themselves—unless one wants to adjectivise everything as modern. Their major claim is to reject the ideology of modernity in order to go back to classical Islam. However, the cultur-

80 Asad 2003.
81 Ibid.
82 Veer 2001; Jones 1994.
83 Hefner 1998; Jones 1994.
84 Masud 2016: 237.
85 Ibid: 238.

al and religious authenticity they marshal in defence of their ideologies is not really of the classical period of Islam at all. It is a contemporary construction of their idealised understanding of it.

Another reaction to modernity is acceptance of some of its core values, the values of the Enlightenment (rationalism, egalitarianism, human rights, women's rights, democracy, etc.). Those modernist Muslim thinkers who do so are then faced with the problem of reconciling them with Islam. This, of course, is done through interpreting the foundational texts in ingenious ways. In short, as Qasim Zaman, in his seminal study of the traditional *'ulamā* in South Asia, has pointed out, both these trends—modernism and Islamist radicalism—'have been largely rooted in modern, Westernized institutions of education'.[86]

In the case of Muslims who develop group-consciousness, the assertion of an identity is a survival tool against perceived grievances or ideological conquest by 'the West'. Thus, the Muslim diaspora in Western countries as well as self-defining groups (sects, sub-sects, ideologically oriented groups) constitute the imagined community—to use Anderson's idiom,[87]which perceives and confronts other equally imagined groups based upon constructed identities. As these constructions, perceptions, and definitions are based upon interpretations of Islam —in this case the crucial concept of jihad—it would be helpful to understand how South Asian interpreters of this concept have understood it.

This brings us to the question of methodology used for analysing the interpretations relevant for our purposes. Primarily, the Quranic verses used by traditional interpreters, modernists, and radical Islamists in Urdu exegeses (except for Sayyid Quṭb's exegesis which has been used in the English translation) to justify their understanding of jihad will be studied. These are:

Table 1: The Verses of the Qur'an

Al Baqrah 2: 190	Repel aggression but in proportion to the offence.
2: 191	Fight those who began hostilities since *fitnah* is worse than war.
2: 193	Fight to end *fitnah* till religion is purely for God.
Al-Anfāl 8: 39	Fight till *fitnah* disappears and religion is only for God.
8: 61	If the enemy inclines towards peace so should you.
Al-Tawbah 9: 5	Kill the polytheists wherever you find them (sword verse).

86 Zaman 2002: 7.
87 Anderson 1983.

9: 29	Fight the people of the Book till they are subdued and pay the poll tax (jizyah) as 'small ones' (*sāghirūn*) (*jizyah* verse).
Al-Mumtaḥinah 60: 8	You may be kind and just to those who have not been hostile to you (for full texts see Annexure B).

While the first verse seems to allow only defensive warfare and that too in proportion to the injury, the three subsequent ones mention a concept called *fitnah*, translated either as persecution or disbelief, which determines the implications of these verses. Two verses, 8: 61 and 60: 8, advocate peaceful and amicable co-existence with non-Muslims both as groups in society and as nation-states. However, two verses, 9: 5 and 29, used very often by Islamist militants to justify their project of eternal warfare with the rest of the world, apparently allow perpetual warfare. Indeed, Osama bin Laden quoted 9: 5 in his *fatwā* against Americans, adding to it:

> Our youths know that the humiliation suffered by Muslims as a result of the occupation of their sanctuaries cannot be removed except by explosions and jihad.[88]

In short, taken at their face value there are verses which imply fighting as well as living in peace. The point is how they are interpreted and which interpretation is privileged by those in power. For instance, the above verse, as interpreted by Afifi al-Akiti, a fellow of the Oxford Centre for Islamic Studies, is not about perpetual war at all. It was, he says, about the Arab polytheists who had broken the treaty of Ḥudaybiyyah and its order is subject 'to specification' (*takhṣīṣ*) and is not general (*'ām*).[89] Indeed, it is their interpretations which distinguishes the traditionalist, modernist-progressive, and radical-militants from each other in South Asia and, indeed, in the rest of the world. Thus, the interpretation of these eight verses by the most significant exegetes of South Asia studied in this book will be discussed in relation to the politics and dominant ideologies of the periods of their writing.

While the focus of this book is on the way the concept of jihad is interpreted in the Urdu-using part of South Asia from the eighteenth century onwards, there will inevitably be some references to jihadi movements in India especially during the colonial era and then again in the contemporary period. In this context, the use of Habermas's concept of 'public sphere' by Deitrich Reetz may be useful. Reetz argues that his study of Islamic groups in India from 1900 to 1947 analyses

88 Euben and Zaman 2009: 456.
89 Akiti, al- 2005: 31.

religious discourse on the assumption that it negotiates 'the hierarchy of values and activist concepts in competition and comparison with other Islamic or religious groups'.[90] In this study then we will analyse one variant of this discourse: that relating to jihad.

The sources of this book are mostly in Urdu and English; not in Arabic. These sources are mostly the various exegeses or commentaries of the Qur'an from the eighteenth century onwards. Only one early exegesis, that by the famous Islamic scholar of the eighteenth century Shāh 'Abdul 'Azīz (1746–1824), is in Persian, but this too is available in the Urdu translation.[91] In any case this exegesis does not cover the verses about jihad or, indeed, those given in Table 1 above. Most of the South Asian Islamic scholars—Sayyid Aḥmad Khān (1817–1898) , 'Ubaydullāh Sindhī, Mawdūdī, Abū'l Kalām Āzād (1888–1958), Ghulām Aḥmad Parwēz, Waḥiduddīn Khān, Ḥāfiẓ Sa'īd, Mas'ūd Aẓhar—whose works have been used as primary sources to understand how jihad has been interpreted wrote in Urdu. The works of Arab theoreticians such as Sayyid Quṭb, Farrāj, 'Abdullah 'Azzām, and Ayman al-Ẓawāhirī, are originally in Arabic, but their English or Urdu translations are available and have been used for this study. Besides the exegeses there are other works—essays, sermons, pamphlets, and books—on jihad by South Asian writers in Urdu or English which have also been consulted. As the author is well versed in both Urdu and English, can read Persian with some understanding, and also knows basic Arabic, this study does not suffer from linguistic impediments. It needs to be reiterated that the author does not claim to be trained in either theology or Islamic jurisprudence. Thus, if some readers are looking for a final theological interpretation of jihad by the author, they will be disappointed. In any case, even if such an interpretation had been offered, it would have been no more than yet *another*, rather than the *only*, interpretation. Indeed, the point of this study is that there are more than one interpretation of ideas; that all interpretations are subject to change because of external dominant discourses, and, hence, there is no fixed, unchanging intellectual monolith called jihad.

While it is conceded that people do not fight only because they are inspired by theory—indeed they fight for various complicated reasons—this is no reason for not trying to understand the history of such theories which do, after all, acquire a niche in the worldview of so many people. A book on intellectual history can put together a historical narrative of an idea to which people ostensibly refer

90 Reetz 2006: 4.
91 *Tafsīr-e-'Azīzī*.

in order to justify their actions without going into the question of their deeper, covert psychological motivations.

After this introductory chapter there are ten other chapters including the conclusion. The one which follows (Chapter 2) is on the interpretation of the Qur'an and the hadith. It gives a brief outline of the interpretative devices used by exegetes in explaining the meanings of these canonical sources. These devices may be used to give a meaning of jihad which promotes either war or peace. Chapter 3 is on 'Jihad in Transition'. It gives a synoptic account of the political uses of jihad by some of the medieval Muslim rulers of India. More importantly, it examines the state of Islamic learning in India during this period of transition to modernity with a view to understanding how jihad was constructed in the available texts of the period. Chapter 4, entitled 'Jihad and The Family of Shah Waliullah', begins with the legacy of the great Islamic scholar, Shāh Walīullah (1703–1762), pertaining to events which went by the name of jihad in India. In this context, his son Shāh 'Abdul 'Azīz's edicts (*fatāwā*) on the question of India's Islamic status—whether it is a land of peace or Islam (*Dārul Islām*) or a land of war (*Dārul Ḥarb*) or something in between—is most important since it influenced Muslim politics in India for more than a century. One of the persons influenced by 'Azīz who actually led a jihad movement in the present-day KP province of Pakistan was Sayyid Aḥmad Barēlwī. His influence over a number of resistance movements during colonial rule will be touched upon in passing. Chapter 5, on 'Colonial Modernists', is on the modernist interpreters of Islam in the nineteenth and the twentieth centuries—Sayyid Aḥmad Khān, Chirāgh 'Alī,[92] Syed Ameer Ali (1849–1928), etc.—who wrote to counter the colonial view that Islam was an aggressive religion and preached violence. Some of their ideas are still used by modernist Muslims in South Asia to defend Islam against the same charges now leveled both by Western scholars and militant Islamists. The next chapter (6), entitled 'Jihad as anti-colonial resistance', looks at the ideas of 'Ubaydullāh Sindhī, some prominent members of the Deobandi clergy, and Abū'l Kalām Āzād. It covers responses ranging from covert attempts at armed resistance to the British to agitational, nationalist politics. Chapter 7, entitled 'The Age of Mawdūdī', describes his ideas of Muslim political dominance, the Islamic state, and jihad as an instrument of power. Mawdūdī's writings on these subjects, with special focus on his exegesis of the Qur'an, will be discussed. The next chapter (8), called 'Radical Imports', provides the link with Islamist militant ideas from the Middle East which establish much of the theoretical basis of the forms of international militancy which is the focus of this book.

---

92 Ali 1885.

This chapter will look at the interpretations of jihad by Quṭb, Farrāj, ʻAzzām, and Ẓawāhirī. The ideas of these writers, though not the primary focus of this study, will be examined briefly in order to understand their influence on Pakistani militants. Chapter 9 is on Pakistani radical interpreters of jihad—Ḥāfiẓ Saʻīd,[93] Masʻūd Aẓhar,[94] Muftī Shamazaī,[95] and others—who have written much on the subject of jihad and inspired young men to fight in Kashmir and Afghanistan. Chapter 10, entitled ʻRefuting the radicals', is about the edicts and interpretations offered by present-day South Asian (and other) writers against the views of the Islamist militants. This is an important chapter since, like the modernists, the aim of these writers is to counter the militant view that jihad can be fought by non-state actors without any permission of the government and that it is justified to fight non-Muslim and even Muslim rulers whether there are treaties with the former or not. The last chapter is the ʻConclusion' in which the whole argument of the book will be summed up. One important question discussed here will be as to which interpretative devices are used to give an aggressive or peaceful reading of verses from the canonical sources.

The book has a bibliography divided into sections. The first section is on the original sources (exegeses, translations of the Qur'an, edicts, and manuscript sources, etc.); the second is on secondary sources in English, Urdu, and other languages. This is followed by annexures of the Quranic verses and *aḥādīth* which makes for convenient reading. In the end there is an index to facilitate researchers.

---

93 Sa ʻīd *Tawbah.*

94 Aẓhar *Fatḥ.*

95 Shamazaī 2012; ʻĀbid 2003.

2 Interpretation of the Qur'an and the Hadith

This chapter attempts to study how the foundational texts of Islam, the Qur'an and the hadith, are interpreted.[1] The interpretation of these sources is, of course, a subset of hermeneutics. One of its pioneers, the German scholar Hans-Georg Gadamer, wrote a book called *Truth and Method*[2] which is considered a path-breaking text in this intellectual project. According to him, hermeneutics is the 'phenomenon of understanding and of the correct interpretation of what has been understood'.[3] Among the concepts which are relevant for the interpretation of the foundational sources of religion, both Christianity and Islam, is the concept of the inevitability of prejudice; our consciousness being historically affected; the fusion of 'horizons' and a sense of 'community' or 'tradition'. By 'prejudice', Gadamer means the ideas, tastes, and axioms which we all bring to the work we interpret. As he points out, 'the fundamental prejudice of the enlightenment is the prejudice against prejudice itself, which deprives tradition of its power'.[4] Tradition, in which we are historically situated, gives us the 'horizon' defined as the 'range of vision that includes everything than can be seen from a particular vantage point.[5]. So, understanding occurs when our present horizon expands when it meets other horizons. Thus 'we regain the concepts of an historical past in such a way that they also include our own comprehension of them'.[6] Such views, combined with other theories about meaning, create an awareness of the inevitable historical and cultural 'prejudices' we bring to a text. In this study these have been called 'ideological assumptions' or the 'ideological imperative' but these terms, as used here, will be defined and explained later.

Responding to this new scepticism about the validity of interpretations—a view which implied such a degree of relativism as to undermine the very concept of meaning itself—some scholars, such as E.D. Hirsch[7], sought to retrieve the notion of validity in interpretation. He argued that 'hermeneutics must stress a reconstruction of the author's aims and attitudes in order to evolve guides and norms for construing the meaning of his text'.[8] Others, such as Stanley Fish, re-

1 Waardenburg 2002: 111–113.
2 Gadamer 1927.
3 Ibid xi.
4 Ibid 239–240.
5 Ibid 269.
6 Ibid 337.
7 Hirsch 1967.
8 Ibid 224.

https://doi.org/10.1515/9783110716986-005

sponded to the fear of extreme relativism expressed by Hirsch, by pointing out that 'the identification of what was real and normative occurred within interpretive communities'.[9] But these communities are not stable. They keep changing though at a given time and place, within a certain tradition, the interpretations which will appear plausible will have 'constraints on the range, and even the direction, of response'.[10] Moreover, semantic competence—the ability to understand the meaning of words of a given age or language—will further restrict 'the range of response'.[11] But despite arguing that such interpretative communities prevent chaotic relativism and solipsism, Fish does agree that communication occurs in *situations* and to be in a situation 'is already to be in possession of (or to be possessed by) a structure of assumptions, of practices understood to be relevant in relation to purposes and goals that are already in place'.[12] In short, the criteria of judgment of communities are also shaped, as Gadamer pointed out, by history and culture.

The idea of interpretative (interchangeable with interpretive) community was used by Merold Westphal in order to understand the interpretation of the Bible. He points out that the naïve-realist view, that the Bible is understood without interpretation, is erroneous since it has always had a plurality of interpretations.[13] Taking into account modern views about hermeneutics, he argues that 'all interpretation is relative to traditions that have formed the perspectives and presuppositions that guide it'.[14] He then suggests an escape from relativistic vertigo by positing that the Church is a community, a 'communal conversation seeking to understand more deeply its founding "classic" text, the Bible'.[15] But the 'Church' is not a singular monolithic community in our age of plurality—nor was it ever one in any age. Thus, there are new methods of biblical interpretation: 'reader-response, feminist criticism, ideological criticism and postcolonial criticism',[16] to name some of them. The basic intellectual change brought about by modernity is that it introduced the historical critical method of research (HCM) which is described by Jonathan Brown as follows:

1. Intial doubt about the authenticity or reliability of a historical text.

---

9 Fish 1980: 15. For Muslim 'Communities of interpretation' see Duderija 2011:7.
10 Ibid 45.
11 Ibid 46.
12 Ibid 318.
13 Westphal 2009: 17–20.
14 Ibid 71.
15 Ibid 120.
16 Davies 2013: 1. Also see Poythress 1988 for the implication of the scientific method on biblical criticism.

2. A general suspiciousness towards orthodox narratives presented in texts.
3. The conviction that by analyzing historical sources a scholar can sift the reliable from unreliable by identifying which parts of the text served which historical agendas.[17]

This method changed the default position beginning with faith in the truth of the canonical texts of religion—all Abrahamic religions—to beginning with doubt. But this new position, which began by destroying the stability of religion, soon began to nibble away at the stability of nineteenth century positivism. It became especially problematic when it took the form of reader-response and subjectivism as it slipped into relativism. It was because of the potentially threatening relativism of the reader-response theory—that the meaning of a text is not determined forever by the author but that every reader interprets the text in his or her own way—which called forth the response of Hirsch noted above. But feminists, postcolonial ideologues, and ethical critics brought their own concerns to interpret the Bible. They discovered the biases of their male, white, interpreters of the Book, pointing out how the interpretions themselves had marginalised, oppressed, or slighted women and coloured people. The most important of these approaches from our perspective is 'ideological criticism' where ideology is defined as 'a set of ideas or a coherent system of beliefs' not, as Marxists do, to 'a system of illusory beliefs created by a social or economic system with the aim of presenting a distortive or deceptive view of reality'.[18] Ideology, if one may use a metaphor, is oxygen which surrounds us. We are not aware of it unless we are in a situation in which we are deprived of it. It is our normality. Thus, ideology makes us see the world in a certain way without being aware that we have a 'prejudiced' and historically-effected—in Gadamer's sense of both terms—view of it. This idea of ideological interpretation has been used in this book when the terms 'ideological assumptions' or 'ideological imperative' are used for the interpretation of the Qur'an. These terms, however, do not refer to that inevitable situatedness in a tradition constituted by history we are all born into. Instead, they refer to those sets of ideas (assumptions) an exegete announces as being fundamental to his or her enterprise prior to embarking on the exegesis itself. Thus, if one begins with the announcement that all the wars of Islam in the early period were defensive in nature, then this assumption will limit the possibilities of interpretation. This is then an 'ideological imperative' which constrains the boundaries of the whole hermeneutical project. With this hermeneut-

17 Brown 2009: 203.
18 Davies 2013: 62.

ical concept, or grounding if you like, in mind, let us go to this specific project, i.e. to trace out how the concept of jihad has been interpreted in the exegeses of the Qur'an, as well as in some other sources, in South Asia.

Since the exegeses of the Qur'an are the major primary documents consulted for this study, a brief introduction to this genre of writing is in order. Basically an exegesis, commentary, or *tafsīr*, is a detailed explanation of the meaning of the Qur'an. Other associated terms are *ta'wīl* and *ma'ānā*. For the first three centuries, 'there appears to be no consistent differentiation between *tafsīr, tā'wīl* and *ma'ānā* when used in titles of books'.[19] Later, however, *ta'wīl* came to be reserved for an interpretation which leaves the obvious sense of the words to go into 'more speculative levels of language (*bāṭin*).[20] *Ma'ānā* refers to meaning which is not always non-controversial, and therefore subject to interpretation, as we shall see below.

Books of *tafsīr* started appearing around 120/727. A long list of early commentators are given in an 'Index of Names' by Gilliot in his article on the history of this period.[21] Among those which were mentioned most often in the curricula of South Asian Islamic seminaries (*madāris*, sing.madrasah) were *Jalālayn* and *Bayḍāwī*.[22] Other commentaries, known to scholars, were by Ṭabarī, Zamakhsharī, Rāzī, Ibn Kathīr, and Nafasī (details about them follow in chapter 3).[23]

If the exegesis is based on the Qur'an and the hadith as the main sources of explanation as understood by the community (*mathūr*), then it is a traditional one (*tafsīr bi' il-ma'thūr*). If, however, the exegete relies mainly on his own opinion (*rā'y*) or rationality (*dirāya*), then it is *tafsīr bi' l-rā'y*.[24] The latter kind of work used to be regarded with a certain trepidation in conservative circles since one's own opinion can be mistaken. For instance, the Tunisian scholar Muḥammad Ṭāhir ibn 'Āshūr (1879–1973), in the second volume of his thirty-volume *tafsīr*, 'seems to hesitate between an explicit rejection of rationalistic *tafsīr* unsupported by hadith and not backed up by a consensus of scholars, and a warning not to be overly subservient to the authority of the ancients'.[25] Sayyid Sulaimān Nadwī

---

19 Rippin 1997: 84.

20 Ibid 84; Waardenburg 2002: 118–120; as an example of chaotic relativism, Fazlur Rahman points out that using ta'wīl, the Ismā'īlīs made 'the Qur'an 'a plaything of their fancy' (2000: 100).

21 Gilliot 1999: 24–27.

22 *Jalālayn* c. 16 C/2008 and *Bayḍāwī* c. 13 C.

23 For Ṭabarī and Ibn Kathīr, see McAuliffe 1988. In this study, the English translation of the first and the Urdu one of the second have been used. For Bayḍāwī (c. 13 C), the Urdu translation and for Jalālayn both the English (2008) and the Urdu (Nūrī 2005.) have also been used.

24 Rippin 1997: 84; Waardenburg 2002: 115.

25 Campanini 2008: 26.

(1884 – 1953), a famous scholar of Islam in India, divided pre-modern South Asian exegetical works into traditional and rational ones. The paradigmatic works in the first category were the exegeses of Ibn Kathīr and al-Ṭabarī, among others. They were based on the medieval, magical worldview with appeal to the supernatural rather than rationality and empiricism. Thus, traditions, anecdotes, and stories of the supernatural kind are found in these exegeses and each exegete follows his predecessors in the field. Among the second variety are the ones which emphasise rationality such as Rāzi's *Tafsīr-e-kabīr* and *Bayḍāwī*. This rationality, however, is based on Greek philosophers like Aristotle and Plato as translated into Arabic.[26]

Tafsīr, like other genres of writing, is anchored into the cosmology, the worldview, of the age as well as the ideological and psychological orientation —the personality—of the individual exegete. This is perhaps what Georg Gadamer means when he says that readers have a 'historically effected consciousness'.[27] In the case of Muslim exegetes, this 'history' is the particular ideology which that particular exegete wants to defend. This method is called the prescriptive methodology. It is used both in exegesis (*tafsīr*) and in the determination of meaning (*ma'ānā*) through translation (*tarjumah*). The starting point is the idea or belief-system which informs the search for meaning. Modernity, with which we have dealt briefly in the last chapter, brought in a consciousness of European power versus the 'Muslim Orient'. As mentioned earlier, if one can abstract from a plethora of reactions to European power and modernity, one may place these reactions under three headings: falling back on the literal meaning of the foundational texts i. e. the Qur'an and the hadith (often called fundamentalism), renewal of society in accordance with the fundamental principles of Islam or revivalism (radicalism is placed under it), and interpretations of Islam in the light of Enlightenment ideas borrowed from the West (modernist or progressive Islam). Exegetical literature is obviously affected by modernity just as Biblical criticism is.

Massimo Campanini, an Italian scholar of Islam, gives detailed examples of the different types of *tafāsīr* in the modern age. He places Ibn 'Āshūr among the traditionalists while Maḥmūd Shāltūt is categorised as a traditionalist influenced by reformist *Salafism*. But this *Salafism* is the doctrine of the modernist Sheikh 'Abdūh (1849 – 1905) another al-Azhar scholar. 'Abdūh and his follower Rashīd Riḍa (1865 – 1935) are known more for their reformist readings than their *Salafism*, though, of course, the imperative for reform is based upon what they con-

26 Nadwī in Shāhjahānpurī 1984: 21.
27 Gadamer 1927: 299 – 310.

sider the authentic (*Salafī*) reading of the sources.[28] These ideas rubbed off on Jamāl al-Dīn al-Afghānī (1839–1897), an Iranian social and political activist, who visited India several times. His only idea which seems to have found resonance in India is the concept of the Muslim community as a single nation (*ummah*).[29] These ideas of pan-Islamism—though they never got translated into geographical world states based on Islam—did create a community of feelings which had important repercussions on the appeal of jihad in contemporary times as we shall see later.

Muslim scholars in India, in common with those of other parts of the Muslim world, were initially impressed with Western humanitarian values, the rule of law, representative government, science and technology. Sir Sayyid Aḥmad Khān, the pioneer of British education in India, in letters to his friends exhibits an extreme awe of Western progress. Nor, indeed, is he alone in his high estimate of the West. However, even Sir Sayyid, loyal to the British though he was, was pained by Sir William Muir's (1819–1905) biography of the Prophet which, in his view, was insulting towards Islam. But Sir Sayyid's response to this biography and, indeed, his own exegesis of the Qur'an, is an extreme example of modernist Islam. Basically, Sir Sayyid writes 'scientific' exegesis. Generally, it is the Egyptian exegete Ṭanṭāwī Jawharī (1862–1940) who is credited with this kind of exegesis,[30] but Sir Sayyid took the lead on him. He takes science as authentic and true and interprets those ideas of the Qur'an which do not appear to conform to this view—with the exception of the belief in God and the mission of the Prophet —as metaphors, distortions of the meaning, and figures of speech.

Exegetes of this school argue that scientific discoveries have been predicted in the Qur'an. To confine ourselves to examples from South Asia, Abū'l Kalām Āzād has been placed by Campanini[31] among the scientific exegetes. However, though he refers to some scientific ideas, he also warns against being so impressed by science as to force the Qur'an into the scientific framework in an obvious reference to Sir Sayyid.[32] Ghulām Aḥmad Parwēz, the founder of the movement for progressive Islam called *Tulū'-e-Islām* (the Dawn of Islam) in Lahore, contends that rationality is the basis of understanding the thought process promoted by the Qur'an and this is also the philosophy of science. In short, at the higher philosophical level, faith and science are one and not antithetical ways of dealing with reality. Āzād and Parwēz, as well as Mawdūdī, refer to modern dis-

28 Campanini 2008.
29 Keddie 1972.
30 Campanini 2008: 37.
31 Ibid 40.
32 Āzād, *Tarjumān* 1931: 16.

ciplines to suit their purposes though, of course, not always to support the same agenda.

Liberation theology, a term borrowed from Christianity, describes the interpretations of the Qur'an using modern hermeneutics of the kind used in Biblical criticism and literature. Such efforts bring literature, history, linguistics, sociology, and other disciplines to reach new explanations of the Book called 'progressive Islam'.[33] Though many scholars are included in the list of progressives, only a few outside South Asia are mentioned below. Notable among them are Muḥammad Arkoun (1928–2010), an Algerian born French academic, who asserts that the Qur'an is a historical narrative which makes flexibility of interpretation possible.[34] Another one, of Egyptian origin, Naṣr Ḥāmid Abū Zayd (1910–1943) also begins with the assumption that the Qur'an is a cultural and historical product, the implication of which is that its meanings are limited to time and place and are not immutable. Both raise the question of 'the historicity of the text' which makes it amenable to human reason.[35] Yet another, Farid Esack (b. 1959), a South African exegete, sees the Qur'an as a book for human liberation. For him, jihad is 'struggle and praxis', not the conquest or rule over non-Muslim peoples. In his interpretation of the verse 'fight against them until disorder (*fitnah*) is no more and God's religion reigns supreme'(2: 193), *fitnah* is defined as an unjust social order like apartheid in South Africa which he experienced himself.[36] In the modern world—while anaysing the political exegeses of Khomeini and Quṭb—Neguin Yavari tells us that exegesis has emerged as a medium of 'the articulation of political thought'.[37] Supporting this observation, Rebecca Sauer, in her analysis of the 'rebellion verse' in *al-Ḥujarāt* (Q. 49)—which says that if two factions of Muslims fight then try to make peace and if necessary fight those who are wrong (49: 9)—she tells us that the traditional exegetes did not refer to the case of the 'Alid and Umayyad conflict—an obvious rebellion—'for pragmatic and mundane reasons'.[38] But now that the political exegesis is common, South Asian as well as other exegetes openly use their exegeses to express political ideas.

In South Asia, Sir Sayyid, Chirāgh 'Alī, Mohammad Ali (1874–1951), Parwēz, and Waḥīduddīn Khān, all wrote what can be called modernist exegeses. Johannes Marinus Simon Baljon (1861–1908), a Dutch scholar of South Asian

33 Waardenburg 2012: 127–128; Ahmed 2013; Sharify-Funk 2008: 23–59
34 Campanini 2008: 48–62.
35 Ibid 59.
36 Ibid 107–113.
37 Yavari 2014: 312.
38 Sauer 2014: 245.

Islam, in his study of modern interpretations of the Qur'an, focuses on the work of Āzād, 'Ināyatullāh Khān Mashriqī (1888–1963), the leader of a semi-fascist organisation called the *Khāksārs*, and Parwēz. He sums us the common features of this kind of interpretation. First, it is to 'strip the text of legendary traits and primitive notions';[39] secondly, 'to minimize as much as possible miraculous elements in the story';[40] thirdly, to make the Qur'an 'appropriate to the thought-world of to-day;'[41] and fourthly, to make the Qur'an conform to modern, Western humanist ideals about war, tolerance, freedom, and human rights. Modernists explain the verses about women, especially the permission to marry up to four wives, or the permission to beat wives in case of disobedience, slavery, and such other issues in a manner which reconciles them to Western, progressive values. Examples will be provided in due course. The result of these hermeneutical approaches is to produce what may be called a liberation theology. While such insights into interpretation may be helpful for us,[42] it is necessary to present the particular hermeneutical devices used for interpreting jihad by South Asian scholars of Islam.

Lexis and Semantics

Lexis refers to words (*lughā*) and semantics to the construction and reception of meaning as well as the whole range of meanings including denotations and connotations (*ma'nā*). One approach towards understanding the Qur'an is to comprehend the meanings of the words used in it. Exegetes and translators of the Qur'an have to determine the meanings of the words they try to explain. This seems fairly simple provided one has an understanding of classical Arabic for which one should master lexicography (*'ilm al-lughā*). Shāh Walīullah, the most famous scholar and reformist of Sunni Islam in modern India, devotes several pages to this pointing out that figures of speech, variations of style, idiom, etc., are complex issues which can only be learnt by immersing oneself in the study of Arabic. He concludes by saying that the criterion is the usage of the Arabs and not contemporary explicators of meaning.[43] Modernist or progressive interpreters of the Qur'an also focus on meanings. For example, Parwēz wrote a

39 Baljon 1961: 21.
40 Ibid 24.
41 Ibid 89.
42 Poythress 1988.
43 Walīullah *Fauz* 84.

dictionary in four volumes called *Lughat al-Qur'ān*[44] in which he points out that by the time the exegeses of the Qur'an came to be written, Arabic had been influenced by Persian and other foreign languages which carried the linguistic baggage of their own belief systems. Thus, it is necessary to find the root of each word, see how it was used in Arabia in the seventh century, and trace out its occurrences in the Qur'an itself to determine its significance.[45] This view is also expressed by Jāwēd Aḥmad Ghāmidī (b. 1951), whose refutation of radical Islamists and traditionalists forced him to live in exile.[46] However, Parwēz's use of semantics is very different from that of Ghāmidī. When Parwēz talks of the roots of words, he takes a position which the linguist Ferdinand de Saussure (1857–1913) would call the diachronic argument instead of the synchronic one. For Parwēz, if etymologically a word, or its root, meant something at one point in time, it can be used to determine its meaning at another. Ghāmidī's position, on the other hand, is that words mean whatever they do at a certain point in time irrespective of their history. So while both believe that the intention of the Author (in this case God) is recoverable and both use language as a means for doing so, they use different linguistic strategies for retrieving this meaning. Ghāmidī's position, it may be pointed out, is in conformity with modern theories of semantics.

A linguistic approach is also followed by Amina Wadud (b. 1952), who gives a feminist interpretation of the position of women. She argues that 'although each word in Arabic is designated as masculine or feminine, it does not follow that each use of masculine or feminine persons is necessarily restricted to the mentioned gender—from the perspective of universal Qur'anic guidance'.[47] This is important for her because she wants to transcend what she calls the androcentric readings of the Book.

Thus, the quest for meaning is not only a matter of one's competency in Arabic. It is much more complex since an exegete might already have an ideological imperative for promoting one meaning instead of another. Thus, out of several possible meanings, the exegete or translator prefers the one which supports his or her belief-system. The descriptive method provides several possible meanings without obviously preferring one[48]. Several examples of the prescriptive method, the one which most concerns us, will be given in due course.

One example is the interpretation of the word *ḍarabā* in a verse of *al-Nisā'* (Q. 4) which has traditionally been translated to mean that husbands can beat

---

44 Parwēz 1960.
45 Parwēz 1960: 8 & 17.
46 Ghāmidī 1990: 15–20.
47 Wadud 1992: 7.
48 Burge 2015 b: 27.

their wives for disobedience (*nushūz*). The relevant part of the verse is translated as follows: 'men are guardians (*qawwamūn*) over women since they spend their wealth upon the latter. Good women obey them and guard their modesty. If they rebel you must admonish them; then separate them from your beds and finally strike them. But if they obey do not find excuses to use force...'(4: 34). It is explained thus by Amina Wadud:

> [*ḍarabā*] is, however, strongly contrasted to the second form, the intensive, of the verb—*darraba:* to strike repeatedly or intensely. In the light of the excessive violence towards women indicated in the biographies of the Companions and by practices condemned in the Qur'an (like female infanticide), this verse should be taken as prohibiting unchecked violence against females. Thus, this is not permission, but a severe restriction of existing practices.[49]

A modernist Muslim, Chirāgh 'Alī, had concerns similar to that of Wadud in the nineteenth century. He argues that the husband is no longer the head of the household in the legal sense. For this there are courts of law and this right, once given in the absence of the legal institutions, has now been taken away. Moreover, this verse has been abrogated (*mansūkh*) by the very next verse (4: 35), which orders that people from the two families of the spouses should be appointed to make peace.[50] Parwēz interprets the whole verse as relevant for men and women in general and not husbands and wives. This does away with the husband's right to strike his wife for certain forms of disobedience. He begins with the word in the beginning of the verse, i.e *qawwamūn* in (4: 34), which is translated as 'rulers' by most South Asian exegetes following Shāh Rafī'uddīn, who translated the Qur'an in Urdu. Parwēz contends that it actually means 'one who provides sustenance'.[51] This means that men are to provide sustenance while women are to look after the other needs of the family. If anyone rebels against this order, the state, and not people in general, can punish them.[52] Thus, in accordance with modern concepts of equality in marriage, men are seen as partners of women rather than their masters. A contemporary progressive interpreter of Islam, Waḥīduddīn Khān, while explaining (4: 34), does concede that physical punishment is allowed as a last resort for constant rebellion by wives but it may be 'like beating with a tooth brush' (*miswāk sē mārnā*).[53] As

49 Wadud 1992: 76.
50 'Alī 1910, part 2: 16.
51 *Maṭālib* Vol. 3: Explanation of 4: 34, p. 363–364.
52 Ibid 359. Also see 365–66.
53 Khān *Tazkīr* Vol. 1: 190. Miswāk is a small, delicate branch of a tree used for cleaning the teeth.

we have seen, in all cases except Khān, the exegetes have resorted to giving different meanings of the verb 'to beat'. These are examples of semantic variations.

Other examples of it are as follows. According to Aziz Ahmad, 'In Āzād's exegetical *lexique technique*, *dīn* (religion) is equated with law' and other concepts are similarly used with different implications.[54] Mawdūdī also distinguishes between revelational religion (*dīn*) and the traditional one which is *madhhab* or Sharī'ah.[55] But perhaps the most ingenious, though least convincing, explanation is by Ziauddin Sardar who suggests that 'its [*ḍarabā's*] function is to generate moral apprehension of that act' so that men may be shamed into not doing it.[56] Sardar goes on to quote with approval the use of semantic expansion—based upon meanings of the word *ḍarabā* other than beat such as pet, tap, to go away, strike out on a journey, and seduce—as an interpretive device by the Iranian-American translator of the Qur'an, Lāleh Bakhtiyār (b. 1938), who renders the last line of the verse as 'and go away *from* them' (emphasis in the original).[57] This meaning has also been used in verses other than the one we have been considering so far. For instance, Baljon points out as an example of 'lexicographic juggling' by Sir Sayyid who interprets it to mean 'going' or 'running' in order to assert that Prophet Moses was told to walk in the Red Sea leaning on his staff across a ford.[58] In short, the miracle of the sea parting to allow him to cross over could be explained naturalistically. This use of semantic expansion has, however, been discouraged by a number of scholars. Ghāmidī, for instance, recommends taking the most ordinary, known, and clear meaning and not the lesser known or esoteric ones.[59]

In some cases, meanings are deliberately suggested, sometimes in parentheses, as in the case of the translation of *Sūrah Fātiḥā* (Q.1: 6–7) which is rendered as follows:

> Guide us to the Straight Way, the way of those on whom You have bestowed your Grace, not (the way) of those who earned Your Anger (such as the Jews), nor of those who went astray (such as the Christians).[60]

---

54 Ahmad 1967: 181–182.
55 Ibid 212.
56 Sardar 2011: 308.
57 Ibid, 309.
58 Baljon 1949: 56.
59 Ghāmidī 1990: 21.
60 Hilali and Khan 1999, Part 1: 2–3.

In the same edition, while translating (2: 193), the parenthetical explanations are as follows:

> And fight them until there is no *Fitnah* (disbelief and worshipping of others along with Allah) and (all and every kind of) worship is for Allah (alone). But if they cease, let there be no transgression except against *Al-Ẓalimūn* (the polytheists, and wrong-doers).[61]

The meanings suggested in brackets do not include 'persecution', 'cruelty', or 'those who turned you out of your homes' etc., thus suggesting that jihad is against a belief system rather than certain aggressive acts. Although Saudi Arabia is 'Wahhābī' not militant, such semantic manipulation privileges the radical Islamists who argue that jihad is against all non-Muslims.

Āzād, and later Parwēz, translates a verse of *Sūrah Hūd* (Q. 11: 78) about the Prophet Lot offering his daughters instead of his male guests to the men of his town in ways which suggest that he is actually persuading the men to marry the girls or go to their wives. Let us begin with the words of the Qur'an first: 'O People! these are my daughters who are pure for you...'. The translation of these words by Shāh 'Abdul Qādir, the first translator of the Qur'an in Urdu, is: 'these are my daughters, they are offered to you. They are pure for you, with them... (*yē mērī bētiyā̃ haẽ ḥāḍir haẽ, yē pāk haẽ tum ko in sē...*). But he explains in the margin that Prophet Lot offered his daughters in marriage to save his guests since in those days it was permitted to marry unbelievers.[62] Āzād agrees with the translation but writes in brackets that 'the women of this place whom he [Lot] considered in place of his daughters and who had been abandoned by those men' were offered to them.[63] Parwēz goes a step further saying in his translation of the verses in Urdu: 'these your wives, who are like daughters to me, are permitted and appropriate for you'[64] suggesting that Prophet Lot was only persuading them to go to their wives. Waḥīduddīn Khān, though he puts no suggestive remarks in parentheses, explains that these are the nation's daughters and the men should indulge their natural (*fitrī*) desires with them after marrying them.[65] In short, the exegetes' ideology, that a prophet could not offer his daughters to men for forbidden sexual practices even to save guests, precluded their accepting the literal meaning of the verse. This, however, is neither an innovation of South Asian exegetes nor does it originate in re-

61 Ibid part 2: 40.
62 Qadir 1792: 298.
63 Āzād *Tārjumān* 1936: 200.
64 *Matālib* Vol. 6, 1991: 473.
65 Khān *Tazkīr* Vol.1: 594.

cent times. Indeed, classical Muslim exegetes deviated from the exegetes of Genesis (19: 7–9) in the explanation of this incident. Whereas the Biblical exegetes sugggested that Lot 'exposed his daughters to the sexual desires of the Sodomites to protect his male guests from sexual abuse',[66] Muslim scholars and exegetes ('Abdullāh bin Mas'ūd [594–653], Mujāhid bin Jabr [645–722], and Abū 'Abdullah al-Qurṭubī [1214–1273] among others), suggested three alternatives: that the offer was of marriage with the daughters; that all the women of the community were like daughters for Lot; and that it is a rhetorical ploy to shame the Sodomites.[67]

Sometimes, however, there may be confusion about the word itself. For instance, the 'introduction of the variant reading of *īmān* to replace *ayman* in Qur'an 9: 13—exhorting Muslims to fight those who break their pledges—by Al-Wahidi on the authority of the Syrian *qārī*' Ibn 'Āmir' changes meaning. As the word *ayman* refers to pledges while *īmān* is faith, so if the first reading is privileged the order to fight is against those who violate their oaths while the latter meaning connects it to belief in Islam.[68] But while there is ambiguity of meaning in some cases, certain meanings became privileged over time. By the time of the classical exegetes, such as al-Ṭabarī, the meaning of jihad which had become more predominant was that of 'fighting in the path of God', not of other forms of endeavour.[69]

Besides the philological focus on the meaning of words and phrases, there is the mystical approach to meaning. Among others, Ṣadr al-Dīn Shīrazī or Mullā Ṣadrā (1571 or 2– 640) is known as a paradigmatic exegete and philosopher in the mystical tradition. Mullā Ṣadrā believes that the Qur'an has several layers or levels of meaning. There is the literal meaning (*ẓāhir*) as well as the esoteric (*bāṭin*) meaning. Moreover, there are several other semantic levels some of which are gnostic and not available to lexicographers. The verses of the Qur'an are either explicit (*muḥkamāt*) or ambiguous or undecipherable (*mutashābihāt*).[70] The latter are not amenable to the tools of the lexicographer anyway, but even those which are do not exhaust their meanings once they are decoded. Based upon these hermeneutical principles, Mullā Ṣadrā writes a gnostic exegesis of a verse of the Qur'an Q. 24 (*al-Nūr*) which is available in English translation.[71] Not only mystics but others who preferred heterodox explanations, such as the

66 Ahmed, W 2011: 415.
67 Ibid 419–423.
68 Afsaruddin 2013: 63.
69 Ibid 23.
70 Vishanoff 2011: 17.
71 Peerwani 2004.

Mutazilites, established the 'binary opposition between literal (*haqīqa*) and figurative (*majāz*) usage' which traditionalists like Abul Ḥasan al-Ash'arī (874–936) 'resisted'.[72] The latter are called the essence of the Qur'an by the mystics. The classical Persian poet Jalāluddīn Rūmī (1207–1273) says:

> *Māz-ē-Qur'ān rā bardāshtaem*
> *Istakhwān pēsh-ē-sagā̃ andākhtaem*
> (The essence of the Qur'an I carry/the bones I throw to the dogs).

But the esoteric meanings can change the very nature of the text and Islam itself. As the Urdu poet Muḥammad Iqbāl (1877–1938) says:

> *aḥkām terē ḥaqq haẽ magar apnē mufassir*
> *ta'wīl sē Qur'ān ko banā saktē haẽ pāzhand*
> (Thy orders are true but our exegetes/with esoteric interpretations can turn the Qur'an into Zoroastrian sacred texts)

Iqbāl refers to the infinite creativity—misleading in his view—of esoteric interpretation.

However, mystical commentaries are not relevant for our understanding of jihad in the contemporary world and are mentioned here only to suggest that meaning is not a fixed entity from several points of view.

Exegesis is not the only thing affected by the meanings of words. As suggested by some of the examples given above, the translation of the Qur'an itself relies, among other things, on its linguistic aspects. Every word one chooses has a semantic load which commits or inclines one to a certain interpretation. As Gadamer pointed out[73] and Rashīd Riḍā reiterated in 1908, 'every translation is at the same time an interpretation'.[74] Discussing the several translations of the Qur'an in English, Ziauddin Sardar points out how they were meant to convey certain points of view. 'Abdullah Yusuf 'Alī (1872–1953) and Marmaduke Pickthall (1875–1936) had their translations revised by Saudi authorities in such a way that they now support the Wahhābī point of view.[75] This makes it impossible to escape the processes of conferring pre-existing meaning onto the text with or without being conscious of one's biases.

Given these apprehensions, it is possible to understand why there was so much resistance to Shāh Walīullāh's translation of the Qur'an in Persian and

72 Vishanoff 2011: 21–22.
73 Gadamer 1927: 346
74 Quoted by Sardar 2011: 40.
75 Sardar 2011: 46–48.

his sons', 'Abdul Qādir and Rafī'uddīn's, translations of it in Urdu. Sometimes the translation may be seen to promote a certain sectarian ideology and, if that is construed as being heretical, it is banned. For instance, the English translation of Mohammad Ali was banned and burnt in Cairo in 1925 as the translator was a member of the Lahori faction of the Ahmadiyya sect which is considered heretical by mainstream Islam.[76] Even Marmaduke Pickthall, whose translation of the Qur'an was welcomed in India, was opposed in Egypt.[77]

As mentioned above, one aspect of the words chosen to translate a concept is the semantic load they carry. This is because this load carries certain associations for certain people in their minds. For instance, the Ḥanafī jurist Abū'l-'Abbās al-Mustaghfirī (d. 432/ 1041) has recorded in his book *Faḍāi' l al-Qur'ān* the translation of the *Sūrāh Fātiḥā* (Q1: 1): (in the name of God the most compassionate the most merciful) as follows:

Ba-nām-i īzad bakhshāwand bakshāyishgār

Īzad is the Persian concept of the good god (Yazdān) in the Zoroastrian religion which carries the connotations and ideological vestiges of there being a deity of evil (Ahrimān) also. In short, the words 'could very well evoke a set of non-Islamic religious practices and beliefs'.[78] In the same way, the translation of Shāh Rafī'uddīn of (Q.1: 3) in Urdu is as follows:

Mālik-i yaum al-dīn
(Khudāwand din jazā kā)

The word *Khudāwand* refers to the Persian concept of the deity which is no longer preferred by South Asian Muslims because of increased Arabization and Islamization.

Similarly, the word for worship used in the translation of Rafi'uddīn is *pūjnā*, which is associated with Hinduism and is now substituted by the Arabic word *'Ibādat* in Qur'an (109:2):

Lā a'budu mā ta'budūna
(maẽ nahī̃ pūjtā jis kō tum pūjō)

76 Zadeh 2015: 378.
77 Ibid 378.
78 Ibid 402.

Shāh 'Abdul Qādir, in his Urdu translation, used the Arabic alternative in the translation of the same verse.[79] Thus, in the eighteenth century, both the indigenous *pūjā* and the Arabic *'ibādā* were considered permissible substitutes. This, however, is no longer the case when the Arabic word is mandatory in modern Urdu as the boundaries of the Muslim identity are drawn more tightly in India and Pakistan now than they were in the early nineteenth century in British India.

Abrogation as an Interpretive Device

One of the concepts used to interpret the Qur'an is that of abrogation (*naskh*). Among the classical writings on it are Abū 'Abdullāh ibn Idrīs al-Shāfi'ī's (767–810) *Risālāh* (c. 9 C) and 'Ubayd al-Qāsim ibn Sallām's *al-Nāsikh wa'l-mansūkh fi'l-Qur' ān* (d. 839) (c. 9 C).[80] In order to understand them, it is necessary that the technical register in which they are given should be explained. First, the word *naskh* has two meanings. The first is copying a book; the second is 'replacing a practice with another'. The understanding of the concept by scholars of Islam is that it refers to 'abrogation or annulment of a divine ruling by a later divine ruling'.[81]

Another important distinction is between the Qur'an and the *muṣḥaf.* The term Qur'ān is derived from *qara'ā* (read) while *muṣḥaf* comes from *ṣaḥīfah*, the plural of which is *ṣuḥūf* (written pages) which occurs in the Qur'an. Thus, the Qur'an is the total revelation of the word of God in Islamic belief while the *muṣḥaf* is that part of the revelation which is recorded on paper. According to most Muslims the two are identical but scholars, especially those who believe in some forms of *naskh*, believe on the evidence of the hadith that some verses were 'caused to be forgotten' or were not recorded.[82]

With these concepts in mind we can conclude that there are three forms of *naskh:*

1. Legal abrogation: the ruling of a verse does not apply but it is recited as it remains in the Qur'an (*naskh al-ḥukm dūnā al-tilāwah*).

---

79 Shāh 'Abdul Qādir's and Rafī'uddīn's translations of the Qur'an.

80 For an introduction, see Powers 1988; for a detailed account, see Burton 1990. For the classical sources in translation, see Shāfi'ī c. 9 C; Sallām c. 9 C.

81 Fatoohi 2013: 13.

82 See Burton 1977 for an account of the collection of the Qur'an and Muslim traditions about this theme. Arthur Jeffery (1998) quotes at length a tradition from Abū 'Ubaid about such verses (1938). Quoted from Warraq 1998: 150–153.

2. legal-textual abrogation: both the words and the orders do not apply (*naskh al-tilāwah wal-ḥukm*).
3. Textual abrogation: the words do not exist in the *muṣḥaf* but its ruling still applies (*naskh al-tilāwah dūnā al-ḥukm*).

Legal abrogation is explained by many scholars but, for a concise account, see Burton.[83] His primary example is about the *'iddah*—the waiting period for a widow or a divorced woman—which was first prescribed as a period of one year in (2:240). Later, it was reduced to four months and ten nights in (2: 234).[84] Burton argues that the law (*fiqh*) 'is formulated on the basis of something other than the *Ḳur'ān* wording' which means that this invocation of abrogation is a legal-exegetical device to reconcile theories of law with the Qur'an.[85] Another example, apparently more plausible, adduced by exegetes is that people were asked to pay '*ṣadaqāt* (goods sanctified to God, contribution to obtain recompense from God, alms) in *al-Mujādalah* (58:12) but then this order was withdrawn (58: 13). Burton as well as modern Muslim commentators do not consider this a case of abrogation on the ground that the offering was not insisted upon anyway.[86] Such considerations have led scholars to suggest that abrogation was a legal device to reconcile texts with legal principles. Abū 'Ubayd, a jurist, gave attention to the use of *naskh al-ḥukm dūnā al-tilāwah* for reconciling legal difficulties.[87] Al-Shāfi'ī contends that 'what He abrogated from the Book is abrogated only by the Book', and that 'the *Sunnah* cannot abrogate the Book'.[88]

The second category, legal-textual abrogation, is about certain verses which were said to be recited but are not recorded in the *muṣḥaf*. The belief is that they were not forgotten but 'caused to be forgotten' since it was not the divine will that they should be remembered.[89] The belief that there are such verses is based on evidence such as the testimony of the Companions and the hadith. One example is about the verses pertaining to the Bi'r Ma'unā incident in which some Muslims were killed at the place of that name. The great compiler of hadith Imām Bukhārī (810 – 870) reports on the authority of a chain of narrators ending on the Companion Anas bin Mālik (612–709) that 'we used to read: "Tell our people that we have met our Lord. He has been pleased with us and He

83 Burton 1990: 56 – 57.
84 Ibid 57– 62.
85 Ibid 80.
86 Ibid 190.
87 Sallam c. 9 C: Introduction.
88 Shāfi'ī c. 9 C: 53.
89 Burton 1990: 45 – 55.

has pleased us....".This was then abrogated'.[90] However, since they do not exist any longer, there is controversy about their identity, length, number, and dates of revelation and cancellation.

The third category, textual abrogation, has one famous example, i.e stoning married adulterous pairs till they die.[91]There is no such punishment in the Qur'an now since it prescribes only giving the adulterous couple a hundred stripes in *al-Nūr* (24: 2). However, it is contended that this punishment was given by the Prophet and the first four Caliphs, so there must have been such an order in the Qur'an which is still valid though it is no longer recited. Al-Shāfi'ī cites hadith to argue that stoning (*rajm*) for adultery is still valid. However, he does not call it the Prophet's own initiative but only that he [the Prophet] was conveying what God had directed him to do.

Among classical scholars, the number of abrogated verses ranges between twenty-two (in the work of the Egyptian scholar Jalāl al-Dīn al-Khuḍairī al-Suyūṭī [1445–1505]) to two hundred and forty seven (in the work of the Hanbalite Baghdad scholar 'Abd al-Raḥmān Ibn al-Jawzī [1126–1200]).[92] Ibn Sallām's own list of abrogated verses is given in tabular form by Powers.[93] Indian scholars of Islam were also aware of abrogation and referred to it in their works. Shāh Walīullāh, in his study of the principles of exegesis of the Qur'an, discusses *naskh* in detail. His conclusion is as follows:

> Allāma Suyūṭī agreeing with Ibn ul 'Arabī says that twenty-one verses stand abrogated but even in these there is disagreement. But for three the claim of abrogation is not correct... [here he mentions three verses in which there is no abrogation]...which leaves only nineteen verses which are abrogated. I say according to my previous writing [here he refers to the previous pages [32–38 in the source given below in which he has mentioned every verse in which abrogation is claimed but does not actually occur] it is only in five verses that abrogation can be proved.[94]

Shāh 'Abdul Azīz gives a brief introduction to the idea of abrogation without, however, giving his own opinion as to what he considers abrogated.[95] Sir Sayyid denies *naskh* in the usual sense in which it is understood. He believes that it refers to the abrogation of previous religious laws (that of Judaism for instance) but

---

90 In Fatoohi 2013: 139.

91 Burton 1990: 122–164.

92 Ibid 184; Fatoohi 2013: Table 5.1, p. 88.

93 Powers 1988: Appendices A & B, 137–138.

94 Walīullah *Fauz* 38.

95 *Tafsīr-e-'Azīzī*, Vol. 2: 175–193.

not to the verses of the Qur'an.[96] Since this refers to divine law as promulgated for Jews and Christians, this brought an angry denial of *naskh* from the missionary polemicist Karl Gottlieb Pfander (1803–1865) who argued that this would imply that 'God could give an impractical and imperfect command which he would have to repeal later; this would put into question the wisdom and omnipotence of God'.[97] Perhaps one of the most interesting views put forward in South Asia is that of Ḥifẓ al-Raḥmān Seohārwī who argued that 'the repertoire of abrogated passages should not be seen as fixed in all their implications: evolving circumstances should be allowed to resuscitate what was once a dead letter and vice versa'.[98] However, the majority view in South Asia was a denial of abrogation as commonly understood. For instance, Mawlawī 'Abdullāh Chakṛālwi (1900–1932), a denier of the authenticity of hadith, considered *naskh* as 'simply issuance of a religious command in place of the other on the condition that the first command can, due to some temporary problem, no longer be abided by'.[99] Fazlur Rahman argues that the original meaning of *naskh* is the 'substitution' of 'certain verses for others' and distinguishes it from the 'juristic doctrine of abrogation which later developed in Islam and which is an attempt to smooth out apparent *differences* in the import of certain verses'.[100] Parwēz believes that when circumstances change, new rules are needed so a new prophet is sent by God who abrogates the previous orders. Since the Qur'an is the last such divine order, none of its verses have been abrogated.[101] This, indeed, is a trend one observes in other modern Muslim scholars too. They generally deny that any verse of the Qur'an could be abrogated. For instance, Louay Fatoohi contends that abrogation is not supported by the Qur'an. It is an invention by later scholars to reconcile certain legal contradictions. In this context, he refers to the work of John Burton who reaches similar conclusions in his study of the collection of the Qur'an and the role of *naskh* in it. Fatoohi writes:

> My analysis will agree with the three modes of Burton's conclusion. Even in the unlikely case that the Qur'an contains an instance or two of abrogation—which I can accept as a possibility only in case of legal abrogation—there is absolutely no ground to suggest that the Qur'an introduces [it] as a principle of any prominence in Islamic law.[102]

96 Khān 1887 in Pānīpatī Vol. 11: 489–504.
97 Troll 1978: 91.
98 Zaman 2012: 32.
99 Quoted from Qasmi 2011: 137–38.
100 Rahman 1980: 62.
101 *Matālib*, Vol. 1: 130.
102 Fatoohi 2013: 113.

One major reason for modern Muslim scholars to deny the doctrine of *naskh* is explained by Fatoohi as follows:

> The so-called "verse of the sword"[Q 9: 5] is claimed to have abrogated as many as 140 specific verses and many more unidentified verses. Today's interest in this particular abrogation claim stems from the fact that it has been used by some terrorist individuals and groups to justify atrocities, as it is claimed to give Muslims the right to unjustifiably kill non-Muslims. The case of this abrogation claim embodies everything that is wrong with the unhistorical phenomenon of abrogation.[103]

This, as we have seen in the last chapter, is also Qaraḍāwī's reason for denying *naskh*. In the case of the concept of jihad, the conflicting interpretations take on the form of an intellectual battle. As Afsaruddin says:

> Tensions between dovish and hawkish camps continue to manifest themselves in this exegetical material, especially in connection with the controversial hermeneutical tool of *naskh*, which was wielded to privilege more belligerent readings of the Qur' ān.[104]

The battle of interpretations goes on with the moderates and the militants giving conflicting interpretations of the Quranic verses. In November 2002, for instance, Muḥammad al-Massārī, a Saudi dissident in self-exile in the UK, published an interpretation of jihad which accused moderates of trying to 'water down Islam' in order to make it acceptable to Christians and Jews though it meant 'having your blood spilled'.[105] The battle of interpretation goes on.

Explanation by Citing Occasions of Revelation

This kind of commentary takes cognizance of the occasion for the revelation of a Quranic verse, the *asbāb al-nuzūl* (*reasons for revelation*), to determine its significance.[106] In his translation of the words of Ḥājī Khalīfah, an Ottoman bibliographer of the 11th/17th centuries, Andrew Rippin defines it as follows:

> *'ilm asbāb-al-nuzūl*, one of the subdivisions of *'ilm al-tafsīr*, deals with the transmission of the *sabab* of the revelation of a *sūra* or verse and the time, place and so forth of its reve-

103 Ibid 244.
104 Afsaruddin 2013: 94.
105 E-mail circular quoted from Burke 2003: 32.
106 Rippin 2001b: 1–15.

> lation. It is verified by the well-known principles of transmission from the pious ancestors [*salaf*]. Its goal is the precise rendering of these matters.[107]

Rippin goes on to give several names of such exegetes beginning from 'Ikrima (d. 105/723). However, the main work mentioned in this kind of exegesis is by Abu'l Ḥasan 'Alī ibn Aḥmad al-Wāhidī al-Nīsāburī (d. 468/1075). The book, called *Kitāb asbāb nuzūl al-Qur'ān,* became a model for later exegetes and is widely available even now.[108]

Some South Asian scholars, such as Ḥamīduddīn Farāhī (1863 – 1930) and Amīn Aḥsan Iṣlāḥī (1904 – 1997)[109]were critical of this method on the grounds that the *asbāb* make a chapter of the Qur'an 'like a completely disjointed discourse'.[110] Iṣlāḥī says that 'the *shān-e-nuzūl* should be taken out from the Qur'an itself and only those things may be taken from the corpus of hadith and historical legends which support the Qur'an and not those which destroy its system'.[111] Parwēz, another exegete who has reservations about the way this method of interpretation has been used, points out that exegetes give meanings related to particular incidents and not with reference to the roots of words and their usage in seventh century Arabia thus obscuring or changing the meaning of the Qur'an.[112]

Specification

The method of appealing to the circumstances of revelation mentioned above can be used as a hermeneutical device by exegetes. It may, for instance, make verses 'specific for a certain time and place' (*takhṣīṣ al-zamān wa'l-makān*). This would restrict them to a certain group of people making it a special case

107 Ibid 1.
108 Ibid 4.
109 Amīn Aḥsan Iṣlāḥī writes in the preface (*muqaddimah*) of his exegesis of the Qur'an entitled *Tadabbur al-Qur'ān* and again in the preface of its last volume (8) that he had become a student of Mawlānā Farāhī in 1925 and studied with him for five years (*Tadabbur*, Vols 1: 19 and 8: 8 – 9). Farāhī's main work, according to him, is that he has given an analysis of the verses of the Qur'an as a coherent whole and not as scattered accounts of events. More importantly, he has grouped verses in seven categories in such a manner that their themes appear as clusters. The aim of the whole exercise is to bring out the internal harmony (*naẓm*) and coherence of the Qur'an (*Tadabbur* Vol. 1: 9 – 42).
110 Guezzou 2008: xiii.
111 Iṣlāḥī, *Tadabbur*, Vol. 1: 32.
112 Parwēz 1960: 9.

and not a general one. For instance, Muḥammad 'Abdūh and Rashīd Riḍā, who have been mentioned earlier, argued that jihad was defensive. They interpreted the 'sword verse' (9: 5)—and similar verses about fighting the polytheists—as applicable only to the Arab polytheists of the seventh century.

A general rule for the interpretation of the Qur'an, basing itself on the presence of general and particular (restricted) verses, is also found in Jalāl al-Dīn al-Suyūṭī's, *Al-Itqān fi 'ulūm al-Qur'ān*, which gives a comprehensive scholarly digest of all aspects of the interpetation of the Qur'an including abrogation, grammar, and the causes of revelation. One of Suyūṭī's rules is as follows:

> ...if it [the verse] is a command or a prohibition, then it will apply to the individual concerned as well as those who fall in this category. If however, it consists of praise or dispraise then too it will apply to the individual concerned as well as those who fall in this category.[113]

If this is applied to the orders for jihad, they are to be taken as applicable everywhere provided the same conditions obtain. In this context, Chirāgh 'Alī points out that 'the Mohammadan legists, while quoting the Koran in support of their theories, quote some dislocated portions from a verse without any heed to its context, and thus cause a great and irreparable mischief by misleading others, especially the European writers'.[114] Jihad, asserts 'Alī, is only defensive, or it refers to non-military struggle for betterment. This meaning of jihad was changed by scholars, he continues, because of the political pressures of an expanding empire. Peaceful interpretations of jihad are also created by restricting aggressive warfare only to Arab polytheists (*takhṣīṣ*) on the basis of the causes of revelation.

Among others, Ziauddin Sardar explains verses pertaining to women's dress code and alcohol consumption with reference to the circumstances of revelation. He reasons that 'the dress worn by women of the time had a deep cleavage which exposed the breasts', so what is being suggested in the Qur'an is modesty and not a specific form of veiling.[115] As for alcohol, he continues, the prohibition is to reform binge drinking which was the norm of Arab society. However, he stops short of permitting drinking though he does go into a philosophical discourse about the relativism of good and evil and ends up saying that 'what is "wholesome" in one context may not be so in another'.[116]

113 Suyūṭī, c. 15 C. *Al-Itqān:* 7.
114 'Alī 1885: 129.
115 Sardar 2011: 332–333.
116 Ibid 227.

Some of the *'ulamā* are not comfortable with this mode of interpretation because, in their view, this undercuts the immutability of the Qur'an and makes it possible to suspend the application of its rulings on the grounds that they were bound by time and place. Shāh Walīullāh, for instance, approved of those explanations which were historical in nature but not those which were in the nature of 'general applicability'.[117]

Privileging Principles over Particulars

A major protagonist of this approach is Fazlur Rahman who calls it 'double movement' and explains it as follows:

> First, one must move from the concrete case treatments of the Qur'ān—taking the necessary and relevant social conditions of that time into account—to the general principles upon which the entire teaching converges. Second, from this general level there must be a movement back to specific legislation, taking into account the necessary and relevant social conditions now obtaining.[118]

Shiblī Nu'mānī (1857–1914), a nineteenth-early twentieth century Indian interpreter of Islam, also touched upon the idea of a 'lasting, universal in the societal norms of Islamic *sharī'ah*',[119] but he did not develop this insight into a hermeneutic principle. Amina Wadud also uses this approach in her book mentioned earlier. She posits a 'hermeneutics of *tawhid*' which makes her reject 'interpretations which ignore the basic social principles of justice, equality, and common humanity'.[120] What she means by this is that the Qur'an must not be interpreted literally but that its general spirit of reform should be adjusted according to circumstances. This makes her conclude that the 'Qur'an adapts to the context of the modern woman as smoothly as it adapted to the original Muslim community fourteen centuries ago'.[121] Ziauddin Sardar also advocates the same approach but goes to greater lengths than Fazlur Rahman when he claims that the interpreter may 'reject, enhance, go beyond and differ significantly from the interpretations of earlier times'.[122] Without this hermeneutical tool, his own progressive interpretation would not be possible.

117 Guezzou 2008: xiii; for the detailed discussion see Walīullah Fauz: 38–43.
118 Rahman 1982: 20.
119 Murad 1976: 77.
120 Wadud 1992: xii.
121 Ibid 95.
122 Sardar 2011: xx.

An example of how diverse interpretations of the same verse are possible using the hermeneutical tools given above, one may look at Patricia Crone's history of the interpretations of (2: 256) (*lā ikrāha fī'l-dīn*, i.e. there is no compulsion in religion). While the arguments given below are from Crone,[123] the name of the hemeneutical device in parentheses used by the interpreter is by the present author. One of the traditional Sunni interpretations is that it has been abrogated by verses ordering aggressive war. The second, also advanced by traditional interpreters, is that it was only meant to prevent parents from forcing a certain faith upon their children since that is what was happening in Medina (*asbāb al-nuzūl*). In short, it was meant for a specific group and does not have general implications (specification or *takhṣīṣ*). Yet another traditional interpretation is that it applies to those from whom *jizyah* can be taken (this excludes Arab polytheists and ex-Muslims). The Mutazilite position is that while God does not force people to convert, human beings can do so to promote societal solidarity or to confer benefits upon their children (as was done in the case of Arab polytheists). Yet another view, again Mutazilite, is that '*ikrāha*' in the verse which is usually translated as 'compulsion' also means 'dislike' (*karāha*). If this meaning is granted, the verse means 'there is nothing to dislike in religion' (semantic expansion). Modernist Muslims, going for the literal meaning of the verse, argue that this is a verse which outlaws religious intolerance, aggressive jihad, and forced conversion (ideological imperative). It is, as Crone points out, 'a timeless grant of universal tolerance'.[124] The Islamists, on the other hand, use it to allow war. Quṭb, for instance, argues that this verse is to be read in conjuction with (2: 193) (fight them till *fitnah* ends and religion is all for God). If thus understood, it means that Muslims should fight to bring about an end of all political systems which prevent the worship of God in the Islamic manner. And, Quṭb continues, this can only happen when Islam is politically dominant. Only this, he further argues along with Mawdūdī, can bring about the freedom in which one can choose Islam freely or reject it.[125] To sum up, one verse can be interpreted using different hermeneutical devices to yield not just different but even opposite meanings.

123 Crone 2009.
124 Ibid 150.
125 Ibid 154–155.

The Interpretation of Hadith

The interpretation of hadith, besides involving the debate over meaning, revolves around the basic question: how authentic are they? Hadith, which literally means 'talk', 'statement', or 'speech', has now come to mean accounts of the words and deeds of the Prophet of Islam.[126] Thus, the authenticity of these sayings and reports of actions and behaviour is related to how they were collected and transmitted. The orthodox Muslim view is that they were preserved as sacred wisdom by the Companions mostly orally but some were also preserved in writing even during the early period, i.e the 1st/7th centuries.[127] European scholars—and some Muslims too as we shall see later—feel that, since they were mostly transmitted orally, their authenticity is open to question. One of the foremost of the former group is the Hungarian scholar, Ignaz Goldziher (1850–1921), whose monumental work on hadith laid the foundation of that discipline in Europe. Goldziher's main argument is that the hadith were fabricated for various reasons: for instance, during Umayyad rule, the 'impetus to these inventions and falsifications often came from the highest government circles;'[128] as the law (*fiqh*) developed the hadith rulings were invented to provide authority;[129] heretics invented them deliberately to support their opinions;[130] they were created for 'ethical, hortatory and ascetic purposes'.[131] His other main objection was that the references (*isnād*) were invented 'without much scruple' to complete the chain. Schacht confirmed this scepticism about hadith with reference to the work of jurists.[132]

Muslim scholars, most notably Muḥammad Mustafā Azmi, refute the theories of both Goldziher and Schacht. Among other things, Azmi points out that: there were writings in the first century; there is nothing definitive against recording them; that the theory of 'projecting back' of the *isnād* is 'difficult to imagine' since the number of transmitters and their dispersal across a vast area makes this improbable.[133] There was, however, a third group of Western scholars who took what can be called the middle road. They accept that some *aḥādīth* purport-

126 For a comprehensive introduction see Brown 2009.
127 See Azmi 2001: 1–6; 25–26 for the traditional Sunni point of view and refutation of European scholars such as Goldziher 1890 and Schacht 1950. Also see Motzki 2004: xxiv-xxv.
128 Goldziher 1890: 44.
129 Ibid 81.
130 Ibid 126.
131 Ibid 146.
132 Ibid 148. See Schacht 1950.
133 Azmi 2001: 237.

ing to be early ones are authentic but that others in their present written form are doubtful.[134] Juynboll talks of a 'position that could be taken between the two points of view represented respectively by Muslims and Western scholarship'.[135] However, since the Muslims believed that the Companions were free from falsehood, this represented a point of departure between Muslims and Western scholars.[136] Burton, while agreeing that the *isnād* could be made up and the texts were sometimes anachronistic, concludes that 'the wholesale rejection of the *ḥadīths* as mere invention and fabrication misses the point that many of the *ḥadīths* can be shown to spring from an ancient source in the primitive exegeses'.[137] Apart from the argument of 'freedom from mendacity' in respect of the Companions which Muslims believed in, their major point of departure from Western scholars was the chain of transmission expressed through the names of narrators (*asmā'al rijāl*) which traditional Muslim scholars did not doubt, provided certain criteria were satisfied, but which the first group of Western scholars, as well as some Muslim scholars to whom we will come below, doubted. The *isnād* tradition itself emerged at an uncertain time in history. Three dates are given: during the lifetime of the Companions (60/679 – 80); in the generation of their successors (60 – 120/679 – 80 – 737 – 8); between 120 – 180/679 – 80 – 797 – 98).[138] Here again the controversy between those who agree with the traditional Muslim view and those who do not remains unresolved primarily because there are hardly any extant written texts which unambiguously refer to a large corpus of hadith.

Another method of using hadith is by looking at their subject matter (*matn*) and *'ilm al-dirāyā*, i.e criticism of the *matn*, with reference to reason and historical fidelity. Both Goldziher and Schacht used the criteria based on the *matn* for placing the hadith in time. Clearly, the implicit reasoning behind these criteria is the assumption that the *aḥādīth* were created later in order to provide legal support to jurisprudence which emerged to meet the exigencies of the time. Thus, scholars sceptical of the hadith accepted the less developed texts as more authentic since they were not necessitated by the legal requirements of the time.[139] Wael B. Hallaq, however, attempts to solve the problem by bringing in

---

134 Juynboll 1983; Burton 1994.

135 Ibid 1983: 1.

136 Ibid 190 – 191.

137 Burton 1994: 181.

138 Motzki 2004: xxxiv.

139 Ibid xlv. Muslim scholars laid down that the transmitter should be scrupulously religious (*'ādil*); sober; deeply versed in hadith; reliable (*thiqā*); accurate (*thābit*), and of excellent memory (*ḥāfiẓ*). The reports of such a man are in the highest category of being sound (*ṣaḥīḥ*). Those

the theory of probability: 'We have been told that except for a score of *ḥadîths*, the rest engenders probability, and probability, as we know—and as we have been unambiguously told by our sources—allows for mendacity and error. What more do we want?'[140]

The 'more' which traditional or the stricter Muslim scholars wanted was to begin with faith, not doubt in the hadith as a system. Moreover, the scholarly use of probability Hallaq was talking about was not part of the ordinary Sunni faith in India. Indian scholars used criteria different from European ones to classify hadith according to their authenticity.[141] However, scholars like Shāh 'Abdul 'Azīz, whose work has influenced modernists in various ways, laid down certain criteria for accepting the validity of a tradition. Among these are the criteria of not being 'contrary to reason' or the *shari'ah* and not laying down disproportionate punishments or rewards etc—in short, criteria similar to those suggested by people whose attitude towards the hadith was more critical than that of traditional scholars.[142]

The traditional Sunni view in India was to believe in the six canonical collections of hadith as authentic and accept their guidance, as representing the Prophet's own commentary on the Qur'an and the good Muslim life (for details, see Chapter 3). Those who wanted to deny aggressive jihad, prohibit polygamy, or ban slavery—the very concerns of the nineteenth century modernists and now progressive Muslims—had to re-examine the hadith in order to give interpretations which, in their opinion, presented a humane and soft image of Islam—an image they believed was the 'true' one. So, in order to save Islam from the attacks of Western critics, Muslim modernists (or apologists as they were called) used all the hermeneutical devices mentioned earlier to give progressive interpretations of Islam. For this, they denied the validity of the hadith or, without any explicit denial, did not use them at all.

The pioneers of hadith criticism in India were European scholars writing on Islam. Aloys Sprenger (1813–1893), an Austrian scholar who worked in India for most of his career, wrote an article to demonstrate that there was writing among

nearly of this standard are fair (*ḥasan*). If the narrator is liable to err then his reports are weak (*ḍa'īf*) (for details, see Brown 2009: 100–110).

140 Hallaq 1999: 90.

141 Schacht gives the categorisation of hadith in use by the time of Shāfi'ī and still used by traditional Muslims in a succinct form as follows: *thābit* 'well authenticated', *mashhūr* 'well-known', *mawṣūl* or *muttaṣil* 'with an uninterrupted *isnād*', *maqṭū* or *munqaṭī'* 'with an interrupted *isnād*', *mursal* 'lacking [the mention of] the first transmitter', *ḍaīf* 'weak', *majhūl* 'unknown, not identified', *munkar* 'objectionable' (1950: 36).

142 Rizvi 1982: 139–140.

Christian Arabs, and that even Muslims did write the hadith. He adds, however, that there was an opinion in early Islam that it should not be written but, nevertheless, it was. Sprenger wrote an article in which he claims that he was 'the first writer who attempted to submit the sources of the biography of the prophet of the Arabians, to a critical enquiry' in his work on the subject published in 1851.[143] However, it is Sir William Muir's biography entitled *The Life of Mahomet from Original Sources* (1858–1861) in three volumes which is better known since its first volume is devoted to the discussion of hadith which the author dismisses as being unreliable. Sir Sayyid was specifically distressed by the attacks of Muir in this book. However, he noted that Muir had used Arabic sources which were not available in India. To refute the book, therefore, it was necessary to go to England. On this project he spent his own money and accompanied his son Sayyid Maḥmūd (1850–1903) to Cambridge. He stayed in England between May 1869 and October 1870 and used the libraries of London for his work. The result was a series of articles in Urdu, which were translated into English and published in 1870 in London. The original version is now available in twelve essays compiled by Isma'īl Pānīpatī.[144] Both Muir and Sir Sayyid were concerned with the authenticity of the sources for their undertaking and both found the hadith scholarship by the traditional *'ulamā* questionable. Although Sir Sayyid began with the idea of exposing Muir's work for its prejudiced approach, which he did clearly, he also imbibed Muir's scepticism towards the sources of the hadith. Indeed, he declares in the preface that even the traditions in the six collections of *aḥadīth* believed to be authentic by the Sunnis are not necessarily true.[145] He also states that the traditions were written two hundred years after the migration to Medina and that they were often invented to suit the occasion.[146] Indeed, though he begins by criticising European scepticism of hadith, he ends by doing the same himself which makes Thomas Patrick Hughes (1838–1911), his missionary adversary, observe facetiously that he (Sayyid) is 'his own refutation'.[147]

Sir Sayyid goes on to find fault with biographical accounts (*kutub al-siyār*), especially with the accounts of Ṭabarī and Abū 'Abdullāh ibn 'Umar ibn Wāqid al-Aslamī (130/747–207/823) known as Wāqidī which, he claims, are used by Christian authors to vilify Islam.[148] Thus, Sir Sayyid is highly critical of Muir

143 Sprenger 1856: 303.
144 Khān 1887 in Pānīpatī Vol. 11: 382–548.
145 Ibid 123.
146 Ibid 364.
147 Hughes 1875: 59.
148 Khān 1887 in Pānīpatī Vol. 11: 370.

who relies on such stories and takes the most disparaging *aḥadīth* as true despite the fact that he himself says that most of them were invented by later generations in order to legitimise the standpoint of warring parties. So, in Sir Sayyid's view, Islam could only be defended if texts like the histories and the *aḥadith* were treated sceptically.

In contrast, Sir Sayyid establishes the Qur'an as the criterion for the acceptability of a hadith text. If a tradition contradicts the Qur'an, he rejects it. Moreover, the *dirāyāt* of a tradition rather than its *isnād* are given more value.[149] He also claims that Muslim scholars of the traditions did not find the time to test each one of them with reference to the *dirāyāt.*[150] This makes him claim that it is now up to any Muslim to test any tradition on the basis of the criterion of *dirāyāt* and accept or reject it.[151] In a letter to a certain Sheikh Mīran, who had questioned him about his scepticism towards the hadith (letter of 7 August 1897), he writes that many of them are not authentic and, while he does respect them, especially *Muslim* and *Bukhārī*, 'he believes that *dirāyāt* should be used while consulting them'.[152] He also refers to the criteria of accepting a hadith as authentic in Shāh Walīullāh's works.[153] Among other points, one is that it should not go against rationality. This is in the context of his discussion of the Prophet's ascension to the heavens (*mi'rāj*) which, Sir Sayyid argues, could only be a dream. Thus, while refuting Muir, Sir Sayyid eventually comes to accept only five *aḥadīth* as being authentic on grounds of chain of narration while for the rest he emphasises rational analysis. Indeed, he was at pains to impress upon critics like Muir that 'there was a tradition of rational criticism of the content of the Hadith in Islam'[154]. Sir Sayyid's circle of friends and admirers, the modernist reformers of Indian Islam discussed below, also shared his views about the hadith.

For instance, Chirāgh 'Alī, who has been referred to earlier, points out that the *aḥādīth* are not reliable on the usual grounds that they were written in the third century (*hijrā*) and reliance was placed on the chains of narrators rather than rationality and subject matter.[155] In his writings on Islam, he rejects a number of traditions because they were either 'repugnant to the dignity of prophet-

149 Ibid 383.
150 Ibid 403.
151 Ibid 419.
152 Khān 1898: 97.
153 *Tafsīr-e-Sayyid*, Vol. 2: 114–131.
154 Troll 1978: 138.
155 'Alī 1910 part 2: 48–49.

hood', contradicted the Qur'an, or were incredible for other reasons.[156] Indeed, proceeding from Shāh Walīullāh's hypothesis that a hadith could convey the sense 'but not the exact words of the Prophet', Chirāgh 'Alī uses it 'when it suits him to reject a particular rejection'.[157] Sayyid's other admirers and friends, such as Alṭāf Ḥusain Ḥālī (1837–1914), a famous intellectual, poet, and reformer, also pointed out that some of the *aḥādīth* were fake.[158] Mahdī 'Alī Khān, better known by his title of Muḥsin al-Mulk, (1837–1907), another follower of Sayyid, argues that the principle of abrogation 'must necessarily operate in the *ḥadīs̱*'.[159]

Another famous intellectual loosely connected with Sir Sayyid's circle, Shiblī Nu'mānī, who has been mentioned earlier, also wrote about the hadith. Shiblī's major theory on the hadith is in his biography of the jurist Abū Ḥanīfah al-Nu'mān bin Thābit (80/699–150/767) entitled *Sīrat al-nu'mān*. First, he points out that the orthodox Caliphs narrated very few apostolic traditions: Abū Bakr (17); 'Umar (50); 'Uthmān and 'Ali also narrated in numbers in the same neighbourhood. On the other hand, Abū Hurayrah al-Dawsiyy (d. 681) narrated 5,340, Anas 2,286, and so on.[160] Secondly, Abū Ḥanīfah, whose eponymous school of law is followed by most Indian Muslims, used rational grounds for evaluating the veracity of *aḥādīth* and was, therefore, called 'One who reasons on opinion' (*ahl al-rā'ay*).[161] Though the Imām knew *aḥadīth*, having studied them from several masters of the age, he considered most of them inauthentic since they depend on narrators who suffer from human limitations of memory and other weaknesses.[162] Shiblī also used Abū Ḥanīfah's distinction—also followed by Shāh Walīullāh—'between legislative (*tashrī'ī*) and non-legislative (*ghayr tashrī'ī*) commands and *aḥādīth*'.[163] The former concern prophethood and are to be obeyed. The second, on the other hand, are habits, adaptations, or responses to situations or exigencies. These were not binding on all Muslims.[164] Shibli expanded the same theories in the first chapter of his biography of the Prophet, *Sīrat al-nabī*, which came in manuscript form in the hands of Sayyid Sulaimān Nadwī, a historian and Islamic scholar with training at Deoband (1884–1953) in 1914. Nadwī edited and published it in 1918. Shiblī points out that there

156 Ahmad 1967: 50.
157 Ibid 59.
158 Ḥālī 1879:13.
159 Ahmad 1967: 69.
160 Nu'mānī 1893: 104.
161 Ibid 108.
162 Ibid 127.
163 Murad 1976: 67.
164 Ibid 67–69.

were some written records during the Prophet's lifetime but the compilations of *ḥadīth* which we have are all from a hundred years later. He then lays down certain criteria for distinguishing between implausible *aḥādīth* from valid ones. These criteria (*dirāyā*), as mentioned in the case of Abū Ḥanīfa's acceptance of traditions, are mostly rational. For instance, the tradition should not be against reason; should not contradict observation and empirical realities; should not threaten dire punishment for minor transgressions or disproportionate rewards for minor acts; should not contradict the Qur'an and repeatedly occurring traditions (*mutāwātar*), etc.[165] He then adds that even less reliable than the traditions in compilations are the books of history. Among those he names are the Abbaside historian Wāqidī mentioned above, Ṭabarī, the Abbaside historian and biographer Ibn Isḥāq (85/704 – 150 or 159/761 or 770) and the historian Abū 'Abdullāh ibn al-Sa'd also known as the 'scribe of Waqidi' (*kātib al-Waqidī*) (168/784 – 230/845).[166] Shiblī was, however, not entirely convinced by Sir Sayyid's heterodoxy. But even Shiblī himself, despite his caution, was criticised by the Ahl-e-Hadith who said that he 'has nevertheless done irreparable damage by promoting such [rationalistic] views'.[167] On the whole, then, Sir Sayyid and his circle—including Shiblī who was only at the peripheries of it and that too temporarily—did challenge the orthodox view about the unquestioning acceptance of the six canonical works of hadith.

Both Chirāgh 'Alī and Sir Sayyid had argued that hadith was 'unreliable long before Goldziher's work came out in the West'.[168] However, while scholarly work published in Europe did not influence India immediately, there were critics among missionaries and Evangelical colonial officials who offered critical discourses on the validity of the hadith. One of them, T. P. Hughes, whom we have mentioned earlier, called for 'a science of evaluating the traditions'. Ironically, he had 'taken the rules and categories for the reception and rejection of traditions directly from Aḥmad Khān's *Essays*'.[169] But some of the missionaries, for instance Hughes and Sell, mellowed down their earlier views while Indian scholars developed even more sceptical views of hadith than the pioneers mentioned above.

These Indian scholars were the so-called 'deniers of hadith' (*munkirān-e-ḥadīth*). Both Brown and Qasmi, writing about them, point out Sir Sayyid's role in this movement—commonly called the Ahl-i-Qur'ān movement. Sayyid, along

165 Nu'mānī and Nadwī, Vol. 1, 1918: 43 – 44.
166 Ibid 48.
167 Brown, D 1996: 130.
168 Rahman 1982: 120.
169 Guenther 1997: 123.

with other Muslim modernists, were 'the first to reopen the question of Prophetic infallibility in the modern period'.[170] The most detailed book-length study of this movement is by Qasmi but Brown too has written about them.[171] Both point out that they differ from the traditionalists in that they accept only the Qur'an as the sole authority in religious matters excluding the hadith as well as the edicts of jurists.[172] Qasmi gives detailed accounts of the ideas and writings of the most well known members of this group such as Mawlawī 'Abdullāh Chakṛālawī (1900–1932), Aḥmad Uddīn Amritsarī, Aslam Jayrājpūrī (1882–1955), Tamannā 'Imādī (1888–1972), and Ja'far Shāh Phulwārwī (1902–1982). Although their ideas and forms of argumentation and presentation varied considerably, they agreed that the hadith does not have the binding force or authenticity which the Qur'an has. Chakṛālawī came out with Quranic prayers since it was pointed out by his opponents that prayers cannot be said if hadith is not taken as a guide.[173] Aḥmad Uddīn emphasised the historicity of the hadith arguing that they were written by human beings and God never promised to keep them unchanged which is the case with the Qur'an.[174] Apparently, his thought influenced Iqbāl who wished that he (Aḥmad Uddīn)would write a book about Islamic practices based only on the Qur'an.[175] Jayrājpūrī, however, accepted Prophetic practice which is repeated very often and by large segments of people (*sunnat-i-mutawātir*) as valid. But he too rejected most of the *aḥādīth* on the ground that they were reported by only one person. Phulwārwī distinguished between the Prophet's religious and human roles making the point that it was only the first where he was divinely guided.[176] 'Imādī, a scholar from Bihar, used the *isnād* paradigm to argue that the hadith were fabricated by Iranians to undermine the Arab version of Islam.[177] Parwēz also used the Qur'an itself to interpret it pointing out that the *aḥadīth*, historical accounts, and stories recorded by exegetes were not reliable. In his book *Muqām-e-ḥadīth*, he gave a detailed account of how the *aḥādīth* were compiled and why he did not use them to interpret the Qur'an.[178] Although a few scholars, for instance the Egyptian doctor Muḥammad Tawfīq Sidqī (1881–1920), did present views similar to the Indian scholars pre-

170 Brown, D 1996: 64.
171 Ibid 44–48; Qasmi 2011.
172 Qasmi 2011: 140–143.
173 Ibid 138–144.
174 Ibid 178.
175 Ibid 184.
176 Ibid 191.
177 Ibid 192.
178 Parwēz 1953.

sented above, such views remained isolated in the rest of the Muslim world.[179] Among modernists, Fazlur Rahman gives a 'situational interpretation' of hadith in order to 'resurrect the norms which we can then apply to our situation today'.[180] He begins by arguing that the *sunnah* is 'either a continuation of the pre-Islamic Arab practices or the result of assimilative-deductive thought-activity of the early Muslims themselves'.[181] Further, 'the majority of the contents of the *Ḥadīth* corpus are, in fact, nothing but the *Sunnāh-Ijtihād* of the first generations of Muslims'.[182] Gradually the hadith became part of orthodoxy taking on the 'character of an eternal truth, unchangeable and irrevisable' and blocked progress.[183] Fazlur Rahman challenges this view by rejecting *aḥādīth* which, in his opinion, go against the spirit of the Qur'an which, he asserts, is one of reform, progress, and humanism. Thus, he rejects the predictive *aḥādīth* about 'political troubles' which are given in *Muslim* and *Bukhārī* with impeccable *isnād.*[184] Even more relevant for us is his interpretation of the Caliph 'Umar's orders that the land of the vanquished in Iraq and Syria was not to be distributed to the Arab fighters. As the Prophet himself had confiscated the land of the tribes he vanquished, this order apparently opposed his *sunnah.* However, explains Fazlur Rahman, the Prophet was operating in the tribal milieu. If this practice was extended 'where vast territories and whole peoples are involved' it violates 'the very principles of justice for which the Prophet had been fighting all his life'.[185] Thus, it is the spirit of the tradition, not the words nor the exact meaning, which is to be used for moral living. In short, as Brown points out, Rahman feels that he is 'free to accept, reject, or reinterpret traditions without appearing to flout the example of the Prophet'.[186]

Even scholars who defended orthodox Sunni views about the authenticity of hadith kept a certain flexibility of interpretation for themselves. Ghāmidī, for instance, laid down seven principles for accepting a hadith as authentic. The gist of his work is that it should not contradict the Qur'an and the actual conduct of the Prophet and also that it should not be incredible from a rational perspective. Even if a tradition is in *Bukhārī*, *Muslim*, or *Muwaṭṭā*, he declares, it should not

179 Brown, J 2009: 245–46.
180 Rahman 1964: 80.
181 Ibid 6.
182 Ibid 45.
183 Ibid 141.
184 Ibid 72.
185 Ibid 181.
186 Brown, D 1996: 106.

be taken for granted if it does not fulfill these conditions.[187] In short, like the doubters or non-users of *aḥādīth*, Ghāmidī, who does make use of them, reserves for himself the right to use them selectively in the light of the principles and criteria laid out by him.

This position, however, is more famously associated with Mawdūdī who often defended traditional positions and took issue with the deniers of hadith. Indeed, it was in the context of refuting the position of these deniers that he wrote essays in his journal called *Tarjumān al-Qur'ān*, the gist of which is that the Prophet is to be obeyed in all matters pertaining to religion. As this is not possible unless one believes in the guidance provided in the *aḥādīth*, they are of utmost importance. However, it is also true that some of the *aḥādīth*, even in the six authentic books of hadith (*Ṣiḥāḥ Sittah*), may not be authentic. To separate them from those which are, one has to be extremely well read in the Islamic sciences. This he expresses as follows:

> By excessive study and thinking and practice one develops a capability to understand the personality of the Prophet (*mizāj shinās-e-Rusūl*) and the real spirit of Islam goes into his heart and mind. Then, upon seeing a hadith, he understands at once whether the Prophet, Peace be Upon Him, could say or do such a thing or not.[188]

Mawdūdī expressed this idea several times comparing it to a goldsmith's insight into precious stones. He even goes to the extent of saying that if one has this insight one can reject a hadith which is *mutawātir* and accepted by others. Indeed, one does not even need the references (*isnād*) any more. Thus, one can then accept a single, weak hadith, provided it is according to the personality of the Prophet.[189] However, such a license is not to be given to those whose forte is not Islamic studies of the traditional kind. Thus, he had the following to say to Justice Sheikh Abdur Rehman (spelled as Rahman also) (1903–1990) of the Supreme Court of Pakistan in 1958:

> *Dirāyāt* is authentic of only those people who have spent a considerable part of their lives in the study and research of the Qur'an, hadith and jurisprudence.[190]

This rules out secular intellectuals with only Western type of learning. But because Mawdūdī's criterion to accept the *aḥādīth* was subjective, the *'ulamā* at-

187 Ghāmidī 1990: 62.
188 Mawdūdī 1940: 338.
189 Ibid 362.
190 Mawdūdī 1958: 303.

tacked it as heresy.[191] However, the fact is that all those who have given any but the most traditional and literal reading of the hadith, have done something like Mawdūdī without necessarily declaring it. Indeed, Shiblī refers to several scholars during the time of Abū Ḥanīfah who made similar claims. According to some scholars, insight into hadith is a psychological state one experiences 'on their hearts' (*'alā qulūbihim*). Shiblī adds to this in Urdu: 'this claim of the traditionists is absolutely correct. Without doubt the command of the art of narration [of *aḥadīth*] gives a certain taste or expertise which makes it possible to decide whether a certain saying could be of the Prophet or not'.[192] These descriptions are not far removed from Mawdūdī's claims.

The questioning of hadith on the basis of its exact meaning or validity on rational grounds, rejecting some or all of them and taking them as suggestive of tendencies rather than strictly authoritative orders are all strategies for interpreting the concept of jihad. For instance, the hadith often quoted by radical Islamists to justify their ongoing global war—'I have been ordered to fight humankind [*nās*] till people say there is no god except God'—is interpreted as advocating eternal war against non-Muslims. Al-Qaraḍāwī, however, uses the hermeneutical device of specification (*takhṣīṣ*) for the hadith. Thus, '*nās*' does not mean 'all human beings' but a specific group of them, i.e hostile Arab polytheists. In the case of the tradition 'I was sent with the sword', he argues that it is weak.[193]

Asma Afsaruddin examines early hadith as well as the six canonical collections to reach conclusions which challenge the predominantly combative meanings of jihad. Her main contribution is her study of the *Muṣannafs* of 'Abd al-Razzāq al-San'anī (126/744- 211/827) and Ibn Abī Shaybah (d. 235/ 849). She reports that 'several of these archaic reports preserve the most expansive, non-combative significations of the term *shahīd*'.[194] Combative meanings were apparently a requirement of the time since the 'Umayyads were at war with the Byzantine Empire. Since much of this warfare was naval, the *aḥādīth* proclaiming greater merit for this kind of warfare is also a product of the political climate of the period. Another important point made by the same author is that the six standard collections of the *aḥādīth* contain more reports about the combative aspects and their high value than the early works. She says:

191 Parwēz c. 1950s; Zakariyya 1975.
192 Nu'mānī 1893: 135.
193 Ghannouchi, al- 2015: 337.
194 Afsaruddin 2013: 125.

> The *faḍā'il* [blessings of *Jihād*] reports promising exaggerated posthumous rewards to the military martyr continued to be added to and put in circulation after the third/ninth century.[195]

But even among the standard works there are non-combative meanings of jihad which are ignored by the militants while the combative ones are similarly ignored by the modernists. Both parties use the same interpretive strategies—dismissing *aḥadīth*, dubbing them weak and interpreting them differently.

Three overriding hermeneutical principles for all kinds of sources, not normally described separately in their own right, are: ideological imperatives, emphases, and selection. Ideological imperatives, as mentioned earlier, are like the lenses through which the interpreter sees reality. They are *a priori* beliefs which are not to be questioned but for which evidence is to be marshalled in support. For instance, if an interpreter starts with the belief that jihad is only defensive then this assumption will not be questioned at all. Instead, all interpretations will be made with this imperative in mind. Sometimes, appeals to common sense or some other branch of knowledge, are made to support a certain argument. As in the case of translation, parenthetical remarks may be provided to lead a reader on to the interpretation preferred by the exegete. Sometimes this ideological imperative—the very reason for the interpretation—may not be consciously known to the interpreter, or, it may be known but not explicitly stated. However, it influences the use of hermeneutical devices in the project of interpretation.

Yet another way of constructing an interpretive narrative is that it deploys sources selectively to favour a certain interpretation. This method also leads to emphasis or lack of it but, in contrast to the method of emphasising certain aspects, selection bias will miss out a source altogether while in the last method it is mentioned but carries such emphasis as the interpreter thinks necessary. One factor which also affects the whole interpretive project is the interpreter's personality (inherited traits, psychological makeup and life-experiences). But this is so complex a factor that one can only point to it without attempting to operationalise its effect on interpretations.

To conclude then, the foundational sources for the interpretation of jihad are the Qur'an and the hadith which we have covered in some detail. Others which are used are the books of jurisprudence (*fiqh*). They are useful in order to understand how the history of the actual declarations of religious war, migration, and Muslim attitude towards non-Muslims played out in history. However, they are not necessary to understand how the concept itself has been interpreted by

---

195 Ibid 148.

South Asian spokespersons of jihad. That is why the methodology used by jurists and the way the religious edicts (*fatāwā*) are actually written have not been discussed in this chapter. Ultimately, the basis of the reasoning of jurists as well as exegetes and others, is 'derived in principle from the Ḳur'ān and *ḥadīth*'.[196] Religious edicts also refer to the consensus of opinion (*ijmā'*) 'and might include intellect', analogy (*qiyās*), 'juristic preference (*istiḥsān*), and public welfare (*maṣlaḥa*)',[197] but the ultimate court of appeal are the Qur'an and the hadith.

As for jurisprudence, there is indeed a legal hermeneutics about which David R. Vishanoff has written a detailed treatise. It is useful in so far as we learn that it can be both flexible and inflexible. The flexible 'law-oriented hermeneutic has allowed more rapid changes' but they were guided by 'a priori social norms and values of jurists'.[198] This notion is crucial since, in all interpretations of jihad as a concept, flexibility is not an outcome of the hermeneutic. Rather, one chooses the hermeneutic in the light of *a priori* commitment to change (flexibility) or conservation (inflexibility).

While not affecting interpretations of jihad itself, certain juristic edicts do have great practical consequences. For instance, it does matter whether jurists declare a country a *Dārul Islām* (land of peace) or *Dārul Ḥarb* (land of war). In the latter case, people have to know whether jihad becomes a *farḍul 'ayn* (duty for all) or *farḍul kifāyah* (duty for some). They also want to know whether a practicing Muslim is supposed to migrate from such a country or not. But, despite the practical importance of such matters in peoples' lives, jurisprudence does not have bearing on how the phenomenon of jihad is itself understood. Thus, it is not necessary to analyse the reasoning of individual *fatāwā* or the institution of jurisprudence itself. As religious edicts are necessary in order to provide the historical context of events which were understood as jihad in South Asia, they will be mentioned in passing wherever necessary. However, the focus of this study remains the idea of jihad itself as it is interpreted primarily in the genre of *tafsīr* and secondarily in other writings about it.

---

196 Hooker 1997: 321.
197 Ibid 325.
198 Vishanoff 2011: 277.

3 Jihad in Transition

This chapter describes the transition of the practice and theory of jihad from the medieval to the modern periods in South Asia. The first section, which is very brief, refers to the actual use of the concept of jihad by Muslim rulers. The second deals with the broad consensus of views about it amongst orthodox, traditional Sunni *'ulamā*. The sources for the first are historical documents; those for the second are the religious texts available to the *'ulamā*.

The rulers of India, whether Turks, Pathans, or Mughals, used Islamic vocabulary to legitimise their rule in the eyes of their Muslim chiefs and the *'ulamā*. Amīr Taimūr (1336–1405), the Turco-Mongol conqueror who attacked India in 1397–99 with legendary cruelty and devastation, uses purely religious language in defense of his action in his memoir *Malfūẓāt-e-Taimūrī*.[1] Ẓahīruddīn Bābar (1483–1530), the first ruler of the Mughal dynasty of India, in his memoir *Bābar-Nāmah*, also uses the vocabulary of jihad when he confronts the Hindu ruler Rānā Sangrām Singh (1484–1528), the ruler of Mewar, in the battle of Tarain but not when he defeats the Muslim ruler Ibrāhīm Lodhī (r. 1517–1526).[2] However, Taimūr did not actually rule over India while Bābar chose to do so. Hence, in the case of Bābar and the other Mughals, the religious language is used only selectively so as not to alienate the Hindu chiefs with whom the Mughals allied themselves.

Some of the use of the language of jihad is, however, merely conventional. For instance, in the *Fatḥnāmah* of Abū'l Ḥasan Yamīn al-Dīn commonly known as Amīr Khusraw (or Khusrau) (1253–1325), possibly the most famous poet and intellectual of medieval Muslim India, written during Ghiasuddīn Balban's (r. 1266–1287) victory in the battle of Lakhnauti, the words 'jihad', '*ghāzī*', and the 'victory of Islam' are used. It seems that Khusraw was merely practicing how to draft documents of this genre but this only suggests that, whatever the reality, the language of documents announcing victories of Muslim rulers rhetori-

---

1 Sensing reluctance among his chiefs, he opened the Qur'an to suggest the course of action (*fāl*). It read 'O Prophet! Struggle against the unbelievers and the hypocrites' (*yā ayyuhannabīyū jāhidil kuffār wal munāfiqīna*)[i.e al- Tawbah 9: 73] (Taimūr c. 14 C: 67). Elsewhere, while describing his conquests, he claims that he wanted to spread Islam.

2 Bābar calls his war against Rāna Sanghā jihad. Both his order (*farmān*) and his declaration of victory (*fatḥ nāmah*) are full of verses from the Qur'an including 9: 73 used above by Taimur. His force is the 'army of Islam' (*Lashkar-i-Islām*) while his opponents are 'infidels' (*kuffār-i-nāfarjām*). He publicly stops drinking and declares that he who dies is a martyr (*shahīd*) and he who survives is a *ghāzī* which is also the title he adopts when he wins the war (Bābar c. 16 C: 551–576).

https://doi.org/10.1515/9783110716986-006

cally appropriated the legitimacy conferred by religious concepts for purely worldly aims[3]. A number of documents of this type exist in the *Munsha'at-i-Namakīn* compiled by Abū'l Qāsim Namakīn. An important *Fatḥnāmah* issued at the victory of Chittor, in Persian as usual, cites the same verse which Taimūr and Bābar had used to justify their conquests (*jāhidil kuffār wa'l munāfiqīna*) as well as others exhorting to fight against the unbelievers and the hypocrites, and goes on to record:

> *Wa jihād masrūf sāzand* i.e [we]... remained busy in Jihād.[4]

Iqtidar Alam Khan writes that the Mughal emperor Jalāluddīn Akbar (1542–1605) wanted to be recognised as the head of the Muslims of India. Thus, he is called the *amīr al-mu'minīn* in a document (*maḥḍar)* of 1579 which is the title conventionally used by the caliphs.[5] However, according to Zilli, 'the tradition of Indo-Persian historiography as well as *fatḥnāmah* writing was familiar with only religious idiom'.[6] Later, under the influence of Abū'l Faḍl (1551–1602), Akbar's minister, such terms were changed. Thus *ghāziān-i-Islām* was changed to *ghāziān-i-daulat* and *ghāziān-i-iqbāl* but in Aurangzeb 'Ālamgīr's (r.1658–1707) time we are back with a vengeance with the vocabularly of jihad which is used in the campaigns of the emperor against the Assamese and against the Marhattas as Khafī Khān's history of his rule *Muntakhabāt al-Lubāb* (1722) testifies.[7] In short, the recourse to the vocabulary of jihad was part of seeking legitimacy through religion if the occasion demanded. The frequency of its use might increase or decrease according to the ruler's known preferences but it remained a handy resource for most part of Muslim political ascendancy in India.

Religious vocabulary for legitimation, seeking endorsement from the *'ulamā*, sanctifying past history and other such purposes, is also reported from other Muslim empires such as the Ottoman. For instance, the term *ghāzī* (veteran of a holy war), and the activity which gives him the honorific, *ghazā* (armed expedition), were used for all these purposes. As Linda T. Darling points out, 'the uniformity of motive implied by terms like "the *ghāzis*" is illusory' since the term did not mean the same thing to all actors.[8] Apparently, the *ghazā*, as used in the Anatolian and, more to our purposes, in the Indian ones, was not jihad in the

---

3 Nizami 1961: 357–363.
4 Zilli 2007.
5 Khan 1968: 124.
6 Zilli 2007: 60.
7 Ibid 61. For Aurangzeb's period see Khān, Khafī c. 17 C.
8 Darling 2000: 138–139.

strictly theological sense of the term. One could, for instance, take help from non-Muslim troops in order to fight. A certain commander and relative of Sulṭān Maḥmūd of Ghaznī (971–1030), called Sālār Mas'ūd (1014–1034) and nicknamed Ghāzī Miyā, used local soldiers to subdue Hindu rulers and yet had a certain religious aura because of which he is called *ghāzī*.[9] Indeed, such titles and the literature celebrating their holders, may all be part of the legitimisation of Muslim rulers through recourse to symbols which have a certain sacral value. This is true of Indian rulers no less than the Ottomans.

An important but under-researched subject is the perception of the attacks of Muslims by the victims of these attacks. Romila Thapar (b. 1931), possibly the most famous historian today writing on ancient India, gives a highly interesting analysis of Somnath—the famous Hindu temple which was attacked and looted by Maḥmūd of Ghaznī in 1026. She points out that it was only from 1843 onwards that this event began to resonate in the Hindu consciousness in India as a collective trauma. Earlier, 'there are multiple groups with varying agendas, involved in the way in which the event and Somnātha are represented'.[10] Indeed, the very categories of classification of people vary from time to time. Arab Muslims were called Tājikas while the Turks, the people who attacked north India, were called Turuskas.[11] The people of Somnath might have seen Maḥmūd's forces as the rapacious Turuskas rather than as Muslims since there is evidence that a certain Vohara Farīd, a Muslim of Arab origin, fought 'against the Turuskas' when the temple was attacked.[12] Since representations are constructed by groups, it is important to remember that one function of such representations is to create, uphold, and legitimise identities. Since most of the legends about Muslim iconoclasm are 'to be found largely only in the Turko-Persian chronicles',[13] it seems likely that the chroniclers wanted to create a legend of domination and subordination of the conquered people to support their political ambitions. And since the major ambition was to govern India, where Hindus were the majority, they might have considered such images of ferocity helpful in suppressing the very idea of rebellion among the defeated people. If so, the idea was to create docile subject people and for this the rules of Islamic jurisprudence were used selectively.

Before we synoptically review the way these rules were articulated and applied in medieval India, let us pause to observe that this is a highly relevant de-

---

9 Ibid 147.

10 Thapar 2013: 471.

11 Ibid 466.

12 Ibid 467.

13 Ibid 470.

bate nowadays. According to Anver M. Emon, 'predominant myths hovering over the dhimmi rules are those of harmony and persecution'.[14] According to the first myth, non-Muslims lived in harmony with Muslims, whereas in the second one they were persecuted. The latter myth is supported by rules in the books of jurisprudence one of which, the *Hidāyah*, will be mentioned below. Those who propagated it also buttressed their position by referring to the views of the classical exegetes towards the *dhimmīs*. For instance: Al-Suyūtī talks about them being 'humbly submissive'; Maḥmūd al-Zamakhsharī, a famous exegete of Mutazilite views, says that the tax-payer is 'seized by his collar' and 'pushed on the nape of his neck'; al-Ṭabarī mentions the *dhimmīs*' 'lower' posture; al-Bayḍāwī, an exegete whose work was popular in India, mentions that the *dhimmī's* 'neck is being hung low'.[15]

Moreover, there are documents available which suggest that the *dhimmīs* were discriminated against. Moreover, the treatment given to them is not the same in different versions of the covenant of 'Umar.[16] In some versions, they were not allowed to make new churches, preach their religion, or even practice it openly, hold positions of power, build houses as high as those of Muslims, and wear the same kind of clothes.[17] Perhaps the most forceful expression of this discrimination is by Bat Ye'or[18] whose work was quoted by the Oslo terrorist Anders Breivik in justification of his rage against Muslim intolerance.[19] The other myth, that of harmony, is defended by pointing to the harmonious relationship among Muslims and non-Muslims in various ages and places, such as Muslim Spain.[20]

This was one of the issues on which the Muslim modernists of India spent a lot of time writing in the apologist mode. Defending some of these actions, Shiblī Nu'mānī argues that the above restrictions should be placed in context. For instance, the *dhimmīs* were not to call people for worship but only when the Muslims were praying; pigs, considered unclean by Muslims, were not to be driven into the living quarters of Muslims; children of men who had converted to Islam were not to be baptised to enable them to have a free choice of religion when they grew up, etc. As for sartorial distinction, this was because of Caliph 'Umar's fondness for group identity and not due to Islamic exclusivity. Hence, the Caliph insisted that both the *dhimmīs* and the Arabs wear their traditional

14 Emon 2012: 34.
15 Excerpts of exegeses in Bostom 2005: 127–128.
16 Tritton 1930.
17 Ibid 6–16.
18 Ye' or 1980.
19 Emon 2012: 40.
20 Akasoy 2010; Bouhdiba 1998.

clothes and not just the former.[21] Nu'mānī is critical of the *Hidāyah* as well as the *Fatāwā-e-'Ālamgīrī*, claiming that these were the excesses of the jurists who gave orders in the name of Abū Ḥanīfah, not the eponymous pioneer of the law himself who, in fact, gave much more tolerant orders for *dhimmīs* than the other schools of Islamic jurisprudence.[22] Shiblī and the other modernists established two major lines of explanation which remain valid. One is that, though the rules did exist, they were rarely applied or, as in the case of *jizyah*, it was merely a tax the equivalent of which was paid by Muslims under another name.[23] The other one is that the rules do not represent the spirit of Islam but are, as Shiblī asserts, the excesses of jurists.[24]

An alternative way of looking at the position of the *dhimmī* is to see it as an issue of governance. Anwer M. Emon, who offers this approach, presents the *Sharī'ah* as a rule of law 'situating debates about law in a mutually constitutive relationship with the enterprise of governance'.[25] The jurists who created the specific rules comprising the *Sharī'ah* were trying to balance Islam's universalism (the idea that it should be eternally normative for everyone) with the fact of diversity. This idea of governance is useful for us when applied to medieval India. Here a small minority was ruling a huge majority. The rules this minority took as its faith were man-made and, more to the point, made in countries in which Islam was ascendant and expanding. In India it was politically triumphant but demographically besieged. Hence, no matter what the theologians and other intellectuals might say, the rulers had to exercise caution lest they alienate their non-Muslim subjects beyond the point of no return. It is with this understanding that we can look at the reception of the *dhimmī* rules in India.

Ziāuddīn (Ḍiauddin) Bārānī (1285–1357), a medieval historian, writes in his *Fatāwa-i-jahāndārī*[26] that the ideal Muslim ruler should treat the Hindus harshly. He goes so far as to write:

> You should not content yourself merely with levying the poll-tax and the tribute from the infidels ...You should strive day and night for the degradation of infidelity so that (on the Day of Judgment) you may be raised ... among the prophets and be blessed with the sight of God for all eternity.[27]

---

21 Nu'mānī 1898: 321–323.
22 Nu'mānī 1893: 190–194.
23 Rahman 1986.
24 Nu'mānī 1893: 193; Faruqi 1980; Hussain 1993.
25 Emon 2012: 172.
26 Bārānī c. 1358–9.
27 Ibid 47.

In his *Ta'rīkh-e-Fīroz Shāhī*, Bārānī also narrates the story of the answers of Qāḍī Mughīth of Bayana pertaining to the *dhimmīs* before 'Alāuddīn Khiljī (r. 1296–1316). The Qāḍī was so inordinately prejudiced against Hindus that he first spoke approvingly of the opinion that they should be converted or killed saying that all the schools of jurisprudence except that of Abū Ḥanīfah, the very one followed in India, agreed with this. Then, very reluctantly, he confessed that the 'Imām-i'Āzam [Abū Ḥanīfah], whose school [of jurisprudence] we follow' allows 'the taking of *Jizya* from the Hindus'.[28] Despite that, he goes on to suggest that the *jizyah* should be taken while humiliating the tax payer. He goes on to express such inordinate prejudice for Hindus that the King smiles and tells him that he may be highly educated but is not well versed in practical matters.[29] Although the vitriolic language and the obvious animus are the Qāḍī's own, his words do suggest that medieval jurists—like medieval people among Christians and Hindus too—were prejudiced so they did recommend discriminatory treatment of the religious 'Other'. Thus the canonical book of Hanafite jurisprudence, the *Hidāyah*, also speaks of the tax collector being seated while the payee stands and, according to one report, of the former shaking the latter by the collar at the outset.[30]

Bārānī was probably more influenced by his personal prejudices through which he interpreted the classical theory on the *dhimmīs* ignoring the actual practice towards them which varied enormously across time and space. The reality in his time was that non-Muslim subjects of the rulers could enjoy a good lifestyle. This, indeed, is Bārānī's major complaint: that 'Muslim king's [sic] not only allow but are pleased with the fact that infidels, polytheists, idol-worshippers and cow dung (*sargīn*) worshippers build houses like palaces, wear clothes of brocade and ride Arab horses caparisoned with gold and silver ornaments...'.[31] Indeed, Muslims serve these rich and powerful Hindu *rānās*, *ṭhākurs* and *pundits*, and this is what makes Bārānī wax vitriolic in his political advice to Muslim rulers.

---

28 Bārānī, *Ta'rīkh-e-Fīrōz Shāhī* c. 14 C: 425–428. Qāḍī Mughīs's prejudice is so extreme that he told the King that the payee should remain polite even if the tax collector spits in his mouth in order to show the prestige of Islam and to humiliate all other beliefs. The Qāḍī refers to the word '*ṣāghirūn*' in 9: 29 to support his argument. The translator, Moin ul Haq (Note. 1, p. 426) calls this statement not only wrong but also 'stupid' and adds that such kind of irresponsible statements give a false image of Islam. Of course, no Indian ruler followed the advice of such an extremist. Also see Alam 2009: 286.

29 Ibid 286–7.

30 *Hidāyah*, Vol.7: 140.

31 Bārānī 1358–9: 48.

In Shaykh Aḥmad Sirhindī (1564–1624), called the renovator of the second millennium (*mujaddid alfthānī*), this political imperative of keeping up a hostile attitude towards Hindus is equally manifest. In his letters (*Maktūbāt*), he rebuffs the Hindu Harday Rām's desire to join the Naqshbandi *ṣūfī* order without converting to Islam. Moreover, he goes on to reject the Hindu deities and asserts that '*jiziyah* should be mercilessly levied upon them [Hindus]'.[32] In another letter, this time to Farīd Bukhāri, Sirhindī celebrates the execution of Gurū Arjun Singh (1563–1606), the fifth spiritual leader of the Sikhs. He says: 'These days the accursed infidel was very fortunately killed. It is a cause of great defeat for the reprobate Hindus. With whatever intention and purpose they are killed, the humiliation of infidels is for the Muslims life itself' (*dar ī waqt kushtan-e-kāfir-e la 'īn goindiwāl bisyār khūb waqi' shud wa-ba'th-e shikast-e 'azīm bar hunūd-mardūd gasht bi-har niyat kih kushtāh bashand wa-bi-har gharaz halāk kardāh khwari-ye kuffār khwud naqd-e waqt-e ahl-e Islām ast*).[33] It may be noted, as Freidmann points out, that the anti-Hindu letters are mostly addressed to officers in the Mughal court.[34] In short, Sirhindī, like Bārānī, was apprehensive of the possibility of losing political dominance since non-Muslims (Hindus and Sikhs) constituted a vast majority. For both, a continuous form of jihad, in the form of obvious social and political subjugation, was a political necessity which they justified through the Islamic idiom of jihad and its related concepts like *jizyah.* This does not mean that their use of the idiom of Islam was purely pragmatic and cynical. That idiom came naturally to them through their socialisation and formal learning but the way they chose to interpret it was probably because of the constant fear of a small ruling elite losing its power and being eternally dominated by the majority it had ruled over.

Aurangzeb 'Ālamgīr got the legal document *Fatāwā al-Hindiyyah*, popularly called *Fatāwā-e-'Ālamgīrī*, composed during his rule.[35] Although the document talks about jihad being one of the alternatives to be used for those who do not accept Islam, the King's practice was to fight for reasons of state. Among those reasons one was to extend his rule as a conqueror. Even his re-imposition of *jizyah* in 1679, according to Satish Chandra, was for political and not purely theological reasons. The state, though it could not be entirely Islamic as the clerical establishment clamoured for, could at least pacify the clerics by adopting the symbolic practices associated with Muslim political dominance. Thus, Chan-

---

32 Sirhindī's letters, *Maktūbāt*. Quoted from Friedmann 1971: 73.
33 Ibid 73–74.
34 Ibid 74.
35 Guenther 2003.

dra concludes, what 'generally prevailed during the eighteenth and nineteenth centuries under Muslim rulers was the eclectic compromise of Shah Jahan' (i.e not giving real power to the clerics but proclaiming orthodoxy through the idiom of Islam and discrimination against Hindus at some levels).[36] We now come to the Islamic material available on jihad from the eighteenth down to the twentieth centuries.

Hadith Literature

As mentioned earlier, Sunni Muslims in India considered six canonical works of hadith—*Bukhārī* (d. 256/ 870), *Muslim* (d. 261/ 875), *Ibn Mājah* (d. 273/ 886), *Abū Dāwūd* (d. 275/ 888), *Tirmidhī* (d. 279/ 892), and *Nisā'ī* (d. 303/915)—as completely authentic. The 'Indian Hanafī scholar, al-Saghānī (d. 650/1252)' added to this list 'the *Sunan* of al-Dāraqutnī as well'[37]. They do not include Imām Mālik bin Anas's (711–795) *Muwaṭṭā* (136/753) about which Shāh Walīullāh says in his magnum opus, *Hujjat Allāh al-Bālighā*.

> Investigation has established that only three books belong to the first rank: *The Muwaṭṭā'*, the *Ṣaḥīḥ* of al-Bukhārī, and the *Ṣaḥīḥ Muslim*. Al-Shāfi 'i said, "the most sound book after the book of God is the *Muwaṭṭā'* of Mālik.[38]

By first rank Shāh Walīullāh meant those *aḥadīth* which are 'confirmed from the beginning by many reports (*tawātur*)'.[39] Mawdūdī, the doyen of revivalist scholars in the Subcontinent, also considered '*Ṣiḥāḥ Sittah* and *Muwattā* of exceptional quality'.[40] The *Muwaṭṭā* must have occupied an important place in Indian hadith studies since Muḥammad Zakariyya (1898–1982), an eminent scholar of hadith from Deoband, wrote a twenty-nine volume commentary on it entitled 'the shortest of paths to Mālik's Muwatta' (*Awjāz al-Masālik ilā Muwaṭṭa' Mālik*).[41]

According to a study of the teaching of hadith in India, the first centre of such study was Sindh and the second was Lahore under the Ghaznawids. During the Delhi Sultanate period, the law (*fiqh*) was privileged while the hadith was ne-

36 Chandra 1969 in Eaton 2003: 143.
37 Brown 2009: 39.
38 Walīullāh, *Hujjat:* 389.
39 Ibid 387.
40 Mawdūdī 1958: 300.
41 Brown 2009: 54.

glected. The mystics (*ṣūfīs*) did teach it, however, in their hospices.[42] Out of the forty-six scholars of religion during the reign of 'Alāuddīn Khiljī, only one, Shamsuddīn Yaḥyā (d. 747), was interested in hadith.[43] Two collections of hadith are, however, mentioned in the sources before the eighteenth century. One was *Mashāriq al-anwār* of Raḍī al-Dīn Ḥasan bin Ḥasan Saghānī (1181–1252) which is mentioned as having been read by many scholars. It embodies 2,253 select *aḥadīth* from the most authentic collections of *Bukhārī* (327) and *Muslim* (827). The rest 1,051 are common to both. It has twelve chapters (*bābs*) with some *aḥādīth* on jihad also. This book was introduced to India by Burhān al-dīn Maḥmūd (d. 676/), a pupil of Saghānī. It was the only book on hadith available during Ghyath al-Dīn Muḥammad Tughlaq's time (r.1321–1325) as the Sultan received the fealty (*bay'ah*) of his courtiers on it and the Qur'an.[44] Its translation in Urdu, which must have been used by more readers than the Arabic version was, carries remarks by the translator in keeping with the values and social norms of India of that period. The usual *aḥādīth* about the great value of fighting are present but even more common are those about women who, India being a very corrupt country in the eyes of the translator, are not even allowed to go to the mosque.[45]

The other book of hadith introduced in India in the 9th century, is the *Mishkāt al-Maṣābīḥ* by Abū Muḥammad al-Farrā' al-Baghawī (433 or 436/1041 or 1044–516/1122) and later expanded by Muḥammad bin 'Abdullāh al-Tabrēzī (d. 739/ fl. 1337).[46] The *aḥādīth* on jihad are in volume 3 (Book XVIII). There are sections on jihad, instruments of war, actual fighting, humanitarian law, security, international law in war, treaties and peace, war booty, property called *fai*, poll tax on non-Muslims, war captives, expulsion of the Jews from Arabia, and the emancipation of slaves. The *aḥādīth* in praise of jihad are that one would wish to be killed again and again to enjoy the high value of martyrdom. There is also the hadith that a party of Muslims will always continue the war. Both are given below with reference to the six canonical books of hadith. Indeed, out of 4,719 items, only 2,468 are from sources other than *Bukhārī* or *Muslim* or both.[47]

The most important change in the eighteenth century in the field of Islamic learning was the dissemination of the *Dars-e-Niẓāmī* curriculum all over India. This curriculum was devised by Mullā Niẓām Uddīn (d.1748). Its distinguishing

---

42 Isḥāq 1955: xii & 49.
43 Ibid 50.
44 Ibid 76.
45 *Mashāriq* 1874: 152.
46 Ishaq 1955: 78.
47 Robson c. 19 C: introduction.

feature was that it 'incorporated the new *ma'qulat* [rational] traditions, balancing them against the traditional manqulat [revealed] subjects'.[48] It too included the *Mishkāt* in hadith.[49] Shāh Walīullāh, writing in the eighteenth century, tells us in his autobiography that, at the age of fifteen, he 'studied the whole of Mishkāt, and a portion of *Ṣaḥīh-i-Bukhārī*'.[50] The *Mishkāt* continued to be taught in the Subcontinent, as we shall see below, even when the other books of hadith were in print and, therefore, easily available.

Shāh Walīullāh, despite the fact that he places the *Muwaṭṭā* in the highest category of authentic collections of hadith, did not limit himself only to that book. Instead, he 'introduced a systematic teaching of *hadith* as a compulsory subject' which meant a thorough grounding in the canonical books of hadith.[51] However, Hadith studies were beginning to become important in India even before his period. According to Barbara Metcalf, 'from the time of 'Abdu'l Haqq Dihlawi (1551–1642) and the establishment of close ties to scholars in the Hijaz, Delhi was known as an important center for the study of *hadis* as well'.[52] Shāh Walīullāh himself had access to books on hadith even when many were not available since they were not printed. He mentions some names which are not commonly known in his *Toḥfah Athanā 'Asharīah.*[53] It was Shāh Walīullāh's emphasis on the hadith which changed the orientation of Islamic studies in India from jurisprudence to theology. Robinson places this in perspective by comparing the Indian curricula with the Ottoman and the Safavid ones. According to him the Ottomans taught the six canonical books of hadith and two books of *tafsīr* while the Safavids taught six *Shī'a* books of hadith and nine books of *tafsīr.*[54]

However, ultimately it was not even the effort of Shāh Walīullāh but the introduction of printing by the colonial state which made hadith a major subject of study in India. Mawlānā Naẓīr Ḥusain (1805–1902), a leading scholar of hadith and reformer of the Ahl-i-Hadith movement, tells us that only eighteen copies of *Bukhārī* were available in Delhi and he himself studied *Tirmidhī* by sharing one copy of the book with three other students.[55] Indeed, as Robinson suggests, initially the *'ulamā* were distrustful of the dissemination of a large number of reli-

48 Robinson 2002: 46.
49 Rizvi 1980: 391.
50 Husain 1912: 163.
51 Ashraf 2005: 69.
52 Metcalf 1982: 19.
53 In Sayyid Aḥmad Khān's Urdu translation, Khān 1844 in Pānīpatī 1965: 826.
54 Robinson 2002: Appendixes 1 & 2.
55 In Metcalf 1982: 205–6

gious books because it undermined their monopoly over the interpretation of faith—something which did happen as we shall see.[56]But the immediate result —the availability of books and their low cost—was praised by everyone.[57] Among other things, the Indian Muslims appreciated that, because of the installation of the printing presses in the early nineteenth century, the six canonical books became widely available.[58] Manāẓir Aḥsan Gīlānī (b. 1892), in his biography of Mawlānā Qāsim Nānawtwī (1833–1880), not only testifies to the availability of books of all kinds hitherto considered rare in the early nineteenth century, but also praises their publishers such as Munshī Newal Kishor (1836–1895) who presented books to Deoband where Gīlānī was a student.[59]

Indian publishing houses started publishing the hadith as soon as they were established. Among them was the Matb'a Aḥmadī and Mawlānā Aḥmad 'Alī Sahāranpūrī (d. 879) who published *Tirmidhī* and *Bukhārī* in 1850.[60] The Ahl-i-Hadith *'ulamā* were especially active in the dissemination of hadith. Ṣiddīq Ḥasan Khān of Bhopal (1832–1890) is said to have published twenty-three works on hadith from the Mufīd-ē-'Ām press in Agra.[61] Other presses, especially the Newal Kishor Press which has been mentioned above, were also active in this field.[62] Indeed, the situation was such that Gīlānī could boast that 'tomes of Arabic which could not be published in any Islamic country were being published in India' and he goes on to credit Deoband in general and Mawlānā Qāsim in particular on this development.[63]

The *Mishkāt* remained popular in Indian madrasahs. Sir Sayyid studied it from famous tutors of Delhi as well as *Tirmidhī* and parts of *Muslim*.[64] The Farangī Maḥall school taught it even in 1916 when all the six canonical texts were widely available. 'Abd al-Bārī (1876–1926), a highly influential and politically active *'ālim* of this family, established 'a Dar al-Hadiths, funded by the Rani of Jahangirabad' where the *Mishkāt* was taught 'alongside the commentaries of Mullā 'Alī Qārī (d. 1605–6), the great Hanafi scholar of Herat, and Shah Abd al-Haqq Muhhadith of Delhi (d. 1642), the leading hadith scholar of the Mughal period'.[65]

---

56 Robinson 1996.
57 Gīlānī Vol. 2, 1953: 307–315.
58 Rahman, T 2011: 321.
59 Gīlānī, Vol. 2, 1953: 314. For Newal Kishor's contribution to Islamic literature and its dissemination in India see Stark 2008.
60 Metcalf 1982: 201.
61 Ibid 204.
62 Stark 2008.
63 Gīlānī Vol. 2, 1953: 311.
64 Ḥālī 1901: 59.
65 Robinson 2002: 163.

Maulānā Zakariyya, who has been mentioned before, writes in his autobiography that he was taught the *Mishkāt* as a student but even as a child some of its sayings were narrated to him by his father, Mawlawī Yaḥyā Kāndhalwī.[66] It is taught even today as Muftī Shamazaī (d. 2004), a figure associated with radical Islam during the Musharraf era, was examined on it in the Madrasah Faruqia where he studied.[67]

The fame of the teacher one had studied from carried a lot of weight. Mawlānā Muḥammad Qāsim of Deoband went to Arabia for pilgrimage by sea. The ship anchored in a port where he was told that a famous teacher of hadith lived nearby. He went to call upon him and asked him for a certificate. The Arab teacher asked him the name of the person who had taught him the hadith and when he answered Shāh 'Abdul Ghanī (1819–1878), the Arab did not recognise him. He also did not recognise Shāh Isḥāq who had taught 'Abdul Ghanī but he did recognise Shāh 'Abdul 'Azīz who had taught Isḥāq and agreed to give Qāsim the coveted certificate.[68] In Deoband, the most important subject was hadith and the most important teacher was the *shaikh al-ḥadīth*. Among its legendary teachers were Mawlānā Rashīd Aḥmad Gangohī (1826–1905) and Zakariyya.[69] Indeed, the study of hadith also had mystical and emotional value as some biographies of the period suggest. For instance, in the case of Mawlānā Zakariyya, it 'ties him to the Prophet and thence to Allah'.[70] Such kind of mystic ideas remain active in South Asian Islam even now.

Jihad in the Collections of Hadith

Let us see which particular *aḥādīth* from the collections available in India are used in the discourse about jihad. As mentioned above, *al-Muwaṭṭā*, though not counted among the canonical books, is nevertheless praised by Shāh Walīullāh as equal in status to *Bukhāri*. It has two sections relevant to jihad, the *Kitāb al-jihād wa 'l-siyar* (11th part) and the *Kitāb al-maghāzī* (16th part). The first has 372 items, thirty of which are about actual fighting. The rest are about travelling for war, the sale and buying of horses (presumably for martial purpos-

---

66 Zakariyya Vol. 1, 1987: 25; for an academic appreciation of this biography see Metcalf 2004: 67–95.
67 Abid Vol. 1, 2003: 47.
68 Zakariyya Vol.1, 1987: 57.
69 As testified in numerous biographical accounts of the age. See Gilani 1953 and Zakariyya 2 vols.
70 Metcalf 2004: 90.

es), prognostication of future victories, incidents in the Prophet's life, and other matters. The themes of the great merit of fighting in the way of God, the high position of the martyr, and the desirability of sacrificing one's life are emphasised. The *Kitāb al-maghāzī* deals with subjects concerning the life of the Prophet and the nascent Muslim community and some incidents relating to battles, though the title would suggest that only the latter would be its subject. The collection called *Muslim*, also held in high esteem in South Asia, has a *Kitāb al-jihād wa 'l-siyar.* It too features *aḥādīth* which are found in the above mentioned anthologies.

Most of the *aḥādīth* relevant for the interpretation of jihad in all the collections used in South Asia fall under the following broad themes:

1. Praise of jihad: Extolling its virtues and the high merit of those who sacrifice their lives.
2. Desirability of martyrdom: That the martyr will desire to go back to be killed again and again.
3. Excellence of martyrs and their rewards: That the martyr's body will smell of musk and the soul will wander happily in paradise in the shape of green birds.
4. Continuation of jihad: That jihad will go on forever or till Islam becomes politically ascendant or, according to another version, everyone accepts it.
5. Non-violence towards non-combatants: These include women, children, old men, hermits, and those who cannot fight.

Traditions pertaining to these themes are repeated in different forms with reference to several narrators. A few are given below by way of example and at least one from each category is given in relevant detail in Annexure C.

The following hadith of theme 2 is one of the earliest to be recorded in the *Muwaṭṭā:*

> According to Abu Hurairah the Prophet (Peace be Upon Him) said: I desired to fight in the cause of the Lord and be killed, to be rendered back to life only to be killed again, again to be rendered back to life and be killed.[71]

This is repeated in *Muslim* (4859), *Bukhārī* (63, 64, 82), *Nasā'ī* (5045) and *Ibn Mājah* (2753) also (the numbers refer to the hadith items not to pages).

Two *aḥādīth* often quoted by radical Islamists are about jihad going on forever (theme 4). There are several versions of this: one which says that 'jihad will go on till people (*al-nās*) say there is no god except God' (*Bukhārī* No. 204). Afifi

71 *Muwaṭṭā:* No. 974.

al-Akiti, in common with some interpreters cited earlier, claims that *al-nās* 'refers to the same "mushrikīn" [polytheists] as the Verse of Sūra al-Tawba' refers to, i.e those Arabs who had always been hostile to Muslims and had broken the treaty of Ḥudaybiyyah 'and to no other non-Muslims'.[72]

Another hadith, also quoted by militants, again on the authority of Abū Hurayrah, is that 'paradise is under the shadow of swords'. In *Mishkāt*, perhaps the most accessible work of hadith for ordinary people including madrasah students before the twentieth century, this is the version which is given.[73] But in its most authentic version in *Bukhārī*, these words actually occur in a larger context of not wishing for war but being steadfast once it does take place. Quoting from *Bukhārī:*

> Then he [the Prophet upon whom be peace] stood up among the people and said: 'do not desire to confront the enemy and pray for protection from God. If you encounter the enemy then be patient and understand that paradise is under the shadow of swords ...[part left out].[74]

It is mentioned in the same way in the second-most authentic compilation of hadith, i.e *Muslim* (4042). *Tirmidhī*, however, narrates it without the part about not wishing for war as follows:

> Abū Bakr bin Abī Mūsā al-Ash'arī narrated: "I heard my father saying in the presence of the enemy: 'The Messenger of Allah [Peace be Upon Him] said: "Indeed the gates of Paradise are under the shadows of swords"'.[75]

This is followed by the story of a man with 'ragged appearance' who first confirms its authenticity and then salutes his companions, breaks the sheath of his sword, and fights till he is killed. This version, although it is classified as rare (*gharīb*), is often found in the works of radical Islamists.[76] Sometimes, only the line about paradise being under the shadow of swords is mentioned which supports aggressive interpretations of jihad.

A hadith quoted by those arguing that jihad is moral endeavour, such as Ayesha Jalal, refers to the concept of the smaller and the greater jihad.[77] The former refers to fighting and the latter to moral struggle against one's baser desires

---

72 Akiti 2005: 31.
73 *Mishkāt* Vol. 3 n.d: 817
74 *Bukhārī* Vol. 2 item 285
75 *Tirmidhī* Vol. 3. Item 1659.
76 Pakistani radicals use this version. See Yūsufzaī 1999: 274–75.
77 Jalal 2008: 9.

(see Annexure C for the text). This hadith, however, is not found in any of the collections regarded as authentic among the Sunnis. For those who present Islam as a religion of peace, it is a major supportive argument. However, it is refuted both by academic scholars and radical Islamists. Cook, for instance, points out that this tradition 'is entirely absent from the canonical collections and appears only in the genre of *zuhd*, asceticism, and then in comparatively later collections'.[78] However, he adds that while the mystics (*ṣūfīs*) did emphasise moral perfection, the early ones combined it with fighting, so not all of them can be said to negate the core meaning of jihad as fighting.[79]The militants argue that this hadith has been planted by the enemies of Muslims who want them to abandon fighting. They also argue that it is a saying by Ibrahīm bin 'Ablā, one of the early narrators of hadith, but one who is not regarded as reliable. Hence it was never accepted by any of the compilers of the canonical collections.[80] Ayesha Jalal, who uses it to argue that jihad is moral struggle as we have seen, explains its omission in these collections on the ground that they were compiled during the expansionist Umayyad and Abbbaside periods and adds that its absence itself 'reveals the mindset of the compilers and the political climate of the times'.[81] However, no proof is offered by anyone of its authenticity.

The point is that one interpretive device, very often resorted to especially when arguing from the hadith, is to choose them selectively. They are chosen or ignored depending on the ideological imperative one brings to the interpretive exercise. For traditions which are not in any of the authentic compilations of hadith, it is easy to dismiss them as being weak. For others, the devices mentioned earlier (Chapter 2) may be used or they are ignored altogether.

Exegeses of the Qur'an

Tafsīr studies did not progress much in India. According to Fazlur Rahman, much 'fruitless ingenuity' was spent in writing commentaries and super commentaries and this resulted in the Qur'anic commentary of Faizī (1547–1595), a courtier of Akbar, who 'dispensed with the Arabic letters of the alphabet having diacritical marks, thus reducing the number of letters he could use from twenty-eight to only thirteen'.[82] However, some of the traditional books of exegeses

78 Cook 2005: 46.
79 Ibid 44–46.
80 Yūsufzaī 1999: 51–52.
81 Jalal 2008: 9.
82 Rahman 1982: 37.

known in the rest of the Muslim world were also taught in India though, until the British introduced printing in India, these books were not easily available. G.M.D Sufi gives the names of the following books of exegesis which were taught throughout much of history in India. During the time of Sulṭān Iltumish (r.1211–1236), three commentaries on the Qur'an were taught: 'Abdullāh ibn Aḥmad an-Nasafī's *Madārik al-tanzīl wa ḥaqā'iq al-ta'wīl* (domains of the revealed text and truths of interpretation); al-Zamakhshirī's *al-Kashshāf 'an ḥaqā'iqal tanzīl* (the revealer of the truth of Divine revelation) and al-Bayḍāwī's *Anwār al-tanzīl wa Asrār al-tā'wīl* (the lights of revelation and the secrets of interpretation). The exegeses are usually referred to by the names of their authors or abbreviated forms of the titles, e.g *Madārik, Kashshāf*, and *Bayḍāwī*.[83]

The *Dars-e-Niẓāmī*, which was taught in various forms in all Indian madrasahs, also prescribed the *Jalālayn* and *Bayḍāwī* as textbooks in *tafsīr* studies.[84] In the Madrasah-e-Rahīmiyā, the school of Shāh Walīullāh's father, the *Jalālayn* was taught. As he himself tells us in his autobiography, at the age of fifteen, 'becoming disciple to his father', he 'studied a portion of the Baiẓāvī the same year' and later *Tafsīr-i-Madārik*.[85] Shāh 'Abdul 'Azīz also outlined a course of studies for students in which, besides Arabic grammar, he also recommended translations of the Qur'an and the *Tafsīr Jalālayn*.[86] The *Jalālayn*, which means the book by two Jalals, is a commentary in two parts, one by Jalāl al-Dīn al-Maḥlī (d. 864/1459) and the second by Jalāl al-Dīn al-Suyūṭī.[87] The Farangī Maḥallīs taught the *Bayḍāwī* even in the early twentieth century when other books of *tafsīr* were available on the ground that it was difficult, and if students understood it they could understand the other exegeses.[88] While only two books of exegesis were prescribed in the curriculum, scholars did have other books available to them. In *Tuḥfah Athanā-Asharīah*, Shāh Walīullāh mentions the following books on *tafsir: 'Tafsīr Bayḍāwī, Zahidī, Nizām Naishāpurī* and *Jazb ul Qulūb'*.[89] By the time Deoband started teaching on a large scale printing had made more texts available and communications had facilitated travelling for students, but still the *Jalālayn, Madārik* and *Bayḍāwī* were all taught.[90] Even when 'Ubaydullāh Sindhī was a student in Deoban in the 1890s *Bayḍāwī* was taught there.[91]

83 Sufi 1941: 74.
84 Gīlānī 1953.
85 Husain 1912: 163. Also see Sufi 1941: 70.
86 Rizvi 1980: 385.
87 Kariminya 2012 a: 35–39.
88 Robinson 2002 a: 161.
89 In Sayyid Aḥmad Khān's Urdu translation, Khān 1844 in Pānīpatī 1965, Vol. 16: 826.
90 Sufi 1941: 131.

The wider availability of printed copies of exegeses, like that of hadith texts mentioned above, needs a comment since it is one of the most significant changes made possible by the advent of modernity in India. A number of contemporary and near-contemporary accounts bear witness to this change. For instance, Naẓīr Ḥusain, who has been mentioned above, tells us in his travelogue and diary about Delhi and its surroundings that the King had a copy of *Tafsīr-e-Kabīr* and even Shāh 'Abdul Azīz had to borrow it from him[92]. One effect of the availability of these canonical texts was the new emphasis upon them in religious education. Thus, for the first time, the 'Qur'an and *hadis* were given a centrality unknown in the Mughal period or in the later *dars-i nizami*, which had stressed "rational studies"'.[93] As Francis Robinson argues, the Farangī Mahallī or Dars-e-Niẓāmī emphasis on the rational subjects declined 'under the impact of Muslim revivalism and the imposition of the colonial state'. The "'ulama turned to manqulat, the revealed sciences, to bolster up the community in its loss of power".[94] Paradoxically then, although modernity brought in secular studies in the British system of education, it also created a new vigour in pursuing religious education with emphasis upon the canonical sources now made available to more people than ever before.

Let us now see, with reference to some of the most widely used *tafsīr* texts widely taught in pre-Modern India, as to how they interpreted jihad. First, let us look at the *jalālayn* both in its English and Urdu translations since the latter is still taught in Pakistani madrasahs. The material below, however, is taken only from the English translation.

Table 2

Verse	Commentary (*Jalālayn*)	Interpretive device
2: 190	Revealed in the year of the treaty of Ḥudaybiyyah. Muslims were afraid of being attacked while performing the pilgrimage. It was, thus, a permission to fight aggression. It has been abrogated by 2: 191 and 9:5 (*Jalālayn* 2008: 28).	Abrogation
2: 191	Revealed after the conquest of Mecca. *Fitnah* is sedition which is idolatry. Thus 'killing and expulsion, is the requital of disbelievers' (Ibid 29).	Semantic expansion

91 Sindhī 2009.
92 In Metcalf 1982: 205.
93 Metcalf 1982: 349.
94 Robinson 2002: 67.

Table 2 *(Continued)*

Verse	Commentary (*Jalālayn*)	Interpretive device
2: 193	*Fitnah* is idolatry so the order is to stop fighting only when idolatry comes to an end. The word 'desist' means 'desist from idolatry' not from fighting (ibid 29).	Semantic expansion
8: 39	Same as above. Fight the unbelievers till idolatry comes to an end and God alone is worshipped (Ibid 160).	Semantic expansion
8: 61	Ibn Abbās said 'it has been abrogated by the "sword verse". Mujāhid b. Jabr al-Makkī (d. 104/722), a disciple of Ibn Abbas, often cited in Sunni commentaries, said it applies exclusively to the People of the Book as it was revealed regarding Banū Qurayzā (Ibid 162–163). It is, therefore, not general but restricted to the People of the Book only.	Abrogation/ restricted by *asbāb al-nuzul*
9: 5	Fight the unbelievers till 'they repent, of unbelief, and establish prayer and pay alms' (ibid 163).	General not particular
9: 29	Fight the Jews and Christians who were given books which have been abrogated by Islam. They must pay the poll tax by being subdued and acknowledging the authority of Islam (Ibid 168).	General
60: 8	This verse enjoins treating unbelievers kindly and justly but it was revealed before the final command to struggle against them (Ibid 543).	Abrogation

Source: *Jalālayn* c. 16 C. In English translation, 2008.

The Urdu translation taught in Pakistani madrasahs follows the English one closely. The translator, Mawlānā Muḥammad Na'īm, gives the meaning of *fitnah* and *fasād* as polytheism. He makes it clear that the injunction to allow those who do not resist the Muslims by force of arms to live in peace, was not relevant after Arabia became *Dārul Islām*. It was a concession but it has since been abrogated.[95] The hermeneutical devices used to interpret the verses to allow perpetual warfare against unbelief have been listed above. This translation can easily be used to support contemporary militant interpretations of jihad especially if the teacher does not inform the students about the restrictions on jihad mentioned in other interpretations.

The other exegesis which has always been taught in South Asia is *Bayḍāwī*.[96] Even at present the first two chapters (up to Q. 2) are part of the curriculum in some Pakistani madrasahs. This part has been translated into Urdu in 2005 by

95 Na'īm Vol. 1, 2012: 183–185.
96 *Bayḍāwī*, 2 Vols.

Muḥammad Khān Nūrī who has been teaching it in the Dārul 'Ulūm Muḥammadiya Ghauthiah at Bhera since 1967. In order to understand how the conservative interpretation of jihad is formed in the minds of students, let us look at the first orders about jihad in 2: 190, 191, and 193. Bayḍāwī explains these orders with reference to the occasion of the revelation (*asbāb al-nuzūl*). He says the verse was revealed when the Muslims went for pilgrimage to Mecca after the treaty of Ḥudaybiyyah. As they were unarmed they feared a sudden attack by their enemies the Quraish. They also considered fighting in the sacred precincts (the *ḥaram*) of the Ka'bah taboo. The verses allowed them to retaliate if attacked even within the sacred space reserved for worship till *fitnah* and *fasād* came to an end.[97] He explains *fitnah* etymologically—the criterion for melting gold to refine it—and then says it is used for some great trial or difficulty such as associating some power along with God and that too in the *ḥaram*. *Fasād*, which he defines elsewhere, is oppression. He then presents three alternative interpretations: first, that the Prophet had only fought those who had fought him but not those who had not; second, that fighting was not allowed with non-combatants (women, old men etc); third, that it is permitted to fight all non-believers on account of religious antagonism.[98] Bayḍāwī does not give his own preferred interpretation but his alternatives suggest that a stringent view is normative though a milder view is not ruled out explicitly. This is also evident in another exegesis which has influenced the formation of the traditional worldview towards jihad in South Asia.

This is the famous exegesis of Ibn Kathīr (d. 1373) who is now probably better known in South Asia as a traditional exegete than the others we have been considering so far. This, like the *Bayḍāwī* of the South Asian madrasah courses, will enable us to understand the classical influences on contemporary views about jihad.

Table 3

Verse	Commentary by Ibn Kathīr	Interpretive device
2:190	Has been abrogated by 9: 5. Transgression is not disproportionate aggression in war but mutilation of the enemy fighters and killing non-combatants etc.	Abrogation/ semantic expansion
2:191	*Fitnah* is unbelief and preventing the worship of God.	Semantic expansion
2:193	Fight till associationism (*fitnah*) ends and Islam is dominant (Vol. 1: 48–51).	Ideological assumption

97 Ibid 105.
98 Op. cit.

Table 3 *(Continued)*

Verse	Commentary by Ibn Kathīr	Interpretive device
8:39	Fight till associationism (*fitnah*) ends and religion is only for God. However, he also considers persecution as *fitnah* (Vol. 2: 100–102).	As above
8:61	Enter into a treaty of peace if the enemy offers it. Abrogated. Do not fight if the enemy is too powerful. 9: 29 (Vol. 2: 17–19).	Abrogation
9:5	Cancels all peace treaties and makes it necessary to fight the associationists till they accept Islam. Does not make it specific to Arab polytheists. Quotes one opinion that it has been abrogated but several that it abrogates peaceful verses (Vol. 2: 31–33).	Abrogation/ generalization
9:29	The People of the Book are to be fought for their false beliefs and subjected to *jizyah* for humiliation. Discriminatory *dhimmī* rules are given. (Vol. 2: 45–47)	Generalization
60:8	Explains 60: 8, which is about living in peace with non-hostile people, by defining non-hostility with reference to non-combatants. Uses the cause of revelation (*asbābul nuzūl*) as a hermeneutic device to specify it to non-combatants (Vol. 5: 45).	Specification to non-combatants

Source: *Ibn Kathīr* 5 Vols.

Ibn Kathīr is often quoted by militants because of his interpretation of jihad as an aggressive enterprise as the above interpretations bear out. While *fitnah* is explained as persecution at places it is also called, again using semantic expansion, as disbelief. First, Ibn Kathīr refers to the words of 'Abdurraḥmān ibn 'Umar, the son of the second caliph, who stayed neutral in the wars between the Companions. When asked to explain his neutrality, ibn 'Umar said that he was ready to fight to end the persecution of Muslims but now that it had ended he need not fight in the civil war between Muslims themselves.[99] However, Ibn Kathīr goes on to quote the opinion of Ibn 'Abbās who asserts that *fitnah* is associating other powers with God (*shirk*). This makes him conclude that fighting is to continue till religion is pure, i.e. everyone converts to Islam. This assertion, not found in the literal meaning of the text, is a consequence of Ibn Kathīr's ideological imperative that Islam should dominate. In support of it he quotes the opinion of Zaid bin Aslam who, in turn, quotes the tradition we have encoun-

99 *Ibn Kathīr*, Vol. 1, Part 2: 50. While explaining 2: 193.

tered in the works of Islamists earlier, i. e. that the Prophet was sent to fight the non-believers till they said 'there is no deity but God'[100](for the text of the hadith see Annexure C). In short, because of the alternatives he presents, read along with his overall tone, one can see why he is used to defend extremist positions. As for 9: 29, Ibn Kathīr gives a long explanation of it saying that its beginning—'fight against those who believe not in Allah, nor in the Last Day...'—refer to the defective belief-system of the People of the Book. Since their prophets had already prognosticated the birth of the Prophet of Islam, their faith was not complete. He also says that the polytheists of Arabia had been subdued so this was the time to deal with the Jews and the Christians. That is why the Battle of Tubuk was initiated. Incidentally, he does not say that the Romans had already planned an attack on the Muslims which is given by other exegetes. The new order, says Ibn Kathīr, is for the People of the Book to be subjugated and made to pay the poll tax with humility. The word *ṣāghirūn* (smaller ones) is explained in terms of social inferiority. He explains that the subjugated people were to be placed in a socially inferior position. Thus, restrictions as to the dress they may wear or the animals they ride or houses they live in were necessary.[101]

In this context, Ibn Kathīr's interpretation of 60: 8, mentioned above, may be relevant. He points out that this verse was revealed because Asmā bint Abū Bakr (595–692), sister of the Prophet's wife Ayesha, was visited by her mother who was still a polytheist. Initially she was not ready to accept the gifts she had brought nor to allow her to stay with her. Then she asked the Prophet about it and he allowed her to play host and treat her mother with kindness. Ibn Kathīr does state that the real enmity of Muslims is with people who threw them out of their homes and were hostile to them but adds that Christians and Jews are also like them. In short, instead of taking this verse to apply to all non-hostile people, Ibn Kathīr, using the hermeneutic device of restriction (*takhṣīṣ*), applies it only to non-combatants.[102]

In short, on the whole Ibn Kathīr's overall interpretation of jihad is that it is justified against non-believers and may be aggressive. However, he also subordinates it to ethical behaviour (no harm to non-combatants) and the usual rule of it being ordered by a *bona fide* Islamic state only for the sake of religion.

100 Ibid 50.

101 Ibid Vol. 3 Part 10: 46–47.

102 Ibid Vol. 5 Part 28: 45. While explaining 60: 8.

Books on Jihad

Traditional views on jihad were expressed by a number of the early scholars of Islam. Here Ṭabarī and Sulamī's books relevant to the subject are briefly mentioned. Ṭabarī's *Kitāb al-jihād* is in the genre called *ikhtilāf* (differences) which expresses the differences as well as consensus among jurists about specific issues under consideration. A typical example is as follows:

> There is unanimous agreement [among Muslim jurists] that the Messenger of God did not fight with his enemies from among the polytheists before [first] making the call [to embrace Islam] and showing proof [of this invitation], and that he used to command the leaders of detachments to invite [to Islam] those whom the calling did not reach.

However:

> They disagreed on the obligation of invitation by Muslims [to embrace Islam] [in the time of the jurists] when waging war against the polytheist people.[103]

The other sections deal with: the conduct of Muslim combatants; rules about duels with enemy individuals; rules about peace and treaties; rules about Muslim combatants committing illegal acts in the land of the enemy; the distribution of the spoils of war; rules about prisoners, etc. In all of these sections, Ṭabarī follows the same pattern of giving the points of consensus and then going on to quote the jurists who differ and their reasons for doing so.

An important point, highly relevant to modern-day conflicts called jihad by their proponents, is that jurists do not recognise only two kinds of states, the *Dārul Ḥarb* and *Dārul Islām*. There is also a third condition called *Dārul Ṣulḥ* (land of peace) or *Dārul 'Ahd* (land of treaty). Section (6.2) says: 'they disagreed on [what constitutes a] permissible peace agreement between Muslims and polytheists if the latter are more powerful [than the former]'. However, these treaties are temporary. Basically, the state of war continues, in theory, till the whole world does not convert to Islam or is ruled by Muslims. While some jurists say that the treaty should be for a short time, others contend that it can be of any length. The other important point expressed here is that if the enemies are militarily more powerful then they need not be confronted. This second point is relevant for understanding the stance of Islamist militants who believe that in situations of such differentials of power, jihad should be continued by unconventional warfare such as bombings and suicide attacks.

103 Ṭabarī a: 59.

The other source is ‘Alī ibn Ṭāhir ibn Ja‘far ibn ‘Abdullāh Abū’l Ḥasan al-Qaysī al-Sulamī al-Naḥwī (431/1039–40 500/1106). He was, among other things, a grammarian as the reference to his *naḥw* (syntax) indicates, and is noted in contemporary sources for his piety.[104] His *Kitāb al-jihād* is meant to incite his listeners to undertake jihad as this was the age of the Crusades. He follows Imām Shāfi‘ī in his judgments and quotes profusely from his works. His concern seems to be what he saw as the waning of Muslim power since Spain (al-Andalus) and Sicily both had gone out of Muslim control. In his view, this was because the Muslims were not united and, even worse, they failed to show military preparedness or bravery. He considers it a ruler’s duty to keep the pressure on the enemy by initiating raids into their territory. In a crucial passage, he attributes the following saying to al-Shāfi‘ī:

> The least that the *Imam* must do is that he allow no year to pass without having organized a military expedition by himself or his raiding parties, according to the Muslims’ interest, so that the *jihad* will only be stopped in a year for a valid excuse.[105]

The book goes into details about the usual concerns about war: the role of women, booty, captives, and so on. He also quotes from authorities justifying raids on enemy lands and using all kinds of tactics, including some against which there are Prophetic injunctions which make them controversial. For instance, he quotes al-Ghazālī: ‘if the *imam* considers it appropriate to burn their date palms and wealth out of anger against them, it is permitted’.[106]

Averroes, whose name was Abū al-Walīd Muḥammmad Ibn Rushd (1126–1198), is another scholar whose book *Bidāyat al-mujtahid wa nihāyat al-muqtaṣid* (the beginning for him who interprets the sources independently and the end of him who wishes to limit himself) carries a chapter on jihad. Ibn Rushd was born in Cordoba when Muslim power was secure but there must have been the fear of Christians reversing this dominance because Spain represented only a foothold of the Arabs in Europe. He was a jurist and the book belongs to the genre of *ikhtilāf* works as does Ṭabarī’s treatise mentioned above. He deals with the question as to what is the general rule and what the exception and whether a verse, or a Prophetic saying or practice, is abrogated (*mansūkh*) by another source.

He begins by raising the question whether jihad is compulsory for all Muslims or only some of them (i. e., whether is it is a *farḍul kifāyah* or *farḍul ‘ayn*). He asserts that the idea that it is compulsory for all is suggested by the Quranic

104 Christie 2015: 4–5.
105 Sulamī in Christie 2015: 207.
106 Ibid 251.

verse in *al-Baqarah:* 'fighting is prescribed for you, though it is distasteful to you' (2: 216). However, this order is cancelled by another one in *al-Tawbah:* 'it is not for the believers to march out all together' (9: 122). Then he comes to fighting the unbelievers under the section on the 'aims of warfare'. Here the verses 9: 5 and 9: 29, the ones used to justify unending war against non-Muslims by militants, are used several times. Ibn Rushd says that the poll tax should be accepted only from the Jews and Christians (*ahl al-kitāb*) whereas polytheists and Zoroastrians were to be offered three choices: conversion to Islam, payment of the poll tax or war. He begins by stating that the general rule is based on the verses we have been citing earlier: 'fight them until there is no persecution and religion becomes Allah's' (2: 193 and 8: 39). As usual, he cites the hadith stating: 'I have been commanded to fight the people until they say: "there is no god but Allah"'. The particular rule—that of offering the choice of paying the poll tax—he continues, is based on the actual Prophetic practice of offering the three choices mentioned above. However, he adds, the practice of giving the three choices came before the revelation of 9: 5 and 9: 29 and, hence, the last word of the Qur'an is to fight the polytheists. The general rule, having been revealed at the same time as the exception granted to them, puts the People of the Book in a special category. To this he adds that, since some jurists believe that the general rule should be interpreted in association with particular ones, the poll tax is an alternative for all kinds of unbelievers.[107] Like other jurists, he too raises the question of asymmetrical warfare. His opinion is based on the verse in *al-Anfāl* (8: 66) which says that God, cognizant of human frailty, permitted Muslims to fight a host twice in strength but not a stronger one. In this context he mentions peace treaties with the enemy. Here he points out that the injunction to make peace is based on 8: 61: 'if they incline to peace, incline thou to it'. However, 9: 5 and 9: 29 command fighting against the polytheists and the People of the Book respectively. This contradiction is resolved through the interpretative device of *naskh* according to which the verses which were revealed later have abrogated the verses advocating peace. However, other jurists say that the verses must be read in conjunction with each other and only the *Imām* can decide when to 'incline to peace' and when to fight. As a concluding argument, Ibn Rushd refers to the authority of Shafi'ī who argues that the general principle is that 'polytheists must be fought until they have been converted or until they are willing to pay poll tax'. The example of Ḥudaybiyyah is the exceptional case not valid for every-

107 Averroes (Ibn Rushd) in Peters 1977: 24–25.

body.[108] Other subjects which are discussed are the same as those in other traditional sources.

Perhaps the most well known book on jurisprudence available in India was the *al-Hidāyah fī sharh bidayāt al-mubtadī* by Burhān al-Dīn al-Farghānī al-Marghinānī (530/1136–593/1197) which contains Islamic law as interpreted by Abū Ḥanīfah. Indeed, it was used, along with its commentary called the *Sharh al-Wiqāyā* by 'Ubayd Allāh bin Mas 'ūd al-Maḥbūbī (d. 1346–7), in Indian seminaries for teaching the law by all sub-sects and is still a textbook in madrasahs. The *Hidāyah* was translated into Urdu in the nineteenth century and published from Calcutta. It was also used by the British as a source of Muslim law in the courts. Since most Indian Muslims were and remain Sunnis, it is an important source about jihad. The Urdu translation of this work has several sections dealing with the subject. For instance, the *Kitāb al-siyār*, on reasons for Jihad and what kind of duty it is, has sub-sections (*abwāb*): on fighting itself, on making pacts with the enemy, giving security of life (*aman*), the distribution of spoils, the duration of the peace treaty, the imposition of *jizyah*, and so on. In the context of India, the most relevant question is whether Hindus were to be treated like the Arab polytheists who could not be pardoned by paying the poll tax if they did not convert or were they like the Zoroastrians who could exercise this option. In the *Bāb kayfiyyat al-qitāl*, the author mentions two categories upon whom *jizyah* could not be levied: the apostates and the idol worshippers.[109] In the *Bāb al-jizyah*, however, he mentions the above view attributing it to al-Shāfi'ī but argues that since Zoroastrian and other non-Arab idolators were not killed but *jizyah* was levied upon them, all idolators can be given the option of paying *jizyah* to avoid both conversion and death.[110] The second forms the legal reason for justifying Muslim rulers' attitude towards their Indian non-Muslim subjects even when some *'ulamā* preached otherwise. Other differences between Ḥanafī jurisprudence about jihad and its attendant issues are small and need not detain us here.

Besides the *Hidāyah*, Indian views about jurisprudence were summed up in the *Fatāwā-e-'Ālamgīrī*. One of the scholars who participated in this project was Shāh Walīullāh's father, Shāh 'Abdul Raḥīm (1644–1719). According to Walīullāh's own account of his family history in *Anfās al-'ārifīn*, his father joined the team of scholars working on this major project on the insistence of Mullā Zāhid who was his class fellow. However, his spiritual preceptor did not want

108 Ibid 23.
109 *Hidāyah*, Vol. 7: 17.
110 Ibid 133.

him to continue with the project and eventually the emperor let him go.[111] Among other matters it also deals with jihad in *Kitāb al-siyār.* It defines jihad as 'calling towards the true faith and fighting that person who does not accept it, or rebels against it or disobeys it (*tamurrad*), by wealth or life'. However, aggressive jihad is only allowed if Muslims are expected to gain power and glory but not otherwise.[112] The *fatāwā* go on to deal with a number of issues connected with fighting. For instance, it says that the *shahīd* is not to be given a bath but prayers of burial (*namāz-e-janāza*) are to be said before burying him in the same clothes along with blood on his body.[113]

Our main interest in the *fatāwā* is in the views it promoted among Muslims, especially the *'ulamā*, ordinary prayer leaders and other religious figures, during the eighteenth century. Of special importance, in view of later developments about the concept of jihad, is to understand what kind of duty it is considered to be. The *fatāwā* declares that when the enemy is about to attack and a general alarm is sounded, those who will be immediately affected must consider it a duty for themselves (*farḍul 'ayn*). However, those who are far removed or not in imminent danger of attack will consider it a duty for some (*farḍul kifāyah*).[114] If it is the first, women and slaves can go to fight without anyone's permission but young women should not take on nursing duties or cook for soldiers.[115] As for aggressive jihad, it is permitted with those who refuse to be converted to Islam or pay *jizyah* 'even if they do not attack us first'.[116] Moreover, rebels can be attacked if the *Imām* orders even if they have not initiated hostilities.[117] The Muslim ruler is to be obeyed in jihad 'if there are equal chances of gain and loss. But if the loss is certain, then he may be disobeyed in battle conditions only'.[118] *Jizyah* can be taken from all non-Muslims—except the Arab polytheists who are no more—so the author(s) of the *fatāwā* also allow(s) it for Hindus though, without naming them. However, it is also mentioned that there is disagreement about this.[119] *Jizyah*, however, is not the same for every type of *dhimmī*. Those who have accepted Muslim rule without fighting can come to agreement as to its amount with Muslims while those who were defeated after fighting do

111 Rizvi 1980: 209.
112 *'Alamgīrī* Vol. 3: 322.
113 Ibid Vol. 1: 266.
114 Ibid Vol. 3: 323.
115 Ibid 325.
116 Ibid 323.
117 Ibid 468.
118 Ibid 329.
119 Ibid 331.

not have this privilege. Here the book suggests a sum of forty-eight *dirhams* for the affluent and twenty-four for the less affluent able-bodied men.[120] As for the treatment of *dhimmīs*, it is based on repugnance for their religious views but neither cruelty nor injustice is permitted. Exhibition of repugnance for them, however, is not included in cruelty. For instance, it is suggested that 'shaking hands with *dhimmīs* is not approved (*makrūh*) and if this is done while in a state of ablution, a Muslim should wash his hand'.[121] However, the *dhimmīs*' property, life, the honour of their women, etc., are to be safeguarded by law.

To sum up, traditional jurists held the following views: that jihad is both defensive and offensive; it is normally *farḍul kifāyah* but if Muslims are attacked it becomes a *farḍul 'ayn*; it should be for propagating the faith and not for glory, lust of power, or to rule more land and people; it should be undertaken by the order of the ruler of the Islamic state; the ruler can also enter into peace agreements if he thinks they are in the interest of Muslims provided they are not for ever; it should not be undertaken if the enemy is more than two times more powerful than the Muslims; it has rules of engagement and dealing with women, male non-combatants, children, and property, etc. Shiblī Nu'mānī narrates that Abū Ḥanīfah was informed by his friend Ibrahīm bin Maimūn, about the cruelties of the Abbaside ruler Abū Jā'far al-Manṣūr (r. 754–775) towards all, but especially towards the Prophet's family. The complainant probably expected the Imām to permit active resistance. However, Abū Ḥanīfah said that though doing good (*al-amr bi'l-ma'rūf*) is a duty, it should only be carried out if one is adequately equipped, i. e. being armed and wealthy enough to sustain the struggle.[122]

To conclude, the understanding of jihad in the age of Shāh Walīullāh, inherited from the orthodox exegetes, was traditional. First, it was believed that jihad is both defensive and offensive. The People of the Book were to be conquered in such a manner that they should be psychologically subdued and manifestly subordinated. However, it was not assumed that all non-believers were to be killed at random everywhere. Secondly, jihad was not against Muslims even if they were not observant of the religious law. Thirdly, it was to be declared by the leader of the Islamic state (*imām* or *caliph*) and not by non-state actors or individuals without any state authority.

120 Ibid 422–23.
121 Ibid Vol. 9: 73.
122 Nu'mānī 1893: 49.

4 Jihad and the Family of Shāh Walīullāh

'Ubaydullāh Sindhī, who figures prominently in the next chapter, asserted in his book on Shāh Walīullāh (1703–1762) that the great Indian scholar of Islam was the pioneer of an Islamic, revolutionary, political movement which Sindhī called the *Walīullāhī Taḥrīk* (the movement of Walīullāh). In a nutshell, for Sindhī, Walīullāh and his family—those members of it whose writings or actions might have contributed to the discourse of anti-colonial resistance—are the mainstays of this movement. Besides Walīullāh himself, there are his three sons: his spiritual and academic successor Shāh 'Abdul 'Azīz (1746–1824) and the translators of the Qur'an in Urdu, Shāh Rafī'uddīn (b. 1749–50) and Shāh 'Abdul Qadīr (b. 1753–54). Sindhī further posits a genealogy of the jihad, which excludes some immediate members of Walīullāh's family such as his son Shāh 'Abdul Ghanī (1819–1878) and Muḥammad, a son from his first wife, but includes his nephew Muḥammad Ismā'īl (1779–1831), his son-in-law 'Abdul Ḥayy, Shāh Muḥammad Isḥāq, and Sayyid Aḥmad Barēlwī—all of whom participated in the war against the Sikhs in which Barēlwī was killed in 1831. Sindhī believed that this was the first phase of jihad personally inspired and organised by Shāh 'Abdul 'Azīz on principles laid down by his father.[1] The second phase of this jihad, comprising the 'silk letters conspiracy', also included in the jihad movement of Walīullāh's family by Sindhī, is the subject of the next chapter. This chapter, then, focuses on the first phase of movements which Sindhī includes in the revolutionary jihad movement of Shāh Walīullāh without, however, subscribing to his notion that there was indeed an organised jihad movement initiated by the prominent members of the family.

Neither Walīullāh nor 'Abdul 'Azīz left behind complete exegeses of the Qur'an which are the main sources for this study. However, Walīullāh did leave behind a Persian translation of the Qur'an and some material which has bearing on the idea of jihad. 'Abdul 'Azīz did write an exegesis of the Qur'an in Persian but the part of it which survives does not cover the crucial verses about jihad. His religious edicts (*fatāwā*) do, however, constitute a landmark development in the way discourses about jihad shaped up in South Asia till independence. Moreover, his letters, like those of his father's, also provide insights into how he reacted to the loss of Muslim political power in the colonial era. As for the Urdu translations of the Qur'an by Shāh Rafī'uddīn and 'Abdul Qādir, they also provide some understanding of how they thought about the sub-

1 Sindhī 1941.

https://doi.org/10.1515/9783110716986-007

ject. Since there is a lot of writing on Shāh Walīullāh and Shāh 'Abdul 'Azīz,[2] most of it hagiographic, only details relevant for our purposes have been touched upon to avoid repetition.

Information about the life of Shāh Walīullāh is available in his autobiography, *Juz' al-laṭīf fī tarjamat al-'abd al-ḍa'īf* (an elegant chapter in the life of the weak creature).[3] His real name was Aḥmad, to which Quṭbuddīn was added later. He was born to Shāh 'Abdul Raḥīm at Phalit in February 1703 and is considered the most important influence on Indian Muslims from the eighteenth century onwards.[4] His father had contributed to the compilation of the *Fatāwā-i-'Ālamgīrī*, as we have seen. 'Abdul Raḥīm, like most religious figures of the age, was a mystic, though he also pioneered scholarship, especially on hadith studies, in his seminary, the Madrasah-i-Rahimiyah at Koshal Anwar Mahdian in the premises of the fort of Feroz Shah in Delhi. Walīullāh also studied there and his curriculum comprised works on mysticism and hadith. To this he later added jurisprudence by self study.[5] 'Abdul Raḥīm died in 1719 and the young Walīullāh, still in his teens, became the head of the madrasah. In 1731, he went to Mecca and stayed there for two and a half years to learn hadith under Abū Ṭāhir Muḥammad bin Ibrāhīm al-Kurānī al-Kurdī (d. 1733).[6] While the hadith studies in India elevated the six Sunni canonical collections of hadith above all else, in Mecca he learned to value the *Muwaṭṭā* which he eventually came to place above the other books of traditions.[7] Thus, Shāh Walīullāh formed his own interpretative tradition which eschewed blind adherence to the orthodoxy of the traditional Indian *'ulamā*.

As mentioned above, Shāh Walīullāh did not leave behind a complete exegesis of the Qur'an but two of his writings relate to it. First, his translation of the Qur'an into Persian, entitled *Fatḥ al-Raḥmān ba-tarjumah al-Qur'ān*; the second, his account of the principles of exegesis, *al-Fauz al-kabīr fī uṣūl al-tafsīr*. The translation is mostly in straightforward, accessible Persian with occasional notes or leading remarks to guide the reader. The crucial verses about jihad in *al-Baqarah* (2: 190, 191, and 193) are explained briefly in laconic footnotes. Verse 2: 193 is translated as 'fight with them till polytheism [*fitnah*] comes to an end and religion is only for God' (*va bejangīd bā īshān tā ã kē nābūd shuvad*

---

2 Ibid; Ghazali 2001.

3 Husain 1912.

4 Rizvi 1980; Baljon 1986: 1–7.

5 Rizvi 1980: 215.

6 Husain 1912: 166.

7 Brown 1996: 23.

shirk va shivad dīn maḥeḍ barāe khudā).[8] The term *fitnah* is also translated as the dissemination of beliefs which associate other powers with God (*shirk*) in a note to 2: 217—fighting in the sacred months is bad but turning people away from their religion and expelling them from their homes is even worse. As for 9: 5 and 9: 29, he gives a literal translation of the verses with no explanatory note. In the latter verse, the term *ṣāghirūn* is translated as being disgraced (*khwār shudgān*). In short, throughout his translation, Shāh Walīullāh shows no special interest in jihad nor does he guide the reader to any interpretation of the verses concerning it by parenthetical intervention, notes, or semantic expansion.

The second work, the book on the principles of exegesis, was a part of the *Dars-e-Niẓāmī* between 1732 and 1747.[9] What is relevant here are his explanations of some verses in the context of the controversy about abrogation (*naskh*). These explanations suggest that Walīullāh's understanding of jihad was traditional, i.e. that it was justified to wipe out unbelief provided one had sufficient means to execute it. While discussing the debate on abrogation he refers to the view that verse 2: 217 quoted above is abrogated by 9: 36 which is about fighting the enemy as a united force. While not evoking the theory of abrogation, he says that this verse is not about forbidding but permitting war. While fighting in the forbidden months is wrong, it is an even greater wrong to evict people from their homes and persecute them if they want to worship God and force them to associate anyone or anything with the powers of God (*shirk*). Hence, to wipe out these evils it is permitted to fight even in these months.[10]

His concept of being at least minimally provided for in warfare is given in his explanation of 9: 41, which orders Muslims to 'go out [to fight] whether light or heavy' (*unfirū khifāfā wa thiqālā*). This he says is not abrogated by the verse exempting some people (the blind, the sick, the weak, and the very poor) from fighting (as given in 9: 91). In fact, he says, *khifāfā* refers to the necessities of fighting such as slaves, food, etc., which must be there in at least some necessary quantity, and *thiqālā* refers to the presence of the same necessities but in excess.[11]

Shāh Walīullāh also mentions, though only in passing, warfare and political domination, in both *al-Budūr al-bāzighāh* and *Ḥujjat Allāh al-bālighā*.[12] Both books are about the establishment of a just and moral society. In both there is the concept of moral evolution (*irtifāq*) though in the latter it is dealt with in

8 Walīullāh *Tarjumah:* 30.
9 Rahman 1982: 40.
10 Walīullāh *Fauz:* 34.
11 Ibid 36.
12 Walīullāh *Budūr* and *Hujjat*.

more detail. Both have no separate chapters on jihad itself. In *Budūr*, however, there is a brief section on war translated as 'Military Expedition'.[13] This, however, does not deal with the theological aspects of conflict. Instead, it offers a theory of war from the point of view of politics, logistics, and the military sciences. The author asserts that the commander must be clear about the purpose of war which 'may be the removal of injustice, attainment of fame, possession of properties, lands, or drawing attention of his subjects towards himself when he fears war may erupt'. Of course, its purpose may also be ethical, i.e. 'the annihilation of persons wicked by nature', but Shāh Walīullāh does not make it out to be the only reason for it.[14] In *Ḥujjat*, however, he gives three arguments to justify war: first, defence; second, to end oppression; third, to create a moral order to ensure that humans progress to higher levels of moral existence. The first is exemplified in his letters and actions to which we will turn later. The second is illustrated by his assertion that 'jihād was legislated for promoting the word of God and making sedition cease, as God, may He be Exalted, said, "Then fight them until there is no Sedition and religion is all for Allah"'(8: 39).[15] The third covers the duties of individuals, groups, and leaders (or *imāms*). First, he takes up the case of the individual arguing that God inspires a righteous man to kill one who 'harms the collectivity'. Next, he takes up the larger case of tyrannical states which oppress people. Here it is the duty of the prophets (*imāms*) to fight them. Here he brings in the concept which is best described as the 'way of God' (*sunnat al-Ilāh'iah*). According to this concept, it is God's way to make his prophets fight evil doers or, alternatively, He destroys them Himself. Thus, because of their impieties, God 'decreed the extinction of their rule such as Persia and Byzantium…'.[16] He also mentions that the Prophet 'established the greatest Caliphate, and with those who accompanied him he waged jihād on those who opposed them until the command of God was fulfilled despite the unwillingness' of these people.[17] The third case is that of a group which becomes aware of true morality so that it saves 'oppressed ones from the predatory ones' so as to bring 'peace and contentment'.[18] These seem to be permissions granted to individuals and groups to take militant action, but Shāh Walīullāh's other writings indicate that this action is subject to rules. He mentions that the Prophet received rules such as

13 Walīullāh *Budūr:* 87–89.
14 Ibid 87.
15 Walīullāh *Hujjat:* 13.
16 Ibid 355.
17 Ibid 369.
18 Ibid 230.

'*Kharāj* tax and the *jiziyā*, rules for jihād...'.[19] In both books he devotes whole chapters to the caliphate defining a caliph as a person 'who has an army and equipment which makes it clearly impossible for someone else to usurp his domain'.[20] In *Budūr*, he seems to be apprehensive of the weakening of caliphal authority and gives much practical advice to 'prevent the public from taking the sword in its hands'. Indeed, his view of becoming a caliph to begin with is free from theological scruples. He remarks judiciously that 'it is not possible unless great persons, well-versed in the art of war join the aspirant for caliphate, and his superiority is accepted by them'.[21] There is no theoretical agonising over the piety of the aspirants or the legitimacy of the process itself. Indeed, it appears as if, in this age of crumbling Mughal authority, what Shāh Walīullāh really wants is to establish a strong Muslim ruler at the centre. So the picture which emerges is that Shāh Walīullāh, theologian though he was, was also surprisingly practical in his advice to a would-be Muslim military adventurer. In the section on military expeditions in *Budūr* mentioned above, he lays down practical advice for military undertakings: collection of weapons and equipment, training of soldiers, gathering of intelligence, arrangement of forces, and so on. Similar advice, in the tradition of the mirror for princes writing, follows in *Ḥujjat*.[22]

In short, Shāh Walīullāh does not deviate from the traditional Muslim position that the primary function of the state is to keep order. Thus, ideas which turn the subjects 'against their king, the servant against the master, and the wife against her husband' are against the ideal city (*madīnah*). He does not believe that aggressive jihad had come to an end—an assertion which was made in the nineteenth century by modernist Muslims—since he argues that the *Imām* 'must make his religion predominate over all other religions, and that he not leave anyone unless religion has gained ascendancy over him'.[23] But this is subject to the condition of the *Imām* possessing military power to pursue jihad. In short, Shāh Walīullāh's ideas do not lend themselves either to insurrection against a Muslim ruler or to guerrilla warfare without the authority of an *Imām*. Only in the case of defensive warfare, he felt, again in keeping with traditional ideas, that a Muslim ruler may be called upon to help beleaguered Muslims gain political domination over their foes. Since the threat of rule by the Mar-

19 Ibid 355.
20 Ibid 137.
21 Walīullāh *Budūr:* 98.
22 Walīullāh Ibid 87–88; *Hujjat* 138–139.
23 Walīullāh *Hujjat:* 343–344.

hattas (or the British) is a case of Muslims being politically dominated, his letters give an insight into his ideas of jihad to deal with such a situation.

But before we consider his own letters, it may be instructive to recall that his father, Shāh 'Abdul Raḥīm, could have been his role model in the matter of writing letters to powerful princes to undertake jihad. For it was the *pater familias* who wrote a letter to Mīr Qamar al-Dīn Khān Ṣiddīqī popularly known as Āṣaf Jāh (1671–1748), the pioneer of the Deccan based state whose rulers were called Niẓāms, exhorting him to undertake jihad to weaken the infidels. 'Abdul Raḥīm begins his letter with the assertion that it has already been decided that the infidels (*kuffār*) will be defeated and humiliated and if Āṣaf Jāh wants to take credit for this he should defeat them. He ends on the mystical note that 'things said even with confidantes in secret are being revealed here on the tip of the pen so that no excuse should remain' (*sukhanē kē bā mehrmā-e-khud dar pardā adā mi-kardēm ī jā bē pardā navishtā shud tā 'uzr namānd'*).[24]

Baljon, otherwise an erudite writer on Shāh Walīullāh's ideas, begins his book by doubting the authenticity of his letters.[25] However, he brings no proof in support of his assertion. In any case, the letters of both his father's and his own—even if they are not genuinely his—are very significant in understanding how jihad was conceived of in pre-modern India. However, since the consensus among the Muslims of South Asia has been that they are genuine, they remain as exemplars or paradigm-setters helping us understand how jihad was perceived in this part of the world. Hence, the letters must be given attention. Considering that his father wrote the letter cited above, Shāh Walīullāh may be seen as continuing a known tradition when he wrote his famous letter to Aḥmad Shāh Abdālī (1722–1772), the ruler of Afghanistan, inviting him to subdue the Marhattas who were the greatest threats to Muslim power in India. In this letter, '*Banāmē Shāhē*' (to a king, letter 2),[26] written in Persian but with quotations from Arabic in its last part, Shāh Walīullāh begins with a synoptic historical account of Muslim rule in India. He makes the point that different areas of India were ruled by Muslim rulers who established mosques and seminaries and encouraged Muslims from other lands to come and settle down in India. Rajputana, however, was never directly ruled by Muslims, though the Rajput rulers did acknowledge Mughal suzereignty and paid money to the Mughal emperor as a token thereof. He then comes to the Marhattas and the Jats who had captured large parts of India. The Marhattas, he said, did not succeed in ruling major

24 Cited from Bhatti 2013: Vol. 2, 976–977.
25 Baljon 1986:1.
26 Walīullāh *Maktūbāt:* 51–52.

parts of areas ruled by Muslims but were so powerful that they collected one-fourth of the revenue (*chauth*) from these areas. Then he describes Jats who were tillers of soil between Agra and Delhi and who, he approvingly mentions, were not allowed to ride horses, make fortresses, and keep guns with them. But they too had become powerful recently. Troops sent to punish them were appeased by token submissiveness. When they found a dynamic leader in the form of Sūraj Mal (1707–1763), they conquered urban centres of Muslim civilisation in India not sparing Delhi itself.

Walīullāh goes on to support this historical narrative by an economic argument. He begins by mentioning the approximate revenue of India which, in his reckoning, comes to millions of rupees. This income, he asserts, is manipulated by Hindus who are getting richer while the Muslims are descending into poverty. After describing this sorry state of affairs, he makes a direct appeal to Aḥmad Shāh, invoking his duty of jihad as follows:

> At this time if there is a king who is powerful, has vision and is an experienced warrior who can defeat the opponents, then it is you. Jihad then is a personal duty (*farḍul 'ain*) on you. [So] come to India and defeat the Marhattas and liberate the Muslims from the power of the non-Muslims. For, if the domination of the infidels remains, Muslims will forget Islam and after some time this Muslim people (*qaomē*) will be indistinguishable from non-Muslims.[27]

Later in the letter he makes promises of both spiritual as well as material rewards for the king and his army. He invites the Afghan ruler to 'enter his name in the list of the fighters for the sake of God and incomputable wealth will come in the possession of the fighters of Islam and Muslims will be liberated from the hands of the unbelievers' (*nām-ē-nāmī nawishtā shiwad ō dar duniyā ghanāem bē hisāb badast-ē-ghāziyān-ē-Islām uftand musalmānān az dast-ē-kuffār nijāt yāband*).[28] But here he sounds a warning. Abdālī should not behave like Nādir Shāh (1688–1747), the Persian King who had sacked Delhi in 1739. This act had weakened the Muslims while leaving the Marhattas unharmed and as powerful as before. This is followed by the last section which comprises Arabic verses from the canonical sources of Islam and the last words of the orthodox caliphs.

According to Sindhī and those who support Walīullāh's idea of inviting a foreign ruler to defeat local powers, he was right to do so since he (Abdālī) did inflict a military defeat upon the Marhattas and this was the immediate danger to

27 Ibid 52.
28 Ibid.

Muslim civilisation in India[29]. For Ayesha Jalal, who begins with the idea that jihad is ethical improvement, this was a kind of falling off. She writes: 'in exhorting Abdali to fight the Marathas and the Jats to eradicate polytheism, Waliullah let his own high standards of jihad fall by the wayside'.[30] Walīullāh, however, does not subscribe to the theory of jihad as moral struggle to the exclusion of armed conflict. Indeed, his decision is contingent upon the latter component of his understanding of jihad. Two points need to be made about this understanding. First, in his view the Muslims of India needed help, which makes it a defensive war. Secondly, only a powerful ruler with an adequate army was asked to fight and not the weak Indian Muslims. In the last section of the letter, he makes it clear that if a Muslim ruler fears defeat, then he should wait and convince people to join him for jihad so that Muslims are not killed unnecessarily.[31] The point then is that, like other traditional jurists, Shāh Walīullāh believes in defensive and offensive jihad provided there is a ruler (*imām*) who is powerful enough to defeat the enemies. Moreover, he rejects insurrections and rebellions against political authority unless the ruler refuses to obey 'the rules of the faith and turn apostate' in which case fighting against him was a jihad; but otherwise not.[32] These points are important when contrasting the theoretical justification for unequal warfare (including suicide attacks) and rebellion against rulers by contemporary radical Islamists.

Shāh Walīullāh did not confine himself to this letter to Abdālī alone. He wrote on the theme of jihad and the governance of India in several other letters to important people among the Muslims of India. Among his correspondents was Najīb ud Dawlah (1707–1770) who was the *de facto* ruler of Delhi from 1761 to 1770. He joined Walīullāh in inviting Abdālī to fight the Marhattas. In a letter to Najīb ud Dawlah, Walīullāh says that 'behind the curtain of the unseen' it had been decided that the Jats and Marhattas would be vanquished and ruined.[33] In another letter to him he adds that, once the Marhattas are defeated, the Jats and the Sikhs should be subdued.[34] Shāh Walīullāh's views about politics and governance are spread in many of his works. It is quite clear that he admires conquerors provided they are Muslims and the conquered people are non-Muslims. Thus, he praises Maḥmūd Ghaznawī as a hero of Islam in India.[35]

---

29 Sindhī 1941: 46.
30 Jalal 2008: 55.
31 Walīullāh *Maktūbāt:* 55.
32 Rizvi 1980: 290.
33 Walīullāh *Maktūbāt*, Letter No. 5
34 Ibid Letter No. 6.
35 Rizvi 1980: 294.

The main reason for the downfall of Muslim power in Shāh Walīullāh's eyes was, besides Muslims not observing the injunctions of the *Sharī'ah*, their involving Hindus in the affairs of the state. In his letter to Tāj Muḥammad Khān Baloch, he says that Hindus would not like stern action against them. Still, he recommends show of power based upon an aggressive assertion of Muslim power.[36] With such views about Hindus, it was only to be expected that he would recommend treating Hindus as inferior *dhimmīs* in his ideal state. Moreover, he also recommends that *Shī'as* be treated in the same manner. This is suggested by a letter he wrote to the Mughal ruler Aḥmad Shāh (1725–1775). The king was ineffective and ruled only between 1748–1754 when he was blinded and set aside. Thus, even if he wanted to, he could not follow Shāh Walīullāh's advice contained in the letter. This letter was probably so problematic for Niẓāmī, the editor of the political letters of Shāh Walīullāh, that he excluded it from his collection of his letters which has been used above.[37] The relevant part of the letter given in the Rampur manuscript reads:

> Strict orders should be issued in all Islamic towns forbidding religious ceremonies publicly practiced by infidels (such as *Hōlī* and ritual bathing in the Ganges). On the tenth of Muharram Shi 'is should not be allowed to go beyond the bounds of moderation and in the bazaars and streets neither should they be rude nor repeat stupid things, (that is, recite *tabarra* or condemn the first three successors of Muhammad).[38]

However, Shāh Walīullāh's model government was never set up by anyone. His dream of Marhatta power being shattered was partially fulfilled but Mughal Delhi was also looted and its citizens, both Muslims and Hindus, were slaughtered in January 1757 when he entered the city. Evidence for this abounds in the sources of this period.[39]

In view of this evidence, there is no reason why one should not agree with W.C. Smith that Shāh Walīullāh's invitation to Abdālī in order to restore Muslim power was 'what most of us would call at least disastrous, to use no more pejorative a term'.[40] Rizvi also says that the letter 'was in reality a vain dream'.[41] It is only fair to point out that Shāh Walīullāh did not subscribe to the European idea

36 Walīullāh *Maktūbāt*, Letter No. 23.
37 This letter is not included in Nizami 1950.
38 English translation of Walīullāh's letter in Rizvi 1980: 294.
39 A Marathi letter bears witness to Abdālī's looting of India (Rizvi 1980: 294). Also see the poet Mīr Taqī Mīr's moving account in Persian comparing the devastation of Delhi as the doomsday (*qiamat būd*) (Mīr 1808: 184).
40 Smith 1981: 206.
41 Rizvi 1980: 206.

of nationalism nor, indeed, had Indian nationalism emerged by that time. He did believe in the Islamic *ummah* which, in his view, could regain power in India if someone came from outside to crush its enemies. This idea of jihad—jihad without frontiers, so to speak—is once again part of the worldview of radical Islamists.

To sum up, although Shāh Walīullāh is counted as a major figure both in the mystical as well as the scholarly traditions of India, he is also the inspirer of heterodox trends in Indian Islam. His position was not traditional in all cases. For instance, despite traditional scholars not accepting Malik's *Muwaṭṭā* as a canonical work of hadith, Walīullāh considers it equivalent to *Bukhārī*. He also allows Muslims to be eclectic in their approach to *fiqh*, whereas traditional scholars insist that if one was a Hanafite then only the Hanafite version of *fiqh* had to be adhered to in all cases. These positions, called 'anti-traditionalist dialectics' by Aziz Ahmad, 'had been absolutely unconnected with any western influences' being inspired by his own studies and interpretation.[42] In his writings on jihad, though he does not deviate in principle from the traditional line. However, his approach is so practical as to be more in the Mirror of Princes tradition rather than in the theological one. Despite his letters on jihad and his disparaging remarks on Hindus and *Shī'as*—attitudes common among Sunni scholars of his age —Shāh Walīullah was not a pioneer of aggressive jihad either of the kind which was practiced by some Deobandi scholars we shall be concerned with in chapter 6 or of those who arose in contemporary South Asia (Chapter 9). Indeed, his will, or rather the document of his last advice (*waṣiyyat nāmah*), does not mention jihad at all. It is preoccupied with personal piety and moral improvement.[43] In conclusion, while one cannot agree with Sindhī that Shāh Walīullāh was the pioneer of a revolutionary jihad movement, he was not a conservative scholar either. He did emphasise the exercise of judgment in order to deal with new realities (*ijtihād*) whereas the traditional emphasis among most Sunni scholars in India was on blind adherence to accepted practice (*taqlīd*).[44] More importantly, he categorised the content of religion into essence and form, i.e., the universal and the local or the eternal and temporary. He did not, however, develop these embryonic concepts. Because of his original opinions there were some misgivings about him in orthodox circles. As Qasim Zaman points out, 'he is that rare figure in modern South Asian Islam who is claimed by the Salafis, the Deobandis, *and* the modernists'.[45] Yet, Waliullāh also valued consensus so 'despite

42 Ahmad 1967: 41.
43 Waliullah *Waṣīyat.*
44 Khan, M 1959; for the debate on taqlīd versus ijtihād in India, see Zaman 2012: 56, 103–107.
45 Zaman 2012: 316.

[his]... personal distaste for the practice of taqlid' he 'had considered it justified in the interest of maintaining a local consensus'.[46] But others who claimed to follow did not, however, value consensus as much. Thus, Sindhī, with whom we began this section, took the essence of Walīullāh's teachings to be revolutionary jihad.[47]

Shāh 'Abdul 'Azīz (1746–1824), the son of Shāh Walīullāh, was given the name of Ghulām Ḥalīm at birth. He learned the usual Islamic sciences from his father succeeding him both in a spiritual and an intellectual sense in the eyes of the Muslims of India. His work represents a compromise between confrontation and accommodation of British power in India. The first example of this is his edict (*fatwā*) about the legal status of Muslims in India under British rule issued probably in 1804, one year after the British conquest of Delhi. He was asked: 'Can a *Dārul Islām* become a *Dārul Ḥarb?*' He gave a long reply which is often quoted. He said that it could, provided that three conditions obtained: first, the laws and rules of the infidels (*mushrikīn*) prevailed; secondly, the *Dārul Islām* joins a *Dārul Ḥarb*; thirdly, there was no Muslim or even a protected non-Muslim (*dhimmī*) left in that country.[48] He then says that the laws of the British (whom he calls 'infidels') prevail all over India except in some Muslim princely states but these too are obedient to the British. Thus, despite the fact that Friday and Eid prayers are going on, India is now a *Dārul Ḥarb.*[49] At another place he says that congregational Friday prayers can be held even in a *Dārul Ḥarb*, provided Muslims elect someone their leader (*Sulṭān*) for this purpose.[50] However, he makes it clear elsewhere that it is not necessary to emigrate from all kinds of *Dārul Ḥarb.* If, however, the infidel rulers prevent Muslims from calling people for prayers (*ādhān*), or if Friday prayers and other Islamic rituals are forbidden, then one should emigrate; but not otherwise. In this context, it may be noted that there is at least one other example from the same period about two places being designated *Dārul Ḥarb.* One was the Rajput state of Jodhpur and the second was some territory of Sindh which Makhdūm Ibrāhīm Thattawī placed in this category on the grounds that the call to prayers was forbidden, killing of birds and animals for food was an offence, and some mosques had been desecrated.[51] This, of course, was seen as a case of persecution of Muslims which did not apply to British India.

---

46 Ibid, 56.
47 Sindhī, 1941.
48 *Fatāwā-e-'Azīzī:* 454
49 Ibid 455
50 Ibid 474–475.
51 Rizvi 1982: 70.

Mushirul Haq, who wrote a dissertation on attitudes towards the British in the early colonial period at McGill University in 1964, gave a detailed analysis of the questions directed at Shāh 'Abdul 'Azīz. He makes the suggestion that Indian Muslims, who had been paying interest earlier when India was considered to be a *Dārul Islām*, were now 'anxious to know whether the new situation has opened the door of interest in the field of economy'. In short, the 'question of *Darul Islam* and *Darul Harb* was a product of an economic problem'.[52] This position, though convincingly argued, goes against the strong post-colonial trend of equating the family of Shāh Walīullāh with jihad. Naeem Qureshi, a historian of the Khilafat Movement in India (1918–1924), points out that the *fatwā* was not supportive of either migration or jihad but 'was interpreted as preaching' both. Since this corresponds with the modern insistence on the anti-colonial attitude of the *'ulamā*, 'some modern Muslim writers have enthusiastically supported' it.[53]

Let us look at the relevant questions and answers which constitute the *fatwā* to determine the validity of these varying claims about the motives of Shāh 'Abdul 'Azīz. To the question 'is it allowed to take interest from the non-Muslims?' he said: 'according to *Fiqh* the interest between a Muslim and an infidel of a *Dārul Ḥarb* is allowed'. He goes on to clarify that the authorities are divided about how a *Dārul Islām* becomes a *Dārul Ḥarb*. Some say that if even one Islamic rite is forbidden then it becomes *Dārul Ḥarb*, while others argue that it becomes that only if infidel rites are practiced openly. He also said that the non-believers can become legal owners of property and one can accept gifts from them. In the same context, he does, after all, trace out a connection with jihad. He says that as long as the Muslims keep resisting the infidels and do not become completely obedient to them, and as long as the rulers do not become so powerful as to stop any religious observance they want to, the country does not become a *Dārul Ḥarb*. However, if Muslims stop fighting and Islamic rituals continue unimpeded simply because the rulers are not against them *per se*, then the country does become *Dārul Ḥarb*.[54] This is a very crucial development in Shāh 'Abdul 'Azīz's thought and one which may have promoted the initiation and continuation of jihad in India. That this edict is very different from the ones given before is something which has not been adequately noticed by scholars, but it is the one which might have affected the conduct of people like Sayyid Aḥmad Barēlwī and others. There is no evidence in this matter but it should be pointed

52 Haq 1995: 44.
53 Qureshi 1999: 177.
54 *Fatāwā-e-'Azīzī*: 578.

out that 'Abdul 'Azīz, like his father, was deeply concerned about the decline in Muslim political power. One of his letters to his uncle Shāh Ahl-Allāh has the following lines:

> May God revenge the atrocities of the Sikhs and the Marathās,
> A painful revenge and very soon
> They (both) have killed a large number of people,
> And have committed atrocities even against the illiterate shepherds.[55]

According to Rizvi, Shāh 'Abdul Azīz's position underwent a change from the time he issued his first *fatwā* in 1804 and the later ones. In the beginning he was 'critical of them' (i.e., the British) but later when he found that peace had been restored, he became more conciliatory.[56] This is hinted at in the answer he gives to the question: 'Please write about the march of the Commander of the North'. To this, Shāh 'Abdul 'Azīz gives a long answer in which it becomes clear that the Northerners were the Marhattas and those who fought and defeated them, called Easterners, were the British. Their commander, General Lord Gerard Lake (1744–1808), is mentioned by name as *līk* (in Urdu lake and *līk* are written in the same way). The word *līkh*, which is very close to it, means louse in Urdu-Hindi, so 'Abdul 'Azīz shows approval for the victory of Lord Lake in the Anglo-Marhatta war of 1803. He ends by observing that the 'Easterners' (the British) 'much against their disposition, had started plundering and had set aside their peaceful nature'.[57] That the Marhattas did not have a 'peaceful nature' is assumed since they had been collecting one fourth of the revenue of Muslim lands by loot anyway. Thus, it appears that in the victory of the British, Shāh 'Abdul 'Azīz saw relief from the depredations of the Marhattas. It is also possible that his personal experience of British rule was positive. It is known that the resident of Delhi, Archibald Seton (1758–1818) (resident 1806–1811), wrote a long note to the Governor-General about a case of 'Abdul 'Azīz's property dated 24 October, 1806, in which the following passage occurs:

> As the general character of the Moulavee is most respectable and as his conduct upon the occasion of tumult at this place was no less marked by mildness and moderation than regulated by sound judgment, I think it is my duty to recommend his request to the favourable consideration of the Hon'ble the Governor-General in Council.[58]

55 'Azīz's letter cited from Rizvi 1982: 79.
56 Rizvi 1982: 236.
57 *Fatāwā-e-'Azīzī:* 615.
58 Extracts from British Official documents cited from Rizvi 1982: 89.

According to Rizvi, the 'tumult' was probably about the *fatwā* about India being a *Dārul Ḥarb* which his followers expected to be either about '*hijrat* (emigration) or *jihād*'.[59] He also allowed his nephew, 'Abdul Ḥayy, to work for the British despite the criticism of his ('Azīz's) peers.[60] Indeed, as Barbara Metcalf mentions with reference to someone's participation in jihad: 'it was after Karamat 'Ali refused to join the jihad that 'Abdu'l-'Aziz appointed him *khalifah*'.[61] Thus, though Shāh 'Abdul Azīz was not at all a supporter of British rule over India, there is no evidence to suggest that he encouraged his followers to fight them.

However, even if Shāh 'Abdul 'Azīz's edict that India was a *Dārul Ḥarb* is taken to promote or legitimise jihad, as some later religious figures associated with Islamic militancy, such as Muftī Shamazai, claim,[62] it still does not make it compulsory for Muslims to emigrate from India because the religious observances of Islam had not been stopped by force by the British. Indeed, according to Haq, Shāh 'Abdul 'Azīz's edicts did not ask the Muslims to either fight or emigrate from India nor in his lifetime did they do so.[63] However, influence can take long to work and sometimes action is precipitated only when a leader is born.

It may be noted that Shāh 'Abdul Azīz's concept of jihad is not predominantly militant. In fact, he said it was of three kinds. The first is the verbal jihad (*jihād-e-zubānī*), the second is preparation for fighting, and the third is actual fighting. He further added that the Prophet 'was busy only with the first two kinds of Jihād'.[64] This was not an answer to any question but a clarification which he must have thought necessary. Unfortunately, his exegesis of the Qur'an in Persian, though in four volumes, only covers up to verse 184 of *Surāh Baqrāh* and the verses in the last two parts (*sipārās*) of the Book. About the rest, which is no longer available, opinions differ. Some scholars suggest it was never written, but Rizvi points out that 'Azīz has referred to it in his explanations of other verses in his writings; but that the drafts were not published.[65] The few verses we do have are almost mute on jihad. However, he gives a mystic interpretation of the word *shahīd*, normally translated as martyr, who, in his opinion, is one 'whose heart has the quality of observation' and that is why, per-

59 Rizvi 1982: 90.
60 *Fatāwā-e-'Azīzī:* 600 – 601.
61 Metcalf 1982: 55, Note 23.
62 Abid Vol. 1, 2003: 213.
63 Haq 1995: 43.
64 'Azīz as cited in Haq 1995: 51.
65 Rizvi 1982: 106 – 107.

haps in mystic ecstasy, he can give the supreme sacrifice of life.[66] He makes much use of the hadith quoting the one which says that the souls of martyrs will appear as green birds in paradise. However, in explaining 2: 154—that the martyrs are alive—he clarifies that this is not life as we know it. Not to die is against the *Sharī'ah,* he claims, and argues that the property of the martyrs is divided as for other dead people.[67] He also says that the verse of *al-Kāfirīn* (Q. 109)—to you your religion; to us ours (109:6)—has not been abrogated by the verse on *qitāl* (he probably means 9: 5).[68] He asserts that the actual meaning of this verse is that the two belief systems are extremely far removed from each other so there is no compatibility in them. Further, he adds, '*jihād* and *qitāl* is part of Islam so there is no reason why this verse should be considered abrogated'.[69] In short, the exegesis in its present incomplete state does not suggest that Shāh 'Abdul 'Azīz gave an aggressive or heterodox interpretation of jihad. He explains concepts with reference to meaning and grammar, and refers to the hadith as well as traditional stories from popular mystical lore to make a point. He is more in the mystical and conservative tradition of Indian theologians than in the ones born out of the encounter with Western modernity, the liberal-humanist one, or the fundamentalist/revivalist one. And, of course, none of his known views remotely suggest that he would agree with the radical Islamist interpretations of jihad which appeared later.

To sum up, it was in keeping with his overall ideology that Shāh 'Abdul 'Azīz argued that it is not necessary to migrate from a *Dārul Ḥarb* unless Muslim rites are prohibited. However, as mentioned above, he did write poetry in which he showed a clear understanding of the British takeover of India.[70] Thus, while it cannot be said that Shāh 'Abdul 'Azīz inspired Indian Muslims to fight against the British or emigrate from India, he understood the reality of colonialism and was critical of it—at least in private.

One of the ways in which Shāh Walīullāh and his sons might have contributed to an increased dissemination of the meaning of the Qur'an and hence, indirectly, making Indian Muslims more aware of jihad, is by their translations. That these translations were known to Indian Muslims even in the 1920s is attested, among other evidence, by one of the leaders of the Khilafat Movement, who spells his name as Mohamed in his magazine called *Comrade* but who is now spelled as either Muhammad or Mohamed Ali in English sources (1878–1931).

66 *Tafsīr-e-'Azīzī* Vol. 1: 58.
67 Ibid Vol. 2: 482.
68 Ibid Vol. 4: 562.
69 Ibid.
70 Cited in Haq 1995: 1–4.

Mohamed Ali tells us that both the Persian translation of Shāh Walīullāh and the Urdu ones of his sons were in print and read during his youth.[71] However, the theory of 'Ubaydullāh Sindhī, that these translations were meant to inspire people to revolutionary jihad, is not supported by proof, since none of them actually mentions this as its objective.[72] What does emerge from the written statements of the translators is simply that they wanted to bring the Quranic message as a whole nearer to the Muslims of India. Shāh 'Abdul Qādir, the first translator of the Qur'an into Urdu, says that he has used 'Hindi *mut'arif*', not *rēkhtā*, for his translation, so that it should be accessible to ordinary people. This preface is part of Munshī Ẓahīruddīn's introduction (five pages) to the edition published by Nawal Kishor in 1788.[73] Hindi is the word used for varieties of the ancestor of the languages which changed into modern Persianised Urdu and Sanskritised Hindi.[74] However, *rēkhtā* referred to that variety of the language which had more Persian words and was therefore considered more appropriate for certain forms of poetry (especially the *ghazal*) while the expression 'Hindi *mut'arif*' (ordinary Hindi) was used for the variety used for conversation in the cities of north India and Hyderabad.[75]

There is a controversy about the date of the translation by the two brothers. Some historians of Urdu give the date of Rafī'uddīn's translation as 1786 while that of 'Abdul Qādir's is 1792.[76] However, Saleem Khalid, who has written about the translations of the two brothers, points out that Shāh 'Abdul Qādir mentions his father's translation but not his elder brother's in his preface which suggests that Rafī'uddīn's translation was completed later in 1788 or 1807. It was finally published in two volumes in 1840 much after 'Abdul Qādir's translation which, according to Khalid, was completed in 1790.[77] The matter of dates, however, is not directly relevant to this study. What is relevant is to understand what light the two translations shed on the intellectual construction of jihad.

Shāh 'Abdul Qādir translates 2: 190 – 193 almost literally like his brother, though he uses idiomatic Urdu. *Fitnah* is defined as 'cruelty'. The verse means that 'cruelty should come to an end and the unbelievers should not be able to

71 Ali 1920s: 33.
72 Sindhī 1941: 18 – 19.
73 Zaheeruddin 1788: 4.
74 Faruqi 2003: 806; Rahman 2011: 23 – 25.
75 Rahman 2011: 22.
76 Rizvi 1982: 104.
77 Khalid 2000: 117.

turn Muslims away from their faith'.[78] To argue that Muslims should not transgress certain limits when fighting, he explains that 'boys and women and the elderly should not be killed knowingly nor should non-combatants be killed'.[79] He translates 9: 5 literally, but adds in the margin that some of the polytheists were given four months while others were given time till their treaties remained valid. No more details are given. As for 9: 29, again there is a literal translation of the words, but on the margin there is a note saying that the orders to fight the *ahl-e-kitāb* arrived since they do not believe in God as they should. As for the word *sāghirūn*, he translates it as 'being made worthless' (*bē qadar hōnā*). But then he explains this in the margin in terms familiar from other medieval jurists when he specifies that the *dhimmīs* should not be considered equal to Muslims in the transport they use, their use of roads, the display of weapons, and other matters.[80] Shāh Rafī'uddīn, who translates from the Arabic word by word, renders *tāghūt* as Satan in *al-Nisā* (Q. 4) (those to whom a portion of the Book was given worship idols and false deities (4: 51)) and *fitnah* as unbelief (*kufr*), thus making 2: 193 an order to fight the unbelievers till unbelief ends and religion is for God. In 9: 5 and 9: 29, he does not differ from his brother, except that *sāghirūn* is translated as 'be humiliated' (*dhalīl hōnā*). He himself gives no explanation of any verse but the copies of his translation published in Pakistan carry 'Abdul Qādir's comments on the margin.[81] In the absence of detailed commentary, it is difficult to determine what interpretive devices the two brothers used to reach their understanding of jihad. However, from what is available, it appears that they did not deviate in any strikingly original way from the traditional interpretation of it, i.e. that it was both defensive and aggressive and that non-Muslims did not have the right to be treated as equals under Muslim rule. As to any special action which may be required in eighteenth century India when Muslim rule had come to an end, the translations do not enter into that debate.

Thus, though it is not clear that the ideas of Shāh Walīullāh or his followers, notably those of Shāh 'Abdul 'Azīz, actually inspired the jihad movement initiated by his followers, it is undeniable that one of them did lead a militant movement which he called jihad. This follower was Sayyid Aḥmad Barēlwī (1786–1831), popularly adjectivised *shahīd* (martyr) in textbooks used among South Asian Muslims. He is known as the pioneer of jihad in modern India. Though he himself fought against the Sikhs and disappeared after the Battle of Balakot

78 Qādīr 1792: 37.
79 Ibid 37.
80 Ibid 248.
81 Rafī'uddīn 1840.

in which the Sikhs defeated him in 1831, he inspired a number of movements of militant resistance against the British which lasted almost till the partition. In a sense, the present militant movement in FATA and Swat have parallels with these earlier movements. Both types of resistance movements, for instance, are based in the present borderlands of Pakistan and Afghanistan, called FATA nowadays but also known as Yaghistan during the British period.[82] The term 'Yaghi' is roughly translated as rebel and '*tān*' (from the Sanskrit *thān* meaning place) renders it 'the land of rebels'.

There are some parallels between the way the Taliban in Afghanistan (1996–2001), Mullā Faḍlullāh (spelled Fazlullah in the literature) in Swat (2008–9), and parts of FATA established their version of the Islamic state. The pattern seems to be that, initially, the common people were enthusiastic about converting to the idea of the Islamic state. Later, however, the same people were disillusioned and even attempted to rebel against the repressive state. However, while the regions that have been taken over by the Taliban and the IS have reported atrocities of various kinds, there are no such reports in Sayyid Aḥmad's case. Another difference is that Sayyid Aḥmad sent a letter to Ranjīt Singh (1789–1839), ruler of the Punjab, inviting him to accept Islam. Faqīr 'Azīzuddīn (1780–1845), a minster of Ranjīt Singh, hesitated to read it aloud initially. However, upon being exhorted to do so by the ruler, he did. The letter promised Ranjīt Singh further conquests and spoils of war if he converted to Islam. If he refused, the Sayyid promised to fight him. Ranjīt Singh is said to have promised to accommodate him with offer of land if only he would not fight him. This, however, the Sayyid refused.[83] Apparently, Sayyid Aḥmad believed in fighting according to the traditional ideas of the conduct of jihad, i.e. that it was his duty to offer Islam to his opponents and, upon their refusal to accept it, to fight them; not to kill non-combatants. Most importantly, he believed that an *imām* (in this case himself) should have ordered the order to fight. In short, for him, jihad was not a purely defensive war as it came to be interpreted in Indian modernist Islam later.

For modernist apologists like Sir Sayyid, however, it was necessary to argue that Sayyid Aḥmad was only fighting against the Sikhs since they oppressed the Muslims. Sir Sayyid's main defense was that Sayyid Aḥmad never fought against the Christians. Even Ja'far Thānēsarī (1838–1905), who was himself involved in Jihad at one point of his life, now tried to argue that the Sayyid had no quarrel with the British.[84] Abū'l Ḥasan 'Alī Nadwī (1914–1999), a biographer of Barēlwī,

---

82 Haroon 2007: 29–30.

83 Khan, N n.d.: 2228–2234.

84 Bari 1954: 219.

refutes this apologist reconstruction of events by reproducing letters which refer to Christians openly. Even more tellingly, Ghulām Rasūl Mahar (1893–1971), in his detailed history of the movement of Sayyid Aḥmad,[85] points out that Ṯẖānesarī actually changed the words of the Sayyid's letters in order to absolve him of the charge of having included the British among those whom he wanted to fight.

For instance, the actual words of a letter, probably to a ruler of Chitral, refer to Christians by name: 'Christians of certain habits and pagans of bad habits have captured a large part of India from the banks of the River Indus till the shore of the saltish sea' (*nasārā-ē nikohidā khiṣāl ō mushrikīn bad ma āl bar akthar bilādē hindustān as labe daryae abasīn ta sāḥil daryae shōr...tasallut yāftand*).

Ṯẖānesarī changes them to:

> 'Sikhs of certain habits ... have captured a large part of Western India' (*Sikhān nikohidā khiṣāl... ...*).[86]

In another letter the original reads: 'the European unbelievers have captured Hindustan..' (*Kuffār-e-Farang ke bar Hindustān tasallut yaftā and..*). Ṯẖānesarī's version reads: 'Unbelievers with long hair have captured the Punjab..' (*Kuffār darāz mūiyā ke bar mulk-e-Punjāb....*'.In short, Ṯẖānesarī substitutes the reference to Christians (*naṣārah*) by Sikhs (who have long hair) and their conquest of Hindustan (the Urdu-Hindi belt) by Western India (the Punjab and present-day KP). Mahar cites other such crucial changes which suggest that Ṯẖānesarī went out of his way to prove that Sayyid Aḥmad Barēlwī's jihad was not directed against the British.[87] Other scholars, including Francis Robinson, also refer to the letters to suggest that 'from the beginning the movement was directed no less against the British'.[88]

This study, agreeing with the scholarly opinion adduced above, also relies more on Sayyid Aḥmad's letters to different people than the opinions of his biographers. In these letters, Sayyid Aḥmad says clearly that the British had taken over all of India and that it was necessary to confront them. To Ghulām Ḥaydar Khān he wrote:

> A great part of the country of Hindustan has fallen into the hands of foreigners (*ba dast-ē-begangā uftādah*) and they are bent upon cruelty and oppression everywhere. The rule of the rulers of Hindustan has been destroyed. Nobody dares confront them but instead every-

---

[85] Mahar 1952: 248–250; Nadwi 1939: 403.
[86] Mahar 1952: 248.
[87] Ibid 249.
[88] Robinson 2002: 187.

> one has started considering them their master (*harkas īshā rā āqāē khud mī shumārad*). Since all the great rulers have given up the idea of confronting them hence some weak and insignificant people have resolved [to resist them] (*lāchār chand kas az zu'afā ē bē maqdār kamar bastand*).[89]

In the letter to Shahzādah Kāmrān, he clearly states that, after defeating the Sikhs, he would go to India since his 'real aim is fighting a Jihad in Hindustan not settling down in Khurasan' (*ke maqṣūd-ē-Aṣlī-ē-Khud aqāmat jihād bar Hindustān ast na tawaṭṭan dar Khurāsān*).[90] Muḥammad Ismā'īl, his close confidante, clarified in a letter to somebody in Hindustan that Sayyid Aḥmad, whom he calls the *amīr al-mu'minīn*, has all the qualities of an *imām*, hence, it is incumbent upon all Muslims to accept him as the leader of jihad. Secondly, he refutes the argument that jihad is only allowed if one has a strong force. In his view, one's force may not be at par with the antagonist but if it exists and if one has sufficient enthusiasm for jihad it is enough. One has to begin struggle and not consider assumed weakness as ground for postponement of jihad forever.[91] Since both these ideas—that the *imām* may be appointed amongst the fighters and does not have to be a *de jure* ruler of a country, and one's military power should not be less than half that of the antagonist—are used by contemporary Islamist militants, it is significant that they were expressed in India during the movement of Sayyid Aḥmad Barēlwī.

Sayyid Aḥmad himself was not a scholar of Islam nor did he leave behind a written interpretation of the concept of jihad. However, his example did inspire many resistance movements against colonial rule which justified themselves either as reform movements or as jihad. Indeed, there were many works by his followers which were in circulation. However, Shāh Ismā'īl, the major theorist of the movement, wrote most of his books on theological subjects. Only in *Ṣirāṭ-ul-mustaqīm* do we 'find four and a half pages out of 376 pages on the explanation of *Jihad*'.[92] In these pages, the author praises jihad but does not instigate people to undertake militant activities on their own in India. Indeed, the only reference to the India of 1817 is that it is mostly a *Dārul Ḥarb* while it was a *Dārul Islām* 'when the Muslims were following the Sharī'ah'.[93] The emphasis upon textual rather than folk Islam, puritanism, and spiritual elevation, at least in the religious writings of the Ṭarīqah-e-Muḥammadiyyah, the movement inspired by Sayyid

89 Nadwī 1939: 404.
90 Ibid 408–409.
91 Cited from Nadwī 1939: 549–552.
92 Haq 1995: 77.
93 Ibid 77.

Aḥmad, was also noted by British authors who pointed out that jihad is only incidentally touched upon in *Ṣirāṭ-ul-mustaqīm.*[94]

However, there were other popular writings advocating fighting. For instance, W.W.Hunter mentions 'the prophecy of Ni'mat-ullah' in which, after a hundred-year rule, the 'the followers of Jesus will be defeated/Islam will prevail for forty years'. Also, 'The King of the West' who will defeat the 'Nazarenes' will be the Afghan ruler. This prophecy was in circulation along with other material—such as the hadith about the black flags coming from Kurasan—spelling the end of British rule.[95] Hunter then goes on to give a list of thirteen works which, in his opinion, are used by the 'Wahabis' to incite people to resist the government. Among them are the *Ṣirāṭ-e-mustaqīm* and the *Taqwiyyat al-īmān* by Muḥammad Ismā'īl; *Sharḥ-i-Waqāya* giving instructions about whom to fight; *Qaṣīdah* (spelled Kasida by Hunter) which sets forth 'the obligation of waging war against the infidel', and Karam Ali's *Naṣīḥat al-muslimīn.* However, Ismā'īl's and Karam 'Alī's books were not about jihad. They were more about moral reform in the Islamic paradigm as defined by the reformers.[96] The centre for this kind of propaganda was Patna from where the printed work was distributed to those who sympathised with the movement. However, occasional poems in praise of jihad were produced elsewhere too. For instance, Momin Khān Momin (1800–1851), a major poet of Urdu who is famous for his amorous *ghazals*, praised Shāh 'Abdul 'Azīz and wrote poems inspiring readers for jihad.[97]

Since 1870, as noted by 'Azīz Aḥmad, a 'lively controversy has raged' whether Barēlwī's movement 'was directed primarily against the British as much as against the Sikhs on India's north-western frontier'.[98] This movement—associated with Shāh Walīullāh, Shāh 'Abdul 'Azīz and members of their family 'Abdul Ḥayy and Muḥammad Ismā'īl in addition to Barēlwī himself—has been used to build disparate discourses about jihad according to the ideology of the time. Sir Sayyid and Ja'far Thānēsarī, both keen on presenting the two religious figures as promoters of peace under *pax Brittanica*, suppressed evidence which suggested otherwise. Thānesarī, as we have seen, deleted parts of his letters while Sir

94 JRC 1832: 487.
95 Hunter 1871: 42–44.
96 Ibid 46–47.
97 Jalal 2008: 58–59; Metcalf 1982: 66. The most detailed, albeit fanciful, treatment of the poetic response of Urdu poets towards jihad in British India is by Husain (1978). However, the author's view that the figures of speech in the *ghazal* (the beloved is an armed fighter, she/he is a killer, a murderer; the lover is killed but is willing to die, etc.), such as that of Ghalib, refers to jihad is not accepted by any scholar of Urdu literature.
98 Ahmad 1967: 20.

Sayyid ignored those which mentioned British dominance. During the Indian freedom movement of the twentieth century,'Ubaydullāh Sindhī invested Shāh Walīullāh's theological ideas with his own revolutionary discourse.

After the freedom of India, some Indian[99] and Pakistani scholars have taken to strengthening 'Ubaydullāh Sindhī's narrative that the family of Shāh Walīullāh were the architects of anti-colonial jihad in India.[100] The Pakistani historian Ishtiaq Qureshi (1903–1981) waxes lyrical about the jihad movement, saying: 'it was the first popular movement born of a consciousness of a political duty' and credits it to the Walīullāhī school, since 'it was born of a consciousness created by the writings of a thinker, who had found in their moral regeneration the remedy of his people's ills'.[101] According to Hasan, '[f]or Barelvi, jihad was ennobling. He did not seek to wage war against non-Muslims out of hatred but only to ensure that injustice against the Pathan tribesmen ended'.[102] Jalal, however, believes that armed struggle, despite its momentous effect on Indian Muslims, was a kind of falling off from the high ideals of jihad. The war, with its accompanying 'sharp distinction between Muslims and non-Muslims blunted the effect of Sayyid Ahmad's ethical teaching' and it became a 'political movement' but his death 'remained sacred'.[103] Both of Jalal's observations follow from her unexamined axiom that jihad is a purely ethical ideal and, hence, precludes aggressive warfare. Hasan and Jalal also emphasise the differences between Sayyid Aḥmad's movement and present-day terrorism on the Pakistan-Afghanistan border.[104] In short, the thrust of the argument for these writers is to distance their anti-colonial jihadi heroes from contemporary terrorism while building up their credentials for anti-colonial struggle and moral improvement.

There are, however, writers who have a less positive view of Sayyid Aḥmad's movement. According to Altaf Qadir, the jihad movement soon turned against Shī'as and, in any case, 'waging jihad in private capacity without adequate resources is not legitimate according to *sharia*'.[105] In India, Waḥīduddīn Khān also pointed out that there was no legitimate ruler (*amīr al-mu'minīn*) at that time and that Sayyid Aḥmad Barēlwī was opposed by some great *'ulamā*, one of whom was Maulanā Mīr Maḥbūb who, having learned that Barēlwī had based his jihad on a dream (i.e. mystic insight), left him and went back to

99 Hasan 2015.
100 Qureshi 1977; Jalal 2008.
101 Qureshi 1977: 231.
102 Hasan 2015: 39.
103 Jalal 2008: 107.
104 Ibid, 107; Hasan 2015: 39.
105 Qadir 2015: 189.

India.[106] Rizvi, after a prolix discussion of the movement, concludes that Ḥusain Aḥmad Madanī (1879 – 1957) and other nationalist Muslims wrongly assume that Sayyid Aḥmad 'was concerned only to drive the British out of India and intended to leave power in the hands of the Indian heads of states'.[107]

Evidence, as we have noted, does not bear out the claims that the family of Shāh Walīullāh gave a particular interpretation of jihad and ordered or inspired a jihad movement in India consciously and deliberately. Sayyid Aḥmad's armed conflict with the Sikhs was more of his own initiative than any specific order from Shāh 'Abdul 'Azīz. 'Ubaidullāh, however, 'fathers on him [Abdul Aziz] a social philosophy which is largely his own creation'.[108] However, Walīullāh, 'Abdul 'Azīz, and Sayyid Aḥmad Barēlwī reacted to Muslim loss of political power through different strategies. Walīullah relied upon foreign Muslim rulers to break non-Muslim (Marhatta) power while his son, despite being distressed by it, found a means of co-existence with British dominance by issuing *fatwās* which did not commit Indian Muslims either to actual armed revolt or to emigration from India. Only Sayyid Aḥmad led an armed struggle, which he called jihad, against the Sikhs who were one of the powers which had subdued Muslims and were also seen as being cruel and oppressive in social and religious matters. But if he had defeated the Sikhs, the kind of state he wanted to create might have proved to be even more intolerant of non-Muslims than the Sikhs were. This possibility is seldom addressed by those who praise him.

106 Khan 2002 b: 239 – 240.
107 Rizvi 1982: 535.
108 Ahmad 1967: 198; Baljon 1977.

5 Colonial Modernists

The term 'modernist' is used for interpreters of Islam who seek to 'rethink or adapt Muslim institutions, norms, and discourses in light both of what they take to be "true" Islam, as opposed to how the Islamic tradition evolved in history, and of how they see the challenges and opportunities of modernity'.[1] They have especially launched a trenchant and heterodox critique of many aspects of Muslim intellectual and social ideas—especially those pertaining to women, slavery, and war[2]—the latter two of which are relevant for our study. In this chapter, the term will be reserved for nineteenth and early twentieth century interpreters of Islam, especially South Asian ones. The term 'progressive' is reserved for contemporary Muslim interpreters with basically the same concerns, except that they operate in a post-colonial situation rather than a colonial one. There are, despite some continuities, differences between the two situations which warrants the use of disparate terms for both.

Colonial rule brought about major changes in the way the Indian society was organised and in its intellectual makeup. Printing, education, employment, entertainment, and commercial activities all changed India in fundamental ways. Printing, as we have seen, made hitherto rare texts, religious and otherwise, widely available. The former sharpened 'the awareness of religious—even sectarian and sub-sectarian—differences'[3] *parri passu* with increasing secularism amongst Muslims. The British system of education, with officials reporting on percentages of students according to their religious labels,[4] intense rivalries between Hindus and Muslims for quotas in state employment,[5] the appeal of printed material and later the radio,[6] and the very fact of the census which categorised Indians in religious terms—indeed 'the very idiom of British rule after 1857'—also heightened the sense of religious identity.[7] Thus, even if a particular individual Muslim was non-observant and secular, he or she had to be part of the group, i.e the Muslim community in social behaviour. Hence, the increasing significance of appeals to Islam as part of the Indian Muslim experience of modern-

1 Zaman 2012: 2.
2 Baljon 1961: 111–120.
3 Rahman 2011: 337.
4 Brass 1974: 143–146 ; Robinson 1974: 34–42; 102–105.
5 Hardy 1972: 80–81 and 123–125; Robinson 1974: 20–23, 26, 144–145, 180–181; Brass 1974: 143–152.
6 Rahman 2011: 348–365; for changes in games and consumption patterns in Lahore, see Talbot and Kamran 2016: 81–123.
7 Hardy 1972: 116.

https://doi.org/10.1515/9783110716986-008

ity. South Asian historians generally call this a deliberate policy of 'divide and rule' but evidence, as Robinson points out,[8] does not bear this out. Documents only suggest that the British, as a group, wanted to consolidate the empire. To do so, different policies were pursued at different times and officers differed with each other. Indeed, in order to maintain law and order, officers tried to create harmonious relationships between antagonistic groups of Indians (in *Muḥarram*, during Hindu-Muslim disputes, etc.). The nature of the colonial state, however, was such that, *ipso facto*, it encouraged group cohesion which implied the exclusion of out-groups.

The modernist interpreters of Islam of the nineteenth and twentieth centuries accepted some values of modernity while rejecting or challenging others.[9] Among those they accepted was the legitimacy of British rule subject to their freedom of conscience, private living, worship and norms of behaviour. They also accepted certain enlightenment values such as peace, the desirability of monogamy and the end of slavery. However, they opposed and challenged those—British officers, Christian polemicists and Muslim traditional *'ulamā*—who claimed that Islam allowed aggressive jihad, polygamy or slavery. They presented explanations and interpretations and were called apologists in return. This phenomenon was not confined to India alone. It was prevalent all over the Muslim world. In India, 'the defence against the unfavourable image of Islam was only timidly voiced' initially, but eventually it came to be framed in the theoretical model of anti-colonialism.[10]

One reason for this spirited defence of Islam by Muslim scholars is that this was the period when Western writers, both scholarly Orientalists and polemical missionaries, accused Islam of having been spread by the sword. This is called the 'scimitar-syndrome'and those Muslims who refute it are called apologists. Of course, not every Western writer agreed with this. For instance, T.W. Arnold, in his major study of conversion to Islam in the world, says: 'the common hypothesis of the sword as the factor of conversion seems hardly satisfactory'.[11]

---

8 Robinson 1974: 348–9.

9 Masud 2016: 240–250.

10 Peters 1996: 109.

11 Arnold 1896: 69. Richard M. Eaton points out that the Muslims were distributed in the east and west of the Subcontinent while the seat of the empire was in upper north Indian plains where the Brahmanical tradition was strong. Hence, it is the weakness of this tradition which explains the spread of Islam, neither Muslim 'scimitar' nor Brahmanical oppression. Moreover, Islam spread in Bengal because of 'the cultivation of wet rice' which required adventurers venerated as religious figures. In the Punjab, it spread around the shrines of the mystics such as that of Baba Farid at Pakpattan (Eaton 2017).
Besides, Arnold, another famous Westerner who defended jihad as struggle against 'sin', which

The Muslim modernists were much indebted to such people and often referred to them in their own writings.

This chapter focuses on the way the modernists of India dealt with jihad in particular though, while doing so, other concerns such as polygamy and slavery will also be referred to in passing. For this we will study the thoughts of Sir Sayyid Aḥmad Khān, Mawlawī Chirāgh 'Alī, Syed Ameer Ali (written as Sayyid Amīr 'Alī on the titles of his translations in Urdu), Shiblī Nu'mānī, and Mirzā Ghulām Aḥmad (1835–1908). The last, being the pioneer of the sect called the Aḥmadīs, Mirzā'īs, or Qādiyānīs, is considered outside the pale of Islam. Sir Sayyid too is considered a heretic since he dismissed traditional Muslim beliefs in supernatural beings (angels, genies, etc.) and scriptural events (the parting of the water of the Red Sea for Moses to cross over, etc.). The others, however, were considered Muslims, though orthodox opinion always remained ambivalent towards them.

To understand the work of modernist Muslims, it is necessary to understand the period in which they wrote. The major anti-British armed upheaval of the nineteenth century was the revolt of 1857. The earlier armed conflict of Sayyid Aḥmad Barēlwī against the Sikhs had come to an end in 1831. Both events had proved to most Indians that armed conflict was useless. Indeed, a number of the figures mentioned below, notably Sir Sayyid, believed that British rule was good for India as 'no one else was in a position to govern'.[12] Even when enthusiasm for accepting the Ottoman ruler as the caliph of all Muslims was building up, Sir Sayyid as well as others who shared some of his views such as Shiblī Nu'mānī, refused to accept him as such. Sir Sayyid even said that 'if he [the Turkish Sultan] is a caliph then he is the caliph of the country and of its Muslim inhabitants over which he rules'.[13] Developing this argument, which he expressed in writing elsewhere too, he concludes that the Indian Muslims are not the subjects of Sulṭān 'Abdul Ḥamīd Khān II (1842–1918), 'we are the subjects of the British government'.[14] This was to become a major point of opposition by anti-colonial

the English as well as even Indian Muslims misunderstood to be aggressive warfare, was the Hugarian-born Gottlieb Wilhelm Leitner, the father of both the Government College and the Punjab University of Lahore, and an influential person in official circles in India and England. His article, 'Jihad—misconceptions about Islamic teaching', *The Asiatic Quarterly Review* 2:4 (October 1886), 338–353, had much resonance in policy-making sectionsof British society (Germain 2015: 297–311).

12 Ḥālī 1901: 73.

13 Khān 1898: 100.

14 Ibid 101.

Muslims to Sir Sayyid's conciliatory stand towards British rule during the Khilafat Movement with which we shall deal in the next chapter.

While most of the major thinkers of India, both Muslims and Hindus, accepted the idea of coexistence with the British and acquired whatever power they could as individuals and as a community by becoming junior partners in the administration of the empire, minor figures and groups kept alive the idea of anticolonial resistance, even armed conflict, alive. One major reason for being impressed by the British was that they had brought new forms of knowledge. Delhi College (*Dillī Kālij* in Urdu) stood as a kind of centre of the Indian renaissance where Indians acquired modern knowledge. Mawlawī Zakāullāh (1832–1910) learned the methodology for writing history, as distinct from hagiography, and Master Rāmchandra (1821–1880) practised modern mathematics. Naẓīr Aḥmad (1831–1912), the renowned Urdu novelist, learned British law and tried to reform education.[15] However, colonialism also brought a trenchant critique of Indian culture, knowledge systems, and, above all, belief-systems. This last led to debates (*munāẓarah*)—highly polemical Christian-Muslim and Hindu-Muslim ones—and attempts by the modernists to defend Islam using the knowledge and technologies of the West.[16] In Sir Sayyid's case, for instance, John William Colenso (1814–1883)[17]and Sir William Muir (1819–1905), the first a bishop and the second a highly placed British officer in India, presented ideas which Sir Sayyid took special pains to refute.[18] Nor was he the only one to do so. Indeed, other modernists of the nineteenth century—notably Chirāgh 'Alī and Ameer Ali —were also engaged in a lively debate with missionaries like Thomas P.Hughes (1838–1911) and Edward Sells (1839–1932) and both parties made intellectual adjustments during these exchanges.[19] Indeed, the very fact that the modernists used the research methodology of the West, meant that they eventually either accepted some of the implicit scepticism of Western authors or interpreted the canonical texts to bring them in consonance with what the nineteenth century called 'civilized values'. All evidence suggests that both discrepant, and even conflicting, trends of thought were genuine and sincere. Thus, the modernists' interpretation of jihad as being defensive, abolition of slavery, and the issue of concubinage and womens' rights, etc., is as genuine a part of the worldview they

---

15 Hasan 2005.

16 Ibid 91–105.

17 Colenso in his book entitled *The Pentateuch and Book of Joshua Critically Examined* (4 parts) (1862) doubts the historical validity of Noah's worldwide flood, but Sayyid calls it a 'partial flood' which does not negate the laws of nature (Quoted from Troll 1978: 110).

18 Troll 1978: 74 & 132.

19 Guenther 1997.

constructed through their reading of Western sources as their equally genuine resistance against Western critiques of Islam and impassioned pleas to save the Muslims of the world from harm.

Sir Sayyid (1817–1898) (for a contemporary, albeit sympathetic, biography see Ḥālī)[20] was a prolific writer and was the first to use arguments from the canonical sources of Islam to prove that Indian Muslims were not fanatics who had waged religious war in his book entitled *The Loyal Mohammadans of India* (1860–1861). But here the author merely scratches the surface. His detailed views pertinent to jihad are found in his exegesis of the Qur'an in Urdu, entitled *Tafsīr al-Qur'ān wa huwā al-hudā wa al-Furqān* (the exegesis of the Qur'an and the guidance from the Book). The work was never completed as 'only two-fifths remained to be done when he was overcome by death'.[21] However, all the important verses pertaining to jihad have been explained as are most of Sir Sayyid's other novel ideas.[22] Its main feature is that it is based on the theory that 'the word of God' cannot be different from 'the work of God'.[23] However, he does not reject the basic ideas upon which religion itself is based; thus, he is not wholly a rationalist but a believer in 'rational supernaturalism', as Baljon calls him.[24] This attempt at conforming to scientific rationalism makes Sir Sayyid's interpretations heterodox to say the least. For instance, he dismisses the physical hell and heavens, genies, the birth of Jesus from the Virgin Mary, and so on as either metaphors or misunderstandings.[25]

This chapter, however, is not concerned with Sir Sayyid's theological doctrines. It focuses on his interpretations of the verses pertaining to jihad which are given in a synoptic form below.

Table 4

Verse	Commentary by Sir Syed	Interpretive device
2:190	Defensive war is allowed with those who persecuted Muslims. (Vol. 1: 196–197).	Literal meaning
2:191	*Fitnah* means cruel persecution in order to make Muslims leave Islam (Vol. 1, 198).	Usual meaning

20 Ḥālī 1901.
21 Ibid 1901: 256.
22 Nafisi 2012.
23 *Tafsīr-e-Sayyid* Vol.1: Introduction.
24 Baljon 1949: 86.
25 For a summary, see Baljon 1949: 45–67; Ahmad 1967: 42–48; detailed analysis is in Troll 1978: 144–193.

Table 4 *(Continued)*

Verse	Commentary by Sir Syed	Interpretive device
2:193	Fighting is to end persecution. The phrase 'and religion is only for God' does not mean that no religion but Islam should exist (Vol.1: 199).	Ideological imperative
8:39	It means fighting is only till persecution ends. i.e. Muslims can worship freely without being stopped (Vol.4: 54).	As above
8:61	Peace treaties, such as Hadaybiyyah, are allowed as peace is the aim. (Vol. 4: 49).	Literal meaning
9:5	The Arab polytheists who had initiated hostilities were fought with to establish peace and not to convert them to Islam. This does not allow Muslims to fight those who have not initiated hostilities (Vol. 4: 555).	Specification
9:29	Only those who had initiated hostilities among the non-believers could be fought with while *Jizyah* was a small tax to make *dhimmīs* secure (Vol. 4: 104–105).	Specification/ ideological imperative
60:8	Regarding those who have not been hostile, you may be kind and just towards them and be at peace with them (Vol. 4: 51).	Literal meaning

Source: *Tafsīr-e-Sayyid* 5 parts in 2 Vols.

Sir Sayyid's ideological assumptions are that jihad is purely defensive and that none of the wars of the Prophet were aggressive in nature. He uses the device of specification (*takhṣīṣ*) to argue that jihad was restricted to a particular period and foe.[26] Moreover, he also specifies the conditions for fighting. One can fight non-Muslims if they: (a) fight Muslims; (b) break their oaths; (c) capture Muslim women and children.[27] As for those who have never been hostile towards the Muslims, peaceful coexistence is prescribed. Sir Sayyid supports this argument with reference to *al- Mumtaḥina* (Q. 60) (that Muslims can treat those non-Muslims with justice who have not been hostile to them (60: 8)). This passage occurs in his commentary of *al-Tawbah*. Since Sir Sayyid's ideological imperative makes him deny that any war of the Prophet was aggressive, he calls the expedition to Tabuk as a defensive step to the news that Byzantine forces were heading towards Arabia. Ibn Kathīr, it may be noted, had justified this expedition on the ground that the Romans had to be chastised for their wrong beliefs. Sir Sayyid also explains the expeditions to subdue the polytheist Arabs involving the break-

26 *Tafsīr*, Vol. 2: 51–54. While explaining Q.9.
27 Ibid Vol. 2: 53. While explaining Q.9.

ing of their statues, with reference to the belief that the Arabs, being the children of Abraham, were monotheists and idol worship was a post-Abrahamic accretion.

As Sir Sayyid was in constant dialogue with Christian missionaries, he refers to the New Testment in which Jesus tells his followers to turn the other cheek. This, he says, is not practical as it is not in accordance with human nature which, in Sir Sayyid's view, implies that it is only Islam which gives the correct guidance to human behaviour.[28] He selects for special criticism the view that the part of the verse declaring that 'religion is only for God' refers to the establishment of Islam as the only belief-system in the world. This, he remarks acerbically, 'is foolish' (*nādānī kī bāt hai*) since it would go against the Quranic order of not forcing the faith upon other people.[29] Thus, Sir Sayyid lays down the principle that all orders for fighting in the Quran refer to those who had persecuted the Muslims, prevented them from following their faith, expelled them from their homes, and attacked them. For 9: 29 too, he first restricts it to the hostile people of the Book of that period, and then gives a detailed apologetic explanation of the poll tax claiming that it was lower than the tax on Muslims and that it ensured that the non-Muslim payer was protected and not sent to dangerous military expeditions.[30]

Some battles of the Prophet have been mentioned above. Let us now come to his first battle, that of Badar which, like the others, he explains in the light of his ideological imperative that all Prophetic wars were defensive. He begins by refuting all the Muslim historians or writers of hadith who have said that the Prophet wanted to intercept the caravan of the Quraish being led by Abū Sufyān ibn al-Ḥārith (d. 636 or 641). In order to do so he uses the Qur'an while ignoring the hadith. He explains other events, both when the Prophet went with the fighters (*ghazwah*) and when he sent others (*sariyah*) one by one proving that each one of them was defensive or in retaliation to aggression or treason.[31] As mentioned above, the breaking of the statues of the Arabs was explained by him on the assumption that they had originally been monotheists. This has an important implication for India i.e if the original religion is polytheistic—and here Sir Sayyid must have had Hindus in mind— then that community should not be molested.[32] Here he uses the hermeneutic device of reserving a verse to a specific group (*takhsīs*) which ensures the possibility of living in peace in the contemporary world. In short, jihad is to bring about peace and not to convert non-Muslims

28 Ibid Vol. 1: 193. While explaining 2: 190.
29 Ibid Vol. 1: 199. While explaining 2: 193.
30 Ibid Vol. 2 : 102–103. While explaining *jizyah*.
31 Ibid Vol. 2: 56–101. While explaining the wars of the early Muslim community.
32 Ibid Vol. 2: 108. While explaining the breaking of idols.

to Islam or oppress them. Having already established the doctrine that all *aḥādith* are not to be trusted, he does not refer to those traditions which seem to suggest that jihad is to convert the whole world to Islam since that would go against the idea of peace.

In addition to his ideological imperative which affects all his interpretations, Sir Sayyid uses semantic manipulation, specification, and *asbāb al-nuzūl* as his major hermeneutical devices. Comparing Sir Sayyid's methods with those employed by another famous modernist, Shaykh 'Abdūh of Egypt, Troll points out that whereas in points of conflict between reason or science and scripture, 'Abdūh uses *tafwīḍ*—'entrusting the solution to God who alone knows'—Sir Sayyid rarely uses this method. As for Arabic lexicology, 'he is less assured in his knowledge of Arabic than 'Abduh and thus proposes, at times philologically, rather doubtful interpretations'.[33] For instance, *Sunnat Allāh*, which for 'Abdūh (and most others) refers to divine custom, means natural law as discoverable by modern science in Sir Sayyid's work [semantic expansion in terms of this study]. Also, he does not accept the word *'arsh*, literally the throne, in *al-Ā'rāf* (Q. 7)—referring to God sitting on the throne (7: 54)—on the grounds that this would imply that the throne was empty before the act of sitting upon it. Such instances of semantic expansion are called 'lexicographic jugglings' and 'metaphorising of supernatural notions' by Baljon.[34] For him, therefore, like many other expressions in the Qur'an, this use of words is metaphorical (*ta'wīl*). This enables Sir Sayyid to give naturalistic explanations of miracles such as angels' help to Muslims in battles.

Sir Sayyid's *tafsīr* was defended by his admirers such as Alṭāf Ḥusain Ḥālī (1837–1914) who begins one of his essays with the question whether a new exegesis of the Qur'an is required or not. During the discussion he makes the point that metaphors, similies, and symbolic language have been used in the Qur'an, thereby implying that merely literal interpretations can be misleading.[35] He finally concludes that a new interpretation of the Qur'an is justified.[36] However, the traditional *'ulamā* refuted Sir Sayyid's views,[37] among them the learned Muḥammad Qāsim Nānawtwī of Deoband. In a nutshell, Nānawtwī says:

33 Troll 1978: 226.
34 Baljon1949: 55.
35 Ḥālī 1899: 95.
36 Ibid 96.
37 Ḥālī 1901: 257–258.

> We should not consider our own ideas and conceptions to be real and then stretch the Word of God and of the Prophet to make it conform to our own views.[38]

It was also attacked by others who complained that Sir Sayyid gives meanings of the Qur'anic verses which put him outside the pale of Islam.[39]

But Sir Sayyid was also a practical man and his role as a champion of Muslim interests should be pointed out, not only in education as that has been done in detail in many other works, but also for representing Muslims as a peaceful community. He wrote his books pointing out the wrong policies of the British responsible for the events of 1857 and exonerating Muslims of the blame for it soon after British rule was re-established even at the risk of annoying the rulers. Indeed, the Foreign Secretary dubbed his *Causes of the Indian Revolt* (1873) as 'an extremely seditious pamphlet'.[40] Sir Sayyid also criticised W.W.Hunter's book describing how the Wahhābīs had organised a conspiracy to keep up the resistance against the British. The book was entitled, *Indian Muslims: are they bound in conscience to rebel against the Queen?* (1871).The sub-title seemed to imply a mistrust of all Muslims, including those of the gentry (*ashrāf*) of North India. However, the book was written at the order of Lord Mayo, the Viceroy, and its purpose was to show that 'Muslims did not need to rebel provided the ruling power was sympathetic'.[41] But the implication that their religion, or some interpretations of it, could justify rebellion against the government on religious grounds was too much for Sir Sayyid. Thus, he entered into the fray since he always defended Muslim interests against perceived Western prejudices. He had, after all, spent much time and energy to convince the British government of the loyalty of his own class (the *ashrāf* class of U.P.) in particular and all In-

38 Nānawtwī 1890 in Ahmad and Grunebaum 1970: 61.

39 While Mawlānā Qāsim Nānawtwī's critique was courteous, the common cleric and ordinary people carried their animosity against Sir Sayyid and the modernist intellectuals to an extreme. The clerics declared before one of the speeches of Mahdī 'Alī Khān that anyone who listens to his speech would go straight to hell and his marriage would be automatically annulled (Zubayri 1934: 73). Also, when it came to be known that Sir Sayyid and Mahdi 'Alī dined with an Englishman, their sweeper, water carrier, and other service providers stopped working for them till they assured them that they were not Christians (Zubayri 1934: 209). Even the Christian missionaries (Hughes and Sell for instance) argued that the 'true nature of Islam is not to be learnt from the rationalistic statements' of the Western-educated modernists (Guenther 1997: 111; for similar views, see Sell 1880: v-xv). Even now the rejection of progressive Muslim thought, especially that which is related to jihad, comes from the traditional *'ulamā*, the radical Islamists, and Western scholars.

40 Ḥālī 1901: 94.

41 Robinson 1974: 103–104.

dian Muslims in general so he could hardly brook that his work should be wasted. Among other things, Sir Sayyid pointed out in his review of the book that Hunter misrepresents Wahhābī doctrine since Muslims are bound to obey a non-Muslim ruler 'as long as he does not interfere with their religion'.[42] Moreover, the Pashtuns who are associated with these jihad movements are Ḥanafīs and not Wahhābīs at all. Sayyid's major argument is that Sayyid Aḥmad and Shāh Ismā'īl, who were the pioneers of jihad, were not anti-British. They left their families in British India under the protection of the British government when they went to fight against the Sikhs. Even the money which was transferred during this episode was known to the British authorities who did not block it. One of the followers of Sayyid Aḥmad, Mahbūb 'Alī, was asked by Bakht Khān (1797–1859), the commander of the Indian forces in 1857, to sign 'the proclamation of a religious war against the English' but he refused to do so.[43] Sayyid also pointed out that the *fatwā* given by the seven 'Law Doctors of Northern India', among whom five happened to be Farangī Maḥallīs,[44] was in support of British rule and against jihad.[45] The relevant *fatwā* is given in Hunter's own book as an appendix. A part of it reads as follows:

> The Musalmans here are protected by Christians, and there is no Jihad in a country where protection is afforded, as the absence of protection and liberty between Musalmans and Infidels is essential in a religious war, and that condition does not exist here. Besides, it is necessary that there should be a probability of victory to Musalman and glory to the Indians. If there is no such probability, the Jihad is unlawful.[46]

Sir Sayyid had given a laudatory sketch of the life of Sayyid Aḥmad Barēlwī, emphasising his piety and mystical orientation but giving little space to his jihad. When he does mention it, he says: 'he had fixed his Jihad on the race of Sikhs'. Ḥālī points out that this review changed even English peoples' perception of Wahhābīs and was much admired by contemporaries.[47] In his *'Shāhjahān Ābād kē lōgõ kā bayān'* (an account of the people of Shahjahanabad), Sir Sayyid writes laudatory accounts of both 'Abdul Ḥayy and Muḥammad Ismā'īl. In both, he does mention that they went for jihad, but only against the Sikhs outside British India. Sir Sayyid's editor and compiler, Ismā'īl Pānipatī, wrote a footnote of two pages arguing that the jihad was not against the British and that Sir Sayyid

42 Khān 1872: 9.
43 Ibid 16.
44 Robinson 2002: 199.
45 Jaffar 1992.
46 In Hunter 1871: Appendix 2:164.
47 Ḥālī 1898: 371–372; Ḥālī 1901: 204–205.

was a near contemporary of his namesake so his word should be considered authentic.[48]

Chirāgh 'Alī (1844–1895), next in importance as a modernist Muslim writer of the nineteenth century, was of Kashmiri origin, his grandfather having worked in the Punjab and then settled in Meerut. His father, Maulawī Muḥammad Bakhsh, worked in Meerut and then in Saharanpur as a clerk. He also served in the Punjab in the lower bureaucracy but died early, leaving Chirāgh 'Alī an orphan at the age of twelve. The family came back to Meerut and eventually the young man entered British service. In 1874, Sir Sayyid introduced him to the service of the Niẓām of Hyderabad, and here he rose to high rank receiving the title of Nawwāb A'ẓam Yār Jang. Here he also had enough income to enjoy intellectual pursuits for which he learned many languages, becoming proficient in Arabic and Persian. He also learned English and seriously indulged his passion for defending Islam from the attacks of both British officers and missionaries as well as conservative Muslim *'ulamā*. [49]

Chirāgh 'Alī's most relevant book for this study is *Critical Exposition of the Popular Jihad* (1885). It was specifically for the purpose of proving that 'all the wars of Mohammad were defensive; and that aggressive war, or compulsory conversion, is not allowed in Islam'—this being the sub-title of the book.[50] The book was later translated into Urdu as *Taḥqīq al-Jihād* (1913). Like Sir Sayyid Chirāgh 'Alī too argues that all the wars of the Prophet were in response to wars initiated by the enemies or a phase of the same struggle. For some, like Tabūk, he reproduces Sir Sayyid's argument. In short, concludes Chirāgh 'Alī, jihad in the prophetic practice was a defensive undertaking to ensure that the Muslim community should survive. In his appendix A, Chirāgh 'Alī takes up the meaning of the word jihad. He begins by giving the etymological roots of the word as 'strove, laboured or toiled'[51] and then argues that 'it is only a post-classical and technical meaning of *jihád* to use the word as signifying fighting against an enemy'.[52] Then he takes up fourteen occurrences of derivations from the morphological root *-jhd-* and argues that the commentators and translators of the Quran 'deviate from the original meaning, and prefer the subsequent unclassical and technical significa-

---

48 Panipati, 1965 Vol. 16 of *Maqālāt-ī-Sir Sayyid*, Note 1: 318. This note (pp. 318–319) is in explanation of Sir Sayyid's claim that Muḥammad Ismā'īl went to fight only the Sikhs. In Khān 1847: 312–321., note 1; see Mahar 1952: 241 for refutation of Sir Sayyid's view.

49 Rahman, W : 57–62; also see Ahmad 1967: 57–71.

50 'Alī, C 1885.

51 Ibid 163.

52 Ibid 164.

tion of waging war or crusade'.[53] He spends much effort in refuting translations of Western scholars who equate Jihad with war bringing forth translations where it means effort. In one paragraph, he does concede that the words '*katal*' and '*kitál*' [he spells them both with a 'k'] are used in the Qur'an but these, he argues, refer to 'a defensive war, but not to one of aggression'.[54] Throughout the book it is clear that Chirāgh 'Alī is engaged in a conversation with the Western Orientalists and clergymen who attack Islam as a religion of violence and warfare. This, indeed, is the major objective of the modernists who were pained by the charge of Islam being a religion of violence.

Chirāgh 'Alī's other book, comprising his spirited defence of jihad as defensive warfare, monogamy, and the role of Islam in ending slavery, is called *Tahzīb al-kalām fī ḥaqīqat al-Islām*. It is a collection of four pamphlets, one of which is by a Mawlawī Muḥammad 'Abdullāh, the compiler and publisher of the collection, in 1918. The other three are by Chirāgh 'Alī. The pamphlet, which gives its title to the book, is a refutation of a book by Mawlawī Sayyid Muḥammad 'Askarī, called *Haqīqat al-Islām* (1874). It begins with the aim of refuting 'Askarī's claim that Islam permits the killing of unbelievers and enslaving their women and children. Chirāgh 'Alī argument is based on *Sūrah al-Muḥammad* (Q. 47)—which says that prisoners of war should either be exchanged for money (*fidyah*) or released as a favour (*iḥsān*) (47: 4). This being so, he insists, there is no third alternative of taking prisoners. So, no matter what might have happened before, slavery is forbidden after this revelation. To this he adds arguments from history: that prisoners of war in the Battle of Ḥunain were not enslaved; the release of slaves was highly recommended as an act of virtue; and that traditions apparently supporting it were weak. He also mentions that some Hanafite *'ulamā* consider it restricted to the unbelievers of the Battle of Badar while most claim it has been abrogated (*mansūkh*) by Q. 9 which was revealed later. But the latter assertion, in his view, strengthens his argument that enslaving prisoners is not a viable alternative since otherwise the theory of abrogation would not have been invoked.[55]

He also defends the rights of non-Muslim citizens against the traditional explanation of 9: 29—the verse advocating fighting the People of the Book and taking the poll-tax from them—in which the word *ṣāghirūn* has been used for the defeated party. His arguments are in response to an essay by an orthodox opponent called 'Askarī. In 'Askarī's view, the verse refers to the imperative of humiliating (*ṣaghār*) the Jews and the Christians once they are defeated. 'Askarī then

53 Ibid 171.
54 'Alī, C 1885: 192.
55 'Alī, C 1918: 219–221.

goes on to enumerate the ways in which this is to be done: taking the *jizyah* in an insulting manner; not wishing peace upon them (*salām*); not dining with them; considering them unclean; harassing them in their daily lives. Chirāgh ʻAlī refutes these views by arguing that the verse refers to the Byzantine Christians against whom Tabuk was undertaken, i.e. the use of the hermeneutical device of specification.[56] Moreover, the act of accepting the political power of Muslims by paying them a tax is humiliation enough. The conduct of Muslims towards them should thenceforward be courteous and just.

He also uses the same device of specification for the verses apparently ordering Muslims to fight the unbelievers. These verses, he says, are for those Arab opponents of the early Muslim community who had attacked and persecuted them. According to Chirāgh ʻAlī, any act leading to the death of human beings now is governed by the verses of *al-Nisā'* (Q. 4). One verse (4: 92), fixes a penalty for killing a Muslim, or a non-Muslim with whose people there is a treaty of peace; the other (4: 93), threatens eternal punishment for wilful murder. This means that any treaty or arrangement of amicable civil co-existence with non-Muslims cannot be disturbed under the pretext of jihad nowadays.[57] In this context, it is relevant to discuss his interpretation of 9: 5. His argument is that it is a part of this verse—kill the polytheists—which is used to justify aggression against them. Again using specification, he argues that the verse is for those specific polytheists who broke treaties with Muslims and were aggressive and cruel. It is neither valid for everyone nor applies to people after that specific period. Moreover, an atheist or one who adopts another monotheistic religion is not a polytheist (*mushrik*). In short, 9: 5 does not justify either the killing of apostates nor attacks on non-Muslims.[58] Thus, by using the hermeneutic device of specification, Chirāgh ʻAlī makes aggressive jihad a thing of the past with no relevance for the present.

His third book, from which we have quoted above, originally written in English like his famous book on jihad, is called, *Proposed Political, Legal and Social Reforms Under Muslim Rule*. This was written in response to the critique of reverend Malcolm Michael in 1881. It too was translated into Urdu under the title of *ʻĀẓam al-kalām fī irtiqā' al-Islām* (1910) which is being used here because this, rather than the English version, was read in India. Michael claims that Muslim law (*fiqh*) cannot change because it is based on the Qur'an and the hadith and the opinions of the four major schools of law—*Mālikī, Ḥanafī, Shāfiʻī,*

56 Ibid 87.
57 Ibid 41.
58 ʻAlī, C 1910, part 1: 90.

Ḥanbalī—for Sunnis. Chirāgh ʻAlī refutes these arguments by pointing out that not four but at least nineteen people made schools of law which did not, however, survive. The Hanafite school, which most Indian Muslims follow, was derived largely from the writings of Abū Ḥanīfah's students, Yaʻqūb ibn Ibrāhīm al-Anṣārī, known as Imām Abū Yūsuf (735 or 739 – 798) and Imām Muḥammad ibn al-Ḥasan al-Shaybānī (749 – 805), rather than those of the originator himself. Next, he takes the sources of law and argues that the Qur'an has only a few definite legal commandments and some of the hadith is unreliable. Mostly, laws are responses to the exigencies of the times and peoples they were meant for and do not have the status of sacred and permanent principles. Thus, he concludes, Muslim societies can change them and adopt progressive legislation.

He then takes up specific aspects of legal theory including the terms relevant for war. Among them are the concepts of *Dārul Islām* and *Dārul Ḥarb* which had been discussed earlier in India and which, he points out, W.W. Hunter had written about in his book on Indian Muslims. Chirāgh ʻAlī says that these terms too are not from the Qur'an nor are they found in unambiguous terms in reliable *aḥādīth*. They were constructions created by legal minds in order to devise rules of conduct for Muslims and non-Muslims for travel, business, daily living, and conduct. Muslims are not bound to conquer the *Dārul Ḥarb* nor to initiate hostilities without cause. India, in his view, is *Dārul Amān* (land of protection) or *Dārul Dhimmah* (land of responsibility) and Indian Muslims are supposed to be loyal to the British government which provides them security.[59] The rest of the first part deals with Turkey and the differential treatment of non-Muslim subjects of the Ottomans which, he says, is being replaced with equality. The second part deals with his pet subjects: rights of women, end of slavery, polygamy, and other modern values.

Missionaries who wrote on Islam, did not agree with the kind of modernist interpretations of Islam we have been discussing above. For example, Thomas Hughes, in his entry on 'Jihad' in his *Dictionary* quotes verses (9: 5 and 29) apparently promoting unrestricted warfare against non-Muslims. In his *Notes on Muhammadanism*, he wrote a chapter on Jihad (xliv) in which he noted that the whole matter 'hinges upon the question whether India is *Dár-ul-Harb*, the land of enmity, or *Dár-ul-Islám*'. And this, he suggests, despite *fatwās* to the contrary, goes against British interests since, in private, Muslims do consider it a *Dārul ḥarb*.[60]

59 Ibid 63.
60 Hughes 1875: 207 – 209.

As mentioned above, one of the claims of these Western critics of Islam was that Islamic law was inflexible and unchangeable. Hughes says in the preface to his first edition (17 August 1875) that Islam 'admits of no progress in morals, law, or commerce'.[61] Edward Sell, the author of *The Faith of Islam*, also argued the same. This, in turn, implied that all the efforts of the modernists to interpret it as being compatible with human rights and peace were misguided. Thus, in order to contradict Chirāgh 'Alī who had asserted that jihad was only defensive, Hughes adduced verses, books of jurists, and traditions, suggesting just the opposite. In the end he concludes patronisingly: 'it is undoubtedly the best position for enlightened Musalmans to adopt, although it brings them into conflict whith all the canonists of preceding ages, and with the views of commentators and theologians of all the various sects'.[62]

Mahdi 'Alī Khān (1837–1907), like Chirāgh 'Alī, was also a supporter of Sir Sayyid in all matters, especially in the establishment of the Aligarh College. Like Sayyid, he too rejected traditionalist interpretations of jihad using both doubt about the authenticity of the hadith and rationalist exegesis.[63] Co-existence with non-Muslims rather than confrontation is the cornerstone of this interpretation.[64] Indeed, he assured the British that Indian Muslims consider it wrong to think of jihad against the British since they had given them freedom of worship and conscience.[65] Instead of confrontation he advised Indian Muslims to be loyal to the British as subjects even in cases where Muslim nations—this is in the context of the Turkish caliph's having the right of obedience from Indian Muslims—had to suffer because of imperial political exigencies.[66]

Shiblī Nu'mānī (1857–1914), who has been mentioned in other contexts several times earlier, followed a similar but more nuanced trend of thought: defense of Islam as a religion of peace and tolerance while, at the same time, taking pride in early Muslim conquests.[67] In his book on the life of the second caliph,

61 Ibid xii.

62 Sell 1880: Appendix B, 336.

63 Ahmad 1967: 69.

64 Zubayri 1934: 162.

65 Ibid 40.

66 Ibid 175.

67 Shiblī Nu'mānī's thought manifests the major antagonistic tendencies of the age: traditionalism and modernism. He was educated informally in Arabic and Persian in the traditional way but when he moved to Aligarh, accepted Sir Sayyid's desire for change. After a stay of sixteen years at Aligarh, he left for Hyderabad and Nadwatul 'Ulama which, he desired, would be an Islamic seminary but with some modernist elements in its curricula. One of his biographers, Sayyid Sulaimān Nadwī (1943), emphasises the first aspect of his thinking while S.M. Ikram, contradicting Nadwī, gives a more balanced view (Ikram 2015).

'Umar ibn al-Khaṭṭāb (584–644), both trends are manifest. Shiblī repeats the narrative of early Arab histories that the sword or the poll tax was offered to the non-Muslims.[68] Verses of the Qur' an, such as *Sūrah al-Anfāl* (Q. 8), were recited in a war against the Romans to inspire soldiers to fight valiantly.[69] He refutes the European scholars who explain the conquests with reference to the decadence of the Iranian and the Roman Empires. Instead, he claims that militant enthusiasm and moral superiority of the Muslims were the real reasons for their-victories.

His most important work on the subject of jihad, however, is in his biography of the Prophet. In volume 1, he explains both 9: 5 and 29. About the first, he says that the Arab tribes had broken all treaties and were given four months to convert to Islam or face death. As for the second verse, he translates '*ṣāghirūn*' as small, saying laconically that the wayward *Ahl al-kitāb* should be fought 'till they give *jizyah* like subordinates'. He uses the Urdu word '*chhōṭē*', which means small, but which has been translated as subordinate here. Neither verse is explained in any detail nor are they applied to any period after that of the Prophet.[70] Like Sir Sayyid and Chirāgh 'Alī he too goes on to explain all wars of the Prophet as defensive pointing out that the large number of *Sariyahs* mentioned in history, and inevitably translated as attacks, were actually reconnaissance parties since they never had more than a dozen people in them.[71] Volume 5 has a chapter entitled 'Jihad'. However, it is not clear whether it was written by Shiblī and added to this volume or originally written by Sayyid Sulaimān Nadwī. The author emphasises forms of struggle (called jihad) against one's own evil desires, against idleness, and against oppression. He quotes the hadith about returning from the small jihad and going towards the greater one with approval. However, he adds that this hadith does not conform to the criteria established for evaluating the authenticity of traditions, but it supports other *aḥādīth* which are reported in *Ṣiḥāḥ Sittah*. For instance, in *Muslim* it is reported that 'the struggler is one who struggles against his self' (*al mujāhid min jāhid nafsahū*). He also quotes the hadith about the Prophet wanting to be killed again and again in God's way, again, with reference to *Muslim*. However, he points out the Prophet did not say 'I want to kill others'.[72] Thus, while jihad is eternal, he concludes, it is

68 Nu'mānī 1898: 101, 123 etc.
69 Ibid 136.
70 Nu'mānī and Nadwī, *Sīrat* Vol. 1, 1918: 340.
71 Ibid 349.
72 Ibid Vol. 5: 224. According to Ikram, only the first volume was written by Shiblī himself. The others were probably written, or significantly added to or altered, by Sayyid Sulaimān Nadwī (Ikram 2015: 426–430).

only to help the oppressed, spread Islam, help the poor, and reform sinners.[73] The ideas expressed in this piece of writing are more in conformity with some of Shiblī's ideas expressed in his other works; hence, it is possible that he was the author of this piece but, since it is in volume 5, which is said to be written entirely by Nadwī, one cannot be sure of the authorship. In his *Maqālāt*, however, Shiblī takes the unusual step of blaming Muslims for having committed acts of aggression against Hindus. He says: 'It is we who invaded their country and destroyed their famous temple Somnath and others in Banaras and Muthra.' The Hindus, on the other hand, have been very forgiving, generous, and amiable towards Muslims.[74] This was a unique admission of the inadmissibility of wars of conquest in the guise of jihad.

According to Mehr Afroz Murad, Shiblī was a modernist but he had a sense of Islamic history and referred to Islamic thinkers, such as the Mutazilites, for justification of his appeal to rationality.[75] The traditionalists supported the theological views of Abū'l Ḥasan al-Ash'arī (874–936) which denied causality, emphasised predestination and lack of human freedom, and taught that divine commandments are unfathomable by the human intellect.[76] These, like the Mutazilites, Shiblī denied, in order 'to show the reasonableness of Islam in the nineteenth-and early twentieth-century humanistic world dominated by natural rationalism'.[77] But Shiblī is often called a staunch Hanafite as he wrote a biography of Abū Ḥanīfah and added the Imam's name Nu'mān to his own. However, his Hanafite views changed overtime. To begin with, he insisted on debating points pertaining to ritual or jurisprudence with the Ahl-i-Ḥadīth. But in the end, he praised Hanafite law since 'he is subconsciously looking for a support for the destined reformulation of the Islamic law in accordance with the needs of the modern age'.[78] And one of these changes was to redefine the position of non-Muslims in Islamic states so that, instead of being second rate citizens, they should be treated as equals. In this matter, as well as others, notably those concerning women, Shiblī suggests that Islamic jurisprudence is influenced by Arab customary law. Indeed, Murād speculates that although he made no statement to this effect, he 'obviously did not regard the Qur'ānic *nuṣūṣ*, at least those which pertained to criminal law, as final and eternal'.[79]

---

73 Nu'mānī and Nadwī, *Sīrat* Vol. 5: 224.
74 Nu'mānī *Maqalāt* Vol. 8: 173.
75 Murad 1976: 19.
76 Nu'mānī n.d in Troll 1982: 94–98.
77 Murad 1976: 22.
78 Ibid 59.
79 Ibid 73.

Be that as it may, one would agree with Murād when she says that he 'was a true forerunner of the breed of Islamic modernists typified by Fazlur Rahman whose *Islam* comes in the direct line of Shibli's religious writings'.[80]

Ameer Ali (1849–1928) was another modernist but, unlike the others we have seen so far, he was brought up more in the English intellectual tradition than the traditional Islamic one.[81] In his memoirs he tells us of his repectable Sayyid family. His father, Sa'ādat 'Alī, died in 1856 and he studied at Hoogly College taking his master's degree in history and political science as well as his first law degree (LLB) in 1868. Apparently, he was inspired to follow Sir Sayyid's example for seeking knowledge in England since he had read an article by him describing his travels in that country.[82] Thus, in 1868, Ameer Ali went to England for higher studies and was called to the bar in 1873. With these qualifications, he easily rose to the height of the legal profession in India culminating in a judgeship of the Bengal High Court in 1890. He was highly anglicised so he not only got married to an English lady but, in 1904, also settled down in England with his wife and two sons where he spent time serving the London Branch of the Muslim League and writing articles on Indian subjects and in defense of Islam.[83]

Ameer Ali wrote two major books: *The Spirit of Islam* (1891) and *A Short History of the Saracens* (1889), along with a number of articles in the press which have been collected by compilers and editors of his works.[84] All this work is originally in English but much of it has been translated in Urdu. Like other modernists, Ameer Ali too described jihad as defensive warfare for the preservation of the faith under threat. In his book *The Spirit of Islam*, he says: 'Islam seized the sword in self-defence, and held it in self-defence, as it will ever do'.[85] Like other modernists he too describes the wars of the Prophet, concluding that they were defensive in essence. As for the conquest of Iran, he claims that the dependencies of the Iranian Empire were engaged in petty feuds with Muslims. The Persians, under the energetic ruler Yezdjard, brought 'an imposing force to bear on the Moslems'. The Caliph 'Umar offered the alternative of Islam which, the author explains, would have meant humanitarian reform since the empire was exploitative. And here he claims that the Muslim conquest of Iran was 'not different from that of the British in India and due to similar causes'.[86]

80 Ibid 120.
81 Forward 1999: 38.
82 Ali, S.A. n.d: 5–20. Evidence of having read Sir Sayyid is in Ḥālī 1901: 178.
83 Ali, S. A. n.d.
84 Wasti 1968 a and b; Aziz 1968.
85 Ali, S.A. 1891: 218.
86 Ibid 217.

These causes, we find from his writings, are the introduction of compassionate, civilised values, and institutions to a society under anti-human laws and usages. In short, Ameer Ali defends some forms of colonialism with reference to the doctrine that they are in the interest of the advance of civilisation.

Ameer Ali's writings are historical and his style of writing is rhetorical so, unlike Sir Sayyid and Chirāgh 'Alī, he does not quote much from the Qur'an and the hadith. However, he does quote from *Surah al-Baqarah*, i.e. 2: 256 (about there being no compulsion in religion) and 2: 190 (which allows fighting aggressors in proportion to their aggression), to support his views. His concept of defensive jihad brings him to the subject of bondage, which as we have seen, was another issue which opened Islam to attacks by Europeans. His defense of Islam rests on two arguments: first, by laying the responsibility for all wars of conquest on Muslim rulers and not Islam itself, and, secondly, by blaming Europe for its wars of aggression, colonisation, cruelty, and exploitation. He also argues that it is only in *bona fide* lawful warfare, *jihād-i-sharī'at,* that slaves may be acquired. This was 'a guarantee for the safety and preservation of the captives'.[87] Muslims, probably because of the influence of other civilisations, wrongly continued with the practice but now they should join to denounce and abolish it. As for concepts like *Dārul Islām* and *Dārul Ḥarb*, they are like the concepts of Christendom and Heathendom.[88] Ameer Ali's history—*A Short History of the Saracens*[89]—like the historical parts of his first book, conforms to his established principle that jihad is defensive and the history of Muslim rulers is not the history of the faith *qua* faith. Moreover, even this history, reprehensible though it is in parts, is actually better in actual conduct towards the minorities, heretics, and the conquered peoples than the history of the rest of the world. His articles also defend Islam against the charges of allowing polygamy,[90] concubinage,[91] making divorce too easy for men,[92] and allowing bad treatment of religious minorities (*dhimmīs*).[93] However, because of our focus on jihad we cannot go into details of his reasoning in these cases. As for his standing as a modernist scholar of Islam, let us confine ourseves to Martin Forward who said that Ameer Ali's use of sources was faulty and, since he wrote in English, he 'provoked little re-

87 Ali, S.A. 1891: 256–266.
88 Ibid 215.
89 Ali, S.A. 1896.
90 Ali 1891: 8.
91 Ibid 8; Ali, S.A. 1927: 454.
92 Ibid 9; Ali, S.A. 1895.
93 Ali, S.A. 1906.

action from Indian Muslims'.[94] Indeed, Forward dismisses him as being 'more of an apologist and even polemicist for Islam to a Western audience than a creative reinterpeter of Islam to other Muslims'.[95]

So far we have been considering people whose ideas—especially their views about supernatural beings and the physical conditions in hell and heavens being metaphors or allegories—were considered as being outside the pale of Islam by orthodox sections of Muslim scholars. However, outside these circles they were considered champions of Muslims in an age of arrogant Western attacks on Islam itself. Now we come to a thinker who is anathemised as a heretic by the *'ulamā* whether Sunni or Shī'a. His name is Mirzā Ghulām Aḥmad (1835–1908), and he is worth attention in this book since he gave a completely new interpretation of the concept of jihad. However, because of his ideas being considered heretical, his ideas on jihad too have not been influential in the mainstream. That is why the exegeses of one of his foremost followers, Mohammad Ali,[96] or those of his successors, have not been analysed in this study. His own views have, however, been summarised here as they need to be addressed to understand the background of the pejorative references to them by the traditional *'ulamā*.

One of Mirzā Ghulām Aḥmad's most straightforward work is his Urdu article on jihad published on 22 May 1900. It was translated into English as it was meant for wider dissemination and reprinted in 1910. He begins with his own status as the promised Messiah which connects with the eschatological doctrine of the Mahdi as the just ruler of the world before it is finally destroyed. His major argument is that the Messiah 'shall not take sword in hand, nor shall he have recourse to any other earthly materials of war.[97] To this he adds the familiar argument of modernists that the Prophet Muḥammad fought only defensive wars. Muslims could have fought against the infidel Arabs in Mecca too but they were ordered to live peacefully till defensive warfare was permitted in Medina. However, even this was allowed for those special circumstances and is not an open and eternal permission for continuing aggressive warfare. Thus, the only jihad which remains is for the 'purification of the soul'.[98] To this must be added, he suggests at other places, effort made by the pen or the tongue to increase virtue and set a good example.

94 Forward 1999: 116.
95 Ibid 131.
96 Ali, M. 1917.
97 Aḥmad 1900: 453.
98 Ibid 461.

According to Yohanan Friedman, the 'reinterpretation of the idea of *Jihād* is one of the main themes of Aḥmadī religious thought'.[99] For this, besides the strategies described above, Mirzā Ghulām Aḥmad also abolished the doctrine of *naskh*. In its place he substitutes circumstantial necessity, i.e. circumstances determine the continued validity or application of a given verse. In his view, though the *Sūrah al-Tawbah* might have been revealed in the end, it does not abrogate the other, more peaceful verses which have preceded it, as some argue. If circumstances are exactly as they were when the *sūrah* was revealed, then it is valid; otherwise not.[100] This is a variant of the familiar hermeneutic device of specification—the verse was for the Arab idolators and none others since circumstances are different—but Mirzā Ghulām Aḥmad added doctrines which gave rise to the rumour that he had been planted by the British specifically to do away with jihad. Yet, as we have seen, Mirzā Ghulām Aḥmad was not the only one who argued that jihad was defensive. It was, indeed, one of the intellectual fallouts of modernity.

Jihad, indeed, was one of the points of contest in this battle for and against modernity. In this context, Francis Robinson's study of politics in the United Provinces from 1860 to 1923 is relevant. He points out how people of Sir Sayyid's views (the 'Old Party') aspired to a place, albeit a subordinate one, in powersharing through protestations of loyalty. But, in time they were challenged and replaced by people who were more active and aggressive (the 'Young Party'). Such changes, to which the next chapter is dedicated, tell us more about the politics of modernisation in Muslim societies. One important effect of this modernisation is that it created a conflicted, split, schizophrenic society: 'one arranged according to the needs of the modern industrial state and the other according to the laws of Islam'.[101] Islam was the only unifying symbol; but which Islam? Perhaps the one major change ushered in by modernity was that medieval, superstition-ridden, shrine oriented, medieval Islam was rejected, or confined to the ordinary people, while the educated elite moved towards the modernist direction we have been focusing upon or moved 'in favour of early Islam in Arabia'.[102] Both versions of Islam rejected central authority and sidelined the traditional *'ulamā* which is the genesis of the contemporary disruption of legitimate authority in modern and post-modern Islam we witness today.

99 Friedman 1989: 172.
100 Ibid 174.
101 Robinson 1974: 355.
102 Hardy 1972: 59.

However, the modernists were not seen by everyone as champions of Islam and forward-looking progressives. They were also regarded as misguided stooges of the West. Martin Forward, in his appraisal of Ameer Ali, says that they represent 'the world-view of an all-conquering, self-absorbed Eurocentric world' and, in the final analysis, they have 'been content to fashion Islam within parameters set by outsiders who are, at bottom, inveterately hostile to it. They have therefore betrayed Islam into the hands of its enemies'.[103]. While this may be true in so far as the basic ideological imperative of the modernists is concerned, they have not used the foundational texts, especially the Qur'an, any differently than the other interpreters such as the traditionalists or the radical Islamists.

Such conflicted approach to modernity, especially towards jihad, was not confined to India, of course. As mentioned in the introductory chapter, and again in chapter 10 (refuting the radicals), it was also a concern of Arab Muslims. In short, there is a perpetual conflict between the desire for refuting Western critics of Islam and to interpret the faith as being in harmony with modern, humanist values. Since, at the same time, there is also the imperative to defend Islam from the Western critique of being aggressive and retrogressive, the modernists are both pro- and anti-colonial. It is the latter aspect of the world view of Indian Muslim intellectuals to which we turn in the next chapter.

103 Forward 1999: 13.

6 Jihad as Anti-Colonial Resistance: Emerging Trends

The last chapter dealt with one aspect of the fractured modernity of South Asia: that of acceptance of certain modern values while resisting others which touched upon core identities. This chapter emphasises the second aspect—resistance—including its more militant expressions. The period which is being covered in this chapter is that between the death of Sayyid Aḥmad Barēlwī in 1831 till the 1930s'. We notice two types of movements of an anti-colonial type in this period: first, clandestine activities punctuated by militant interludes (such as 1857); and second, a nationalist mass movement. As for other religious movements affecting the public sphere during this period, such as the ones covered by Deitrich Reetz, these have been referred to only if they relate to Jihad.[1]

There are four major movements of resistance: the Faraidi movement of Bengal; the anti-British revolt of 1857; the Wahhābī (the British spelling is Wahabi) networks extending from Patna to Chamarkand in the tribal areas of the North West Frontier leading to the 'Wahabi trials' of the 1860s and the 'Silk Letters conspiracy' involving the Darul Ulum at Deoband. All the movements have been described by historians out of whom two prominent ones are Qeyamuddin Ahmad[2]and Ayesha Jalal.[3] The former describes the role of the Wahhābīs in these movements with reference to primary sources and the latter refers to the ideas of their leading actors and provides a chronological outline of events. This study does not repeat this history in detail but its outlines, based entirely on primary sources, have been provided in the notes for those who may want a ready reference to them.

The Faraidi movement of Ḥājjī Sharī'atullāh (1781–1840) and later his son Muḥsinuddīn Aḥmad, generally known as Dūdū Miyā̃ (written as Mian in other sources) (1819–1862), emphasised the essential ritual modes of Muslim worship (the *farā'iḍ* or duties) and sought to enforce a strict, scriptural interpretation of Islam coloured by the ideas of the Indian reformers as well as Muḥammad ibn 'Abd al-Wahhāb (1703–1792).[4] In some matters, Sharī'atullāh was quite radical since, as Barbara Metcalf points out, he defined 'Bengal as *daru'l-harb*, and prohibited absolutely the community prayers recited on Friday and on the

1 Reetz 2006.

2 Ahmad 1994.

3 Jalal 2008.

4 Khan 1965. For a summary see Jones 1994: 19–22. For a history see Faisal 2010. For Wahhābī ideas and role in the world see Commins 2009.

https://doi.org/10.1515/9783110716986-009

'Id festival' but even this 'did not necessitate a declaration of jihad'.[5] The movement was subsequently led by Tītū Mīr (1782–1831). Although Tītū Mīr's actions have sometimes been called jihad, the final British report upon them does not agree with this opinion, though his followers are called 'fanatics'.[6] In short, not all British officers were inclined to call every uprising by Muslims, even by those whom they recognised as being zealous, as a jihad. However, Qeyamuddin Ahmad, whose account of this movement is still unsurpassed, says that 'the *Farā' iḍīs* prepared the ground for the wide, positive response to the Wahhābīs' activities in many parts of Bengal'.[7]

The revolt of 1857, called mutiny by the British and war of independence by South Asians, has been described by many authors. However, this chapter focuses on the role of the idea of jihad in it. Like the events in Bengal, this too was not a jihad in the traditional sense of the term though, at least nominally, Bahādur Shāh Ẓafar (1837–1862), the Mughal king, could function as a Muslim *amīr* (ruler). In any case, it was not even a purely Muslim-led militant movement, though the *'ulamā* of the areas now in U.P. did play a role in it.[8] It is also said that even the Wahhābīs, who ran India-wide underground resistance movements against the British, did not play a visible role in it. This is refuted by Qeyamuddin Ahmad who points out that, though individuals did join the rebellion at places, they mostly kept aloof because of their view that, India being a *Dārul Ḥarb*, they should resist the British by first emigrating to a *Dārul Islām* and then carrying out jihad from there. So, by 'keeping low inside British India they survived the storm of 1857, and were able to render valuable help to the Wahabi state on the North-Western Frontier during the British onslaughts in 1858, 1863 and subsequently'.[9] In the heartland of the resistance, Hindustan proper, the religious dimension was expressed through the publication of a *fatwā* in *Ẓafar al-akhbār* and *Ṣādiq al-akhbār* of 1857. This document has now been reprinted by the Pakistani scholar Ikram Chughtai.[10] It begins with a question to the *'ulamā* whether jihad has become a duty for all Muslims now that the British

5 Metcalf 1982: 69.

6 The whole series of incidents with all letters and reports is part of the Board's Collections of 1832–33 (Board 1833). Titu Mir's real name was Mir Nithar 'Ali Khan (or Alie as the papers spell it). His first name is spelled as Tetoo and Tito also. His followers took to violence against the local landlords but the movement was curbed by the military. Senior officers ordered a report which was submitted on 8 March 1830 suggesting that the 'disturbance' was of a local kind and not a jihad.

7 Ahmad 1994: 94.

8 Ansari and Qureshi 2008.

9 Ahmad 1994: 171.

10 Chughtai 2007: 532–534.

were about to subdue Delhi. To this the *'ulamā* replied that it is a duty for all (*farḍul 'ayn*) for the people of Delhi who are in imminent danger of attack. As for the areas around Delhi, it is a duty for some (*farḍul kifāyah*) but will become a duty for all if they are attacked.[11] Apparently, the *fatwā* is cautious and does not declare an all-out massacre of all the British which, where it did occur, occurred despite the *fatwā*, not because of it. There are many legends about the *fatwā*, one being that Muftī Ṣadr Uddīn Āzurdah, a well-known intellectual and a friend of the famous Urdu poet Mirzā Ghālib (1797–1869), put his signature but added '*bil jabr*' (by force) to it which led to his being spared the death punishment later.[12] This, however, is not correct since there is no such phrase in front of his signature.[13]

Many of the leading men of India, such as Sir Sayyid, clearly said even during the disturbances that this was not a jihad. In Bijnour, where he was posted as a sub-judge, a certain Munīr Khān asked him 'about the possibility of waging a holy war against the British' to which he replied that 'there was nothing in Islam that could justify such a measure'.[14] Besides such kind of opinions, another reason why the *fatwā* was mostly ineffectual may have been that the allies of the Muslims in this struggle were Hindus. This precluded the invocation of the religious themes which might have alienated them. However, letters exhorting the Punjabis to join the fighters in Delhi appeal to both the concept of martyrdom for Muslims and of a similar concept for Hindus.[15] Letters also reveal that it was called a 'war for religion' by the Muslim clergy and that some of them joined the struggle going from Meerut to Delhi with about '6,000 men to make religious war'.[16] Mawlānā Faḍl-i-Haqq Khairābādī (1797–1861), who was interned for life in the Andaman penal colony upon being convicted for rebellion, also called it a jihad in his memoir written during his incarceration. He begins by saying that the British, whom he calls Christians throughout, had schemed to replace all religions of India by Christianity and it was because of this that:

11 Chughtai 533.

12 Ansari and Qureshi 2008: 160.

13 Chughtai 2007: 532.

14 Ḥālī 1901: 74. Sir Sayyid's detailed account is in his account of the events in Bijnour, the place of his posting. In Khān 1859.

15 Mutiny 1911: 144.

16 Ibid 163.

> there arose a party of strong and brave Muslims for *jihad* and fighting after having asked for a *fatwa* from the pious *'ulama* and their *('ulama's)* declaration of *jihad* had become obligatory in accordance with the *fatwas* of the authoritative *imams.*[17]

The Mawlānā does acknowledge the role of Hindus in the initial stages but for the most part, it was a Muslim undertaking from his point of view. Indeed, he blames the 'Hindus of the West', by which he means Sikhs, for the British conquest of Delhi.[18] Like the Mawlānā, the British in their addresses to the troops also appealed to religion as this was the salient marker of difference in the absence of the modern idea of nationalism. For instance, Sir John Lawrence (1811–1879) addressed the troops of the Bengal Army on 01 June 1857, saying that '[t]he Hindoo temple and the Mahomedan mosque have both been respected by the English Government'.[19]

While the uprising was not an all-India movement, not being much in evidence in the Muslim majority areas now in Pakistan, it was, however, quite widespread in the areas of Awadh, Rohilkhand, and other centres of Muslim religious scholarship in North India. Even members of the Farangī Maḥallī family, who were generally devoted to scholarship, teaching, and mysticism, took some part or were associated in these violent movements. Francis Robinson, in his influential study of this family, points out that 'Abd al-Razzāq 'had played a leading role in the Hanumangarhi jihad to defend Babri Masjid in 1855; he presented his turban to be used as a banner by the Indian forces fighting the British at Lucknow in 1875–8'.[20] Among those who are given special attention in the writings on the events of 1857, one of the most prominent persons is Aḥmadullāh Shāh (1820–1857). He is an enigmatic figure, rumoured to belong to a princely family, and his reputation for being a good fighter is testified by Mawlānā Khairābādī from his jail. The Mawlana says: 'he attacked the Christians and their forces and put them to rout in his first charge' but he was deceived and 'martyred'.[21]

However, despite the use of the idiom of jihad by some of the actors in the events of 1857, these acts of fighting against the British were not treated as an Islamic *bellum justum* by most Indian Muslims who, in any case, had neither de-

---

17 Khairābādī 1860s: 31. The original account in Arabic has no title. It was, however, called *Fitnah al-hindiyyah, Risālāh-i-Ghadariyyah*, etc., in later works. The Arabic version was reproduced by Mawlānā 'Abdul Shāhid Khān Shīrwānī under the title of *Bāghī Hindustān.* Its English translation has been used here. Also see Jamal Malik (2006) for Khairābādī's writings in exile.

18 Ibid 32.

19 Lawrence in *Mutiny* 01 June 1857. Cited from Chughtai 2007: 94.

20 Robinson 2002: 149.

21 Khairābādī 1860s: 48.

veloped a united Muslim identity nor a nationalist Indian one.[22] More importantly, the events of 1857 showed a certain fracturing of religious authority in the sense that while there was a *fatwā* about jihad, and the Mughal emperor was the nominal ruler (*imām*), even so the orders for jihad were not considered binding on all Muslims. Thus, the Muslims of the areas now comprising Pakistan, Bangladesh, and the Muslim ruled states of Hyderabad, Bhopal, Rampur, and several other states remained indifferent to the project of jihad. The most that can be said was that some of the fighters of 1857, such as Ḥājjī Imdādullāh (1814–1896), remained an inspiration for Indian *'ulamā* in his retirement in Arabia.[23] More significantly, Mawlānā Rashīd Aḥmad Gangohī created the seminary at Deoband which featured prominently in keeping alive the resistance against the British in the name of jihad.[24] One consequence of 1857, and clandestine resistance movements led by Muslims, was that the British initially suppressed and then stressed the need to watch them closely and appease them.[25] In Francis Robinson's words:

> The fact was that the British feared the Muslims. They were thought to be the greatest threat not only to British rule in India but to the British Empire. To deal with them, government adopted special measures and made special concessions.[26]

This fear was of revolt or armed resistance which could be articulated in the vocabulary of jihad and then be more difficult to suppress than other mundane forms of anti-colonial movements.

While 1857 was an open revolt notwithstanding its Islamic status, there were other surreptitious movements involving the followers of Sayyid Aḥmad Barēlwī which went on for years culminating in the 'Wahabi trials' of 1864 and 1865 at Amballa and Patna, followed up by further trials in 1870 and 1871 at Rajmahal, Malda, and again at Patna. Documents containing the views of the British intelligence agencies and statements of witnesses were presented at the trials. The main charge was that the Wahhābīs had established a centre of armed resistance against the government in Sittana and they recruited fighters for jihad in India.[27]

---

22 Rahman 2008.

23 Smith 1981: 210–211.

24 Ansari and Qureshi 2008: 171–172.

25 Robinson 1974: 100–103.

26 Ibid 131–132.

27 Briefly, Sittana is the village of Sayyid Akbar Shāh, formerly treasurer and counsellor of Sayyid Aḥmad Barēlwī. After the defeat of 1831 at Balakot, some of Barēlwī's followers came to this village to seek refuge here. Two *mawlawīs* from India, Wilāyat 'Alī and 'Ināyat 'Alī, started a movement involving sending men and material from India to this outpost of the jihadis (for a

The views of the other side, such as those of Ja'far Thānesārī, who was arrested and exiled for abetting the resistance, are also available in their own words.[28] While it may be true that the British had exaggerated the threat from people they called 'religious fanatics' and 'Wahabis',[29] it may be noted that 'twenty-two forts, in the areas of Pakhli, Dhamtaur, Orish, Tanawal and Hazara surrendered and large quantities of arms and other materials were captured' by the Wahhābīs.[30] Thus, the British worries about the area called Yaghistan (FATA), which is still considered a hotbed of Islamic resistance and 'Wahabism', might not have been misplaced.

The trials initiated a debate about the relevance of jihad in British India. British district officers continually came up with reports of the continuing distribution of seditious literature. For instance, in 1868, Nobokishto Ghose, an assistant in the police department, reported that in the village of Kaliachak in the Malda district contributions were made for a '"jehad" or religious war against the English'.[31] Moreover, in Malda, pamphlets described as 'seditious' and the '*Tafsīr-i-Murādiyah*, a commentary on the *Ām Sipārah*' (the thirtieth and last part of the Qur'an) as well as *fatāwā* declaring the legitimacy of jihad were being circulated.[32] The exegesis mentioned above by Murādullāh Anṣārī is meant to be comprehensible by ordinary people and the author points out that it is in Hindi (by which he means the common language of the inhabitants of north Indian cities which may be called Hindi-Urdu) rather than Persian which, by this period, only the learned could understand. The writing of the exegesis finished in 1185/1771 and it was published in 1285/1868. The verses covered in it—from *al-Nabā'* (Q. 78) till *al-Nās* (Q. 114)—are Meccan (though this is disputed by some) which were revealed before the orders for jihad. However, Anṣārī brings in jihad in some of his explanations. For instance, while explaining *al-Ghāshiah* (Q. 88)—which, after describing the rewards and punishments of those who accept or reject Islam, tells the Prophet that his duty is to keep preaching without bothering

---

description of both, see Ahmad 1994: 100–101). The whole operation was called business (*beō-pār*) in code (other code words are given in Ahmad 1994: Appendix III). Personal remarks in the letters suggest that both recruits and recruiters were fully convinced their work was purely religious (Wahabi Trials 1860s).

28 The point of view of the 'Wahhābīs' is presented in the documents written by the actors themselves. For instance, Muḥammad Ja'far Thānesārī, one of the leaders of the operation, writes in his biography *Kālā Pānī* (1879; also see Ahmad 1994: 201–204), that he was full of religious zeal at the age of twenty-five when he was arrested in connection with abetting Jihad

29 Stephens 2013.

30 Ahmad 1994: 103.

31 Ibid 235.

32 Ibid 237.

about the response of the people... (88: 21)—Anṣārī says that this verse has been abrogated (*mansūkh*) by the verses on jihad and *qitāl*. The order now is to fight the unbelievers. However, while elaborating upon the identity of these unbelievers he adds 'those who mislead people and out of mischief do not allow the Truth to be disseminated then beat them, kill them, since this will benefit hundreds of thousands' (*logõ kō gumrāh karẽ kharābī mẽ dālẽ sharārat par kamar bāndhē ḥaqq kō jārī hōnē na dē tō uskō mārō qatl karō jis mẽ lākhõ kā bhalā hō*).[33] Similarly, when commenting upon *al-Kāfirūn* (Q. 109), which suggests that unbelievers as well as believers are to be left to their respective beliefs, he says that this verse too has been abrogated by verses about jihad. The specific order (109: 6): 'to you your religion and to us ours' (*lakum dīnukum waliyā dīn*) is now abolished (*mawqūf hu'ā*) and if the unbelievers do not believe then 'beat them kill them' (*un kō mārō qatl karō*).[34] A fiery preacher might have used such interpretations of Quranic verses, and that too in comprehensible language, for recruitment and indoctrination.

In short, for the British, ideas of jihad and the debate about them were important subjects. Thus, W.W. Hunter's book mentioned in the last chapter touched a nerve among British readers in India. The main question the author set out to determine was whether the Indian Muslims were ideologically bound to initiate a religious war against the British. He reproduced three religious edicts about the question whether India was a *Dārul Ḥarb* or *Dārul Islām*. The one by the *'ulamā* of Mecca says that 'as long as even some of the peculiar observances of Islam prevail in it, it is *dar-ul islam*'.[35] This was also the opinion of the Calcutta Muhammadan society.[36] Here, Karāmat 'Alī of Jaunpur (1786–1873) had delivered a lecture on the invitation of Nawāb 'Abdul Laṭīf (1828–1893) on 23 November 1870 declaring that India was *Dārul Islām* on the authority of the *Fatāwā-e-Alamgīrī*, the *Hidāyah*, and another treatise on Islamic jurisprudence called the *Durr al-Mukhtār*.[37] However, opinion remained divided so 'few Muslims were convinced by Maulavi Karamat 'Ali's lecture who did not already wish to be convinced'.[38]

In short, even those of the *'ulamā* of north India who declared India to be a *Dārul Ḥarb* also declared that jihad was not justified as the Muslims were pro-

---

33 *Murādiyah* 1875: 387.
34 *Murādiyah* 1875: 205–206.
35 Hunter 1871 Appendix 1: 163.
36 Ibid Appendix 3: 165.
37 Jaffar 1992: 95.
38 Hardy 1972: 111.

tected by the Christian rulers.[39] The Shī'as too did not support jihad because the *Imām* had yet to appear. Thus, as Hunter happily concluded: 'the duty of waging war has thus disappeared. The present generation of Musalmans, are bound, according to their own texts, to accept the *status quo*'. In short, the majority of Muslims, if treated justly and educated by the government, would be loyal.[40] However, the more alarming implication was that the minority of those whom the British called 'Wahabis' and the Frontier tribesmen, did, however, consider jihad against the British justified. The movements launched by this minority have several similarities to the militant movements affecting Pakistan and parts of India at present. Most importantly, both kinds of movements are surreptitious; both have no central recognised legitimate authority (*imām*); both act upon decentralised and anarchic legitimisations of jihad without there being a state-controlled body of *'ulamā* authorising the same. In short, this phenomenon of initiating militant movements represents a certain fragmentation of Islamic authority which is a feature of both progressive and Islamist models of Islam nowadays.

Probably the most famous anti-colonial clandestine movement was the 'Silk Letters conspiracy'.[41] Behind it was the idea that foreign powers could be used to defeat or weaken the British in India. Whereas in India, it was probably an indigenously conceived strategy to which we will come later, the idea was also present in the rest of the colonised parts of the Muslim world. Apparently Sayyid Jamāl al-Dīn al-Afghānī (1838/9 – 1897), known as a pan-Islamist, is credited with having expressed such ideas. In this context, he wrote a letter in Persian to the Sultan of Turkey. If the letter was written in 1871, then 'Abdul 'Azīz was the Sultan since his period of rule is 1830 – 1876. In this letter, Afghānī outlines the plan that he will go to India and Afghanistan in order to raise the Muslims of both countries against Russian colonialism. In his view, the Afghans 'do not admit hesitation in war, especially religious war, to a religious struggle and a national en-

39 Jaffar 1992: 94.
40 Hunter 1871: 103.
41 In a note of 14 September 1916, the Criminal Investigation Department (CID) described what came to be called the 'silk letters conspiracy' in British Indian history. The note (Silk 1916 a; called 'First Note') recounted the story of how letters written in Urdu on yellow silk were presented to the commissioner of Multan by a certain Khān Bahādur Rūp Nawāz on 14 May 1915. See the notes (Silk 1916 a, b & c) and other sources under 'Silk' in the bibliography (Silk 1917 a & b). The views of the immediate actors, Mawlānā Maḥmud al-Ḥasan (Mian 1999; Madani 1921), Ḥusain Aḥmad Madanī (1921), 'Ubaydullāh Sindhī (1933), Ẓafar Ḥasan Aibak (n.d), 'Abdullāh Laghārī (1980), Rājā Mahendrā Pratāp (1947), etc., are also available and they confirm the British account. However, the Indian accounts vary according to the time they were written and in details concerning internal politics.

deavour' (*muhārabeh-yī dīniyyeh va mujāhadeh-yī milliyeh*).[42] He declares that he intended to proceed to Baluchistan and then to Central Asia for the same purpose. After the Russians are involved in a debilitating war the British will 'inevitably and forcibly devote their whole efforts to the fight, and will be mired up to their necks and give up the thought of domination'.[43] This part of the letter is very confused but it foretells how this kind of delusional thinking came to be discussed in anti-colonial circles which, in case they were Muslim, was often couched in the vocabulary of jihad.

As 'Ubaydullāh Sindhī (1872–1944), as well as Mawlānā Maḥmūd al-Ḥasan (1851–1920), were both connected with the Islamic seminary at Deoband, called the *Dārul 'Ulūm*, the role of this seminary needs to be understood. It was set up by Mawlānā Rashīd Aḥmad Gangohī (1828–1905) and Mawlānā Qāsim Nānawtwī (1833–1879) in 1867.[44] According to the Deoband legend, cited by Ayesha Jalal,[45] both had fought against the British in 1857 and definitely inspired some of their students to keep alive the idea of armed resistance to the colonial rulers. Let us look at the legend itself as it is recorded in detail by Manāẓir Aḥsan Gīlānī, the biographer of the Mawlānā.

Gīlānī begins with Mawlānā Qāsim's participation in an assembly of the *'ulamā* in Thana Bhawan soon after the rebel soldiers had reached Delhi. Here, initially, all the *'ulamā* had opposed jihad except Mawlānā Qāsim. The main objection, besides disparity of resources between the British and themselves, was that there was no *imām*. Mawlānā Qāsim, therefore, proposed the name of Ḥājī Imdādullāh who was then appointed *amīr al-mu'minīn* and led the subsequent attack on a fortress occupied by the Company's soldiers.[46] Mawlānā Qāsim, however, went underground and was not arrested. His biographer narrates many a legend, most of them appealing to the supernatural, about the way the police was unable to apprehend him even when he was with them.[47] Ḥājjī Imdādullāh migrated to Arabia.

The main objection to this account is that it was published much after the events. Gīlānī is aware of this fact but he attributes it to the fear of the colonial government. Those who voice the objection think otherwise. For instance, Barbara Metcalf points out that this account 'appears only in secondary sources

42 Translated into English by Keddie 1972: 135–136.
43 Ibid 137.
44 Metcalf 1982.
45 Jalal 2008: 122–123.
46 Gīlānī 1953, Vol. 2: 125 for the selection of the amīr. For the attack see Ibid, 138–169.
47 Ibid 172–194.

written after about 1920'[48]—an opinion which Francis Robinson agrees with.[49] However, Ayesha Jalal accepts the narrative of Deoband though she points out that Nānawtwī only joined the jihad when 'it took the form of a popular struggle' which fizzled out.[50] Gīlānī, narrating these events in the next century, asserts that they were not mentioned openly because of fear of British reprisal. It may be that he is right because the fear of 1857 did linger on till much later. However, even if we agree with those who think that this account is a later fabrication, it would appear that the warrior image was promoted by the Deoband elders themselves. This supports the view that these elders, in theory if not in practice, supported jihad against the British. The following conversation of Gīlānī with Mawlānā Maḥmūd al-Ḥasan, the rector of Deoband, supports this assumption. The Mawlānā said to him that 'the Madrasa was established before my own eyes. As far as I know, it was decided in the aftermath of the failure of 1857 revolt to establish an institution which would train the sort of people who could remedy [the effects of] the defeat of 1857'. He added that he had chosen the path of political activism though his colleagues were welcome to lead the academic life.[51] While the Mawlānā does not clarify what he meant by 'remedy' nor what 'political activism' entailed, it is evident that he does support in theory—as he eventually did in practice—anti-colonial resistance. His major role as an activist is in the Silk Letters Conspiracy case along with 'Ubaydullāh Sindhī and this was intended to be armed resistance not a peaceful political movement.

According to the police and his Pakistani admirers, the main person behind the whole plot was 'Ubaydullāh Sindhī. He inspired the exodus of students from Lahore in order to train them in the tribal areas for anti-colonial activities. One of these students, Ẓafar Ḥasan Aibak of Government College Lahore, later wrote a biography giving a detailed account of this whole episode and acknowledging Sindhī as his leader.[52] Sindhī also got in touch with the other actors in the plot: the Deoband clerics, the frontier *mullās*, the foreigners, especially the Turks and the Germans, and the leaders of the Indian *mujāhidīn* in the Frontier. He was also in touch with Abū'l Kalām Āzād of Calcutta and Mohamed Ali of the *Comrade* fame of Rampur. Although Sindhī did get mellowed down later when he participated in the anti-colonial Indian freedom movements under M.K. Gandhi (1869–1948), at the time of his Afghan adventure his language was similar to Osama bin Laden's. In 1919, for instance, he sent a letter to India saying: 'kill the

48 Metcalf 1982: 82.
49 Robinson 2002: 197.
50 Jalal 2008: 122–123.
51 Zaman 2009: 238.
52 Aibak n.d.

English in every possible way, don't help them with men and money, and continue to destroy rails and telegraph wires'.[53]

The presence of Rājā Mahendra Pratāp (1886–1979) does suggest that, at some level at least, Hindus and Sikhs were partners of Muslims in this scheme, but there were suspicions on both sides. According to Mawlānā 'Abdullāh Laghārī, Mahendra was in reality a spy for the Hindus (Pandit Madan Mohan Mālaviya (1861–1946)—the Hindu political leader and educationist whom the Muslims considered prejudiced against them is mentioned by name) and that it was he who informed the British about the impending attack on India from Afghanistan.[54] Ẓafar Ḥasan Aibak felt that the Rājā 'wished to set up a Hindu government in India when it gained independence'.[55] The Rājā, on his part, was worried that Muslims would start ruling India and discriminate against Hindus.[56] If this is true, it was a perfectly legitimate concern since the spirit of the whole movement was to ensure Muslim domination over India. However, such was the naivety of the schemers that they did not think that if Germany, Turkey, and Afghanistan really drove the British out of India, they would rule it themselves and not hand over the government to the schemers. It is this incredible naivety which made a British officer remark about the whole venture that it was 'crazy in the extreme'.[57] Eventually the venture failed and 'Ubaydullāh left Afghanistan.

The venture, while it lasted, was unique in that it used both the idioms of jihad and that of Indian nationalism. This is suggested by the very presence of Rājā Mahendra Pratāp and the whole idea of seeking German help to drive out the British. Moreover, the conspirators wanted to seek the help of English-educated intellectuals—the Aligarh lobby—despite the fact that the latter regarded the '*ulamā* as reactionary. However, notwithstanding their views on lifestyle (the veil, beard, etc.), the '*ulamā* too used the language of anti-imperialism as did the secular intellectuals. Mawlānā Ḥusain Aḥmad Madanī, for instance, condemns European imperialism in the most scathing terms and, like Maḥmud al-Ḥasan, participated in anti-British nationalist movements.[58]But closer inspection yields that the Mawlānā thought in terms of religious categorisation, not nationalistic. His reference to the Christian world (*Masīḥī dunyā*) versus the Islamic world is very similar to the use of such terms of international categorisation

53 For the image see Aibak n.d: page facing 144; for the English translation see Kaye 1919: 128.

54 Laghari 1980: 82.

55 Aibak n.d: 101.

56 The Rājā expresses his doubts about his colleagues' real intentions at places in his biography (Pratap 1947).

57 Kelly 2013.

58 Madanī 1953: 114–491–495. For Madani's views and role in the jihad see Metcalf 2009 a.

used by Islamists nowadays (Crusaders versus Muslims). His views on jihad are rather complicated. He believes India is a *Dārul Ḥarb*. However, the Friday congregational prayers are to be peformed.[59] More importantly, he concedes that in India, jihad is a *farḍul 'ayn*, so every Muslim need not fight the British. But, along with this, he also thinks that it is necessary to fight against any power which subdues Muslims.[60] Perhaps, he thought of the Tribal Area of the Indian-Afghan border as outside British territory. Or, maybe when he wrote the letters from which the above views have been taken, he restricted himself to the political struggle in which he was engaged.

His mentor, Mawlānā Maḥmūd al-Ḥasan has left behind a translation of the Qur'an (dated 1336/1917) which, he claims, is as faithful to the translation of Shāh 'Abdul Qādir as possible. A few obsolete words have, however, been substituted by better known ones and some sentences have been explained. This translation is also known for having the exegesis of Mawlānā Shabbīr Aḥmad 'Uthmānī (1887–1949), a leading Deobandi *'ālim* who was also part of the Pakistan movement, on the margins of its pages (completed 1350/1931). The exegesis has, however, been published on full pages and is far more readable than before. If it is taken as a sample of traditional Deobandi thought, it does not legitimise the jihadi outlook of 'Ubaydullāh Sindhī nor any of the militant Islamic fighters who have studied in the Deobandi madrasahs of Pakistan.

'Uthmānī's exegesis of 2: 191 and 193 explains fighting as a response to *fitnah* which is defined as cruelty and oppression, especially turning people away from the true faith.[61] However, while explaining Q. 9 he equates *fitnah* with polytheism and unbelief which had to be purged from Arabia. He refers to the *asbābul nuzūl* of 9: 5 as the ongoing war against the polytheists of Mecca but does not say whether it is valid nowadays or not. As for 9: 29, he says it refers to the People of the Book in Arabia who could have been impediments in the spread of Islam. After removing the polytheists from Arabia, he says, it was necessary to break the power of Christians and Jews though they were allowed to live as subject people.[62] As for the possibility of living in peace with those unbelievers who had not harmed Muslims, as in *al-Mumtaḥina* (60: 8), he fully agrees with it and calls it a high ethical principle of Islam.[63] While the question of militancy remains obscure, resistance through other means was very much part of the Deobandi worldview. This was evident in the political movements described below.

59 Madanī 2005: 167.
60 Ibid 224.
61 'Uthmānī, *Tafsīr:* 38.
62 Ibid, for 9: 5, see 248–249; for Q.9: 29, see 254.
63 Ibid 729.

The foremost of them was the rise of Indian nationalism between the world wars. During the period of the Khilafat Movement—a joint effort of Indian Muslims and Hindus—to resist colonial authority by supporting the Turkish caliphate, the Muslims used the idiom of religion for political mobilisation though without excluding Hindus.[64] This was a period which saw the entry of the Muslim *'ulamā* in politics. However, 'much more "fatwa-power" was expended in trying to get the better of rival schools than in tackling the implications of British rule for the faithful'. The famous *'ulamā* of Lucknow, the Farangī Maḥallīs, were an example of this fatwa-politics. As Robinson tells us, 'For every fatwa Abdul Bari produced in favour of the Khilafat movement, non-co-operation and Hindu-Muslim unity, they [the Bahr-al 'ulūm Party led by Abdul Majid] fired off one in opposition'.[65] Thus, the *'ulamā* could never take the lead in the agitational politics of the twenties though their *fatwās* of emigration or jihad provided the ammunition for the tactics of leaders like the Ali brothers (Mohamed and Shaukat Ali) and Āzād. The Balkan crisis caused by the efforts of European powers and the former colonies of Turkey in Europe to seek independence from Istanbul was covered by newspapers causing public opinion to shift in favour of Turkey which was seen as a bastion of Islam resisting the onslaught of Christian Europe.[66]

Among other things, Indian clerics issued *fatwās* that India was *Dārul Ḥarb* and not *Dārul Islām*. The debate about India's status, then and now, is summed up by Shāhjahānpūrī.[67] Mawlānā Rashīd Aḥmad Gangohī, despite the general impression of Deobandis being anti-colonial, said that he had done no conclusive research on the question whether India was a *Dārul ḥarb* or *Dārul Islām*. This *fatwā* is dated 1301/1883–4.[68] Shāhjahānpūrī, however, attributes another *fatwā* to him which is undated but was probably written around 1857. In this, Gangohī calls India a *Dārul Ḥarb*. However, according to another writer, he called it *Dārul Amān*.[69] Whether the other two *fatāwā*—since except for the 1883–4 one, none is signed by the author—are authentic, cannot be determined. It is also pos-

64 Qureshi 1999.

65 Robinson 1974: 269 and 271.

66 Qureshi 2014: 29–31. Indian Muslims considered the Turkish Sultan as the caliph of all Muslims even earlier than the 1920s when the Khilafat movement was launched. Thus, the Ottoman Sultan's name was read out in the sermon (*khuṭbah*) of Friday during the reign of the Mughal emperor Shāh 'Ālam II (r. 1759–1806) (Qureshi 2014: 28). T.P. Hughes, however, believes that the Sultan's name was not mentioned 'until very recently, in any of the mosques of India' and that only Queen Victoria deserves that honour (Hughes 1875: 154).

67 For conflicting *fatwās*, see Shāhjahānpūrī 2008; also see Qureshi 1999: 178–179.

68 Gangohī *Rashīdiyyah* 1967: 182.

69 Shāhjahānpurī 2008: 38–42.

sible, as Shāhjahānpūrī suggests, that Gangohī was being prudent. However, the signed *fatwā* could be taken as not *opposing* British rule even if it was not clearly supportive of it.

There were, however, several edicts in support of British rule, some dating from 1909, though some were against it too.[70] There is, for instance, a *fatwā* in Persian by Mawlānā 'Abdul Ḥayy of Farangī Maḥall (1264–1304/1848–1886) which defines a *Dārul Ḥarb* as follows:

> [it] is a country of unbelievers (*wilāyet-ē-kuffār bashad*) and in it even one of the orders of the *Sharī'ah* is not imposed (*dar ā ḥukmī az aeḥkāmē-Islām jārī nashawand*). And the unbelievers forbid the imposition of the orders of Islam (*aeḥkām-ē-sharā' mānē' shawand*) but impose the orders of unbelief openly and do not allow anyone to stay in peace unless permitted [by them]'.[71]

But this was not the condition of British India since in another *fatwā*, this time in Urdu, the Mawlānā says that taking interest from non-Muslims in a *Dārul Ḥarb* is permissible, but specifically adds that 'India which is captured by the Christians is not a *Dār al Ḥarb*' so it is not allowed in India.[72] This edict, though not explicitly supporting British rule, does rule out jihad. To take an example of the latter kind of *fatwā* one may refer to Khwājā Ḥasan Niẓāmī (1878–1957), an intellectual and spiritual personality of this period, who proclaimed India to be a *Dārul Ḥarb*.[73] Perhaps the most anti-British intellectual of the period, who also had wide appeal as well as religious standing, was Abū'l Kalām Āzād, about whom there is more to come later. He is considered the 'principal theoretician of the Khilafat movement' and the 1920 '*Hijrat kā Fatwā*' that Muslims should migrate to Afghanistan as India was *Dārul Ḥarb* under the British was written by him.[74] Āzād 'exhorted the Indian Muslims to undertake *hijrat* as a commendable and mandatory step' but even he did not advise everybody to migrate.[75] There were other such *fatwās* too though 'Abdul Bārī of Farangī Maḥall (1878–1926), who had said that migration was not necessary, was misinterpreted by the Urdu press which declared that he had supported it.[76] The result of this was a huge wave of migration of Indian Muslims towards Afghanistan. One estimate

70 Qureshi 1999: 177–179.
71 Ḥayy *Fatāwā* Vol. 1, 1892: 86.
72 Ibid 223.
73 Qureshi 1999: 63.
74 In *Ahl-e-Ḥadīth*, Amritsar, 30 July 1920. Given in English translation in Qureshi 1999: 188–189. Also see Ahmad 1967: 136.
75 Qureshi 1999: 189.
76 Ibid 184–186.

is that about 40, 000 people went to Afghanistan between March and April, 1920.[77]Kabul's population was only 60, 000 and this influx of so many people strained the resources of that poor landlocked country.[78] According to 'Abdullāh Laghārī, who was an eyewitness of this event, food items became so dear that there was nearly a famine in Kabul. Eventually King Amānullāh was forced to order the army to throw the refugees out or induce them to leave for some far off location.[79]

Āzād even instigated the Muslims of India to declare a jihad against those European powers which were trying to dismember Turkey. However, this was not a movement which inspired all Indian Muslims, or even most of them. Indeed, most of the '*ulamā* and the heads of the tombs of mystics (*mashā'ikhs*), the latter even more influential than the former, continued to support the British, especially in the Punjab, since they were bound to them in nets of patronage.[80] The jihad card with its attendant vocabulary was one factor among many to bring pressure upon the British but it lacked the widespread appeal which the idea of nationalism—composite Indian (Congress) or Muslim (Muslim League) —had on the masses. Religion was at best an influence; not the sole determiner of behaviour in India. And sometimes it was not a 'card' but merely a knee-jerk reaction such as 'Abdul Bārī's angry declaration of jihad against Hindus upon hearing that they had killed Muslims in the Shahabad district of Bihar in October 1917. These being the days of Hindu-Muslim unity, the Mawlānā's sudden fit of temper was not welcomed by the educated Muslims since it could alienate the Hindus.[81] However, the Farangī Maḥall *fatwā*, again inspired by 'Abdul Bārī, about jihad being a duty of all Muslims if the holy places of Islam in Arabia were occupied by infidels, was a more serious matter. However, even this was blunted as it was opposed by Aḥmad Raḍā Khān of Bareilly (1856–1921), 'Abdul Mājid, and 'Abdul Ḥāmid of Farangī Maḥall and Ḥāfiẓ Aḥmad (1862–1928), son of Mawlānā Qāsim Nānawtawī, of Deoband among other divines.[82] Aḥmad Raḍā Khān, being the pioneer of the *Ahl-i-Sunnat-wa'l-Jamā'at* or Barelvi movement, is important because most Muslims of north India and Pakistan belong to this sub-sect of Sunnis. In his several edicts in response to questions about migration to Afghanistan, supporting the Ottomans and boycotting the British in India, he gives the following responses. In a *fatwā* of 1338/1919, he for-

77 Ibid 230–231.
78 Ibid 231.
79 Laghari 1980: 200.
80 Robinson 2002: 191.
81 Robinson 1974: 284.
82 Ibid 293.

bids migration on the grounds that migration is necessary only from a *Dārul Ḥarb*. As for several questions about supporting the Ottomans he says it is necessary in principle to support other Muslims but only as far as one is capable (*baqadr-i-istiṭā'at*).[83] Then, in several edicts he offers such vitriolic criticism of Āzād and the whole Khilafat movement on the ground that it entails uniting with Hindus; inviting them to lecture in mosques; placing the Qur'an at par with Hindu sacred books that it is clear that he does not support any contemporary political movement in favour of the Turkish ruler whom he refuses to accept as a caliph since he was not from the Quraish.[84]

But despite Aḥmad Raḍā Khān's apostotatisation of Deobandis (and Ahl-i-Hadith for that matter) in several edicts, they were considered heroes in anti-colonial circles. As an influence, Deoband continued to play its role in political life, perhaps more so in Pakistan than in India after independence. In an article explaining the rise of Sunni militancy in Pakistan, S.V.R. Nasr points out that the Madani group was always more political, and thus closer to 'Islamism', than other groups including Deobandi ones.[85] However, as Qasim Zaman points out, even the T͟hānawī group—the followers of Mawlānā Ashraf 'Alī T͟hānawī, a major cleric from Deoband (1863–1943)—especially if one takes the work of Taqī 'Uthmānī, is politically oriented.[86] Even in the Musharraf era, Muftī Shamazaī wrote that all subsequent jihad movements were inspired by Deoband. Among these he placed 1857, the resistance movements against the British and the Afghan 'jihad' against the Soviet Union. This claim was supported by the Pakistani academic Tahir Kamran who wrote a comprehensive paper on the contribution of Deobandis to the development of the idea of jihad in the Punjab. In this paper, he mentioned a number of Deobandi clerics who contributed to the rise of jihadi ideas in the Punjab. For instance, an early exemplar was Aḥmad 'Alī Lāhorī (1886–1962) who participated both in the anti-colonial resistance movement in 1921 and then, more significantly, in the Kashmir movement in 1931 and 1947–48.[87] However, it is worth noting that the authors of the British period denied the involvement of the Deoband *'ulamā* in jihad against the British while latter historians emphasised it. This is because of the change in world view since that period. Whereas at that time Muslims were keen to deny their involvement in Jihad against the British, nowadays they are equally keen to prove that their elders did participate in such an anti-colonial movement.

83 Khan, A.R. *Riḍwiyyah* Vol. 6: 6. For a biography of Aḥmad Raḍā Khān, see Sanyal 1996.
84 For three edicts of 1920, see Ibid 8–21.
85 Nasr 2000: 172–175.
86 Zaman 2002: 134.
87 Abid Vol. 1 2003: 235. Kamran 2016: 75–76.

Both this movement and the 'Wahabi Trials' are connected with the Pashto-speaking tribesmen who live between Afghanistan and Pakistan (the area called as AfPak by the Americans nowadays). Let us explore this connection briefly as it is relevant once again with the Pakistan army fighting the Taliban militias which also use the idiom of jihad just as their ancestors did in the early part of the twentieth century. Several clergymen from this area appear in British and other records for having resisted the British militarily using the vocabulary of jihad. The best scholarly work so far on them is by Sana Haroon[88] and there is nothing new which this chapter will add to it. However, the use of the vocabulary of jihad by groups of tribesmen fighting against the British in the first part of the twentieth century, whether for the consolidation of their own power—an important insight of Haroon's book—or out of religious conviction, will be touched upon.

The Frontier resistance movements were generally led by religious men called *mullās*, *pīrs*, and *faqīrs*. The *mullās* formed spheres of influence through what Sana Haroon calls '*pīrī-murīdī*' (preceptor-disciple) lines.[89] First let us consider the Akhund Ghafūr-Haddā Mullā-line. In this line perhaps the most important person from the point of view of initiating movements known as jihad is Faḍl-i-Wāḥid, better known as Ḥājjī Ṣāḥib of Turangzaī. Faḍl-i-Wāḥid came from a family which had participated in Sayyid Aḥmad Barēlwī's movement against the Sikhs. He was a disciple of Najmuddīn from the village of Hadda near Jalalabad in Afghanistan popularly known as the Haddā Mullā. He also stayed for some time in Deoband where he was impressed by Mawlānā Maḥmūd al-Ḥasan who, as we have seen, was himself inspired by anti-British sentiments of jihad. It was here that he got the chance of going on pilgrimage and, since there were very few people who had performed the Ḥajj, he came to be called Ḥājjī Ṣāḥib. It was in Arabia that he became a disciple of Ḥājjī Imdādullāh and promised to keep up the jihad movement of Sayyid Aḥmad alive upon his return to India.[90] He was both a social reformer of Pashtun society and a preacher of anti-British jihad. He also served as the deputy of another cleric called the Bābrā Mullā.[91] The Ḥājjī began his anti-British struggle, much like Ṣūfī Muḥammad of the 1990s in Swat, by trying to substitute a local form of providing justice in place of the cumbersome and corrupt courts of the colonial government.[92] Then he tried to sabotage the authority of the allowance-holders of the British

88 Haroon 2007.
89 Ibid 51–52.
90 Ibid 53.
91 Qadir 2006: 88; Haroon 2007: 53.
92 Qadir 2008: 113–115.

since they were beholden to the colonial masters and could not be expected to look after the interest of the ordinary Pashtuns. This brought him in conflict with these allowance-holders who were heads of tribes, but he too collected an armed force (*lashkar*) and by 1927 he had the power to burn the houses of pro-British tribal chiefs.[93] His military power was enough to make the British commit a large force to the frontier. In this *pīrī-murīdī* line three other *mullās* are also mentioned in British reports. These are: Mullā Chaknāwar (1884–1930), Mullā Sandakī (d. 1939) and Mullā Bābra. These names and those of other *faqīrs* and *mullās* keep cropping up in sources in the context of preaching Jihad, collecting armed tribesmen, raiding British outposts, killing Englishmen, abducting Hindus and occasionally also Muslims, from settled areas.

One of the most famous of these tribal clerical leaders was the Faqīr of Ipī (d.1960). His date of birth is uncertain. Some give the date of 1897 but in 1936 he was said to be thirty-five years old which, if true, makes it 1901. He caught the imagination of writers as witnessed by the title of an article—'One man against an empire'—on him.[94] The Faqīr's real name was Mirzā 'Alī Khān. He was the son of Mullā Arsala Khān and went to the village school (*maktab*) under Mullā 'Ālam Khān of Ipī. In 1920, he moved from Khajuri to Ipi with his brother Sher Zamān who lived with him. His exploits are described in many sources, administration reports, secret correspondence, interviews, and secondary sources. His battles are serious enough to have been the subject of a book-length study by Warren.[95] Because of him, a large British force had to be kept in the Frontier even when soldiers were needed in World War 2. All these movements of jihad, mostly on the Frontier, constituted the practice of the idea in British India. Let us now turn to the interpretations of jihad by anti-colonial intellectuals during this period.

Among these, the first is the revolutionary interpretation offered by 'Ubaydullāh Sindhī whose role as an activist has already been discussed. The second

---

93 Ibid 118.

94 Hauner 1981.

95 The Faqīr is reported upon in numerous British sources: the letters of British officers to their superiors, despatches of military officers to headquarters, reports of the Government of India to the colonial secretary and the administrative reports of the year (Adm. NWFP 1938, 1940, 1941) and the weekly confidential reports of the 1930s (Ipi. Int. 1930s; Ipi. Pol 1930s). For a summary see Ipi. Burrows).
Eyewitness accounts of officers who fought against him (Shareef, Montgomery, Parsons) suggest that he was a formidable enemy since a large British force had to be sent against him during the Second World War when it could be used elsewhere. He survived till the 1960s continuing to create trouble for Pakistan as he did for the British (Ipi. Int 1948–49). See Hauner 1981 for his relations with Germany in the light of German archival sources. For his battles, see Warren 1984.

major theological figure is Mawlānā Abū'l Kalām Āzād who was an important anti-colonial political activist during the crucial years of the nineteen thirties and forties. Both were also champions of Indian nationalism, as was Mawlānā Ḥusain Aḥmad Madanī who has also been discussed below.

Sindhī's most important work representing his movement as a revolution is his exegesis of sixteen chapters of the Qur'an.[96] His exegesis was published in serial form from 1944 onwards but appeared as a complete book in 2009. The first thing which strikes one is that the verses commented upon by the author are not normally chosen by those who give a militant interpretation of jihad. However, Sindhi's hermeneutical practices are such that meanings are constructed through the filter of his ideological imperative—in this case revolution—so that almost anything can be explained as being a form of jihad. Among Sindhī's hermeneutical principles is that the Qur'an is higher than the hadith as far as the derivation of religious meaning is concerned. The *Sunnāh* was 'only meant to be absolutely binding during the era of the Prophet'.[97] Thus, the basic law (*qānūn-ē-aṣīṣī*) is the Qur'an whereas the provisional law (*qānūn-ē-tamhīdī*) is the *sunnāh*. This principle 'allows a large degree of latitude in the interpretation of sunna'.[98] Thus, the hadith does not play a restrictive role allowing Sindhī to interpret verses in the light of his revolutionary philosophy. The gist of his philosophy is that Islam is a revolutionary religion which aims to establish the sovereignty of God on earth. The early Muslims were the vanguard of this revolution and the rule of the first three caliphs was the ideal revolutionary state created by their effort and supported by God. Later Muslim societies left this revolutionary message behind and the European colonial powers took over the dynamism, though not the high moral principles and theological rectitude, of the Muslims. Because of their courage, they rule Muslim lands and peoples. Sindhī, therefore, wants to confront Western colonial hegemony by creating a vanguard, much in the tradition of Marx, which will take up the leadership of the world. This will be an international effort and he defends the establishment of a dictatorship (again like Marx's 'dictatorship of the proletariat') in which there will be no opposition especially from the politically quietist clergy. It will be compulsory for all, including women, to take part in the war necessitated for propagating this revolutionary message.

Sindhī is much impressed by Shāh Walīullāh whose works he quotes with approval throughout his exegesis. He begins the interpretation of *Sūrah Fātiḥa*

---

96 Sindhī, *Tafsīr* 2009: 151.
97 Brown 1996: 68.
98 Ibid 68.

(Q. 1)—the prayer to God to save Muslims from following those who go astray and disobey Him (1: 7)—by identifying these disobedient people as the '*ulamā* who abandon Islamic politics. Those 'who go astray' are Anglicised people who think the Qur'an cannot be followed any more.[99] In short, a verse which has always been taken as part of a general prayer for guidance, is now invested with revolutionary significance. While interpreting *Sūrah Muḥammad* (Q. 47), Sindhī says there are two types of movements in society: evolutionary and revolutionary. Islam is the latter type of movement. Thus, he attacks Chirāgh 'Alī by name, and others like him, who argue that Islam only allows defensive warfare. He also attacks the traditional idea that jihad is not permitted without a caliph or an *amīr* calling it a reactionary excuse for passive acceptance of colonial exploitation.[100] For him the correct Islamic praxis is to belong to the Quranic movement for a militant Islamic revolution. This movement is credited to Shāh Walīullāh and all those who struggled against the British—Mawlānā Qāsim Nānawtwī, Mawlānā Maḥmūd al-Ḥasan, and he himself (though he modestly omits his name)—belong to it.[101] The struggle against those who oppose this Quranic movement will continue until they give up all opposition. In that case they will be protected but the power to rule the state will be in Islamic revolutionary hands.[102] Here Sindhī interprets 2: 256—there is no compulsion in religion—in his typically unique manner. He argues, ostensibly on the authority of Shāh Walīullāh, that since right conduct and belief are so evident, it would actually be wrong to allow people to follow the wrong path. Thus a little compulsion or use of authority is justified in order to make people think correctly in their own interest.[103] In the interpretation of 47: 22, which mentions the evil consequences of obtaining earthly power, he asserts that the targeted group is those who avoid going to war. They should not be given responsible posts in peacetime as that would have negative consequences.[104]

Sindhī's concept of an Islamic revolutionary state is essentially Marxist. His state will encourage militarism and compel women to serve in the military in order to help in the war effort. Here he argues that another reason for the quietism of Indian Muslims is that they are 'the slaves of women'. This is exemplified with reference to a statement in Shāh Ismā'īl's Persian letter saying 'they [Indian Muslims] are busy in the vaginas of women' (*dar farj-ē-zanā mashghūl ha-*

99 Sindhī, *Tafsīr* 2009.
100 Ibid 174.
101 Ibid 356.
102 Ibid 182.
103 Ibid 378–379.
104 Ibid 215.

stand).[105] This, of course, is the old argument that Muslims lost their power in India because of sexual indulgence—an argument not supported by historical evidence as such indulgence was more pronounced when they were politically powerful. As mentioned before, the paradigm of revolution which inspired Sindhī and other revolutionaries of this period was Marxism. He praises the principle of 'from each according to his ability and to each according to his need' saying that this was the principle of rule in the early caliphate.[106] Though he does not deal with the issue of *naskh* in detail, he says that war will continue for ever and no verse of the Qur' an about this has been cancelled.[107] As he himself cooperated with non-Muslims, such as Mahendra Pratāp, in his struggle against the British, he does not rule out such conduct. To justify it he quotes Quranic verses which allow friendship with people who have not transgressed against Muslims nor turned them out of their homes such as *al-Mumtaḥinah* (Q. 60: 8 and 9). In this context, he is even prepared to live with an Indian non-Muslim than with a non-Indian Muslim.[108] However, he calls Q. 60 a blueprint for creating a ministry of foreign affairs while *al-Ṣaff* (Q. 61), which warns about the battles to come, is about the ministry of war.[109] This view is not shared by any other radical or militant Muslim interpreter of the idea of jihad. Sindhī ends his book by interpreting the last few verses of the Qur'an as the gist of the revolutionary philosophy he has been advocating. In his view the verses of *Sūrah al-Kafirūn* (Q. 109)—which declares in response to Arab rejection of Islam 'unto me my religion and unto you, yours' (109: 1–6)—declare a state of war between Muslims and non-Muslims. The last four chapters (from Q. 111 to 114) are about the philosophy of the universe based on the oneness and power of God. This, Sindhī declares, is the basis of the revolution he preaches since, he asserts, Islam is the only political philosophy reflecting this reality.

Sindhī's hermeneutics, as mentioned before, is different from others we have been reading about in that he imposes an overall meaning without the semantic expansion of single words or expressions nor, indeed, does he use specification or abrogation. He gives an entirely unfamiliar and heterodox meaning in terms of his philosophy of revolution which is a unique act in a class all by itself which can only be described as *ta'wīl* of an extreme kind dictated by his ideological imperative. This act of interpretation was not merely an intellectual exercise as far

---

105 Ibid 438.
106 Ibid 275.
107 Ibid 293.
108 Ibid 546.
109 Ibid 431–432.

as Sindhī himself was concerned. In his view, it justified the overall aim of revolution against the British, an aim in which help from non-Muslim citizens of the motherland as well as foreigners was welcome. Thus he welcomed any help from abroad to further his aims even if it involved clandestine activities and mendacity. As mentioned in other contexts, Sindhī's views were not condoned by the *'ulamā*. Ḥusain Aḥmad Madanī, once himself a firebrand, wrote in an essay after Sindhī's death that the views expressed by him (Sindhī) should be evaluated according to traditional principles and that they do not necessarily represent the positions of those he writes about, i.e. Shāh Walīullāh, Qāsim Nānawtwī, Maḥmud al-Ḥasan and others.[110]

It must be remembered that the anti-colonial resistance against the British was not carried out only through the militant means employed by Sindhī and the Deoband *'ulamā*. It was also part of the peaceful political process of the period by supporters of composite Indian nationalism of which M.K. Gandhi was the acknowledged leader. In an important movement of the period, the Khilafat agitation, Gandhi joined forces with the nationalist Muslims who wanted the caliphate to be preserved in Turkey.[111] A prominent leader of this movement was Abū'l Kalām Āzād (1888–1958).[112] The religious ideas of Abū 'l Kalām Āzād have been called 'enlightened fundamentalism'.[113] His enlightenment was at least partly owed to Sir Sayyid whose views he had read and with whom he 'was greatly impressed' at least as far as the necessity of modern education was concerned. Indeed, it was because of this contact that he, otherwise educated on traditional lines, decided to study English.[114] But since he was the son of a scholar of Islam and knew Arabic having been born in Mecca, he also specialised in Arabic scholarship. Thus, he was poised in a sense between the old world and the new one and his work strikes out a new, modernist path though it was different from the modernists of the nineteenth century with their emphasis on reconciliation with the colonial powers. Indeed, there are places where, as we shall

110 Madanī, Essay on Sindhi. Appended in Sindhī's *Dhātī Diary* 1933: 50.
111 Qureshi 1999: 233–316.
112 The name Āzād, meaning free in Urdu, was Abū'l Kalām's own addition to his name. He explains it as follows: 'The ideas I had acquired from my family and early training could no longer satisfy me. I felt I must find the truth for myself....I passed from one phase to another and a stage came when all the old bonds imposed on my mind by family and upbringing were completely shattered. I felt free of all conventional ties and decided that I would chalk out my own path. It was about this time that I decided to adopt the pen name of "Azad" or "Free" to indicate that I was no longer tied to my inherited beliefs' (Āzād 1959: 4).
113 Ahmad 1967: 176.
114 Āzād 1959:3; Douglas 1993: 64.

see, he gives interpretations of jihad more in keeping with the views of radical Islamists.

In his book on the caliphate, called *Mas'alah-i-Khilāfat*, for instance he presents a more aggressive view about jihad than he does in his exegesis which is mentioned below. His main concern in this book is the preservation of the caliphate of Turkey and resisting the British domination of the Middle East. Although he begins with the view that jihad is basically defensive, he qualifies it by expanding the meaning of defensive warfare to include offensive warfare in the interest of peace 'until there is international peace'.[115] He refers to *al-Nisā* (Q. 47)—fight till war itself ends (47: 4)—in support of this end, i.e. the end of all wars and oppression. But in his view this will only happen 'when the whole world bends down to accept the brotherhood of Islam' (*jab tamām duniyā Islām kī da'wat-ē-aman ō akhuwwat kē āgē jhuk jāye gī*).[116] This position is associated more with revivalists and radical Islamists than with modernists. However, though Āzād does not elaborate upon it, he does clarify that offensive war is individual duty (*farḍul kifāyah*) for all Muslim countries separately but only the Turks have been fulfilling it not Indian Muslims.[117] In this context, he mentions Turkish conquests of Europe with approval without noticing that these occupations are similar to European occupations of Muslim countries.[118] Besides jihad, migration (*hijrah*) is also a duty. Āzād explains this concept with reference to the rise of Western civilisation which features navigation of the oceans, exploration of the remote corners of the earth and mobility.[119] The main argument of the book is to inspire the Muslims of India to struggle by every means possible to preserve the caliphate of the Ottomans. He defines *khilāfah* as being the viceregent of God. This implies not just spiritual or theological viceregency but also temporal power over God's earth. Here Āzād comes very near Mawdūdī's concept (to be explained later) that Muslims should be the rulers of the earth in order to impose God's own laws upon it.[120] Indeed, his biographer Douglas says that one of his themes was that 'Muslims cannot be under the rule of others. Submission must be to God alone'.[121] But Āzād, quite inconsistently, twists this to mean 'under colonial rule' while making concessions for others. Indeed, he later served as a minister in India under Nehru's Congress.

115 Āzād 1920: 163.
116 Ibid 145.
117 Ibid 164–165.
118 Ibid 139–141.
119 Ibid 51–53.
120 Ibid 22.
121 Douglas 1993: 135.

Perhaps, for Āzād, all such concepts were to be used for the problems created by colonialism. Thus, he comes from the theory of the ideal caliphate to the reality at hand, i.e. the caliphate in Turkey which, he says, is sacred. He argues that the Muslims of India believed in the Sultan of Turkey as the caliph of all Muslims even before the Khilafat Movement of the nineteen twenties.[122] He also asserts that every age should have a caliph and that it is incumbent upon all Muslims to obey him or any other ruler who has power over them.[123] The defining characteristic of a Muslim society is that it is united. Indeed, *jāhiliyyah* is defined by him as the state of discord which is tantamount to a state of anarchy.[124]

Āzād was one of the first Muslim leaders to give theological arguments to prevent Western and Jewish political domination over parts of Iraq, Egypt, and Palestine. For instance, he refers to the idea of the *jazīrah al-'Arab* (the island of Arabia) which, he says, is called an island because it has the sea on its three sides and the rivers Tigris and Euphrates in the north.[125] As the Prophet's dying injunction was to remove non-Muslims from this area—here Āzād quotes a hadith to this effect (*akhrajū al-yahūd wa'l naṣārā min jazīrah al-'Arab*)[126]—he concludes that it is incumbent upon Muslims to struggle to prevent colonial intervention there.[127] In short, except for the Hindus with whom he advocates peaceful relations, Āzād declares war against colonial powers in general and Britain in particular.

In his speeches and addresses to various organizations, Āzād refers to the ideas he presents in his exegesis about Hindu-Muslim relations in India. In his presidential address to the Majlis-e-Khilafat held at Agra on 25 August 1921, he specifically referred to 60: 8 saying that it orders Muslims to live in a friendly relationship with those non-believers who had not attacked them or expelled them from their homes. But, since the British government was hostile to Muslim interests in the world (he specifically mentions Turkey), it came in the category of 'militant unbelievers' (*harbī kāfir*). That is why it was necessary to fight them along with the help of Hindus.[128] He even goes on to expatiate upon a technical aspect of the hermeneutics of the Qur'an stating that some people think that this verse (60: 8) has been abrogated (*mansūkh*) by 9: 5 and that, therefore, the final

122 Āzād 1920: 134.
123 Ibid 80.
124 Ibid 54.
125 Ibid 180–183.
126 Ibid 184.
127 Ibid 88.
128 Āzād 1920 s: 36–37.

orders are to continue the conflict with all unbelievers. However, 9: 5 is specifically meant for the polytheists of Arabia so it is no longer applicable while 60: 8 still is.[129] This is unusual since specialised matters such as the hermeneutics of the Qur'an are generally not made the subject of public speeches.

But Āzād went beyond his stated theological positions in his political speeches. Indeed, during the heat of the nationalist struggle against the colonial rulers he goes so far as to declare jihad. In a speech on 27 October 1914, during the First World War, he says:

> I say that all true Muslims (*mu'min*) who believe in God and his Prophet and His Books; on them it is incumbent that they rise for jihad. The first jihad is spending one's wealth, and secondly one's self and life. Send your wealth and possessions and take your lives in your hands. If today they are not required it does not matter; tomorrow the occasion may arise.[130]

On the whole, Āzād's work has two conflicting aspects. In the domain of theology, he inclines towards modernist interpretations of jihad as being defensive. And in his politics, he veers towards anti-colonial resistance bordering on violence.

The theological aspect of Āzād's thought is evident in his exegesis of the Qur'an in three volumes the last of which was compiled and edited by Mawlānā Muḥammad 'Abduhu.[131] Āzād tells the reader in the preface of the first volume how he was extradited from all the states of India except two and how, when incarcerated, he lost some crucial papers on which the exegesis was written. The work began in 1916 and ended in the late 1930s, a period of great political turmoil in the Subcontinent and in Āzād's life since he was part of anti-British politics. The exegesis refers to hadith but not to the numerous, mostly incredible, legends which were part of the medieval exegeses such as Ibn Kathīr's. Āzād's translations are by no means literal. Indeed, they are paraphrases in which the parenthetical information directs the reader to his preferred meaning. He begins with an assertion of the basic unity of faiths i.e that they teach the same truths. Thus, Hinduism is called monotheistic-polytheism which keeps the former principle for the highest intellects whereas the latter one is for ordinary people.[132] Like the other *'ulamā*, he is not sympathetic to Judaism and Christianity but, unlike the others, he deals 'more sympathetically,

---

129 Ibid 39–40.
130 Ibid 27.
131 *Tarjumān* Vol. 1 (1930); Vol. 2 (1936 a); Vol. 3 (1936 b).
132 Ibid Vol. 1 (1930: 141).

with the "indic" religions, Buddhism and Hinduism'.[133] But, of course, Islam has central significance in his worldview. Thus, whatever other religious texts might teach, the Qur'an can provide guidance to humanity which has gone astray despite claiming to follow religions which taught the same transcendental truths. In this interpretation, Āzād seems to be desirous of being sensitive to Hindu sensibilities since Hindu cooperation was part of his politics. This being the time of the Khilafat Movement in which, as mentioned above, Gandhi supported the Muslims, two strategies were resorted to. First, the Ottoman caliph was celebrated as the religious head of the Muslim world and, secondly, Hindus were conciliated and wooed. The former trend is evidenced by some of the *fatāwā* of Deoband. For instance, a question was asked whether it is necessary to take the name of the Sultan of Turkey in the Friday sermon. The reply was that it is, since he is the caliph of all Muslims. A note explains that this was written in 1340/1921 when this movement was at its height.[134] As for the second, Hindu speakers were invited to deliver speeches and lectures in mosques. Another *fatwā*, again from Deoband and of the same date, allows such speeches by Hindus adding that 'this is help from the unknown since it is in support of Muslims and God is giving such help through the means of unbelievers'.[135]

Āzād's view of Jihad is defensive despite his record of resistance to the British. A brief summary of his exegetical position is given below:

Table 5

Verse	Commentary by Āzād	Interpretive device
2:190	Defensive war is permitted but do not transgress (Vol. 1: 272).	Literal meaning
2:191	Fight those who began hostilities such as attacking you and expelling you from your homes since oppression and cruelty (*fitnah*) is worse than war (Vol. 1: 272).	Specification
2:193	Fight till oppression (*fitnah*) ends and everyone is free to follow any religion. Human beings should not be so powerful that they intervene forcefully in the relationship humans may have with God. Hence the aim of the war is to make the world safe for the free practice of all religions (Vol. 1: 272).	Semantic expansion/ ideological imperative
8:39	Fight till the cruelty of human beings no longer comes between the freedom of people to worship as they like (Vol. 2: 62).	As above

133 Ahmad 1967: 184.
134 *Deoband* Vol. 5: 91.
135 Ibid Vol. 14: 133.

Table 5 *(Continued)*

Verse	Commentary by Āzād	Interpretive device
8:61	Connects it with 8:59 which instructs Muslims to keep a strong deterrent force to prevent others from attacking them. He emphasises this stating that if Muslims had done this, they would not have been colonised by European powers. However, the aim is international peace so if the enemy wants peace, it should be preferred (Vol. 2: 68).	Literal meaning
9:5	Explains with reference to *asbābul nuzūl*—the breaking of the treaty of Ḥudaybiyyah by the Quraish—and specification of the order for 'killing wherever found' to Arab polytheists who had initiated hostilities and broken treaties. This was a special case as the Ka'bah had to be reserved only for the worship of God. This order is no longer valid (Vol. 2: 78).	Specification/ ideological imperative
9:29	Those out of the People of the Book whose beliefs were perfidious were to be fought with. However, they could live in safety if they paid a tax (*jizyah*) which was similar to the one paid by Muslims (Vol. 2: 82).	Specification
60:8	God does not stop you from being kind and just to those who have not transgressed against you (Vol. 3: 475).	Literal meaning

Source: Āzād, *Tarjumān* 3 Vols.

Like other modernists, Āzād's main interpretative device is specification of the aggressive verses to certain groups, i.e. the Arab polytheists. His ideological assumption is that this was a unique case but otherwise jihad is defensive. He uses the occasions of revelation (*asbābul nuzūl*) for both purposes. As for the peace verses, he privileges the literal meaning, emphasising that they determine the norm to be followed in international relations. However, since he was fighting against British colonial domination, he also advocates that all nations should possess the power to deter aggression. He eschews all mention of killing, especially of prisoners, so he explains *al-Anfāl* (Q. 8)—which tells the Prophet not to take prisoners till there has been a war in which the enemies have been crushed (8: 67)—in completely peaceful terms. It does not behoove a Prophet to take prisoners, he says, till his message does not become 'manifest and dominant' in the country (*jab tak us kī da'wat mulk mẽ ẓāhir ō ghālib nah hō jāyē*).[136] While explaining the order to fight the People of the Book in 9: 29, he again uses the device of specification by suggesting that the order to fight them is not a general

136 *Tarjumān* Vol. 2: 71.

one but refers to those special Jews and Christians who were hostile to Muslims. Only such special types of people were to be combated till they paid the poll tax willingly (*apnī khushī sē jizyah dēnā qubūl kar lẽ*). In keeping with the imperative of making Muslims adhere to the values of international amity advocated in his time, he does not translate *sāghirūn* in 9: 29 as being humiliated but merely remarks that 'their condition should have become such that their rebelliousness should have ended' (*un kī sarkashī ṭūṭ chukī hō*).[137] In a note at the end of the volume, echoing Sir Sayyid, he says that this *jizyah* was equivalent to the tax on Muslims but the non-Muslims were protected and exempted from military service. He also says that, although the term was used in the context of the People of the Book, Hindus too were included. Such interpretations fall in the modernist tradition but, as we have seen in his other writings, Āzād could also express opinions which verged on the radical.

Somewhat unusually, Āzād does not refer to his own political struggle in his exegesis except at a few places and then only in passing. For instance, he says that during World War 1 he asked the Indian *'ulamā* to oppose the war effort. However, only Mawlānā Maḥmūd al-Ḥasan of Deoband agreed with him while the others dismissed this plea by dubbing it as mischief (*fitnah*).[138] At another place too he seems to suggest that lack of warlike preparations had led to the downfall of Muslims. This occurs while explaining *al-Anfāl* (Q. 8)—about preparing one's defense capabilities (8: 60)—to deter the unbelievers from aggression. He says in a note that Muslims are advised to prepare for war as much as possible. They are told not to wait till they have the latest weapons while making excuses that they cannot resist oppression. To this he adds that if Muslims had understood the spirit of this verse they would not have come to the paralysis which has made them stagnant for one hundred and fifty years.[139] In yet another place, he says Muslims should now think whether other people are more intellectually advanced than they are and, if they are, then it is natural that they will dominate them.[140] The implication is that Western people are not intrinsically more intelligent but that they have used their talents in science, technology, and commerce which had made colonial domination possible and it is only by activity in these fields that freedom would be won.

The Indian nationalists responded to the political events happening both in India and abroad through their anti-colonial reading of them. Religious vocabu-

137 Ibid 86.
138 Ibid 95.
139 Ibid 68.
140 Ibid 70.

lary was used to categorise events even though such vocabulary could hardly have resonated positively with their Hindu allies. Mohamed Ali (1878–1931), already mentioned with reference to his magazine *Comrade*, was also a firebrand journalist and leader of the anti-colonial resistance movement. He says in his biography that 'the disastrous war in the Balkans' affected him so profoundly that he 'even contemplated suicide'—such being his passion for Muslim solidarity.[141] In his trial in Karachi, Mohamed Ali's argument is based on the superiority of divine law over the secular one. Thus, if a soldier is going to fight in Iraq then it is the duty of an *'ālim* to tell him that it is wrong.[142] One relevant example of divine law, as constructed by the anti-colonial party, was the declaration of jihad by the Ottomans during the Second World War against the Allies, through a conventional *fatwā*. The *fatwā* declares that there are three major types of wars: first, the war in secret in which 'every unbeliever is an enemy'; the other is by word of mouth which is propaganda to be carried out where fighting is not possible as in the Caucasus; and then there is 'physical war' which is further subdivided into the 'lesser war' which comprise a series of battles by groups of Muslims and finally the 'greater Holy War' which is to be proclaimed by the Caliph himself. However, even for small struggles, permission should be taken from the Caliph 'for prestige sake'. Thus, the *fatwā* takes it for granted that the Ottoman ruler is the only legitimate caliph of the Islamic world. 'Only he can declare a war.' Curiously enough, there is a general statement against Christians and Jews saying they should not be accepted as friends; yet, a little later it is also said that 'the holy war is proclaimed only against those who rule over Islamic countries' and not 'against all unbelievers'.[143] In short, Germany, an ally of Turkey, was spared in the *fatwā*. The *fatwā* tries to use all the biases of the masses which it is possible to evoke but remains confused. The venom against Christians in the early part of the document is not counteracted by the flat statement that the order for fighting is only against colonisers. However, despite its emotional rhetoric, Cook says, 'it did not seem to command as much attention from the masses of Muslims as the Persian and Ottoman leaders had hoped'.[144] And that, it seems, is precisely the problem with the nationalist leadership's use of Islamic vocabulary. They deviated from orthodox positions on jihad, thus alienating the traditional *'ulamā*, and in their eagerness to cooperate with the Hindus they also alienated the ordinary Muslim masses which, by the end of the world war, were looking for leadership to the Muslim League which also used the vo-

141 Ali 1920 s: 40.

142 Jafri 1965: 106.

143 Ottoman *fatwā* of 1915 in Bostom 2005: 221–225.

144 Cook 2005: 92.

cabulary of Islam—though not of jihad—and appealed to their fears of Hindu domination.

What is of interest for us is the use of the idiom of jihad by the actors, the reporters, and the scholars who were writing on jihad. It is arguable that each party does it on ideological grounds in order to further broader objectives. The actors call it jihad if they rely on a religious ideology to gain power as all their actions, whether they satisfy their urge to gain power, recognition and material goods, are then perceived by themselves and others as part of a sacred mission. The reporters, often representatives of the state, are apt to call events jihad if the religious idiom is used by their opponents. Since the image of the fanatical Muslim evokes the response of countering this fanaticism by military force, it facilitates military action. It may be noted that the Gadar Party, comprising mostly expatriate Sikhs from North America, also tried to create an uprising against the British during World War 1. They carried out robberies to finance what they considered a nationalistic struggle against colonial 'exploiters' and also appealed emotively to religion. They too were crushed by force and their ideology, nationalism, also caused as much concern for the British as those of Muslim rebels.[145] However, since the movement was not conducted on religious lines, it did not stigmatise the whole Sikh community nor was it considered as potentially contagious by the authorities as the idea of jihad could be for the Muslim community.

Two thinkers who are not exegetes but who responded to the spirit of the times in their own unique ways were Muḥammad Iqbāl (1877–1938) and 'Ināyatullāh Khān Mashriqī. Iqbāl, as Mawlānā Muḥammad 'Alī of the Comrade fame tells us, 'was a household word throughout the Urdu-speaking Muslim world, and of course I was an ardent admirer and devotee'.[146] It was Iqbāl's Urdu poetry, however, not his Persian one nor his writings in English, which made him so popular. However, for his ideas we shall turn to his book in English called *The Reconstruction of Religious Thought in Islam*. Iqbāl's work is studded with references to the most famous thinkers of the world but there is no clear statement as to what he wants to use, let us say, Ibn Taymiyyah or Shāh Walīullāh, for. It is clear enough, however, that he, like other modernists, wants Islam to adapt to modern life. His lecture on the subject, entitled 'The principle of movement in the structure of Islam', sums up his views on the subject.[147] He begins the essay with the assertion that 'Islam rejects the old static view of the universe,

145 Joshi 1977.
146 Ali 1920 s: 61.
147 Iqbāl 1934: 116–142.

and reaches a dynamic view'.[148] He then points out that innovation (*ijtihād*) was impeded by the defeat of the Mutazilites (whom he calls rationalists) at the hands of the conservatives; the growth of ascetic mysticism; the destruction of Baghdad and the 'fear of further disintegration'.[149] He then praises the Turkish Legislative Assembly for their bold and creative interpretations and concludes by exhorting the modern Muslim to 'reconstruct his social life in the light of ultimate principles, and evolve, out of the hitherto partially revealed purpose of Islam, that spiritual democracy which is the ultimate aim of Islam'.[150] But how does this modern spirit, the alleged dynamism of Islam—whatever both may mean—affect the theory and practice of jihad? Iqbāl gives no clear answer to this in his major theoretical and rhetorical treatise we have been considering so far.

Coming now to his poetry, some of his verse apparently glorifies Muslim conquests and praises warriors. However, poems like Ḥālī's '*Madd o Jazarē Islām*' (the rise and fall of Islam), celebrating the glory of the Muslim past and lamenting the present decadence and weakness, were the rage of colonial India. Indeed, 'the political poem became a form of vitriolic journalism in the verse of Ẓafar 'Alī Khān, and 'was one of the chief attractions of his paper *Zamīndār*'.[151] It is in this context that Iqbāl's *Shikwah* (complaint) and *Jawāb-e-Shikwah* (answer to the complaint) may be placed. In the first, the poet complains to God about the decadence of Muslims; in the second, God replies to it saying that this degradation is only because Muslims have abandoned Islam. The imagery of conquest is part of the glorification of Islam in both:

> *Dasht to dasht haẽ daryā bhī nah chōṛe ham nē*
> *Bahr-ē-Ẓulmāt mẽ daoṛā diyē ghōṛē ham nē*
> (Deserts are deserts we did not even leave rivers
> In the sea of darkness we galloped our horses.[152]

Dynamism, without however specifying what it is, is praised in verse just as it is in prose. The poet admires the dynamism of Satan, Mussolini, and Napoleon and shares aspects of the philosophy of Friedrich Neitzsche (1844–1900) who wrote about the positive aspects of power. As Aziz Ahmad notes: 'In Iqbāl's romantic involvement with power the occasional suspension of a moral criterion stands

148 Ibid 116.
149 Ibid 120.
150 Ibid 142.
151 Ahmad 1967: 101.
152 Iqbāl, '*Shikwah*' [Urdu: Complaint], *Bang-e-Dara* in Maher n.d.: 288.

in contrast with his insistence on a moral purposiveness in the principle of movement'.[153]

In conclusion, neither Iqbāl's prose not verse amounts to any rationalised position on jihad nor did he write an essay, let alone an exegetical work, on the subject. Indeed, in contrast to his apparent praise for dynamism, even fascism in politics, Iqbāl's views are 'counterbalanced in other poems by a denunciation of fascist aggression and the abuse of power'.[154] The final judgment of Fazlur Rahman about Iqbāl's work may be instructive. He says:

> It is true that Iqbāl did not carry out any systematic inquiry into the teaching of the Qur' ān but picked and chose from its verses—as he did with other traditional material—to prove certain theses at least some of which were the result of his general insights into the Qur'ān but which, above all, seemed to him to suit most the contemporary needs of a stagnant Muslim society. He then expressed these theses in terms of such contemporary evolutionary theories as those of Bergson and Whitehead.[155]

Iqbāl, like other modernists, was caught between the desire to adapt Islam to the values and institutions of the modern age initated by colonial rule while resisting Western hegemony. He, like other modernists, responded to the West in this complex, contradictory, almost schizophrenic manner because modernity meant civilisation which was an ethical ideal; but it also meant succumbing to Western hegemony and political domination which, however, was to be resisted.

Dynamism, including celebration of leaders like Mussolini and Hitler, could lead to authoritarianism. This is what happened in the case of Mashriqī (1888–1963) who took four triposes in five years at Cambridge.[156] In his Urdu book *Tadhkirah*, which is prefaced by an introduction (*Iftitāḥiyyah*) in Arabic, the author purports to establish a 'scientific revolution'. He refers to the then current scientific theories about fitness in the Darwinian, or rather social Darwinist, sense.[157] He established the Khaksar party which emphasised both military discipline and public service. While the Khaksars helped both Hindus and Muslims, 'Ināyatullāh Khān moved towards anti-Hindu ideas and supported a militant version of Islam. His speech on 28 May 1950 at Iqbal Park in Lahore was abusive towards India and Hindus. He asked Muslims to 'adopt soldierly [sic] way of life'.[158] However, despite his use of the Qur'an in *Tadhkirah*, he remains a peripheral figure

153 Ahmad 1967: 144.
154 Ibid 145.
155 Rahman 1982: 153–154.
156 Hussain 1991: 14–15.
157 Mashriqī 1924: '*Ifititāḥiyah*'.
158 Hussain 1991: 279.

with almost no influence either on the interpretation of Jihad or in political life in Pakistan.

To sum up, the movements covered in this chapter represent not jihad in the traditional sense as described in the texts pertaining to it, but a kind of non-traditional asymmetrical warfare against an extremely powerful and organised state. This was only possible because Indian Muslims no longer waited for messiahs and saviours from outside (such as Abdālī) or a powerful *imām* sitting in the Red Fort in Delhi. They could only form groups for taking initiatives on their own. As Peter Hardy has astutely pointed out, 'the reform movement of Saiyid Ahmad Bareilly [sic] and of the *fara'izis* contributed to the gradual (and in the event incomplete) transformation of the Indian Muslim community from an aggregate of believers into an association with a will for joint action'.[159] In all the cases, the enemy was the British colonial state and those who fought it were rebels, clandestine groups of zealous individuals and non-state actors. They were mostly from the working classes, tribesmen, or from petty trader backgrounds being 'members of that underworld of which the British were subconsciously aware'.[160] This was one aspect of the democratisation (or anarchisation?) of jihad. The other was that there was no recognised, legitimate religious authority whose *fatwā* was accepted by all (or even most) Muslims (as individuals or rulers of states). Nor, indeed, was there any manifest declaration of war. However, and this may be an important insight, the Wahhābīs did set up an Islamic state under Sayyid Aḥmad Barēlwī and then again under Wilāyat 'Alī and 'Ināyat 'Alī. This has been described in some detail by Aḥmad.[161] Their pattern of awarding punishments for not following Islamic rituals like prayers is very similar to the Afghan state or the Islamic Emirate of Waziristan during the period of Taliban rule over both.[162] The setting up of an Islamic state, like ISIS (Daesh), may be considered necessary by the Islamist militants precisely in order to provide legitimacy to the declaration of jihad. These are important findings because all these features figure clearly in the wars which present-day Pakistan and India have to face. In a sense then, the significance of the movements described is precisely the fact that they are not jihad as understood in the classical texts about it in India. More importantly, this jihad is more a matter of vocabulary and emotion than that of interpretation of religious texts. In a sense, then, it represents a certain democratisation of the theory of jihad which plays into the hands of anyone who takes the initiative to use evocative words.

---

159 Hardy 1972: 58.
160 Ibid 169.
161 Ahmad 1994: 118–119.
162 Ibid 119.

7 The Age of Mawdūdī

When Major General Tajammul Hussain Malik (1924 – 2003), a decorated army officer and a believer in establishing an Islamic state by force, thought of carrying out his ideas in real life, he met Sayyid Abū'l A'lā Mawdūdī (1903 – 1979) in Lahore. He had already been inspired by Mawdūdī's book *Khilāfat aur Malūkiyyat* which he had read in 1967 – 68. He was just as inspired by the author of the book and asked him 'how far his party was ready for a revolution'. Mawdūdī replied that his party had been brought up by him to aspire for non-revolutionary change and it would not agree to such methods.[1] This was not a dishonest answer as Mawdūdī appropriated the idiom of revolution closely resembling Marxist uses of it but actually 'meant by the term... a process of changing the ethical basis of society, which should begin at the top and permeate into the lower strata'.[2] What is beyond dispute is that Mawdūdī did inspire many people who wanted to establish an Islamic state and at least some of these people may have wanted to expedite the process through violent revolution. His journal *Tarjumān al-Qur'ān* lays out arguments for the Islamic state and its blueprint in almost every issue. Indeed, he initiated his efforts to create such a state in Pakistan from the very beginning as one of his interviews broadcasted from Radio Pakistan on 18 May 1948 bears witness.[3]

Mawdūdī is the most influential Islamic thinker of the Subcontinent. As the discourse about jihad changed significantly because of Mawdūdī's input—especially as it pertains to the development of the Islamist interpretation of this phenomenon—the period in which his theories were propounded can be called the age of Mawdūdī. Hence, the focus here will be on Mawdūdī, though the views of his contemporaries, especially those who challenged his views or propounded alternative ones, will be mentioned. Mawdūdī's legacy lives on in forms which he may not have recognised and he commands immense devotion and respect in a sizable community of South Asian Muslims. However, the same legacy is also disputed, resisted, and opposed vehemently for different reasons. Those who criticise him are liberal intellectuals, his political opponents, and traditional *'ulamā*. Before going into his ideas, however, let us briefly touch upon his educational background.

---

1 Malik 1991: 215 – 16

2 Nasr 1996: 77.

3 The official mouthpiece of the *Jamā 'at*, the *Tarjuman al-Qur'*an carried articles on the necessity of an Islamic government in Pakistan in every issue. See Mawdūdī 1948: 112 – 118 in which, though the context is of Kashmir, he advocates the formation of the Islamic state in Pakistan.

https://doi.org/10.1515/9783110716986-010

Although Mawdūdī did not include himself among the traditional Madrasah-trained *'ulamā*, he was actually educated along traditional lines in addition to self-study. First, he came from a religious family and his father influenced him in his early education. Secondly, he attended the local *Dārul 'Ulūm* in Hyderabad where his family moved from Delhi and the principal of this institution was Mawlānā Ḥamīduddīn Farāhī, who is well known as the major influence on Amīn Aḥsan Iṣlāḥī, once a colleague of Mawdūdī in the Jamā'at-i-Islāmī. Thirdly, after the Hyderabad interlude, Mawdūdī returned to Delhi and studied in the Fatehpur mosque's seminary where he obtained his formal *ijāzahs* (permission to teach) in 1926. However, he adopted journalism as a profession choosing not to become a clergyman. As a journalist, and one who used his mother tongue Urdu to great effect, he had a much wider audience for his ideas than were available to the Muslim clergy with their Arabised and stilted Urdu and the formal constraints of working in the seminaries with their attendant discipline and heavy teaching load.[4]

Mawdūdī is often credited with being one of the intellectual fathers of Islamist militancy which is much in evidence nowadays in the form of violent attacks on civilian targets, suicide attacks, and so on. Yet by his own actions and writings he does not advocate the use of force in the way militant thinkers do. Mawdūdī might have inspired them in certain of their doctrines, but he did not personally choose to legitimise violence by non-state actors either against one's own rulers or against non-Muslims in general. Indeed, despite his revolutionary interpretations of jihad, he also remained bound by some of the rules about its conduct by the traditional *'ulamā*. At the end of his essay on Mawdūdī's *Tafhīm*, Charles J. Adams, a scholar of his works, says:

> Were one not acquainted with Mawdūdī's attitudes and his political activities from other sources, it is not at all certain that any strong impulse would emerge from the *tafsīr* clearly to identify him with the resurgence perspective, at least in my opinion.[5]

Mawdūdī's first writing on the concept of jihad was a series of articles later collected together under the title of *Al-jihād fī'l Islām*. The book appeared first as a series of articles in response to the murder of Swamī Shraddhanand (1856–1926), an educationist and activist who tried to convert Muslims to Hinduism

---

4 Nasr 1996: 9–26. Mawdūdī never published a biography but he did write some notes on his life. These are in the possession of his son Hayder Mawdūdī and I am grateful to him for telling me about them. There is information on Mawdūdī 's family in the biography of Mariam Jameela who lived in his house for some time (Baker 2011).

5 Adams 1988: 323.

on the ground that it was their original religion. Thus, Mawdūdī's original conception of his task was to defend Islam which was being attacked as a religion of violence. Yet, despite the idiom of theology he uses and his response to attacks on the faith in what appears to be the genre of modernist apologia, Mawdūdī is an original thinker; a constructor of an ideological edifice; a belief- system, the central point of which is political power in an Islamic state. Mawdūdī begins this book with the value of human life quoting *al-Furqān* (Q. 25) and *al-Māidah* (Q. 5): to be exact 25: 68 and 5: 32—the first saying that one should not kill anyone illegally; the second emphasising the idea further by saying that one who kills one person has killed all mankind and one who saves one life saves all mankind. On the basis of these verses he rules out warfare for all worldly reasons. However, defending lives and religion are also sacred duties. Thus, defensive war to avoid persecution (*fitnah*) is permitted. But the word *fitnah*, which is a key concept in Mawdūdī's thought, is not just physical or economic persecution. It is also ideological. Thus, all attempts to turn Muslims away from Islam, or expose them to other ideologies is also *fitnah*.[6] An equally important term is *fasād*. To explain it, Mawdūdī refers to the Quranic descriptions of ancient peoples who had been destroyed such as the people of Noah and Lot—in short, all manifestations of moral turpitude, which persist despite warning. Moreover, all forms of government which promote moral turpitude or do not stop it by force are also included into this category.[7] This is of crucial importance since, in Mawdūdī's view as expressed in his first book, jihad is to eliminate such systems of rule. The last few lines of this argument are worth reproducing. Mawdūdī writes: 'and if necessary and it is possible, then all such governments should be removed by war (*qitāl*) and, in their place, a just form of government should be established'.[8] By just government, Mawdūdī means a government which follows the rules laid down by God, i.e. Islam as interpreted by Mawdūdī. This adds to the definition of defensive jihad—against attackers—given earlier.[9] Indeed, this semantic expansion in the meanings of *fitnah*, etc., lays down a principle which later developed into a theory of global rule and, by implication, global warfare. Mawdūdī devotes much space (section 6 of his book under discussion) to the concept of war in other religions and contemporary Western practice. He argues that other religions allow harsher conditions of belligerency than Islam. Those which do not mention war, however, are dismissed as being unrealistic.

6 Mawdūdī 1930: 106–108.
7 Ibid 109–117.
8 Ibid 117.
9 Ibid 56–57.

Modern Western practices, and especially the laws of warfare now declared as being legally agreed to by powerful nations, are dismissed by him as being subject to change since they are man-made. Interestingly, he defends his practice of comparing actual Oriental and Western practices of warfare with the ideal of Muslim sacred law about the conduct of jihad in which the latter come out as being the more humanitarian.[10] Here he argues that whereas Islamic law is not dependent on the will of Muslims, all secular laws are.[11] This is important since it is precisely this argument he uses to justify the imposition of *sharī'ah* rule over the world as the desiderated ideal.

This, however, was Mawdūdī's first attempt at tackling the problematic concept of jihad especially because it was under attack by European Orientalists, Hindus as well as progressive Muslims and those, like Mirzā Ghulām Aḥmad of Qadian, who were heretics in his eyes. In this book, despite the initial expression of views which justified global jihad, Mawdūdī's overall tone is such that it has been mistaken for being apologetic by Cook in his own book on understanding jihad.[12] However, Cook does point out that Mawdūdī considers the initial wars of conquests by Muslims as wars of civilisation and liberation whereas similar conquests by Western countries, though they too called them wars of civilisation, were described by him as wars of aggression.[13] The deceptively mild tone, he points out, 'was a response to Christian missionary polemic'.[14] Another notable analysis of the same book is by the Islamic scholar Jamal Malik. He begins his article with the metaphorical allusion (said to be based on a hadith) that 'the ink of scholars is holier than the blood of martyrs'. Whether authentic or not, and rather ironically since the hadith gives high value to scholars, this tradition has been used to justify jihad resulting in martyrdom. In the case of Pakistan, Malik points out, 'the constructions of religious leaders and the ideals of martyrs' eventually 'relate to each other'.[15] Mawdūdī is the initiator of constructions which led to his interpretation of Islam as a political doctrine with jihad as its active sustainer. This doctrine, as we shall see, was expressed in ways which are given below.

Soon, therefore, Mawdūdī came up with a more elaborate theory of the Islamic state, which, he argued, was the logical outcome of the philosophy of the Qur'an. In this context, it is useful to study his book, *Qur'ān kī chār*

10 Ibid 200; 536–537.
11 Ibid 200.
12 Cook 2005: 101.
13 Ibid 101.
14 Ibid 102.
15 Malik 2009: 68.

bunyādī iṣtilāḥē. This book concerns four religious concepts: *Ilāh, Rab, 'Ibādat,* and *Dīn* translated as deity, sustainer, worship, and religion, respectively. Mawdūdī, however, gives their Urdu equivalents only to reject them as inadequate to the revolutionary and essentially political message of the Qur'an. *Ilāh* is not just any deity but really means 'One who Rules'. It is associated with complete power.[16] *Rab* is sustainer but in a complete sense so that not accepting any of the orders of this Sustainer and Nourisher, in the sense of thinking that anyone else can or actually does fulfil these functions, is rebellion. *'Ibādat* means to be fully in control; to be a slave and hence refers to obedience in all aspects of life.[17] *Dīn* too refers to the whole system of complete obedience and, hence, has the meaning of accepting the sovereignty of God. Thus, if a religion is purely for God, it means the non-acceptance of all man-made systems of rule. He adds that there is no word which can give the connotation of *Dīn* and the only one which comes near is state but even this is not exactly like it.[18] These meanings, as we can see, lead to the necessity of the rule of the *Sharī'ah* which, obviously, entails a revolutionary view of political life. In short, though Mawdūdī's method is not outwardly revolutionary his conclusions are. And, since political power is his main concern, the establishment of an Islamic state, and jihad, carry great significance in his works.[19] Here, as we can observe, Mawdūdī uses the hermeneutical device of semantic expansion since he gives new meanings to terms originally created for subjective forms of worship. The new meanings expand the semantic range of these expressions, allowing Mawdūdī to construct political interpretations of not only jihad but also belief, worship, and religion itself.

These were the views which Mawdūdī elaborated upon with reference to Quranic verses in his six-volume commentary on the Qur'an, entitled *Tafhīm al-Qur'ān*. It was begun in 1942 when the author was living in Pathankot now in India. Later a large part of it was written when he was incarcerated in Multan jail in 1948. Finally the first volume appeared from Lahore in 1951.[20] The translation is not verbatim nor is the commentary like those of the traditional exegetes who use the *aḥādīth*, historical anecdotes, grammatical subtleties, and supernatural explanations in their interpretations. Mawdūdī, on the other hand, uses his own opinion and other sources, such as the Bible and modern subjects, in his. Despite the *Tafhīm's* focus on traditional concerns such as the observance of religious law and theological concepts, the commentary does have political

16 Mawdūdī 1953: 37.
17 Ibid 121–129.
18 Ibid 153.
19 Mawdūdī 1962: 49–74.
20 Mawdūdī *Tafhīm* Vol.1.

concerns the major one of which is the establishment of an Islamic state. By the time Mawdūdī came to write the *Tafhīm*, his views about jihad had evolved in important ways as Ammār Khān Nāṣir pointed out.[21] Nāṣir argues that, whereas in the 1930s Mawdūdī had defined *fitnah* in terms of morality and rights—oppression, negation of peoples' rights to belief, preventing people from accepting Islam or turning them by force to unbelief, conspiring against the believers by force and fraud, using force against them and domination over them—he now adopted an expanded definition which included the exercise of political power outside the limits laid down by God, i.e. Islam.[22] This is a consequence of the semantic expansion he practised by defining theological concepts politically. Thus, for Mawdūdī, any form of rule, whether Western democracy, communism, fascism, or kingship, is a revolt against this principle and is called *ṭāghūt*. Since it is a central term used not only by Mawdūdī but by all radical Islamists, let us look at Mawdūdī's definition of it with reference to the Qur'an. In his explanation of 2: 256 (there is no compulsion in religion), he says:

> Here *dīn* means the whole social and moral system which God has designed to rule over the world. One who agrees in theory about complying with this system, but does not do so is a wrongdoer (*fāsiq*). One who does not agree with it is an unbeliever (*kāfir*). One who imposes his own will and does not rule according to the laws of God is *taghūt*. If one is a Muslim one will deny this *taghūt* (Commentaries 285 and 286 on 2: 256).

The word *ṭāghūt* occurs in another verse not related to war in *Sūrah al-Zumar* (Q. 39)—there are glad tidings for those who leave false gods (*ṭāghūt*) and turn to Allah (39: 17). In his commentary on this verse, Mawdūdī again defines *ṭāghūt* as a rebellion against God's laws and also calls it the greatest rebellion. In short, in his exegesis of the Qur'an, Mawdūdī lays down the principles of rule which imply fighting those who do not adhere to Islamic laws in governance. However, in his actual political conduct, Mawdūdī never preached jihad against the rulers of Pakistan who were his political opponents. Indeed, when asked whether rulers who had treaties with India were theologically legitimate; and, if not, then why should those treaties be respected, he replied:

> Pakistan's government whether theologically legitimate or not is, after all, elected by Muslims and its governor general has the confidence of 95 per cent Muslims. Whatever such a government does is on behalf of the people and is responsible before the people and God.[23]

---

21 Nasir 2012: 305–340.
22 Ibid 330–331.
23 Mawdūdī 1948: 12.

He did add to this that religious governments should be elected and the people who did not do so would be responsible to God but he never suggested disobedience of the government, a people's war with India for Kashmir or the forceful removal of Pakistan's rulers through an armed revolution.

Thus, despite differentiating between evil conduct (*fitnah*) and non-Islamic forms of rule (*ṭāghūt*), Mawdūdī keeps the argument at the level of ideas. At this level, he very often equates the two concepts with each other. Mawdūdī says that *fitnah* (evil) is defined as rule outside the boundaries and laws laid down by God. His explanation of the verses 8: 39 and 2: 193—which are about the necessity of fighting evil (*fitnah*) till it is eliminated and 'religion is solely for God'—makes it clear that this condition refers not to certain actions or policies which may be called evil, i.e. unjust, oppressive, or cruel, but only to non-Islamic rule. Thus, Mawdūdī points out that after the conquest of Mecca, where a *ṭāghūt* form of rule prevailed, not only really evil persons, such as 'Uqbah bin Abī Mu'īṭ (d. 624) and Naḍar bin Ḥārith (d. 624), were killed, but the form of rule was also changed (here Mawdūdī ignores the controversy regarding the deaths of both which, according to some, occurred at other times). As noted above, he argues that the words *lā ikrahā fī al-dīn* (there is no compulsion in religion (2: 256) and *lakum dīnukum waliya dīn* (to you your religion; to me mine) (109: 6) mean only that diverse belief systems will be tolerated. However, this tolerance does not extend to the exercise of political power. This must always be in the hands of those Muslims who rule according to the Qur'an and the hadith.[24]

Aggressive warfare, then, is a corollary of desiring moral order in the world. This state of international relations is called *Dārul Islām* in which the Islamic state would be established all over the world. Lands outside the ambit of this kind of state are the *Dārul Ḥarb* since they have both *ṭāghūt* and *fitnah*. Muslims must aspire for the imposition of such a moral order even by force till the vanquished live as their dependents and pay the protection tax (*jizyah*). In this context, his commentary on 9: 29 is that non-Muslims, Jews and Christians, have the right merely to exist but not to rule or impose their laws on the world. But to exercise this right they must pay money and accept their inferior status. By way of example, he cites *Sūrah al-Namal* (Q. 27) in which the Queen of Sheba, Bilqīs, is asked to come to the Prophet Sulaimān's court as a 'Muslim'. In his commentary on the verses relating to the incident (27: 29 – 31), he emphasises that Islam offers either conversion or the payment of the *jizyah* along with the loss of the power to rule. He quotes the words of Sulaiman in 27: 37 to the effect that he did not care about the gifts sent by the queen to appease him and that he would attack her

24 *Tafhīm* Vol. 1, Explanation 204 and 205: 151.

land and subdue her and 'disgrace her and render her among the inferiors' (*azil-latun wa hum ṣāghirūn*). In short, aggressive warfare is justified only because the queen and her people do not follow the religion of Sulaiman which, according to Mawdūdī, is Islam.

However, in his commentary on *al-Mumtaḥina* (Q. 60)—the verse instructing Muslims to live in peace and be just to those unbelievers who have not been hostile to them (60: 8)—he takes a softer line. He begins with the same story as given by other exegetes, i.e. about Asmā bint Abū Bakr's taking permission from the Prophet before treating her non-Muslim mother kindly. However, unlike the others (such as Ibn Kathīr), this reference to the occasion of revelation (*asbābul nuzūl*) is not used to specify the verse to those particular people or non-combatants. Instead, Mawdūdī goes on to say that the order not to make friends with the non-Muslims is not because of their beliefs; it is because of their oppression and cruelty. If these are absent, then it is possible to make friends with them. In short, Muslims should discriminate between those with whom they can have friendly relations and others with whom they cannot.[25] Perhaps this view leads Mawdūdī to suggest that treaties and pacts of peace should not be violated at will. Indeed, he gives much importance to them. Thus, a state of peace between Muslim and non-Muslim countries through treaties called *Dārul Ayman* is recognised.[26] However, according to a verse in *al-Anfāl* (Q. 8), it is allowed to break treaties if treachery by the other party is imminently expected (8: 58). Commenting on this verse, Mawdūdī says that in such cases Muslims have to inform their opponents that the treaty is no longer valid. One-sided, sudden attacks without first warning the enemy that treaties are no longer valid are not lawful. If, however, the opponents have already broken the agreement, as in the case of Ḥudaybiyyah, then it is another matter.[27] These interpretations, taken to their logical conclusion, would delegitimise covert attacks emanating from Pakistan (like Kargil). This, indeed, was Mawdūdī's own objection to the covert war Pakistan had resorted to in 1948 in Kashmir. Mawdūdī was asked why he had opposed this war knowing fully well that the people of Pakistan were very sensitive about this issue. He replied that the feelings of the people were not the criteria he used for taking positions. Rather, he used the Qur'an and the hadith for doing so. He then went on to cite 8: 72—telling Muslims that those who have not chosen to migrate to an Islamic polity can only be helped in matters of religion but not against people with whom there is a treaty—to

25 Ibid Vol. 5. Explanation 13: 432.
26 Mawdūdī 1930: 130–149.
27 *Tafhīm* Vol. 2. Explanation 3: 153.

make the point that if Pakistan wanted to fight with India to help the Kashmiris, then it would have to first openly break the treaties between the two countries and then declare open war as 8: 58 orders. Covert operations carried out by troops or non-state actors are not allowed in Islam. He then added that his opinion was first solicited in a private gathering but it was seized upon by newspapers which disseminated it beyond his expectation. Since the subject was hotly debated, Mawdūdī gave an interview about it on 17 August 1948, which was published in *Kauthar*, another publication of the Jamā'at-i-Islāmī.[28] However, the authorities were incensed and Mawdūdī was jailed. In 1965, yet another covert military action by Pakistan which led to an open war with India, General Ayub Khan (1907–1974), president of Pakistan from 1958 till 1969, otherwise an opponent of his ideas, 'publicly appealed to Mawdudi for support in his war against India by declaring a jihad'.[29] This time, however, Mawdūdī did support the government but probably because now there was an open war between the two countries. That this war itself was the Indian response to the kind of covert attack Mawdūdī had condemned in 1948 was either not known to him or, since now things had gone beyond it, he did not think it was sufficient to warrant non-cooperation with the state. Ironically, after Mawdūdī's death, this policy of low intensity covert warfare through non-state actors was endorsed and enthusiastically supported by the Jamā'at-i-Islāmī.

Mawdūdī knew that his views on jihad would be opposed. In order to neutralise such opposition, he meets it headlong by placing it in the mouth of an opponent who says:

> Islam initiates an unending war in the world and imposes the duty of aggressive warfare on the believers because of which Muslims cannot live in peace anywhere. This exposition [by Mawdudi] makes it compulsory for us that we fight not only against all non-Muslim governments but even those Muslim governments which do not impose Islamic restrictions and laws.[30]

To this objection, he replies that non-Islamic beliefs will be tolerated but rules, laws, and conduct would not be. If the latter are not Islamic, they must be forced to be. That is precisely why the state with its immense coercive power must be captured.[31] For Mawdūdī the rules of God must reign supreme and his objection to democracy is that, in theory, the people are sovereign in it.[32]

28 Mawdūdī 1948: 9–13.
29 Nasr 1996: 45.
30 Mawdūdī 1962: 65.
31 Ibid 68.

Like Sayyid Quṭb, Mawdūdī too uses the analytical category of *jāhiliyyat* (Urdu version of *jāhiliyyah*). In his exegesis of the Qur'an, while commenting on *Sūrah al-Aḥzāb* (Q. 33)—which instructs the wives of the Prophet to stay at home and not show their beauty in public, etc. (33: 33)—he uses the word and gives three other instances of its use. In articles written in the nineteen forties and fifties he talks of what can be described as the holistic view of religion. He says that in pre-Islamic, ignorant (*jāhil*) societies, religion was merely an appendage, an annexure to all other activities. It was not the be-all and end-all of existence. The idea that, among other activities, one also performed religious rites or spent some time worshipping the sacred was, according to him, the *jāhiliyyat* view of religion.[33] The Islamic view, on the other hand, is that nothing one did or thought could be outside religion. It was a way of life and covered everything one did, i.e. politics, culture, values, education, relationships, living, dying, inheritance, and so on.[34] This is his definition of *dīn* which we have already explained with reference to his book, *Qur'ān kī chār bunyādī iṣṭilāḥē*. But to impose Islam in its entirety, one needs the power of the state because of which religious people would be failing in their duties if they only confine themselves to leading prayers and performing religious rituals—merely 'appendages' as he dubs them—as *mawlawīs* do in Muslim societies. What is required is the whole worldview and way of life for which 'political Islam' is absolutely essential.[35] Let us now sum up Mawdūdī's explanation of the eight verses of the Qur'an we have been using earlier in the form of a chart.

Table 6

Verse	Commentary by Mawdūdī	Interpretive device
2:190	Those who prevent you forcefully to reform your system of governance and organization of society should be fought (Vol. 1, Explanation 200:149–150).	Semantic expansion/ ideological imperative
2:191	*Fitnah* refers to persecution. Those who impose their ideology upon Muslim reformers should be fought with (Vol. 1, Exp. 202 P. 150–151).	As above
2:193	Refers to acts (persecution) not beliefs. However, governance cannot be based on false beliefs and hence those who have	As above

32 Mawdūdī, *'Islām aur Jumhūriyyat'* [Urdu: Islam and Democracy], *Tarjumān al-Qur'ān*, 20:3 (June 1963). In Ibid 139–140.

33 *Tafhīm* Vol. 4. Explanation 49: 91–92.

34 Ibid Explanation 55 and 56:95.

35 Mawdūdī 1953:143–153.

Table 6 *(Continued)*

Verse	Commentary by Mawdūdī	Interpretive device
	them should be fought with. Here *Fitnah* is ruling in non-Islamic ways. Exp: 204. *Din* means obedience i.e living according to God's rules. This is 'religion being only for God'. Exp 204 & 205 (Vol. 1: 149–151).	
8:39	The governance should be as God orders. Non-Islamic beliefs can, however, be retained (Vol. 2, Exp. 31: 144–145).	As above
8:61	In international relations cowardice is unacceptable but a treaty of peace may be accepted at the enemy's request (Vol. 2, Exp 45 Vol. 2: 156.	Literal meaning with political undertones
9:5	The Arab associationists were to be fought with till they accepted Islam. Exp 6 & 7 do not generalize the verses to all unbelievers but they do say that apostates may be fought with (Vol. 2: 176–177).	Generalization for certain groups
9:29	Non-Muslims should not be allowed to rule but should be protected in lieu of a tax (*jizyah*). *Ṣāghirūn* means 'small' i.e. subordinate in governance (Vol. 2, Exp. 28: 188–189).	Generalization/ ideological imperative
60:8	Friendship with unbelievers in not allowed only if they are hostile but not because of their unbelief (Vol. 5, Exp 13: 433). Refers to the story of Asma's mother but does not specify non-combatants for its application.	Literal meaning

Source: *Tafhīm* 6 Vols.

As we can see, Mawdūdī's major hermeneutical device is his ideological imperative, i.e. that Islam must be politically dominant since God wants the world to be ruled according to the laws of Islam. It is the only system of being and doing which ensures the sovereignty of God hence no other form of rule can be tolerated. Subordinate to this assumption, he uses semantic expansion—which would probably be called semantic manipulation by his critics—giving political meanings to terms normally used in the paradigm of worship and piety.

Although Mawdūdī remained a theoretician throughout his career since the Jamā'at-i-Islāmī never succeeded in obtaining political power, his blueprint of the Islamic state is relevant today since some aspects of it, especially those pertaining to the position of women and their mobility and especially gender segregation, are discussed in detail by Mawdūdī in his book called *Purdah*.[36] Such

36 Mawdūdī 1939. Such views about women, dissidents, and dhimmīs are common in states

laws, in Mawdūdī's opinion, are part of the social contract made by Muslims when they accept Islam and the ideal Muslim state, as he conceives of it, should insist that its citizens should live according to these divine laws. This ideal state is described in his collection of essays entitled *Islāmī Riyāsat.*[37] We have seen above how Mawdūdī starts with the premise that in the Islamic state it is God who is sovereign so 'the evils that arise from the domination of man over man cannot occur in the Islamic system'.[38] This theme is also repeatedly expressed by Quṭb but neither he nor Mawdūdī goes into the practical reality that it is, after all, only human beings who will claim to interpret the will of God. Thus, there is nothing to prevent rulers, under the guise of their own interpretations, from punishing their political opponents on the charge of heresy. This lack of engagement with practicalities of rule is noted by several of his critics as scholars have described.[39] While Mawdūdī's views about women and dissidents are not relevant for this study, his interpretation of the rules about *dhimmīs* is worthy of note since this subject is connected with jihad. He defends the opinion of some medieval jurists that they should be sartorially different from Muslims. However, the reason he adduces is modern since he argues that this is to safeguard the *dhimmīs'* right to their own identity because conquered peoples imitate the lifestyle of their conquerors and lose their identity and pride.[40] Likewise, Muslims too should not look like non-Muslims.[41]

Mawdūdī had several opponents as mentioned earlier. Within his own Jamā'at too, at least one important thinker, Mawlānā Amīn Aḥsan Iṣlāḥi, did not agree with Mawdūdī's interpretation of jihad.[42] In his own eight-volume exegesis of the Qur'an, *Tadabbur al-Qur'ān*, published from 1958 till 1980, Iṣlāḥi gives ideas which are unique but not revolutionary by Mawdūdī's criteria. Iṣlāḥī's exegesis is like Mawdūdī's in certain characteristics: avoidance of quotations from classical exegeses; reasoning instead of adherence to paradigmatic commentaries; careful and parsimonious use of legends and stories about the *asbāb al-nuzūl* so that they do not dominate the meaning of the Qur'an as understood

---

which call themselves Islamic. These are Saudi Arabia, post-revolutionary Iran, Afghanistan under the Taliban, and the Islamic State (Daesh or ISIS). For a discussion of the ideological controversies about such a state, with special relevance to Pakistan, see Ishtiaq Ahmed (1991).

37 Mawdūdī 1962: 320.

38 Adams 1983: 114.

39 Ibid 129–130.

40 Mawdūdī 1962: 485.

41 Ibid 485.

42 Iṣlāḥī, *Tadabbur* 8 Vols. For the internal friction in the Jamā'at which resulted in Iṣlāḥī's leaving it, see Nasr 1994: 28–43.

by the writer; and special attention to semantics and lexicology. The uniqueness of Iṣlāḥī's work is that he analyses the meanings of verses to manifest a coherence of themes. One major difference between Iṣlāḥī and Mawdūdī is that the latter, as we have seen, explains all Qur'anic concepts with reference to politics and power, whereas Iṣlāḥī does not. For instance, *ṭāghūt* is defined by Iṣlāḥī as 'the powers of Satan' and 'evil spirits' while explaining a verse of *al-Nisā* (Q. 4)—which refers to people who, though given part of sacred scripture, now believe in magic and necromancy (4: 51)[43]as well as Satan himself (The believers fight for God and the unbelievers fight in the way of the Satan...).[44] However, on another occasion Iṣlāḥī explains *ṭāghūt* as the negation of 'the Book of God and the Prophet'.[45] For Mawdūdī, as we have seen, it is governance without the *Sharī'ah* as understood by him. Iṣlāḥī, like Mawdūdī, mentions in passing that sovereignty is the right of God and that this implies obedience of the Prophet but this is in the context of people appealing to the courts of the Jews. The verse 4: 60—the hypocrites go for judgments (in disputes) to false deities when they have been ordered to abandon them altogether—implies lack of faith in the Prophet as the adjuticator appointed by God.[46] Iṣlāḥī, however, does not extend this to contemporary political systems and the necessity of the Islamic state. Let us summarise the ideas of Iṣlāḥī in the form of a chart below.

Table 7

Verse	Commentary by Iṣlāḥī	Interpretive device
2:190	Permission to fight a defensive war (Vol. 1: 475).	Literal meaning
2:191	This order is for those who turned people away from their religion by force (*fitnah*) (Vol. 1: 475).	Specification
2:193	Fight to end religious persecution so tha the Ka 'aba is in Muslim hands who will worship God as He intends. This is connected with 9: 5 below. The main idea is that these verses are only about the Arab polytheists of that period and cannot be taken to be a general order to fight others (Vol. 1: 475).	Ideological imperative/ specification
8:39	*Fitnah* (persecution) should come to an end. In the precincts of the Ka'bah (*haram*), which Abraham constructed so that God could be worshipped, only Islam should remain (Vol. 3: 66).	As above

43 *Tadabbur* Vol. 2: 86. While explaining 4: 48–52.
44 Ibid 109. While explaining 4: 76.
45 Ibid 98. While explaining 4: 60–63.
46 Ibid 101. While explaining 4: 63–65.

Table 7 *(Continued)*

Verse	Commentary by Iṣlāḥī	Interpretive device
8:61	If peace is offered, it should be accepted. Real peace was not expected from the Quraish but even so, offers of peace were to be honoured even at the risk of betrayal of trust (Vol. 3: 94–95).	Literal meaning
9:5	Kill the polytheist Arabs giving no quarter. This was God's way (*Sunnāh Ilāhiah*) so these orders are specifically meant for the Arab polytheists. Thus Muslims are not to fight anyone except in defence (Vol. 3: 13–131).	Ideological imperative/ specification
9:29	Since the People of the Book or that period had deviated from the orders of God's and denied the Prophet they had to be fought with till they were defeated and accepted Muslim rule as subjects (Vol. 3: 150). However, *jizyah* could only be taken from those who had fought the Muslims not those who had entered into a contract with them (Vol. 3: 151).	As above
60:8	Those who have not been hostile can be treated justly and kindly. The operational word is *tawallī* (friendship) which is not permitted with those who have been hostile (Vol. 7: 334–335).	Semantic analysis/ literal meaning

Source: *Tadabbur* 8 Vols.

Iṣlāḥī's ideological assumptions are: that jihad is only defensive nowadays; that the Arab polytheists were a special case who were eliminated by God (*Sunnāh Ilāhiah*); that this case is specific to the polytheists of that period and is, therefore, not to be used to justify aggressive jihad nowadays. Also, the taking of *jizyah* does not apply to non-Muslims who have not been defeated in war. For instance, if non-Muslims are already living in a Muslim state—as was the case of Pakistan in 1947—then this is no longer applicable. Instead, treaties can be made with them and they may be offered the same terms of citizenship as Muslim citizens.[47] Iṣlāḥī emphatically adheres to traditional restrictions on warfare even for defensive purposes: i.e., sufficiency of military power and permission of the Islamic ruler. He uses his explanation of 60: 8 (advocating living in peace and justice with non-belligerent non-Muslims) to argue that Muslim countries can live in peace with friendly countries and only their leaders are allowed to make decisions about military action; not non-state actors or individuals. Nor, he adds, have private persons any right to undermine, compromise, or negate

47 *Tadabbur* Vol. 3: 151. While explaining 9: 29.

these international arrangements. This may be a reference to pro-peace initiatives of groups in Pakistan towards India, but it also rules out the concept of using non-state actors to pursue aggressive policies as well as rebellion in the name of Islam against the state. More importantly, unlike Mawdūdī, Iṣlāḥī never makes the establishment of the Islamic state all over the world an ethical and ideological imperative. Nor does he make jihad a necessary instrument of it. References to the Islamic state, though interspersed throughout his exegesis, do not amount to anything but a vague, romanticised ideal. In short, Iṣlāḥī is not the inspiration for worldwide Islamic revolution which Mawdūdī is. This aspect of Mawdūdī's thought is covered very ably by Asif Iftikhar who compares his views with those of Iṣlāḥī's school, especially with the views of Jāwēd Aḥmad Ghāmidī, as well as Waḥīduddīn Khān in India, who is yet another scholar who broke away from Mawdūdī.[48] Khān's views about jihad will be discussed later but his refutation of Mawdūdī's thought is mentioned below.

Mawdūdī has also been criticised by scholars of Islam, such as Mawlānā Abū'l Ḥasan 'Alī Nadwī and Waḥīduddīn Khān,both major Islamic scholars from India, for defining key concepts such as *Ilāh, Rabb, 'Ibādah,* and *Dīn* as political and analytical constructs.[49] Nadwī, in his book *'Aṣr-i ḥāḍir mē̃ dīn kī tafhīm-o-tashrīḥ,*[50] claims that Mawdūdī's exegesis 'presents a new interpretation of Islam and Qur'an on which the political aspect became dominant' (*us nē Islām ō Qur'ān kī ēk nayī tafsīr kā namūnah pēsh kiyā jis par siyāsī rang ghālib ā gayā*). In short, claims Nadwī, Mawdūdī wants a theocracy.[51] Waḥīduddīn Khān agrees with this opinion in his book, *Ta'bīr kī ghalaṭī,*[52] which attempts to demolish Mawdūdī's political interpretation of Islam through semantics. Khān also wrote an exegesis of the Qur'an as mentioned earlier. Let us now take both publications one by one. In *Ta'bīr kī ghalaṭī,* he points out that whereas Mawdūdī makes the four analytical constructs mentioned above coterminous with Muslim political dominance, they actually refer to the realm of worship. He quotes not only verses of the Qur'an but also the most famous exegetes of the classical era to support his argument. *Fitnah,* he says, does not refer to associating other powers with God (*shirk*), it derives from 'making hot' (*tapānā*), which is a metaphor for putting someone through a hard test. The term came to be used for cruelty, oppression, and disbelief. However, he goes on to argue

---

48 Iftikhar 2004.
49 For a comparison of the use of these words in Mawdūdī and Khān.
See Ibid 23–33.
50 Nadwī, A. 1978.
51 Ibid 15.
52 Khān, W. 1963.

that the order to fight the unbelievers was specifically meant for the Arab polytheists and cannot be extended to others.[53] In short, Mawdūdī builds his whole intellectual edifice justifying war against the world, provided one is sufficiently powerful, on heterodox and inauthentic foundations. While Mawdūdī uses semantic expansion to give new meanings to words used traditionally for worship, Khān reverses this by using the same hermeneutical device to revert to the more traditional meanings of the terms. The main points of his exegesis are summed up in the form of a chart below.

Table 8

Verse	Commentary by Waḥīduddīn Khān	Interpretive device
2:190	Only defensive war is permitted. Moreover, when the enemy stops aggression so should Muslims (Vol. 1: 80).	Literal meaning
2:191	War was a response to the aggression of the Quraish. However, Arabia was a special case since it had to be reserved for Islam. Thus Arab polytheism (*fitnah*) had to be removed by all out war (Vol. 1: 81).	Ideological imperative/ specification
2:193	War should continue with the Arab polytheists till Arabia is purely for Islam. This order is restricted to the Arab polytheists only (Vol. 1: 81).	As above
8:39	*Fitnah* (persecution) should come to an end. In the special case of Arabia, *fitnah* was also the sin of associating other powers with God. Hence, in the precincts of the Ka 'aba (*haram*), which Abraham constructed so that God could be worshipped, only Islam should remain (Vol. 1: 446).	As above
8:61	If the enemy inclines to peace, so should Muslims. Muslims should have such military power as should deter aggression but war should be avoided (Vol. 1: 455).	Literal meaning
9:5	Kill the polytheist Arabs giving no quarter. This was God's way (*Sunnāh Ilāhiah*) and such orders are addressed to prophets only. These orders are specifically meant for the Arab polytheists. Thus Muslims are not to fight anyone except in defence (Vol. 1: 463–464).	Ideological imperative/ specification
9:29	The Jews had been hostile to Islam and its prophet. That is why they had to be fought with till they were defeated and accepted Muslim rule as subjects by paying *jizyah*. Except for the	As above

53 Ibid 112–114.

Table 8 *(Continued)*

Verse	Commentary by Waḥīduddīn Khān	Interpretive device
	Arab polytheists of that period, other groups could exist by paying this tax. (Vol. 1: 473–474).	
60:8	God does not stop Muslims from being kind and just to those who did not fight them nor expelled them from their homes. However, those who committed these excesses or abetted them in doing so, are not to be befriended (Vol. 2: 690).	Literal meaning

Source: Khān, W *Tazkīr* 2 Vols.

As we can see, Waḥīduddīn Khān's special theory, or ideological imperative, is that if a group of people do not accept guidance from a prophet especially sent to reform them, then God himself destroys them (*Sunnah Ilāhiah*). In his exegesis, he explains his ideas about jihad with reference to the *asbābul nuzūl* of the verses. This allows him to use the hermeneutical device of specification so that, except for the specific group of the Arab polytheists, no other group is to be fought with. Otherwise, jihad is only defensive and in proportion to the aggression. The norm should be peaceful co-existence with non-Muslim nations, though preparation for war to deter aggression is always necessary. If this has not happened in history, it is the fault of individual Muslim decision-makers but not that of Islam as a religion. The same hermeneutical device—restricting jihad to a particular age and people with reference to the reasons of the verse's revelation—is also used while explaining 2: 217—which says that, in the sacred months, killing is bad but expelling people from their homes and preventing them from rightful worship and disbelief is even worse. This, he argues, was for the initial period of Islam 'but in the contemporary world this is not necessary'.[54] As for 9: 29, the verse about fighting the People of the Book, he effectively glosses over it, thus deemphasising it. Indeed, he merely confines himself to the statement that the defeated People of the Book should give *jizyah* with their hands. Like Shiblī and others, he translates *sāghirūn* as *chōṭē* (small), i.e. 'they should live like subordinates' (*chōṭē ban kē rahẽ*).[55] On the whole, he makes it clear that he interprets Islam as recommending a peaceful relationship of mutual amity between nation-states.

While Waḥīduddīn Khān, a major critic of Mawdūdī before the September 11 attacks, did not focus on him afterwards, his other critics persisted in demolish-

54 Khān, W. *Tazkīr* Vol. 1: 92.
55 Ibid 473.

ing his views even in the contemporary period when the radical Islamist militants were attacking Pakistan as well as India in the decade beginning in 2005. At that time, the monthly *Al-Sharī'ah* published a special issue on jihad (1 March 2012) which contained some such writings. Among them, the work of Yaḥyā Nu'mānī refutes the theories of Mawdūdī which, in his opinion, allow an aggressive stance in international relations. He begins by saying that there are three views about jihad. First, that it is against unbelief (*kufr*); second, that it is against the government of unbelievers not unbelief itself; and third, that it is purely defensive. He concedes that classical thinking on jihad seems to suggest that peace is to be made only if unbelievers are not allowed to rule anywhere in the world. For Mawdūdī, as we have seen earlier, rule by anyone except good Muslims is the rule of *ṭāghūt* and jihad should be undertaken against it if Muslims are militarily capable of it.

Nu'mānī, however, presents arguments against Mawdūdī's views with reference to general Quranic principles as well as particular interpretations of specific verses. One general principle is that perpetual warfare conflicts with the Quranic commandment of preferring peace over war. In this context, he refers to *al-Anfāl* (Q. 8), arguing that in some of its verses Muslims are exhorted to fight against their antagonists and yet, in the middle of this, they are also told to incline to peace if the enemy is thus inclined (8: 61). This follows the order to create a credible military deterrent (8: 60), so that such desire for peace is not a consequence of weakness but follows from a genuine preference for it. Another argument, again from a principle, is that the aim of jihad is not the elimination of unbelief but only the deterrence of aggression. Islam supports freedom and justice which implies that Muslims cannot take away the right to rule from anyone without just cause.

Nu'mānī then takes up Mawdūdī's use of interpretative devices. For instance, Mawdūdī justifies Muslim rule over the world by the device of semantic expansion, i.e. giving new meanings to terms. He points out that Mawdūdī uses the terms *fitnah* and *fasād* for all actions defined as sins in Islam (drinking, fornication, etc.). If this meaning is accepted, the order to end *fitnah* and *fasād* becomes an order to end all forms of rule other than by those Muslims who enforce the *sharī'ah*.[56] Such a doctrine would allow perpetual war, as was resorted to by the Kharijites in the early period of Islam. This 'neo-Khariji' outlook, as some of the *'ulamā* call it, was emphatically refuted by them.[57] Nu'mānī then takes up the device of *naskh* used by radical Islamists. He argues that Mawdūdī was

56 Nu'mānī, Y 2012: 34–35.
57 Nasr 1996: 114.

much admired by Quṭb who said that verse 8: 61— advocating peace if the enemy so wishes—had been abrogated by 9: 5 which advocates aggressive war. He argues that such abrogation of the peaceful verses was merely asserted but could not be proved. Further, Nu'mānī, like Waḥīduddīn Khān and many others, also uses the hermeneutical device of specifying the verse to Arab polytheists who were aggressors and had a record of breaking treaties.[58] Similarly, the orders for taking the poll tax from the People of the Book and humiliating them in 9: 29 are to be understood in the context of the then ongoing conflict with the Byzantine Empire. Nu'mānī explains the use of the word *ṣāghirūn* (small ones; humiliated ones) as merely those who accept the rule of someone else.[59] Finally, he takes up the case of the medieval scholars whose predominant view was that jihad should be pursued against non-Muslim states. This is explained by reference to the specific historical circumstances of the period in which those scholars formulated their doctrines. He argues that in that age, states were based on religious and racial intolerance. Hence, they were in perpetual conflict with each other. The message of Islam could not be disseminated under such conditions. Now that it can be, there is no need for armed conflict.[60]

In the same publication, 'Ammār Nāṣir, whom we have mentioned earlier, also points out that Mawdūdī's contention that the war with the polytheists of Arabia was because they had transgressed (*fitnah*) against the Muslims was wrong because many tribes remained friendly, broke no treaties, and never initiated hostilities. Yet, they were not allowed to live in Arabia unless they converted to Islam. This is not explained if Mawdūdī's original definition of *fitnah* as transgression or persecution is accepted. It is only comprehensible if the definition of the classical interpreters of jihad—that it was against unbelief—is accepted. Mawdūdī did accept the view that jihad was, indeed, against all Arabs when he wrote the *Tafhīm*,[61] but then he explained this with reference to the necessity of making Arabia an Islamic state. In short, the order in 9: 5 became a political rather than a religious requirement.[62] This political explanation of jihad, implies Nāṣir, is not warranted by the meanings of the verses in question. However, despite his critique, Nāṣir finally concludes that those who think that Mawdūdī's thought about jihad is similar to Quṭb's are mistaken. Though there are some superficial parallels between the two, Mawdūdī is much more profound, hence, much more in touch with abiding rather than contingent political issues.

58 Y. Nu'mānī 2012: 21–33.
59 Ibid 58.
60 Ibid 42.
61 Nasir 2012: 329.
62 Ibid 330.

Quṭb, on the other hand, responds to the politics of Egypt and hence is far less philosophically sophisticated.[63] Coming from a theological opponent, this was high praise indeed.

It is also relevant to present the views of Ghulām Aḥmad Parwēz (1903–1985), who remain a vocal critic of Mawdūdī's ideas. He was born in Gurdaspur, presently in India, and worked in the civil service till his retirement in 1952. Later, he moved to Pakistan. His views on some issues have been mentioned before but here the focus will be on his exegesis of the Quranic verses about jihad. In a major study of his work, Sheila Mc Donough argues that Parwēz is a revolutionary modernist influenced by Sir Sayyid and Iqbāl but he is less concerned with spirituality or personal worship than creating a political system of authority which is meant to end economic and social exploitation though at the cost of making education a tool of propaganda and eliminating dissent.[64] While some of his political ideas at first glance seem to overlap with those of his major adversary, Mawdūdī, in the final analysis, Parwēz has more in common with the modernists. Since the nature of the state was intensely discussed during the early years of Pakistan, both Parwēz and Mawdūdī appealed to the educated middle class—albeit to different sections of it: Parwēz to the Western-oriented, middle and upper-middle classes; Mawdūdī to the vernacular-educated, lower-middle, petty businessman. Both take the Qur'an as their basic source of religious interpretation. Parwēz, however, rejects the hadith while Mawdūdī uses it selectively. Parwēz's organisation, *Ṭulū'-i-Islām* (the dawn of Islam)—the title having been taken from a poem of Iqbāl[65]—is still functioning and keeps publishing and reprinting his numerous works in Urdu and in English, many of them translations of the Urdu works.

Surprisingly, Sheila Mc Donough does not touch upon Parwēz's interpretation of jihad in her thesis, though Parwēz has given attention to it not only in his exegesis of the Qur'an but also in other writings. For instance, one of his pamphlets is entitled *Jihād* and the sub-title says: *It's true meaning in the light of the Qur'ān.* The words of the sub-title are significant and are repeated in his exegesis of the first fifteen chapters of the Qur'an entitled *Maṭālib al-Furqān* (in seven volumes) and sub-titled: the meaning of the Qur'an from the Qur'an itself (*Qur'ān Majīd kī tafsīr khūd Qur'ān sē*).[66] This exclusive mention of the Qur'an is important because Parwēz is a denier of the hadith. He mentions in his book on the subject (as well as in his exegesis) that there is only one collec-

---

63 Ibid 340.
64 Mc Donough 1963.
65 Ibid 4.
66 Parwēz *Maṭālib* 7 Vols.

tion of *aḥādīth* from the first century called the *Ṣaḥīfā Ḥamām ibn Munabbih* and it has only 138 *aḥādīth*. Ibn Munabbih was a student of Abū Hurayrah (603–681) and he (Munabbih) died in 101/719. So, questions Parwēz, how is it that the Iran-born compilers of the six canonical collections of hadith, who lived about two hundred years later, had thousands of *aḥādīth* to choose from? His answer is that they were mostly invented to suit the requirements of the period.[67] When the laws of Pakistan were being brought into conformity with the Qur'an and the hadith in the 1980s, he agreed with using the Qur'an as a criterion but rejected the use of the hadith.[68] Indeed, he argues that most of the incredible stories in the exegeses of the medieval exegetes are based on legends which were recorded in the collections of the *aḥādīth*. Hence, to get an authentic view of Islam one should not refer to them.

In his pamphlet on jihad, Parwēz begins with the sanctity of human life (as does Mawdūdī of whom he is otherwise highly critical). He then declares that it is Western propaganda to call Islam an aggressive religion. Parwēz, like Mawdūdī and Āzād to name two other famous exegetes, uses semantic expansion as an interpretative device. About this Aziz Ahmad says:

> In dressing up modern concepts in Qur' ānic terminology he develops a fantastic exegetical *lexique technique*. *Rabb* (God the Provider) also signifies to him a universal divine law of *rubūbiyyat*, which is the development of the latent faculties of a creature of God. The entire terminology of the Qur'ān is thus given a far-fetched meaning and interpretation to suit the political or economic requirements of present-day Islamic society.[69]

Thus, he distinguishes between *madhhab* and *dīn*, both of which are translated as religion. For him, however, the former is merely a set of beliefs while the latter is a complete way of life of which beliefs about the hereafter and worship are a subset. Islam, he argues, is a *dīn*. This means that it aims to establish the rule of God upon earth. There is no separation of religion and politics and the worship of God is merely the creation of conditions where God's word is obeyed in full. And that is where power comes in – since a state where God rules through His word, requires power to establish it. All other forms of rule are the rule of *ṭāghūt*. This is similar to Mawdūdī's concept of rule. Parwēz's definition of *Rubūbiyyat* again brings him in harmony with Mawdūdī since both believe in 'parmanent values' which 'cannot be vested in man, even in the prophets' and these values

67 Parwēz 1953.

68 Ibid Vol. 4: 176. Explaining Q. 3: 92–93.

69 Ahmad 1967: 227.

come from *rubūbiyya*.[70] In his exegesis, Parwēz defines *ṭāghūt* as 'transgressing boundaries and rebelling against God's laws'.[71] So far, his ideas seem astonishingly similar to those of Mawdūdī. However, he stops short of initiating warfare to establish the rule of God all over the world. In his case it seems to be only a theoretical ideal not translatable into action at least in the present circumstances. Thus, in his exegesis he lays down the following reasons for war:
1. To defend one's Muslim government and land.
2. To help oppressed Muslims everywhere.
3. To save humans from the violence unleashed in anarchy anywhere.
4. To safeguard the religious freedom of everyone (including non-Muslims).[72]

The last can lead to aggressive warfare if it is taken to its logical conclusion but Parwēz denies the train of this logic. Let us take the main points of Parwēz's interpretations of the verses below.

Table 9

Verse	Commentary by Ghulām Aḥmad Parwēz	Interpretive device
2:190	Only fight those who fight you (Vol. 3:324).	Literal meaning
2:191	*Fitnah* is cruelty and persecution so it may be resisted by force in case the enemy does not respect international treaties (Vol. 3:325).	Semantic expansion
2:193	Fight till oppression (*fitnah*) ends and everyone is free to follow any religion (Vol. 3: 325). It does not mean forcing people to accept Islam.	As above
8:39	Fight till people are free to accept whatever religion they want (Vol. 6: 119).	As above
8:61	Incline towards peace since the aim is to end *fitnah* and if this can happen peacefully it is to be welcomed (Vol. 6: 145).	Literal meaning
9:5	Those who do not live as peaceful citizens should be fought with. Others–Muslims or non-Muslims–can live in peace. The order to 'kill wherever found' only refers to war according to rules. Nowadays there is no need for an Islamic state as one can practice Islam in peace anywhere (Vol. 6: 166–169).	Ideological imperative/ specification

70 Ibid 231.
71 *Maṭālib* Vol. 3: 441.
72 Ibid Vol. 6: 192. These ideas are elaborated upon in Parwēz 1967.

Table 9 *(Continued)*

Verse	Commentary by Ghulām Aḥmad Parwēz	Interpretive device
9:29	Islam allows war for (a) defence (b) to help the oppressed (c) to prevent anarchy in order to protect human values (d) to ensure religious freedom for all. *Jizyah* is a small tax to protect those who have lost the war and accepted Islam's governance (Vol. 6: 191–198).	Ideological imperative
60:8	Parwēz died before completing this part.	

Source: *Matālib* 7 vols.

Parwēz, like other modernists, also believes that jihad is not aggressive. This ideological imperative enables him to use specification to restrict the application of verses to the hostile Arabs of the seventh century, thus making peaceful coexistence of Muslims with others possible nowadays. While explaining individual verses, he asserts that it is our exegetes who have argued that Islam supports eternal warfare with non-Muslims. In his own commentary on 2: 190; 191 and 193, he criticises Mawdūdī's explanation of 8: 39 saying that he (Mawdūdī) interprets this verse (fight till *fitnah* [hurdles in religious freedom] ends and religion is all for God) as eternal warfare. This, he says, is wrong and such views give a bad image of Islam.[73]

However, he does not agree with the quietism of his namesake, Mirzā Ghulām Aḥmad whom he takes pains to refute at length saying that jihad, which includes fighting, has not been abolished. He also refutes Christian, Hindu, Buddhist, and Jewish ideas of war saying that it is unnatural not to retaliate and that, in fact, both Hinduism and Judaism allow and actually promote war. However, it is his view that jihad is defensive which brings him ideologically closer to the modernists than his contemporary and nemesis, Mawdūdī. But Parwēz is also similar to Mawdūdī in that he is not in favour of democracy nor does he believe in giving non-Muslims key positions in the state.[74] He does, however, believe in peaceful coexistence with non-Muslim states under treaties.

Parwēz's thought has several strands. Like other modernists, he seeks room for reinterpretation by invoking the rationalism of the Mutazilites;[75] the idea that any particular *sharī'ah* (code of laws) was not valid for all ages; that the *'ulamā* are not the sole custodians of religious interpretation; and that the verses of the

73 Ibid Vol. 3: 267–270.
74 *Maṭālib* Vol. 3: 424–425 and Vol. 4: 194. Explaining Q. 3: 117.
75 Mc Donough 1963: 6.

Qur'an can be interpreted as allegories (thus, like Sir Sayyid, Parwēz too takes angels, the devil, hell, heavens, and Adam to be metaphors, allegories, and myths).[76] He believes in dynamism and change, like the modernists Iqbāl and Sir Sayyid, but his theory of rule brings him close to Mawdūdī's concept of the Islamic state. Parwēz would establish the 'Caliphate on earth'. About the tyranny this envisages it is best to quote Sheila McDonough:

> Parwēz fails to understand authentic modernism because he retains the medieval belief that a particular system is possible and necessary. He rejects that particular system which is expressed in the books of *fiqh*, but he replaces it by another system. In doing so, he changes direction, but does not really advance.[77]

Parwēz's advocacy of totalitarianism—very much part of Marxist rule then prevalent in large parts of the world—and condemnation of all systems of thought other than his own, place him more in the authoritarian tradition of the *'ulamā* than that of the modernists he professes to draw his inspiration from. This makes him something of a complex and eclectic thinker who is not easily categorised, though he is clearly not in favour of Mawdūdī's revivalist ideas which formed the theoretical background of Quṭb's more militant interpretations of jihad. Perhaps, one reason for this emphasis on politics in both popular modernism (Parwēz), revivalism (Mawdūdī), and radical Islamist discourses (Quṭb) is because all of them responded to the political power of the West and the governance of rulers inspired by Western, rather than Islamic, notions of rule. Mawdūdī, as Asif Iftikhar points out, interpreted 'tradition as well as modernity on the basis of preconceived ideology' (called 'ideological imperative' in this study).[78] Parwēz did the same. But Parwēz, like Sir Sayyid before him, was condemned as a heretic by the traditional *'ulamā* because, unlike Mawdūdī, he deviated from orthodoxy in manifest ways whereas Mawdūdī employed the orthodox idiom though he gave new meanings to it. The more perceptive *'ulamā* did oppose Mawdūdī. However, for them, Parwēz's thought is 'nothing more than a re-appearance of the ancient heresy by which individuals claimed the right to possess secret knowledge of the true meaning of the Qur'an'.[79]

While Parwēz's clientele has dwindled in the last several decades as Pakistan has taken a turn to more literal and scriptural interpretations of Islam, Maw-

76 Ibid 159.
77 Ibid 265.
78 Iftikhar 2004: 48.
79 Mc Donough, 1963: 257. The book *Fatāwā* (1962) against Parwēz has been ably summed up in English and has been cited from Mc Donough 239–244.

dūdī's has not. The latter has his enthusiastic and diehard supporters in Pakistan and abroad. His works did inspire many Muslims, including but not exclusively, militant ones. He is acknowledged by name by Quṭb in his exegesis of the Qur'an. Both Quṭb's works and his were read in Islamist circles in Afghanistan in the sixties and seventies.[80] They were also read in Algeria in the eighties by Islamist intellectuals who formed the Front Islamique du Salut (FIS).[81] His followers are part of the British Muslim scene also. The UK Islamic Mission (UKIM) was created in 1962 and now has educational institutions offering BA and MA degrees in Islamic studies.[82] Although the UKIM has been praised for interfaith work, an undercover agent in a Birmingham mosque reported much hostility for British culture from the local preachers. One Saudi-trained preacher went so far as to declare a war against British political institutions by saying: 'Everywhere, King, Queen, House of Commons...if you accept it then you are part of it. You don't accept it. But you have to dismantle it... so, you being a Muslim you have to fix a target'.[83]

But does this influence translate into the creation of the present-day terrorist organisations, radicalised 'lone wolves', and even states which carry out 'jihad' against the world? This question is too complex to be answered. When Mariam Jameela, born in a Jewish American family and named Margaret Marcus (1934–2012), who later converted to Islam and came to live with Mawdūdī, was asked such a question by her biographer Deborah Baker she answered as follows:

> 'I have never preached violence,' she said, punctuating her insistence with high-pitched 'ooo, no, no, oooo, no, no'. I wrote only on a philosophical plane,' she said.[84]

But when and how ideas on the philosophical plane influence people to such a degree that they are ready to die and kill for them? This we may not know for certain but we do know that they do, and Mawdūdī and Quṭb were powerful influences upon radical Islamist thought in the contemporary era irrespective of the differences between them and their actual meanings. However, the influence of theoreticians is one factor as far as human behaviour is concerned. There are others such as the influence of peers; the frustration caused by one's personal or social circumstances and so on. It is because of this plurality and uncertainty of

80 Burke 2003: 201.
81 Ibid 201.
82 Bowen 2014: 85–86.
83 Ibid 92.
84 Baker 2011: 203.

possible motivations for behaviour that one cannot pinpoint one factor to the exclusion of others.

We may conclude with Vali Nasr's words that Mawdūdī's Islamic revivalism 'purported to give Muslims a new identity rooted in an interpretive reading of Islam'.[85] And, in response to the continued domination of the West, revivalism spread all over the Muslim world albeit creating a globalised Islam[86] of which jihad is a part. Thus, while Mawdūdī may not have permitted the kind of global warfare in the name of Islam we are witnessing, he is theoretically connected with it.

85 Nasr 1996: 124.
86 Roy 2004.

8 Radical Imports

The historian Faisal Devji makes the point that global jihad is placed in 'the genealogy of something called global Islam' with its ancestry traced to Middle Eastern movements of the modern period. However, jihad takes place in Chechniya, Pakistan, India, and the Phillipines so it is also the other way round with Arab fighters returning from such places founding new jihad movements. The Taliban, including Mulla Omar, used local and mystical (*ṣūfī*) themes.[1] This chapter traces the history of jihad in Pakistan from the Middle East. However, Devji's point that there are local inputs into jihad movements is well taken and the next chapter is devoted to them. As for the genesis of certain ideas in the Middle East, there is no denying this though, here too, it will be pointed out, there were South Asian intellectual inputs. This chapter then looks at ideas from the Middle East justifying acts of violence by non-state actors under the umbrella term of jihad. Perhaps the major radical idea about jihad which has been imported from the Middle East is that it is incumbent upon individual Muslims and non-state actors to fight against their rulers if the latter fail to implement Islamic rule.[2] To understand the birth of this idea, it may be useful to look at the political situation of the Middle East during the colonial era.

According to Francois Burgat, the Arab response to colonialism is divisible into three phases. In the first phase, the endogenous culture was used to resist the coloniser and an intellectual response, based on reformism with appeal to Islam, was adduced. In the second, which continued from independence till the 1990s, the indigenous elites in power were critiqued for being like the Western ones they had replaced. Moreover, despite the sloganeering about freedom and rights, these elites were highly repressive. In the third phase, the Islamist rebellion, fed on internal coercion and legitimised by the Israeli violence against Palestinians, the ethnic cleansing of Muslims in Bosnia, and the attacks on Muslim lands such as Afghanistan etc., used the diction of jihad.[3] The Muslim Brotherhood (*Ikhwān al-Muslimīn*), were born under these circumstances. They were dubbed as neo-Kharijites in a bid to discredit them in religious terms by the Egyptian government.[4] Their role in Egyptian politics is discussed at length by Kenny in his book entitled *Muslim Rebels*.[5] But Islamist radicalism is not con-

1 Devji 2011: 317–18.
2 Wiktorowicz 2011: 273–279.
3 Burgat 2011.
4 Kenny 2006: 1–16
5 Ibid 2006.

https://doi.org/10.1515/9783110716986-011

fined to Egypt and in this chapter we will see how the ideas of some of its theoreticians, mostly from Egypt but also from some other Arab countries, came to influence South Asia in general and Pakistan and Afghanistan in particular.

Out of these thinkers, let us first look at Ḥasan Aḥmad 'Abdur Raḥmān Muḥammad al-Bannā (1906–1949) and Sayyid Quṭb (1906–1966). Both were perhaps the most influential theoreticians of political Islam in the modern world outside of South Asia. Bannā's biographical details, the conditions of Egypt during the development of his ideas, and the ideas themselves have been elaborated upon by many scholars.[6] He was born in 1906 and eventually became a school teacher. The Muslim Brotherhood was formed in 1928 or 1929 and soon his preaching started influencing people. He was one of the earliest politically oriented Islamists with the belief that he could bring about a form of governance consistent with Islam. Bannā's views about jihad evolved and he modified them according to circumstances. In the 1930s, he said 'that Muslims should honor non-believers and should not fight them, unless they wage religious war on the believers'.[7] Later, he responded to the foreign occupation of Egypt with 9: 29—the verse about fighting the 'People of the Book'—interpreting it to mean fighting imperialism. However, he was still cautious because of the law banning paramilitary organisations since he stipulated that Muslims were to 'act justly in wars against infidels'.[8] Thus, at that time he did not suggest that the only solution to the woes of Egypt, or Muslims, was war as his five tracts originally called *Majmū'āt risā'il al-imām al-shahīd Ḥasan al-Bannā*, indicate.[9] At that time, the waves of nationalism and Arabism were sweeping the world. Bannā condemned both on the grounds that they were the 'revival of the customs of a pagan age',[10] thus anticipating Mawdūdī and Quṭb's ideas of *jāhilīyyah* which were to become so prominent in radical Islamist thought later. Another idea which became common in this kind of thinking was the use of force to impose Islam on the world. Bannā declared that Muslims were 'chosen' for this purpose and called them 'monks by night and knights by day'.[11] In order to give an interpretation of jihad which allows aggressive warfare, he begins by attacking Muslims who gave an 'allegorical interpretation' or avoided this duty on other grounds.[12] He also argues that the hadith that fighting is the lesser jihad while

6 Mitchell 1969; Kramer 2010; Levy 2014; Esposito 2002: 52–62.
7 Levy 2014: 148.
8 Ibid 154.
9 Wendell 1978.
10 Ibid 53.
11 Ibid 81.
12 Ibid 83.

self-improvement is the greater one is weak and, hence, one cannot hide behind it to evade the duty of fighting (for details of this hadith see Annexure C).[13] In the tract on 'Jihād',[14] he gives his detailed views on the subject. He supports them with Quranic verses, thirty one *aḥadīth*, and extracts from the four traditional schools of Islamic law. He quotes from a book of legal opinion called *Majma'al-anhar fī sharḥ multaqa'l-abḥur* (the collection of rivers to explain the forum of sailing) with approval:

> It [*Jihād*] is initiated by us as a communal obligation, that is, it is obligatory on us to begin fighting with them [unbelievers] after transmitting the invitation (to embrace Islam), even if they do not fight against us. It is incumbent on the Imām to send a military expedition to the Dār al-Ḥarb every year one or two times, and it is incumbent on the subject populace to aid him.[15]

Later, in a combination of anti-colonial sentiment and the idiom if Islam, he says that in his time Muslims were ruled by non-Muslims, 'their lands have been trampled over, and their honor besmirched' because of which jihād has become 'an individual obligation' (*farḍul 'ayn*).[16] These two ideas—first, jihad is to ensure that God's sovereignty is acknowledged by the whole world; and, second, that in the modern age of Western ascendancy, jihad has become mandatory for all Muslims—are to be found in the works of all radical Muslim thinkers. Bannā, like most other modern Islamists, combines some themes of modernity—while vehemently condemning its secularism and individualism leading to sexual promiscuity—with his interpretation of Islam. For instance, he constructed '*waṭaniyya* (patriotism) and *qawmiyya* (nationalism) as two Islamic virtues' defining them with reference to faith rather than geography.[17] This made defending Muslim lands a duty for all Muslims.

Bannā's thought was disseminated systematically even during his lifetime. As his style was journalistic, his prose was very accessible unlike that of the clerics which was full of jargon and allusions to learned works not known to the youth. Gudrun Krämer, one of the biographers of Bannā, tells us that his '*Risalat al-Jihād* was required reading for' the participants in the summer delegations (*ba'tha sayfiyya*).[18] In his speeches, he would emphasise that Islam was a struggle to establish piety and this, he suggested, meant struggle, including force,

13 Ibid 155.
14 Ibid 133–156.
15 Ibid 147.
16 Ibid 150.
17 Levy 2014: 147.
18 Kramer 2010: 44.

against the powers that be. His style was forceful with rhetorical questions such as the one he asked in 1938 when speaking to the student's section of the *Ikhwān*. He said: 'tell me, Brothers, if Islam is something other than politics, society, economy and culture…'. The implied answer was that it was jihad.[19] The Brothers soon established contacts with the Free Officers and had a 'secret apparatus' which was meant to prepare the young members to use force.[20] On 8 December, the government dissolved the Brothers who were about 500,000 in number, out of which 40,000 were charged with violence.[21] Bannā was shot dead on 12 February 1949, but his message was carried on with fresh enthusiasm and much more erudition by Sayyid Quṭb.

Quṭb was born in a middle class family, his father being a farmer with enough land to live on comfortably. He became an inspector of schools and visited the United States in 1949 to study educational administration. Apparently his vitriolic animosity against the West was triggered off by seeing couples dancing and drinking.[22] Moreover, the prevailing atmosphere of anti-colonial anger, especially directed against Israel and its Western supporters, obviously affected his thinking.[23] His idea of presenting Islam as an alternative to socialism and capitalism is inspired by anti-colonialism though the idiom of Islam makes it appear religious. According to scholars working on his thought, he was influenced by Mawdūdī whose writings had become available in the Arab world by 1951.[24] Quṭb mentions Mawdūdī in his exegesis of the Qur'an, quoting one of his speeches delivered in Lahore in 1939 which was translated into Arabic.[25] Quṭb's ideas, among which we will focus only on those which relate to radical Islamist interpretations of jihad, are given in several of his writings. The most relevant writings for us are his book *Ma'ālim fī al-ṭarīq* (1964) which has been translated as *Milestones*[26] (n.d) and his exegesis of the Qur'an which he started writ-

19 Ibid 51.

20 Ibid 70–75.

21 Ibid 80.

22 Rejection of Western sexual norms after witnessing them is a common experience described by Muslims. Even Anglophiles like Mahdī 'Alī Khān of India, who advised Indian Muslims never to oppose British rule in India says, in his private letters to his friend Nawāb Waqārul Mulk (whose real name was Mushtāq Ḥusain) (1841–1917) that: 'Such a shameless, lacking in honour and unclean country [as England] there could not be in the world. Faith, honour and justice is not there even in name. One does not know when it will be destroyed like Pompeii' (Zubayri 1934: 38).

23 Sivan 1985

24 Haddad 1983: 70

25 'Editor's note' in *Ẓilāl* Vol. 7: 25

26 The English translation *Milestones* (n.d), has been used throughout.

ing in 1951. Though the book, being smaller and easier to read, has been more influential than the multi-volume exegesis, it is the exegesis which contains the most complete version of his ideas about jihad. This exegesis was revised and completed in jail from 1954 till 1964. The references here are to the English translation of the work.

Table 10

Verse	Commentary by Sayyid Quṭb	Interpretive device
2:190	Fight the aggressors but do not kill the non-combatants among them (Vol. 1: 210). Does not restrict the retaliation to those who stop fighting but only to women and children etc.	Semantic expansion
2:191	Any means of warfare can be used against those who infringe upon the Muslims' right of freedom of belief. War can only be stopped if they (the unbelievers) discontinue 'their denial of God and their rejection of His Message'. The word 'desist' (from continuing the war) has been taken as desist from their continued unbelief (Vol. 1: 209).	Semantic expansion
2:193	Oppression (*fitnah*) must be fought with. The world must accept the political dominance of Islam. These order 'remain valid, and jihad is incumbent on Muslims until the end of time (Vol. 1: 213).	Semantic expansion
8:39	Muslims must continue fighting till the power of unbelievers is destroyed and they can no more deny God's Lordship over the whole universe' (Vol.7: 120). This verse, as well as 2: 193, are used to justify the creation of an Islamic state. The words 'religion is purely for God', he argues, is only possible when such a state is set up in the world (Vol. 7: 34–35).	Semantic expansion
8:61	If unbelievers have an agreement of peaceful coexistence with Muslims, the Muslim leadership can accept it. However, this is a temporary measure. The final orders are in Q.9. Some scholars contend that this verse has been abrogated by 9:5 (Vol. 8: 43–43).	Abrogation/ provisional tactic
9:5	This is the final form of the orders for jihad. All earlier, provisional rulings are amended by these orders to fight people of earlier faiths till they submit to Islam. Though about Meccan idolators, this verse applies to all idolators (Vol. l8: 43–83).	General not specific
9:29	Followers of previous religions must submit to Islam and pay the poll tax (Vol. 8: 27–28).	General
60:8	He does not explain it in a separate volume. However, in his opinion, those who quote 8: 61, 60: 8 and other verses of peace are using 'defeatist logic'. These verses are provisional. As soon	Abrogation/ provisional tactic

Table 10 *(Continued)*

Verse	Commentary by Sayyid Quṭb	Interpretive device
	as Muslims are powerful they shuld implement the final orders in Q. 9 to ensure 'freedom' for all humanity to choose the right religion (Islam) or pay the poll tax.	

Source: *Ẓilāl* Vols. 1, 7 and 8.

Quṭb's basic ideological imperative is that Islam must dominate the world politically since only such a system will ensure the freedom of humanity to worship God, i.e. follow Islam. He either considers the verses for peace abrogated or explains them through semantic expansion so that they do not stand in the way of eternal war. For instance, he explains 2: 256 ('there is no compulsion in religion') in conjunction with 8: 60 (equip yourself against the enemy) as well as 2: 193 (fighting should go on till there is peace and God's religion reigns supreme). He argues that if the idea of 'no compulsion' had been the only one in the Qur'an, then those who argue that 'jihad is a matter of history and is no longer valid or necessary' would be right. However, since Islam opposes tyrannical regimes and establishes a just social order, jihad remains necessary. That is where the order to prepare for war (8: 60) comes in. Thus, the verse about there being no compulsion in religion is not to be read in isolation.[27] This verse is taken up again in volume 4 and Quṭb declares that no other faith except Islam is acceptable to God. However, he also says that compelling people to convert to Islam is not allowed. This implies, as Quṭb says elsewhere explicitly, that political dominance, or rule, should be Muslim, though non-Muslims can live under Muslim rulers as protected citizens.[28] While summing up *Sūrah al-Nisā* (Q. 4), he says Muslims should not live under non-Muslim leaders and they should fight those who oppress Muslims anywhere.[29]

Quṭb especially criticises people who argue that jihad is purely defensive as the modernist Muslims of his time did. As the aim of jihad is to create 'freedom'—a word used by Quṭb in the sense of following God's laws only (i.e. semantic expansion)—all political systems depriving people from this aim must be abolished by force.[30] People are not free, he argues, till they live in ignorance (*jāhilīyyah*) by which he means basically non-compliance with the *Sharīʿah* and obeying author-

27 *Ẓilāl* Vol. 1 1999: 328–329.
28 Ibid Vol. 4, 2001: 152–153.
29 Ibid Vol. 3, 2001.
30 Ibid Vol. 7: 7–9. This occurs at various places. See also Vol. 3, 2001: 232.

ities other than God (*ṭāghūt*). In short, not living under the Islamic state and not obeying Islamic laws is by itself wrong. Indeed, even peaceful co-existence with other nation-states, even if offered by them, will not be accepted unless they pay the poll tax.[31] However, as a temporary measure, the orders in 9: 5—advocating all-out war against the polytheists—can only be suspended if Muslims are very weak but they must be ultimately obeyed. Here he mentions the massacre of Baghdad by the Mongol conquror Halākū (also spelled Helugo) Khān (1218–1265), the killings of Muslim emigrants from India to Pakistan in 1947 (ignoring the Hindus and Sikhs killed in the areas that later became Pakistan) and the 'extermination' of Muslims in Soviet Russia and China. As for fighting Western powers, Quṭb uses both secular (political, economic, social, and cultural) as well as religious arguments to explain 9: 29 (about fighting the People of the Book). His main argument is that the Christians had changed the Bible and both they and the Jews had perverted their beliefs. Thus, they did not worship God in the right way. So, fighting them was a religious duty. To this he adds that there was much awe of the Byzantine Empire in the early period of Islam so that defeating the empire would serve to deter all other would be combatants. At places he uses the narrative of victimisation of Muslims all over the world, Western economic exploitation, and the culture of decadence. However, Quṭb does not develop these arguments choosing to privilege only the religious one.[32] In short, Quṭb uses all hermeneutical devices—suspension of peaceful verses, superseding them by the aggressive ones, and reading verses with others so as to negate them through semantic expansion etc—to present a reading of the Qur'an which supports aggressive warfare in the world.

The same ideas, explained in a simple and forthright style, are given in *Milestones*. The basic idea is that all societies are based upon ignorance (*jāhilīyyah*) as pre-Islamic Arabian society was. Haddad points out that 'Qutb concedes that he has borrowed this definition from Mawdudi's *Mabadi al-Islam*'.[33] Mawdūdī's works began to be translated in the 1950s and one of his followers, Abū'l Ḥasan 'Alī Nadwī, who has been mentioned earlier, 'expounded Maudoodi's Modern jahiliyya doctrine' in one of his books.[34] However, the concept of *jahiliyya* has a much more central place and resonance in the worldview of Quṭb than of Mawdūdī. According to this idea, the only society which is enlightened and civilised is the Islamic society. But this is not any ordinary society of Muslims; it is only that society which is based on the Muslim testament of faith,

31 Ibid 22.
32 Ibid Vol. 8, 2003: 271
33 Haddad 1983: 85.
34 Sivan 1985: 23.

'there is no deity but Allah', taken in the political sense of establishing an Islamic state. Such a society, Quṭb argues, is free in the real sense of the word since no person is subservient to any other. Quṭb, like Mawdūdī, calls the rulers idols (*ṭāghūt*) who have assumed God's power of legislating and imposing manmade laws. The ideal Islamic society, unlike others, Quṭb argues in *Milestones*, will impose the *Sharī'ah*, segregate the sexes, and ban certain forms of arts, literature, and philosophy. This, he clarifies, is the establishment of the sovereignty (*ḥākimiyyah*) of God and it is the duty of Muslims to establish it all over the world. Jihad to be undertaken in pursuit of this ideal is not aggression but actually the spread of freedom.

Such ideas might not have gained such widespread dissemination if Jamal Abdul Nasir's (1918–1970) [also spelled as Nasser in some sources] regime had been less repressive and if Quṭb had not become the hero of Islamist revolutionaries when he was hanged by the regime in 1966. Just as Socrates refused to avoid death by running away from his prison because that would subvert the principle that the law should be obeyed, Quṭb also refused to beg pardon of Nasir's regime. Adil Salahi, his admirer who later edited and translated his exegesis into English, describes how Quṭb's sister visited him in his death cell and pleaded with him that he should sign a letter stating that he had been paid by the Saudi government to oppose the regime. Such a statement would save his life. Quṭb refused to do so and was hanged the next morning.[35] Such accounts of his death, as inspiring for Islamists as the drinking of hemlock by Socrates was for the Europeans, shrouded him in charisma that has stood the test of time. It helped in the dissemination of his views and in making him an icon of radical Islamist thought in the world.

Part of this influence was the use of his ideas to justify the taking up of arms against rulers perceived to be less Islamic by revolutionary Islamists. One such person who took up arms against his Marxist Afghan government was Burhānuddīn Rabbānī, the leader of the Jamī 'at-e-Islāmī of Afghanistan, who had translated Quṭb's works into Persian.[36] Rabbānī was an important figure in the war against the Soviet Union and was inspired by Quṭb. Others in Afghanistan may have been more directly influenced by 'Abdullāh 'Azzām or Osama but Quṭb remains the ultimate source of many of the ideas of radical Islam. Quṭb's works were translated into English, as were those of others, which brought his views to the attention to the growing generation of young Muslims in Western countries. For instance, Adil Salahi, the president of the Federation of Student

---

35 'Preface' to *Ẓilāl* Vol. 11 2005: xi-xv.

36 Burke 2003: 66–67.

Islamic Societies (FOSIS) in Britain, translated *Ma'ālim fī al-ṭarīq* in English in 1966.[37]

Meanwhile in Egypt, ideas even more dangerous than before came to be held albeit by small coteries of activists. One reason for this seems to be that there was much frustration among the youth. Kepel tells us that 'in the 1970s, the number of Egyptian students more than doubled to half a million, while university infrastructure remained unchanged'.[38] Many of these students, having come from the villages, were alienated from the cities, which seemed to them like fleshpots. Moreover, these frustrated students could hardly find satisfactory jobs and, in their frustration, they turned to promises of a better, more honest, and meaningful world which the Muslim Brotherhood announced untiringly.[39] Under the circumstances, given that Anwar al-Sadat (1918–1981), the successor of Nāṣir, had recognised Israel, all efforts to mend fences with the Islamists to bolster the government's hold on Egyptian society, backfired. Consequently, Sadat was murdered in 1981 and it is to the ideas of his murderers to which we turn now.

One of the theoreticians of this assassination was 'Abd al-Salām Farāj (1954–1982). Farāj was a leader of a terrorist network which included the Egyptian artillery officer Khalid Islambouli (1955–1952), who killed President Sadat on 6 October 1981. Farāj provided the intellectual justification of this public execution in his famous treatise, *Al-jihād: Farīḍah al-ghaibah* (the neglected duty) which was written sometime in the late seventies and early eighties. This book has been translated under the title in parentheses by Johannes J.G. Jansen[40] and it is this translation to which references are made here.

Farāj begins by quoting a hadith—'I have been sent with the sword...' (full text in Annexure C)— which he interprets as permission to fight against all unbelievers in all ages. Then he quotes other texts to the effect that Islam will eventually dominate the world. In between, however, there will be a 'King who hinders' (Egypt's royalty) and a 'King who Compels' (military) and then a just caliphate.[41] He then comes to the imperative of ruling according to the *sharī'ah*, this time quoting *Sūrah al-Māidah* (Q. 5), the gist of which is that 'those who do not make judgments according to God's law are unbelievers' (5: 44). These ideas are part of what Cook calls the 'activist trend' towards authority. Based on the Islamic injunction to command right and forbid wrong, the activists 'risk

37 Bowen 2014: 103.
38 Kepel 2000: 81–82.
39 Michell 1969.
40 Jansen 1986.
41 Ibid 164.

armed insurrection against them' while the 'quietist trend' regards even verbal 'confrontation with the authorities with deep misgivings'.[42] Farāj belongs to the activist trend. Like Sayyid Quṭb before him, he condemns the rulers of the Muslim world who do not govern according to Islamic law referring to the religious edicts of the Hanbalite medieval theologian Taqī al-Dīn Ibn Taymiyyah (1263–1328). Ibn Taymiyyah lived during the Mongol era and condemned the ruling Mongols who had converted to Islam but still followed their tribal code of conduct and governance rather than the *sharī 'ah*. Farāj refers to Ibn Taymiyyah's *al-Fatāwā al-kubrā* and especially to the section on 'Jihad' for most of his own views on the subject of governance and fighting.

In *al-Siyāsah al-sharī'ah fī iṣlāḥ al-rā'ī wa 'l ra'iyya* (Governance according to God's Law reforming both the ruler and his people), Ibn Taymiyyah argues on the basis of 2: 193 and 8: 39 that those who do not accept Islam must be fought 'until there is no persecution and religion is God's entirely'. He goes on to assert that 'those who depart from the law of Islam must be fought, even if they pronounce the two professions of faith'.[43] He then goes on to quote other Quranic verses as well as hadith to prove that jihad is the 'best voluntary [religious] act that one can perform'.[44] He distinguishes between jihad for propagating the religion which is voluntary and jihad for defence which is 'out of necessity'.[45] Besides Ibn Taymiyyah, Farāj takes the support of Ibn Kathīr, whose exegesis has been discussed earlier, to argue that Muslims should fight those who do not rule according to the religious law.[46]

These and other such pronouncements were taken to justify rebellion and civil war against Muslim rulers, especially those of Egypt. That Farāj had misinterpreted Ibn Taymiyyah is the view of many scholars. For instance, Fazlur Rahman states that 'under no condition did Ibn Taymiyyah condone in-fighting among Muslims.[47] However, Rahman refers to the in-fighting among the Companions while the Mongols, about whom Ibn Taymiyyah was writing, in his eyes at least, only pretended to be Muslims. Thus, Farāj's justification of war against Muslim rulers found resonance among the radical Islamists.[48]

Before discussing the other views of Farāj, let us pause for a moment and see how Ibn Taymiyyah has been used by others in interpreting jihad. Ironically, Qar-

---

42 Cook 2000: 51.
43 Ibn Taymiyyah (c. 13 C) in Peters 1996: 52.
44 Quoted from Bostom 2005: 167.
45 Ibid 172.
46 *Ibn Kathīr* Vol. 1: 102–109.
47 Rahman 2000: 158.
48 Jansen 1986: 173.

aḍāwī, in his magisterial study of jihad, uses Ibn Taymiyyah for arguing that unbelievers are not to be fought with for their views but only because they may be a threat for Muslims. Again, with reference to Ibn Taymiyyah, Qaraḍāwī also says—something which would be anathema to the militants and music to the ears of the modernists—that the Prophet 'never began hostilities against any unbeliever'.[49] In short, Ibn Taymiyyah lends himself to various uses and interpreters appropriate him according to their ideological assumptions.

Going back to Farāj, we now come to his ideas about creating a *sharī'ah*-governed society. In this regard, he first takes up the alternatives to taking political power which he dismisses one by one. For instance, some people think that joining 'benevolent societies', i.e. pressure groups exhorting Muslims to say their prayers and pay the alms tax etc., is enough; or spending one's life in devotion to God; creating Islamic political parties; occupying influential positions, propagating Islam through non-violent propaganda, emigration, and the quest of knowledge—is inadequate. For him, most of these things require collaboration with the state and making compromises which prevent one from imposing the *sharī'ah.*[50] He does permit emigration according to Islamic precedents but does not dwell upon it. Farāj is highly critical of the ideal of some people called 'the quest for knowledge' because, in his view, it comes from people who do not practice jihad. If they know that jihad is necessary and still neglect it, he does not think they should be taken seriously.[51]

Another point which the radical Islamists are at pains to prove is that jihad is both defensive and aggressive and not just the former. In this context, Farāj, though not an *'ālim* in the traditional sense of the term, nevertheless uses the hermeneutical device of *naskh* to interpret 9:5. For this he refers to past scholars who support his position while ignoring those who oppose it. Thus, he refers to Ibn Kathīr who says that it cancelled every treaty between the Prophet and the infidels. Then he quotes the exegete Ibn Juzayy al-Kalbī (1294–1340) who, in his *Tafsīr al-tashīl lī 'ulūm al-tanzīl* (Commentary on Acquiring the Knowledge of Exegesis) wrote that this verse abrogates the command to live in peace with the infidels found in 114 verses of the Qur'an.[52] He also refers to Muḥammad Ibn Ḥazm's (994–1063/64) book on abrogation in the Qur'an entitled *al-Nāsikh wa 'l-mansūkh* in which he asserts that 'in 114 verses in 48 surahs everything is abrogated by the Word of God', i.e.9: 5.[53]

49 Ibn Taymiyyah's *Qā'idah Mukhtaṣarah* quoted from Zaman 2012: 265.
50 Jansen 1986: 186.
51 Ibid 189.
52 Ibid 195.
53 Ibid.

After this interpretation of the Qur'an, Farāj accepts those traditions which emphasise aggressive warfare while dismissing those which define jihad to mean spiritual or moral effort for excellence. In this context, he dismisses the tradition that the greater jihad is self improvement like Bannā before him and goes on to assert that 'the only reason for inventing this tradition is to reduce the value of fighting with the sword, so as to distract the Muslims from fighting the infidels and the hypocrites'.[54] He then takes up the argument that jihad is obligatory only when one is militarily powerful. On this point he presents no theological argument merely repeating rhetorically that one cannot be strong if the duty is suspended or ignored. He also asserts that jihad is no longer a collective duty (*farḍul kifāyah*) but an individual duty (*farḍul 'ayn*). It becomes an individual duty when: (a) two armies meet; (b) when infidels attack a Muslim country; (c) when the leader of Muslims (*imām* or caliph) orders Muslims to fight. He then argues, as mentioned earlier, that there are two types of enemies. Those who are near (*al-'aduw al-qarīb*) and those who are far away (*al-'aduw al-ba'īd*) and that, contrary to fighting those who are far away such as Israel or the USA, the near ones, who are the rulers of Muslim countries, should be eliminated first. Moreover, he adds, 'there is no (need to) ask permission of (your) parents to leave to wage *Jihād*'.[55] As for leadership, there is no need to look up to the state since it is taken hostage by the enemy. Just as a suitably qualified Muslim may lead prayers so can one such person lead the jihad.[56] These ideas, Aaron Zelin, a researcher, points out, constitute a 'paradigm shift in the intellectual history of Jihādi thought' since Farāj really made jihad an anarchistic device for total warfare and rebellion against all established authority.[57]

Another important Arab thinker, though he has always opposed the Islamist view that aggressive jihad is incumbent upon Muslims, is mentioned here because he permits violence in Israel. He is none other than the celebrated Yūsuf al-Qaraḍāwi. In his book *Jurisprudence of Jihad*, he asserts that Israel is the only *Dārul Ḥarb*. Since the Palestinians are under attack and are much weaker than Israel, he approves of suicide bombing which he calls 'missions of self-sacrifice'. In this context, it is pertinent to point out that Qaraḍāwī resorts to eclecticism as a hermeneutical device here. He refers to the case of the famous Companion Abū Ayyūb Anṣārī (576–674) who, though an old man, voluntarily joined the army and died in one of the raids against the Byzantine Empire

---

54 Ibid 201.
55 Ibid 200.
56 Ibid 203.
57 Zelin 2012: 31.

and is buried in Istanbul. As Qasim Zaman has pointed out, Qaraḍāwi uses this example but leaves out another case of a similar kind by a man fighting in the siege of Damascus. The latter did survive but his commander, 'Amr bin al-'Āṣ (d. 664), reprimanded him, reminding him of God's command by quoting 2: 95—one should not put one's self in the path of destruction—to him.[58]

As suicide attacks are responsible for the deaths of innocent civilians, let us consider the views of the radical Islamists about them. David Cook, in his study of martyrdom in Islam, mentions Nawwāf al-Takūrī's book, *al-'Amaliyyāt al-Istishhādiyyah fī al-mīzan al-fiqhī* (martyrdom operations in the legal balance)[59] which justifies suicide attacks primarily against Israel but also in Bosnia, Kashmir, Palestine, Afghanistan, and Iraq on the grounds that they 'equalize what would otherwise be unequal conflicts'.[60] He adduces eleven occasions from the time of the Prophet in which such operations were launched. However, Cook points out that these were attacks in the heat of the battle and 'the line between bravery in battle and suicide is blurred in this material'.[61] Indeed, the arguments of those who oppose such operations are 'persuasive and strongly rooted in Islamic history and law as well'.[62] The interpretation of Yūsuf al-Qaraḍāwī, who also calls them 'martyrdom operations' but only in the case of Israel, is an example of the way such operations are selectively defended. To meet the objection that such missions result in civilian casualties, Qaraḍāwī argues that all Israelis are combatants since they are given military training and may be called upon to fight any time. With reference to this, Zaman points out that 'there is no mention, for instance, of those who are exempt from military service, for example yeshiva students'.[63] And, one might add, children, the elderly, the mentally challenged, chronic patients, visitors, and so on. In the same way, although Qaraḍāwī restricts the permission of suicide bombing to Israel only, the logic of asymmetrical military power could be used by others, including as it happened, in Pakistan and India. Indeed, at least one Taliban commander, operating in Afghanistan in 2005, did say: 'suicide bombings are a tactic with which we drive the enemy to panic. Without this miracle weapon we would never accomplish our goal of re-conquering all of Afghanistan'.[64] So, views such as Qaraḍā-

58 Ibn Kathīr's exegesis of 2: 195, quoted from Zaman 2012: 279.
59 Cook 2007: 150
60 Ibid 150.
61 Ibid, 151.
62 Ibid, 153.
63 Zaman 2012: 275.
64 Euben and Zaman 2009: 420.

wī's support the narrative of the militants all over the world however much he may oppose them for misinterpreting the canonical sources about jihad.

Others whose radical views reached Pakistan were 'Abdullāh Yūsuf 'Azzām, Osama bin Laden, and Ayman al-Ẓawāhirī.[65] Their radical ideas have been disseminated in Pakistan through translations mostly because of the Afghan war when the Arab fighters came to Pakistan and Afghanistan. First, let us take the views of the Jordanian-Palestinian academic 'Abdullāh 'Azzām (1941–1989). 'Azzām wrote a religious edict (*fatwā*) which is translated as *Defence of the Muslim Lands: the First Obligation after Iman.*[66] His major thesis is that jihad has become an individual obligation (*farḍul 'ayn*) since the infidels have attacked and captured Muslim lands and the present generation of Muslims is sinning if it does not fight to expel them from 'Afghanistan, Palestine, the Philippines, Kashmir, Lebanon, Chad, Eritria etc'.[67] This statement is important for radical Islamists since, as we have seen in Farāj's work above, in such cases they argue that no permission is required for anyone to join the jihad. 'Azzām then goes on to argue that, though Palestine is the crucial problem for the Muslim world since it is occupied by the Jews, it is to Afghanistan that Muslims should go to fight first. The obligation to fight keeps expanding from one area to another since it is not tied to nationalism but to the concept of the Islamic *millah*—a collectivity defined by faith rather than nationality. This theory of expanding circles of jihad is succinctly summed up by Shaikh 'Abdullāh Naṣṣāḥ al-Wān, one of the Islamic scholars to whom 'Azzām showed his work. The Sheikh said:

> If the unbelievers are not beaten back, then, the Fard Ayn of Jihād spreads in the shape of a circle. The nearest to the next in nearness. Until, the Jihād has become Fard Ayn upon the whole earth, the destruction of the enemy and their complete expulsion from the Muslim land.[68]

Like Farāj, 'Azzām too dispenses with the condition that the political head of the state should command jihad. This, he argues, may be true for settled states when they undertake expeditions against the enemies of Islam using their paid troops. However, when jihad becomes a *farḍul 'ayn*, a commander may be chosen and there may be several of them. This doctrine ensures perpetual warfare in the world and especially in Afghanistan and Pakistan.

---

65 Riedel 2009. For the role of charismatic leadership, see Ingram 2013.
66 Azzām 2002.
67 Ibid n.p.
68 Ibid n.p.

'Azzām was enthusiastically supported in Afghanistan and the border areas of Pakistan where he lived and worked. In his *fatwā*, he approvingly produces a letter written by 'Abdul Rabb Rasūl Sayyāf (b. 1946), an Afghan politician and commander fighting the Russians, published in the *Jihād Magazine* (9th issue). The gist of the letter is that Afghanistan needed people who could provide religious legitimacy to the ongoing military struggle against the Russian invasion. Such legitimisation was provided by 'Azzām's edicts from Peshawar to kill 'the infidels in the name of God'.[69] Those inspired by him kept offering their services or, at least, approbation such as Khawlā Bint al-Azoor—probably an assumed name since Khawlā Bint al-Azwar is a role model known for fighting in the battle of Thanīta-al-'Uqāb in 634 against the Byzantine Empire—who wrote that she wished to give her life to 'this pure land' (Afghanistan) but being 'a girl' she was 'not able to do anything'.[70] Thus, 'Azzām provided the crucial service of spreading his ideas which influenced not only the fighters against the Russians but a whole Islamic militant movement which later fought both the Americans and the Pakistanis.[71]More importantly, in the short run these ideas influenced the Saudi millionaire Osama bin Laden (1957–2011), who bankrolled the Afghan war against the Soviets during the eighties and then took to opposing the United States.[72] He issued an order on 23 February 1998, making the same argument as Farāj and 'Azzām that jihad had become a *farḍul 'ayn* so all Muslims had to fight the Americans. This was based on the presence of American troops in Saudi Arabia despite the fact that the Saudi government had invited them in order to deter aggression from Saddam Hussein (1937–2006), the president of Iraq (r. 1979–2003) who had attacked Kuwait and threatened Saudi Arabia itself in 1990. Quoting from the canonical sources, Osama urged Muslims to believe that 'killing the Americans and their allies—civilians and military—is an individual duty for every Muslim who is capable of it and in every country in which it is possible to do so'.[73]

Osama's deputy in the Al-Qaeda organisation, Dr. Ayman Muḥammad Rabī al-Ẓawāhirī (b. 1951), first expressed his ideas in *Farsān taḥet Rāetun Nabī*, written in 2001, which was later translated into English as *Knights Under the Prophet's Banner*.[74] The book has twenty-one chapters and was smuggled out from Egypt to England where it was published. Ẓawāhirī describes the bombing of

69 *Jihād* 27 Feb 1987: 35. Quoted from Bergen 2006: 35.
70 *Jihād* April 1987: 43. Quoted from Bergen 2006: 43.
71 Bergen 2006.
72 Quoted from the translation of Peters 1996: 177.
73 Mansfield 2006.
74 Ibid 25.

the Egyptian embassy in Islamabad and his role in fighting the Soviets in Afghanistan. He makes the point that 'popular Arab sources' donated 200 million U.S. dollars worth of material in ten years to refute the charge that the cost of this mission was borne solely by America.[75] The main benefit of the victory in Afghanistan was that it 'destroyed the myth of a (superpower) in the minds of Muslim mujahideen young men'.[76] His letter to Abū Muṣ'ab al-Zarqāwī (1966–2006), an unusually ferocious Islamist militant, cautioning him gently against killing too many Shī'a as that may alienate the masses, indicates that, on occasions, he could be pragmatic in the larger interest of his mission.[77] His letter to the Americans is important since it presents his justification, repeated by many radicals, that civilians should be killed since they elect the leaders and support pro-Israel policies. Women too may be killed since they fight in the armed forces.[78] More important for South Asia is his letter to Pakistan in which he rants against Musharraf whom he accuses of selling Islamists for money and exhorts the army to 'disobey the orders of his commanders to kill Muslims in Pakistan and Afghanistan'.[79]

Even more important is his critical analysis of the *Constitution of Pakistan* (1973) entitled, in English, *The Dawn of the Day and the Flickering Lamp*. The book was translated into Urdu and the initial print run was of 2,000 copies which were disseminated in Pakistan. Al-Ẓawāhirī begins with the claim that democracy and the Islamic philosophy of rule are based on different systems of thought. While democracy is based upon the will of the majority of the people who choose their representatives to express their collective will, Islam enforces the will of God irrespective of the will of the people. From this premise he argues that, since even the Objectives Resolution of 1949 mentions democracy, the constitution is a device for fooling the people of Pakistan into feeling that it is Islamic.[80] He then points out that there are various constitutional provisions which are contrary to the *sharī'ah*. Among these are: the possibility of a woman's rule; the

---

75 Ibid 38.

76 Ibid 250–279. Al-Zarqāwī, whose real name was Aḥmad Fāḍīl Nazāl Al-Khālāylah, came to Peshawar in 1989 and, after fighting with Hekmatyar, returned to Jordan (Brisard and Martinez 2005: 16). However, he returned to Pakistan in 1999 and, since 100,000 Pakistanis passed through the training camps in Afghanistan, and Zarqāwī was associated with them till 2002, he might have had some influence on the thought of these young men (Ibid 64). He is known for having killed many Shī'as in Iraq and justified the abduction and killing of Westerners (Brisard and Martinez 2005: 133–142).

77 Ibid, 292–294.

78 Ibid, 335.

79 Ẓawāhirī 2008.

80 Ibid 127–137.

possibility of a judge being a non-Muslim; the power of the president to pardon convicts; the bar against punishing anyone more than once for an offense (his view is that if the first punishment is not Islamic, there should be no such bar); the continuation of interest in the economy; and the dominance of secular laws over religious ones; the advisory nature of the Council of Islamic Ideology (in his view this court should be able to change all laws by its superior authority), etc. At one point, he quotes from Ibn Taymiyyah to argue that if rulers are like those of Pakistan it is permitted to fight (*qitāl*) against them.[81] As usual, in the case of radical Islamist scholars, he supports his various claims and arguments by referring to the Qur'an and the hadith in addition to Ibn Taymiyyah and other scholars. He concludes that ordinary Pakistanis want an Islamic system of rule but the ruling elite does not. However, in order to keep the people with them, this elite pretends to establish an Islamic rule which, he asserts, is not Islamic at all. In short, Ẓawāhirī preaches rebellion against the constitution of Pakistan and democracy itself and not just the government of the day. He does, however, name General Pervez Musharraf (b. 1943) and former President Asif Ali Zardari (b. 1955) as the leaders of this iniquitous system which, in his view, favours the American-Jewish global war against Islam rather than Muslims like himself and Osama bin Laden who are out to resist the invaders. However, the real object of Ẓawāhirī's criticism and condemnation are not individuals but the system of rule of the country and the democratic philosophy upon which it is based.

To sum up the ideas of the radical Arab Islamists mentioned above: first, they deviate from the orthodox Sunni norms about jihad, i.e. it can only be waged by orders of a legal Islamic ruler; secondly, they consider the killing of civilians legitimate using the doctrine of 'proportional response'; thirdly, they argue that, though suicide to end one's life for private reasons is taboo, it is allowed as a 'martyrdom operation' since these are a just response to the disproportionate power of the enemies of Muslims. Another idea, often reiterated by Islamists, is that rebellion in the name of Islam against the rulers of the Muslim world is justified since, by radical standards, they are apostates. Most of these ideas are found in the literature produced by Islamic militant groups in Pakistan. However, this is not to say that some of them did not exist, possibly in embryonic form, in the Subcontinent. From the eighteenth century onwards some ideas, later attributed to the Ahl-i-Hadith movement, had come into India. As Brown observes, 'the survival and spread of Ḥanbalī revivalism was also reflected in and further encouraged by the publication and circulation of Ibn Taymiyyah's

---

81 Ibid 149.

works. These first began to appear at the end of the nineteenth century'.[82] Indeed, 'the modern rediscovery of Ibn Taymiyyah and Ibn Kathīr—as well as Ibn Qayyim al-Jawziyya and some lesser lights—was to take place in twentieth-century Egypt and Muslim India'.[83] But this is only to be expected in a world where belief systems, among other objects of thought and culture, have influenced each other. To those Pakistani radicals who appear to be influenced by such views, let us turn to the next chapter.

82 Brown, D 1996: 30.
83 Sivan 1985: 101.

9 Pakistani Radicals

There are many studies of the discourses used by Islamist radical militants in Pakistan. For instance, there are book length studies of all kinds of media used by the Taliban by Mona Kanwal Sheikh[1] and the writings of Ḥāfiẓ Sa'īd's organisations by Samina Yasmeen and Christina Fair.[2] These studies provide a deep understanding of the narratives used by these groups to legitimise their militancy and role in society. This chapter, however, will focus mostly on the exegeses of the Qur'an by Muḥammad Ḥāfiẓ Sa'īd (b. 1948), leader of the LeT/JUD, Mas'ūd Aẓhar, leader of the Jaish-e-Muḥammad, and a few writings by some other militant clerics, which have not been dealt with in detail by other writers.

However, before we go into the discourses themselves, it is necessary to understand, however briefly, the rise of Islamist violence in Pakistan. The section dealing with the rise of the Taliban—an umbrella term for a number of disparate groups fighting in Afghanistan and Pakistan for ostensibly Islamic reasons as well as to defeat Western forces—is based primarily on the information provided by investigative journalists, newspaper accounts, statements, reports, and academic analyses. Among works in the last category are Khalid Ahmed's recent book entitled *Sleepwalking to Surrender* in which he looks at the history of policymaking in Pakistan to give a deeper analysis of the present crisis (which he considers as 'surrender' to extremism).[3] Tahir Kamran too traces out the history of extremist violence by going back to Deobandi activism in the anti-Ahmadi movement of 1953 and 1974 and then the rise of anti-Shī'a factions (SSP and LeJ) in the eighties.[4] Briefly, journalistic writings suggest that Pakistan favoured the Afghan Taliban because of the fear that India, which was favoured by the Northern Alliance which ruled Afghanistan, would encircle Pakistan. The Taliban were anti-Hindu so supporting them was seen as providing 'strategic depth' to Pakistan in case of such a crisis. After September 11, however, General Musharraf (r. 1999–2008) officially severed relations with them handing some of

---

1 Sheikh 2016.

2 Yasmeen 2017; Fair forthcoming.

3 The writings by prominent investigative journalists consulted for the summary of views presented here are by Mir 2008; Hussain, M. 2012; Hussain, Z. 2008; Yusufzai 2008, 2009; Shahzad 2011. The TTP is not one cohesive institution. It is an umbrella term for several groups sharing some aspects of their belief-system. In 2011, according to a rough estimate, there were forty groups under the umbrella of the Taliban (Qazi 2011: 580). These groups keep evolving in response to the forces acting upon them. For Khalid Ahmed's analysis of policy-making, see Ahmed 2016.

4 Kamran 2016: 66–74.

https://doi.org/10.1515/9783110716986-012

the Islamist militants hiding in Pakistan to the United States while, simultaneously, hiding some of them in sanctuaries in the country. Meanwhile, when there was an uprising in the Indian-administered Kashmir in 1989, Islamic militants, called the 'Punjabi Taliban'[5]—mostly led by Ḥāfiẓ Sa'īd and Mas'ūd Aẓhar allegedly with the help of the ISI—started attacking India in order to bring Delhi to the negotiating table about Kashmir. It is to sustain this covert, low-intensity guerrilla warfare, called jihad by the actors themselves, that the narratives we shall be looking at were created and disseminated.

First let us look at the work of Mona Sheikh. She begins by what she calls 'sociotheological approach' which is defined as taking 'stock of the religious justifications for social action' so that social scientists are 'more aware of the social significance of spiritual ideas and practices'.[6] She identifies Islamic law (*Sharī'ah*) and jihad as the central concepts in the religious idiom of the Taliban whom she writes about. In this context she points out that the apocalypse is 'especially germane to the Taliban view of jihad' since it relates to Khurasan of which Afghanistan and parts of Pakistan are constituent units.[7] Her interviews with key Taliban figures, such as Muslim Khān, the former spokesman of the TTP (Swat chapter) and Matī'al Ḥaqq, make it clear that the Taliban frame their war as a defensive struggle for the very survival of Islam. From their point of view, the United States attacked Muslims and this is an existential battle for which all tactics, including suicide missions (Ḥaqq insisted that they should be called missions of self-sacrifice, i.e. *fidāyī ḥamlē*) and the collateral deaths of innocent people, are justified. Thus, when Khān or Ḥaqq use the term *jihād bi'l qitāl* (fighting), they use both the narrative of a defensive holy war as well as the imposition of Islamic law on God's earth.[8]

The Taliban use *shabnāmēh* (nocturnal letters), sermons, flyers, pamphlets, magazines, biographical accounts, inspirational songs, and talks on the radio as well as websites to disseminate their ideas. One such message, signed by the former TTP head Ḥakīmullāh Maḥsūd (1979–2013), dated 18 August 2012, states that Pakistan was created in the name of Islam and is ruled by a 'secular infidel' system of rule (democracy) and prays in the end that it should be replaced by the caliphate so that Islam could dominate.[9] Because of framing democracy itself in such negative terms, the TTP also fights against the state of Pakistan which, in its view, is an ally of America (which attacks Muslims). The TTP has not produced

5 Hussain, M 2012.
6 Sheikh 2016: 13.
7 Ibid 50.
8 Ibid 72–76.
9 Image in Urdu in Sheikh 2016: 128.

serious works of Islamic scholarship so there are no exegeses to analyse concerning its interpretations of the Qur'an. However, Sheikh tells us that the verses against hypocrites are used to justify aggression against the Pakistani state. Verses against making friends with Christians and Jews are also used to blame Pakistan since Musharraf entered into an alliance with the USA and NATO which continued later also.[10] Sheikh does not clarify how these verses are interpreted but it is clear that, to be thus used, they would have to be treated as eternal and general orders and not specific to a period or people. Moreover, other verses of the Qur'an advocating friendship with people who had not initiated hostilities would either be considered as abrogated or simply ignored. They also use Ibn Taymiyyah and some ideas of Ibn ʻAbd al-Wahhāb (1703–1792) as Sheikh tells us[11] though, given their predominantly oral culture, it appears that these must be oral versions imbibed by their leaders through their contact with the Middle Eastern radical Islamists. This is not to say that there are no written and printed works about jihad. These, however, are from people residing in towns and cities.

The main theoreticians of jihad we shall be concerned with here, as mentioned above, are Ḥāfiẓ Sa'īd, Mas'ūd Aẓhar, Nūr Muḥammad, Faḍl Muḥammad Yūsufza'ī, and Muftī Shamazaī. All of them spent their lives preaching jihad and influenced thousands of people who fought in India and Afghanistan and are still active at least as far as India is concerned. Their discourses about jihad are based upon both their theological interpretations of it and the nationalist imperative of conquering Kashmir for the Pakistani state or, as they claim, helping Muslim Kashmiris win their freedom from India.[12] The worldview nurtured by these ideologues has the following core beliefs: that it is necessary to fight non-Muslims; that Jihad is incumbent upon all Muslims; that eventually Muslims will conquer the world and *Sharī'ah* will prevail. In some cases, this last belief is based upon Messianism—the belief that Imām Mahdī will come and lead the Muslims to victory—and apocalypse. This, as Cook points out, is a global phenomenon, but in parts of Pakistan it assumes special significance because these areas are identified as Khurasan.[13] In addition to that, again in common with global trends, there is the narrative of victimisation but in this case, Kashmir and Afghanistan play a major role in it.

Let us begin with the interpretations of jihad by Ḥāfiẓ Muḥammad Sa'īd. Sa'īd was born to lower middle class parents in Sargodha in 1948. His father, said to be a farmer, migrated in the autumn of 1947 from Karnal, East Punjab

---

10 Ibid 138.

11 Ibid 139.

12 Reiterated in the propaganda material used by the militants.

13 Cook 2005: 158–161.

amidst terrible riots. The family lost thirty-six members during this traumatic experience. Saʿīd never actually witnessed these murders but heard about them from the family as a child. Whether the way the events were narrated to him caused post-traumatic stress disorder which causes his inveterate hatred for India and Hindus, is a question for the psychologist. For us, what is relevant are his ideas and how his intellectual life developed. He is said to have liked verses about jihad even in childhood when he memorised the Qur'an—hence the title *ḥāfiẓ* (one who remembers the Qur'an by heart). He graduated from Government College, Sargodha and studied for his MA in Islamic Studies at the King Saud University in Riyadh. Upon his return, he worked for some time in the Council of Islamic Ideology and then as a faculty member at the University of Engineering and Technology, Lahore. Most of his family members, like himself, are involved in Islamic organisations. Indeed, his brother-in-law, 'Abdul Raḥmān Makkī (b. 1948), is his 'close partner and holds a powerful position in his *Markaz* at Muridke'.[14] Saʿīd, accused of major attacks on India, has been arrested several times but has always been released by the courts. He has been declared a terrorist by the United Nations. The USA has placed a bounty on his head. However, despite India's repeated demands and international pressure, the government of Pakistan allows him to spread his ideas about jihad. Saʿīd was influenced by 'Abdullāh 'Azzām, Shaikh 'Abd al-'Azīz bin Bāz (1910–1999), the Grand Mufti of Saudi Arabia, and his organisation was supported at some level by Osama bin Laden.[15] Thus, he imbibed radical Islamist ideas from these Arab militant sources in addition to developing them himself.

His ideas have been disseminated in the form of sermons, pamphlets, and on the website of the Lashkar-e-Tayyaba (LT). They have also been discussed in great detail by Yasmeen, Fair, and Wilson.[16] The gist of studies about the narratives offered by Saʿīd himself as well as other members of his organisation is that jihad is a duty of every Muslim in the absence of the Islamic State. Moreover, Saʿīd negates the ideas that: (a) jihad needs to be ordered by the state; (b) that it is not incumbent upon Pakistani Muslims since they have not been attacked; (c) that international treaties would have to be renounced first before any attack; (d) that Pakistan is too militarily and economically weak to win a war so it should not be initiated. He maintains, like 'Abdullāh 'Azzām and Osama bin Laden, that if there is no Muslim ruler ready to order jihad openly, the Muslim community can choose one for that purpose and, as he himself is the head (*amīr*) of his or-

14 Mir 2008: 162; For biographical details also see Yasmeen 2017: 45–50.
15 Yasmeen 58.
16 Yasmeen; Fair 2018; Wilson 2015.

ganisation, it is implied that he is the one who has been *de facto* chosen. He claims, again like the two Arab militant leaders mentioned above, that Muslims have, indeed, been attacked. In this context, he presents the case of Kashmir which, he says, has been occupied by India illegally and is subject to human rights abuses. This being so, he argues, India has already broken international agreements about peace so he is merely responding defensively on behalf of Pakistan. As for the last point, he refers to the small size of the Muslim army in the Battle of Badar vis a vis the Quraysh, arguing that it is courage and faith which are needed and not military superiority. Indeed, when his fighters as well as regular Pakistani soldiers had to withdraw from the Kargil peaks which they had occupied in 1999, he quoted seven verses of the *Sūrah Māidah* (5: 51–57), to argue that Prime Minister Nawaz Sharif (b. 1949) had 'gone against Qur'anic injunctions that prohibit Muslims from befriending Jews and Christians'.[17]

The relevant parts of the verses are summed up as follows:

5: 51 (do not take Jews and Christians for friends);
5: 52 (spiritually diseased people run towards them [Jews and Christians] fearing a change of fortune whereas God can give them victory);
5: 53 (the believers will question whether they are the same People of the Book who swore oaths that they were with them [the Muslims] but who have failed them);
5: 54 (if you Muslims become renegades from your religion God will bring others to replace you who will strive [*yujāhidūna*] in His way);
5: 55 (Only God and his Messenger can be your friends);
5: 56 (those who take God and His Messenger as friends achieve victory);
5: 57 (do not choose the People of the Book and those who disbelief and make fun of your religion as friends).

That these verses have been interpreted differently and that *al-Mumtaḥinah* (60: 8) has been interpreted to allow friendship with non-belligerent non-Muslims were not privileged by Sa'īd as interpretations are undertaken in the light of one's ideological imperative and this, for him, was to fight all non-Muslims especially Hindus.

Sa'īd and others from his organisation have expressed themselves in print as given in detail in the books mentioned above. One of these pamphlets, authored by 'Abdul Salām bin Muḥammad, is entitled *Ham jihād kiyũ kar rahē haẽ* (Why

17 Yasmeen 96.

are we waging jihad?). It has been reprinted several times. It explains clearly the organisation's point of view about why it is fighting in Kashmir in eight points. It has been analysed in great detail by Christine Fair who explains all the points given below in relation to the overall theoretical framework of the organisation, comments on its theological justifications, and refutes its historical assumptions.[18] The points given below have, however, been adapted from Wilson since they are given in a succinct form in his book.

1. To eliminate evil and facilitate conversion to, and practice of, Islam.
2. To ensure the ascendancy of Islam.
3. To force non-Muslims to pay Jizyah.
4. To assist the weak and powerless.
5. To avenge the blood of Muslims killed by unbelievers.
6. To punish enemies for breaking promises and treaties.
7. To defend a Muslim state.
8. To liberate Muslim territories under non-Muslim occupation.[19]

As one can see, India is the target on many counts, including 5, 6, and 8 as far as the LeT is concerned. Indeed, the website of LeT—which was probably seen by more people than the pamphlet in question and is being cited for that reason —carried names of lands once occupied by Muslims and these include Spain and other parts of Europe, parts of China, parts of Africa and, of course, India.[20]

More appropriate for our purposes is Sa'īd's exegesis of the *Sūrah Tawbah* (Q. 9). Samina Yasmeen gives a historical account of this work placing it both in the context of the political situation after the September 11 attacks and the development of Sa'īd's thought. It comprises lectures to students being trained for jihad in his centre in Muridke in the summer of 2004. This, being the era of America's 'War on Terror', Sa'īd's aim is to inspire Pakistani Muslims not to give up their struggle against India and to legitimise it through the text of the Qur'an itself.[21] In this chapter, aspects covered by Yasmeen will not be repeated. Those which she has not touched upon, especially how individual verses have been interpreted, will be the main focus. First, however, let us understand the arguments of the author as briefly as possible.

Sa'īd begins by saying that the infidels, who most resemble the Arabs of the seventh century, are the Hindus who worship many deities. Then he goes on to

18 Fair 2018: 159–163.
19 Quoted from Wilson 2011: 15.
20 Ibid 42.
21 Yasmeen 2017: 129–135.

classify the Jews as those who associate other powers with God (*mushrikūn*) on the grounds that they called Ezra (Aziz), the son of God. He also alleges that Christians fall in the same category since they worship Trinity. This classification serves the purpose of making the present situation analogous to that which obtained at the time when Q. 9 was revealed.[22] He lays down rules for declaring Muslims heretics (*takfīr*) by arguing that if people call themselves Muslims but neither pray nor give the alms tax then they are not to be taken at their word. However, their confession of Islam would be acceptable till this aspect of their behaviour does not become evident.[23] Sa'īd's main theme is that it is because Muslims have abandoned jihad that they are oppressed and powerless in the world. His ideas as expressed in his exegesis of Q. 9 are given in the form of a chart below. Although the exegesis purports to be of Q. 9 it refers to other verses dealing with jihad which are given below.

Table 11

Verse	Commentary by Ḥāfiẓ Sa 'īd	Interpretive device
2:190 etc.	Since his study is only on Q. 9, he does not write specifically about these verses.	
9:5	Order to fight unbelievers. It is applicable nowadays also e.g in Kashmir, Palestine, Afghanistan and Iraq (p.40). A local commander for jihad can be appointed just as Abū Bakr was appointed the *amīr* of *Ḥajj* and 'Alī was given the responsibility to announce this verse to the polytheists (pp. 39).	Generalisation/ ideological assumption
9:29	Open war with People of the Book is ordered as their beliefs are wrong till they give *jizyah* and live in humiliation (pp. 127–128).	Generalisation
60:8	Does not write specifically about this verse but does quote six verses forbidding friendship with non-believers (p. 94).	Implicit abrogation of peaceful verses

Source: Sa 'īd *Tawbah*

In addition to the Qur'an, Sa'īd also uses the hadith to support his ideological assumptions which are that jihad is necessary to enable Muslims to gain glory and power in the world and that it goes on for ever. To support the latter view, he uses the hadith that the Prophet was sent to keep fighting till everybody recited the Muslim creed. As mentioned earlier, this is one of those traditions

22 Sa 'īd *Tawbah.*
23 Ibid 60.

which is invariably quoted by radical Islamists (see Annexure C). However, the word 'human beings' or 'people' (*nās*) used in it has also been interpreted as meaning the polytheists of that period; not all people of all times.[24] Sa'īd, however, takes the tradition as applying to all people all the time. He goes on to refute the idea that one should enter into peaceful negotiations with infidels without fighting them because the Prophet entered into them according to the treaty of Ḥudaybiyyah. He says that this was only to build up military strength to ensure victory. Thus, instead of making peaceful negotiations the aim, the real aim should be fighting to achieve victory.

The whole commentary is hortatory and is meant to persuade Muslims to join the ongoing jihadist movements in the world. For this, he claims that it is not necessary for the Islamic state or its head to give a formal permission by first revoking treaties. Most of the exegesis does not refer to other exegeses or concern itself with erudite discussions of semantics, preternatural legends, or other such matters. Every explanation refers to the present international situation and the narrative of Muslim grievances—attacks by the USA, NATO, Israel, and India—occupies the centre stage. Muslim rulers are chastised for their cowardice and for not realising that all their expectations of peace will come to nought. In short, the discursive thrust is political rather than theological though, of course, the theological scaffolding sacralises the whole inspirational effort so as to make Pakistani young men join the war for Kashmir.

While Kashmir is Sa 'īd's special concern, he praises all Muslims fighting against invasions by non-Muslims such as the Palestinians. As for Kashmir, however, he does not even conceal the fact that he sent armed militants into the Indian-adminstered part of the former state because, in his opinion, Kashmir is Muslim territory forcibly occupied by India. Indeed, those who have been killed while fighting for Kashmir are remembered in inspirational hagiographies. Christine Fair collected 918 such hagiographies of these fighters and points out that they celebrate rather than conceal the fact that they were recruited for jihad.[25] In the *tafsīr* itself, he mentions how one of his fighters, a devotee, carried out a spectacular attack (*fidāyī ma'rakah*). The fighter found himself in a military camp in Indian administered Kashmir. However, it being night, he drowsed off. When he woke up it was morning and people were up and about. He took aim in the sunlight and killed many soldiers and then walked out peacefully from the camp.[26] Another such case, that of an American called Abū Ādam Jibrīl

---

24 As mentioned by several scholars, notably Qaraḍāwī (Ghannouchi 2015: 377).

25 Fair forthcoming 185.

26 *Tawbah* 66.

al-Amrīkī (d. 1997?), who attacked Indian army posts in Kashmir, is given in sources proudly owned by the Lashkar.[27]

Sa'īd and his associates were temporarily held in custody in the aftermath of the attacks in Mumbai on 26 November 2008. To this adversity, he responded, characteristically, by using the Qur'an. He wrote the *Tafsīr Sūrah Yūsuf.* This chapter of the Qur'an narrates the story of the Prophet Yusuf (the Biblical Joseph) who is betrayed by his brothers by being sold into slavery in Egypt. In the story as given in the Qur'an he resists the advances of the ruler's wife, and finally ascends to a responsible position in the country. In the end, his brothers are humbled and he gains success. The quality Sa'īd emphasises in this exegesis is patience in the face of adversity. His own situation is parallel to that of Joseph, in his opinion. He too is oppressed by the state; his followers are incarcerated and he has to remain steadfast to the cause. He also emphasises public service in order to claim a high moral ground in the eyes of the public and to ensure survival. Jihad must go on, he says, but at times it is necessary to conceal it.[28]The tone of the work is patient though there is implicit criticism of decision-makers who sabotage movements such as his. But even with the usual polemics, Sa 'īd does not advocate an open militant struggle against the rulers of Pakistan.

In this matter, Sa'īd's view is different from the Arab radicals mentioned earlier since they justify fighting their own rulers. Sa'īd, while vehemently supporting militancy against India, the USA, and Israel, rules out any hostility towards the rulers of Pakistan. Indeed, he specifically claims that he does not allow any militant attack within Pakistan.[29] Thus, Sa'īd's views are sometimes taken as being rationalisations for policies pursued by the Pakistani military. This seems to be the reason the Zarb-e-Azb and Radd-ul-Fasad operations, in which other radical groups were targeted by the Pakistan army, did not affect him.

Mawlānā Mas'ūd Aẓhar (b. 1968), whose Jaish-e-Muḥammad is alleged to have attacked India several times, preaches the necessity of jihad through his lectures, pamphlets, and books. Mas'ūd was born to working class parents in south Punjab. He completed his religious education at the Jamia Binoria in Karachi where he came under the influence of Muftī Shamazaī. He was also influenced by the Deobandi cleric and exegete, Aḥmad 'Alī Lāhorī, whose commentary on the Qur'an he quotes with approval for its hard interpretations of the

27 In Cook 2007: 183.
28 Sa 'īd *Yūsuf* 273–274.
29 Ibid 319.

verses about jihad. At the age of twenty, he went to Afghanistan in order to undertake a course on handling weapons and basic tactics. Apparently, he got a chance to fight against the Soviets though the jihad in Afghanistan was winding down. In 1989, still enthusiastic for jihad, he returned to Pakistan and joined the Harkat al-Mujahidin which was training young men for jihad in Kashmir. Mas'ūd was now entrusted with a mission which took him to Srinagar where he was arrested on 01 February 1994. For several years he remained incarcerated in jail but, quite unexpectedly, he was rescued when religious activists hijacked an aeroplane from Kathmandu and landed it in Kabul which was then ruled by the Taliban. Back in Pakistan, Mas'ūd was welcomed and, it is rumoured, facilitated by the ISI in setting up his own militia called the Jaish-e-Muhammad. Mas'ūd is no mere theoretician; he is also an administrator, leader, and military planner. In this book, however, we are only concerned with his writings.

Mas'ūd tells us about his career as an author in the preface of his book which was published as *Faḍā'il-ē-jihād*. This is a genre of writing on jihad of which the first work is 'Abdallāh bin al-Mubārak (d. 181/797). Mubārak's book has 262 *aḥādīth* about the rewards for martyrs.[30] Out of these, thirteen are about large-eyed beautiful women in paradise (*hūr al-'ayn*) who are married to the martyr and whose charms are superior to his earthly wife.[31] This kind of literature was probably written to inspire youths to jihad. In Mas'ūd's case too, the purpose was to recruit youths to the project of jihad against India. The book began as a pamphlet in 1994. The author initially put in some Quranic verses and forty Prophetic traditions from *Bukhārī* to explain the high religious significance of jihad. One of his major arguments is that jihad was aggressive during the time of the expansion of Islam and those who portray it as being merely defensive are simply misleading the world and causing damage to Muslims since such misrepresentations would dilute their spirit of conquest and resistance. He implores Muslims not to abandon jihad. And this is only possible if, to begin with, Muslims do not get into theoretical considerations like the 'lesser' and the 'greater' jihad.[32]

Although the book was reprinted several times, the author always regarded it as an incomplete work.[33] He got a chance to complete it by offering a summary and commentary on a book on jihad by Ibn al-Niḥās Abū Zakariyyā (d. 814/1411) which belongs to a sub-genre of Islamic writing known as *Faḍā'il al-jihād* (the benefits of jihad). This kind of writing was meant to inspire young men to join

30 Jarrar 2004: 320.
31 Ibid 334.
32 Aẓhar 1999: 118.
33 Ibid 3.

expeditions against the Byzantines or the crusaders or other wars of the Muslim empires against their opponents. This particular book captured Mas'ūd's attention who translated it into Urdu with additions and explanations and published it in 1999. It gave the author a chance to disseminate his own views about the ongoing jihad which, he says, is taking place already. He begins by narrating how he wrote this book. Its copy was brought to him in the Tahar Jail in India where he had no books of reference nor did he have any peace of mind.[34] He then constructs his anti-Western narrative in which he sees the English language and even Western medicine as part of the conspiracy to subdue Muslims. There is, however, a way to overcome Europe and eventually 'enslave' it—and that is jihad.[35]

The book itself has chapters on aspects of jihad: the high spiritual position of those who fight, the great rewards of fighters (among them, beautiful women in paradise), and so on. Each chapter begins with verses from the Qur'an followed by a number of *aḥādīth* and quotations from scholars supportive of jihad. At the end of every chapter, Mas'ūd gives his own ideas, applying them to the conditions of Pakistan and Afghanistan in particular and the whole world in general. He distinguishes between jihad being a duty discharged by a few people who fight or are professional soldiers (*farḍul kifāyah*) and that which is incumbent upon all Muslims (*farḍul 'ayn*). The first necessitates attacks, or raids, at least once a year, on territories held by the infidels. This, he says, is not going on. Instead, infidel forces are in Muslim lands which makes jihad a *farḍul 'ayn*. Thus, it is not necessary for anyone to take permission of authorities be they familial or governmental.[36] While discussing the duty of guarding the borders of Muslim lands (*ribāt*), he asserts that Spain, Eastern Europe, and India were all once ruled by Muslims so they are the borders too and it is because they were not guarded that they have gone out of Muslim control.[37]

In common with all radical militants, Mas'ūd takes pains to refute the traditionally held ideas about jihad among South Asian Muslims. This he does throughout the book and, for further emphasis, he also sums up his views in an annexure. First, he says that if one wants to fight either a single unbeliever or a group of them, no permission from a ruler (*amīr*) is required. If the ruler has abandoned jihad, then also no permission is required. If there is no ruler or it is probable that he will not permit jihad, then too no permission is required.

34 Ibid 9–10.
35 Ibid 11–14.
36 Ibid 34–36.
37 Ibid 260–261.

And, finally, a leader (*amīr*) can be appointed by consensus instead of relying on rulers who do not rule according to *Sharīʿah*.[38] He also dispenses with the condition that the opponent should be invited to accept Islam before declaring war. This is necessary if the opponent has never been invited to Islam but not otherwise. Moreover, if the Muslims have already been attacked, such invitation is out of the question. In the same way, he argues that using fire or cannon and attacking at night are all permissible even if women and children are present.[39]

In addition to this work, Masʿūd also provides an exegesis of those verses of the Qur'an which directly or indirectly deal with jihad in a book in four volumes, entitled *Fatḥ al-jawwād* and sub-titled *Fī maʿārif āyāt al-jihād*.[40] Masʿūd uses several interpretative devices to offer the militant meaning of jihad. One of them is interpolation, sometimes parenthetically, while giving the meaning of verses. This is generally done in the explanation of the verse and it leads the reader to his preferred meaning. His translation of 2: 114—which condemns people who forbid others to worship in mosques—deviates from the literal meaning of the text. He claims that mosques should be made secure through jihad. Those who make the mosques desolate will be punished through jihad and their power will be taken away.[41] In 2: 195—which is about spending money in the way of God and not putting one's self in destruction—he adds that this expenditure should be on jihad and defines self-destruction as abandoning jihad.[42] While explaining a verse in *Āl-Imrān* (Q. 3)—which asks Muslims rhetorically whether they would turn away from Islam if the Prophet dies, he substitutes jihad for the faith so that the question becomes: 'would you people turn away from jihad or Islam [if the Prophet dies]?' (3: 144).[43] While explaining the concept of *ṭāghūt*—in this case, in a verse in al-Nisā' (Q.4)—which exhorts people to fight for God not the devil (4: 76)—he uses semantic expansion to define *ṭāghūt* as not just idol, devil, magician, and evil as traditional Arabic dictionaries do. For him, it is any individual, power, or philosophy which opposes Islam. Among the examples he gives of such powers are colonial rulers and, at present, the United States. Moreover, modern ideologies such as nationalism, capitalism, etc., are also included in it. In short, his expanded meaning of the term makes the Qur'anic order relevant for the targets he has in mind for his mission of jihad.[44]

---

38 Ibid 629 – 630.
39 Ibid 630 – 633.
40 Aẓhar *Fatḥ*.
41 Ibid Vol. 1: 14.
42 Ibid 45.
43 Ibid 245.
44 Ibid 385 – 389.

One of Mas'ūd's favourite interpretive devices is semantic expansion. For instance, he uses certain terms interchangeably even if their meaning is distinct. For instance, jihad itself is used interchangeably with *qitāl*, preferring the latter meaning throughout the book. Sometimes, the Urdu text constructs both as a compound name, for example, when he writes: 'taught jihad and *qital*' (*jihād ō qitāl kī ta'līm dī*). This helps to give the impression that jihad is restricted to only fighting. *Fitnah* is explained with reference to other exegetes, especially those who think it refers to unbelief.[45] However, exegetes who have equated it with the sin of attacking Muslims or persecuting them are passed over in silence.[46] At another place, while giving another definition of *fitnah* as sin, he calls it the sin of creating differences among Muslims to weaken their military prowess, innovation, and tardiness in fighting (*jihād mẽ sustī*).[47] These meanings have implications for interpreting the verses relating to fighting. For instance, the orders in 2: 193 and 8: 39—about fighting till *fitnah* ends—become orders to wage an eternal war even in contemporary times if the term refers to unbelief. If, however, other meanings are preferred, they can be interpreted differently. Mas'ūd says that some classical exegetes take both as general orders while others use the hermeneutical device of specification, applying them to the Arab polytheists of that period. He is of the view that, whether these verses are general or restricted, they refer to *fitnah*, meaning 'that power which can threaten Muslims'. Hence, they order warfare to break the power of the unbelievers which actually implies that jihad is an ongoing, valid order, even in contemporary times.[48] Below are Mas'ūd's explanations of the relevant verses.

Table 12

Verse	Commentary by Mas'ūd Azhar	Interpretive device
2:190	Fight those who fight you resolutely but do not transgress against non-combatants. Refers to those (a) who *can* fight Muslims whether they do so or not (b) all infidels always wish to fight Islam, so all must be fought with. Moreover, Muslims are promised dominance in the world hence the verse cannot be restricted to defence (Vol. 1: 29–30).	Semantic expansion/ ideological assumptions

45 Ibid 40–41.
46 Ibid 41.
47 Ibid Vol. 2: 147.
48 Ibid 388–389.

Table 12 *(Continued)*

Verse	Commentary by Mas'ūd Azhar	Interpretive device
2:191	*Fitnah* means that infidels have greater power than Muslims. Though the verses refer to Arab polytheists which he mentions, he makes its order to fight general. (Vol. 1: 33–36).	Semantic expansion/ generalization
2:193	Fight those who associate other powers with God (*mushrikīn*) till their power comes to an end and God's religion is imposed. Some exegetes consider it restricted to Arabs but others consider it of general application. *Fitnah* means unbelief (*kufr*) which must be combated so Jihad is for ever (Vol. 1: 39–41).	As above
8:39	Explains *fitnah* in detail as unbelief and its power. Keep fighting till this power is subdued and Islam rules (Vol. 2: 193–197). Islam has come to dominate so Muslims should rule. It is not enough that the non-believers rule the land, only allowing us to pray (Vol. 2: 197).	Semantic expansion/ ideological assumption
8:61	He refers to the verse 8: 60 which instructs Muslims to keep a force which overawes non-Muslims. However, sometimes peace may be necessary for tactical reasons provided no treaty should be of more than ten years. This is mere permission not an order. For some it is abrogated by 9: 5 & 9: 29 (Vol. 2: 293–295).	Ideological assumption/ abrogation
9:5	Unbelievers may be fought with wherever found. He quotes four swords (a) Arab polytheists (9: 5) (b) People of the Book [9: 29] (c) Hypocrites (9: 73) (d) Muslim rebels who fight other Muslims, *Al-Hujurāt* 49: 9. It is general and still valid and abrogates verses of peace (Vol. 2: 380–381).	Abrogation/ generalization
9:29	Fight the people of the Book and other unbelievers for their wrong beliefs till they accept the political dominance of Islam and pay *jizyah* being humiliated (Vol. 2: 473–481). He also explains it with refer to *dhimmī* rules (Vol. 2: 479).	Generalization
60:8	Muslims can be kind and just to non-hostile unbelievers but cannot make friends with them. However, it is merely permission not an order. In *Jalālayn* and other sources this is abrogated. It may also refer to non-combatants as Ibn Kathīr says. He prefers Ibn Kathīr's explanation (Vol. 4: 351–353).	Strongly suggests abrogation/specification (of non-combatants)

Source: Aẓhar *Fatḥ*, 4 vols.

Mas'ūd Azhar makes efforts to explain away verses which advocate living in peace either by citing exegetes who regard them as having been abrogated (*man-*

sūkh) or giving alternative explanations (*ta'wil*). His ideological assumptions, like those of Ḥāfiẓ Sa'īd, are: jihad is aggressive; the downfall of Muslims is because they have abandoned it; the leaders of Muslims are either cowards, apostates, or Western stooges who have given up jihad. Hence, verses for peace are also turned ineffective through his interpretations. For instance, the offer of peace in 2: 192—but if they desist; you do the same—is interpreted as 'desist from unbelief', not 'desist from fighting' ,i.e. non-aggression is changed to conversion.[49] Another verse (4: 90)—if they do not fight you, or join people with whom you have a treaty of peace, then do not fight them—which allows Muslims to live in peace with non-belligerent non-Muslims, has also been explained in such a way that it does not lead to any tenable version of a peaceful co-existence. He does give the literal meaning of the verse, but then he asserts that it has been misused to justify anti-jihad ideas. However, he says, neither war not peace are the real aims of good conduct according to Islam. The real aim is obedience to God so both peace and war are under divine orders.[50] Obedience is further explained as the establishment of Muslim power; not peaceful relations.

The commentary of Q. 9 gives him a chance to expand upon his philosophy of aggressive jihad and make it relevant to the present context. He explicitly tells contemporary Muslims to obey the order in the verse suggesting, as we have mentioned above, that it has abrogated all the verses allowing peace treaties. Here he also takes the support of the hadith mentioned earlier which says that the Prophet was sent with four swords. Indeed, while explaining 9: 8—which is about non-believers not caring for friendship with Muslims when they are powerful—he asserts that non-believers intrinsically hate believers. Here he explicitly mentions the United Nations and Human Rights organisations which, he claims, are meant to make Muslims lose their spirit for combativeness and give up jihad.[51] He also uses his explanation of 9: 5 to justify *takfīr* which, as we have seen, is a practice of radical Islamists. This he does by reasoning that the verse says that those who say their prayers and give alms will not be killed, which means that these are the only visible signs of being a believing Muslim. So, by the same logic, those who do not adhere to them may be killed by an Islamic state.[52]

It will be observed that Mas'ūd Aẓhar uses two discourses to justify jihad. The first is derived from his use of the commentaries of classical jurists and his own interpretations of the verses of the Qur'an. Using the interpretive devices

49 Ibid Vol. 1: 37.
50 Ibid 423.
51 Ibid Vol. 2: 388–389.
52 Ibid 379.

of semantic expansion, favouring exegetes who consider the pro-peace verses abrogated and giving alternative explanations of them, he promotes the discourse of aggressive jihad on theological grounds. The second, however, combines the Muslim grievance of being under attack from non-Muslim powers. This strand of the narrative refers to Palestine, Bosnia, Kashmir, and Chechnya, etc. This second view enables him to declare jihad as a duty for all Muslims for which individuals do not require the permission of the family or the state. Since all kinds of weapons can be used, scruples about women and children getting killed are dismissed as being unrealistic under the circumstances. He also justifies suicide attacks on the grounds that in the classical era of Islam a single champion did attack an armed host for the greater glory of Islam. If such missions of devotion (*fidāyī ḥamlah*) are to impress the enemy or to benefit Muslims in the war, then they are justified.[53] However, none of the classical battles he mentions featured armed fighters attacking unarmed civilians, especially women and children.

One subsidiary view he promotes off and on is that of an ideal Islamic state. The model for one he mentions approvingly is that of Afghanistan under the Taliban, primarily because Mullah ʻUmar has opened the door of jihad again.[54] These views are not confined to the above books which most semi-educated would-be recruits to the cause of jihad would not read. He also disseminates these ideas through his lectures, pamphlets, and sermons in accessible language and without learned references to classical scholarship. He takes pride in being a major fighter against India though, for tactical reasons, he denies specific attacks such as Pathankot and Uri, both in 2016, which he is blamed for.

There are several other radical writers in Pakistan who have written in Urdu. While noticing all of them would look like a catalogue of very similar views, let us look at two major figures among them. The first is Mawlānā Nūr Muḥammad (d. 2010), whose book entitled *Jihād-e-Afghānistān* is probably the first detailed writing on the armed struggle of the Afghans against the Soviet army in that country. The book is in the form of *fatāwā*, i.e. questions about the Islamic legality of the jihad are answered by the author with reference to sources. The book gives arguments about jihad which were used in the Middle East as we have seen and which are repeated by all the writers we are dealing with in this chapter. Regarding the war against the Soviet Union in Afghanistan, and like all radical Islamists, he refutes two traditional views: that the order for jihad can only be given by an Islamic leader (*amīr*); and that the strength of Muslims should be

53 Aẓhar 1999: 351–354.
54 Ibid 328.

such that there are chances of winning the war (half the number of the opponents is suggested). Like Farāj, 'Azzām, and others we have been reading about, he also calls the first totally wrong and recommends that a leader be appointed by the fighters.[55] As for the second, he asserts that even nine fighters are enough to fight a guerrilla war. The only condition, apart from their being Muslims, is that the fighters should not be wiped out of existence.[56] In support of his view that a guerrilla war can be fought without the explicit permission of the overall ruler, he cites the story of Abū Baṣīr who had run away from Mecca to join the other Muslims at Medina. However, according to the treaty of Ḥudaybiyyah, he had to be returned. But, being a brave man, he broke away from his captors and established himself as a guerrilla leader in an isolated place. Other people, such as Abū Jandal (d. 16/639), also joined him till the Quraysh themselves requested that he should be called to Medina. From this he infers that guerrilla action is possible without permission and, further, that, since Abū Baṣīr and his companions were not explicitly forbidden by the Prophet to fight on their own, such kind of warfare is legitimate.[57] The book is full of the supposed evils (some totally false) of communism (that women are shared; religion is destroyed, etc.), Prophetic traditions in favour of jihad, and Quranic verses urging warfare. Expectedly, 9: 29—the verse about fighting the People of the Book till they pay the poll tax—is interpreted as being valid so as to break the power of the non-believers.[58] Similarly, *fitnah* in 8: 39—which says Muslims should fight till *fitnah* comes to an end and religion is only Islam—is defined as the presence of the non-believers itself. His Urdu translation rendered into English reads: 'You fight those non-believers (*kafirõ*) till the *fitnah* of the non-believers comes to an end and God's law becomes ascendant'.[59] The permission of 'killing them [the infidels] wherever found' (2: 191 and 9: 5) is interpreted as a general permission for guerrilla war which, of course, was going on in Afghanistan at that time.[60] Indeed, the overall purpose of the book is to legitimise the guerrilla war in Afghanistan and exhort young men to join it as a jihad in defence of Muslim lands.

The other such figure, also writing and preaching to motivate young men to fight in Afghanistan, is Mawlānā Faḍl Muḥammad Yūsufza'ī, a cleric and teacher at the Jamia Ulum Islamia Banuri Town in Karachi. He too has written a book in

55 Muhammad, N. 1987: 84.
56 Ibid 86; 128.
57 Ibid 86–87.
58 Ibid 188.
59 Ibid.
60 Ibid 190.

the *Faḍā'il* genre using the same book which Mas'ūd Aẓhar did. Like Mas'ūd, he too uses the book to preach the necessity of jihad to a Pakistani audience. He emphatically rejects the modernist position—especially that of Sir Sayyid, Mirzā Ghulām Aḥmad, Mawlānā Waḥīduddīn, and Maḥmūd Shaltūt—that jihad is merely defensive. Indeed, both the Qur'an and the hadith as well as Muslim history are used to prove that aggressive jihad (*iqdāmī*) is not only permissible but also necessary. Indeed, it is recommended that non-Muslim countries should be attacked at least once a year.[61] As for the excuses given by the deniers of jihad—the absence of an Islamic ruler (*imām*) and disparity of military power —for both matters his position is the same as that of Nūr Muḥammad and, for that matter, all the Islamist militants we have been studying.[62] As the book is meant to motivate people to fight the Americans in Afghanistan, the Taliban are praised as a good Muslim regime which should be defended against 'infidel' attacks.[63]

The last major writer we shall be considering is Muftī Niẓāmuddīn Shamazaī (1951–2008). He was born in Swat, studied in a seminary called Jamia Faruqia in Karachi, and then taught in the Jamia Banuria in the same city. He is reputed to be a fiery speaker and his thoughts are collected together in two volumes of sermons in Urdu. Though the sermons are on a number of subjects, the recurrent themes are based on the conspiracy theories of the post-September 11 period when the American forces had attacked Afghanistan. His world view, often repeated in the Urdu press in Pakistan and quite common among students and other members of the middle class, are that the Jews control the finances of the whole world and dominate the USA. He thinks that the USA exercises complete control on the decision-making process in Pakistan citing General Musharraf's siding with that country against the Taliban. He refers to the *Protocols of the Elders of Zion*, a forged work written to malign Jews, as proof that there is a grand conspiracy in the world to harm Islam. He claims that Pakistan's elite—politicians, bureaucrats, military officers, and secular intellectuals—are the pawns of the Jews and Christians whether knowingly or otherwise. NGOs, in his opinion, are the greatest culprits and their main purpose is to spread atheism, liberalism, Christianity, and diluting Islamic religiosity. Indeed, all non-Muslim powers and the elite of Muslim countries join hands to eliminate the spirit of jihad among the Muslim youth since that is the only thing they are afraid of. The only section of society which resists these nefarious designs are the cler-

61 Yūsufzaī 1999: 77–78.
62 Ibid 67–70; 447–480.
63 Ibid 672.

gy and, of course, the seminaries in which they are trained. The sermons are not in the form of a traditional exegetical work on jihad but Shamazaī gives a short order which would be understood as a *fatwā* by his audience. It is that Pakistanis are authorised to kill American military personnel wherever they find them.[64] In another sermon on jihad, he says that jihad should be against those who are apparently Muslim but do not actually practice Islam.[65] Afghanistan under the Taliban was, for Shamazaī, the ideal Islamic state.[66]

More importantly, Shāmazaī also wrote a book on the emergence of the Messiah towards the end of the world.[67] This is a set of millenarian beliefs which also involve armed struggle hence its relevance for this study. We have seen how Mirzā Ghulām Aḥmad proclaimed himself the promised *Mahdī* in the colonial period. Also, during the same period, the prophecy of 'the ultimate triumph of Islamic power under a reborn *Mahdi,* was gaining currency'.[68] Less well known, because of its remoteness in time, is the Mahdawiyyah movement of Sayyid Muḥammad Jawnpūrī (847–910/1443–1505). According to B.M.Wali's *Insāf nāmah,*[69] in which he refers to a source of 1543, Jawnpūrī claimed to be the *Mahdī* and established communities which practiced mystical worship while living away from the world. He practiced *takfīr* by stigmatising those who did not believe in his Mahdi-ship as non-believers. He also used the language of jihad raising his sword in the air and proclaiming 'for them only this remains'—by 'them' he meant the Mughal judiciary and clergy upon whom he vowed to impose the *jizyah.*[70] In short, the belief in the *Mahdī* has resulted in allegations of unbelief upon other Muslims in Indian Muslim history.

Basically Shamazaī's book, in common with other writers on the subject,[71] constructs a belief system on a number of *aḥādīth.* These are said to be over ninety and have been repeated throughout history which enables their supporters to call them *mutawātir.* However, critics doubt their authenticity on the grounds that they do not occur in the collections of *Bukhārī* and *Muslim* and that there have been pretenders to the *Mahdī*-ship in the past.[72] Shamazaī and others of his view nevertheless hold the doctrine of the emergence of the *Mahdī* as an ar-

---

64 Abid Vol. 1 2003: 417–419.
65 Ibid 307–308.
66 Ibid 247–248.
67 Shamazaī 2012.
68 Qureshi 1999: 112.
69 MacLean 2000 in Eaton 2003: 150–166. All citations are to this source.
70 Ibid 157.
71 Sulaiman 2013.
72 Ibid 82–83.

ticle of faith for Muslims. The belief is complicated since sources about the millenarian tradition mention both Christ and the *Mahdī*.[73]However, Shamazaī distinguishes between the two, saying that both will come, but Imām Mahdī will come earlier. He will be fighting against a wicked ruler with mainly Jewish followers called the one-eyed Dajjāl. When Christ emerges, he will lead the prayers but the Mahdī will continue to exercise power with the blessing of Christ. The Dajjāl will be defeated and eventually die and Imām Mahdī will initiate a righteous war and give just rule to the world before the last day.

These traditions are expressed in variant forms and, as mentioned earlier, there are many of them. However, the one quoted below sums up their salient themes and has been quoted in the books of apocalypse mentioned above. A hadith which is always quoted is that there will be fighters with 'black flags' from the east (of Arabia) in the area known as Khurasan. Khurasan is the area now covered by Afghanistan and northern Pakistan. This makes the Mahdī part of a force coming from the areas in which the Taliban operate. This hadith and several others like it are in common circulation in Pakistan.[74] It is a reference which resonates with the Pashto-speaking Taliban whether from Afghanistan or Pakistan. Moreover, the Punjabi Taliban, fighting to liberate and Islamise Kashmir, also a part of Khurasan in their view, are also thrilled by it. The relevance of the traditions about Khurasan is that they mention a war with India (*ghazwah-i-hind*). This, of course, is a godsend for people who seek narratives, the more sacred the better, to inspire young men to fight with India. No wonder, then, that they too are quoted in Taliban sources.

Here this hadith has been quoted from Saleem Shahzad (d. 2011), the journalist who remained in close contact with them, on the assumption that this is the form which he must have heard from the Taliban. He says that this hadith is from the *Kanz al-'Ummāl:*

> Na'im bin Hammad in al-Fitan reports that Abu Hurayrah said that the Messenger of Allah [Upon whom be peace] said: "A group of you will conquer India, Allah will open for them [India] until they come with its kings chained—Allah having forgiven their sins. When they return back [from India], they will find Ibn Maryam [Jesus] in Syria".[75]

73 Shamazaī 2012: 37–38.

74 The Ahmadis too have millenarian beliefs among which one is that Christ died a natural death in Kashmir and that Mirzā Ghulām Aḥmad was the promised Messiah. This is expressed in many places including Ahmad 1900; 1880 and Ahmad and Grunebaum 1970: 83–84).

75 Shahzad 2011: 200–201.

According to Shahzad, this kind of indoctrination, capitalising on the appeal of the sacred, played a notable role in radicalising the youth of Afghanistan and FATA.

To sum up, the Pakistani radical Islamist militants start with the ideological assumptions that jihad is a duty which is now incumbent on all Pakistani Muslims; that the leaders of the state have abandoned it; and, that it is now their duty to appoint a leader (*imām*) among themselves to carry it out. Moreover, they also believe that jihad is aggressive and, if it is against powerful enemies, unconventional methods of fighting can be used (including suicide missions). In an important sense then, they usurp the state's narrative that it has the monopoly over the means of violence. This is an important change in the conventional view about jihad, which, as we have seen, was first noticeable in the war of Sayyid Aḥmad Barēlwī against the Sikhs. It was then witnessed in subsequent anti-colonial resistance movements and now manifests itself in the war of certain *jihadi* groups against established states in South Asia. Indeed, in a sense, the militants themselves constitute a state in the offing. Thus, they, like the conventional state, claim their monopoly over power. But does this narrative go unchallenged? Or do Muslim religious scholars—not to mention other people—challenge it on theological grounds? To this question we turn in the next chapter.

10 Refuting the Radicals

There is a common perception that Muslim scholars, clerics, and academics do not aggressively condemn bombings and suicide attacks on civilians. However, such attacks have been condemned and the ideas thought to have legitimised them have, in fact, been challenged and refuted by Muslims. The Shaikh al-Aẓhar Jadd al-Ḥaqq (1917–1996), regarded by many as the highest authority of Sunni Islam, gave a long and detailed *fatwā* against Farāj's *Farīḍah al-Ghaiba* arguing that the ruler is the representative of the people (*wakīl al-ummah*) and does not become an infidel simply by not applying the *sharī'ah*. Ḥaqq goes on to argue that only by renouncing the *Sharī'ah* in its entirety does the ruler, or anyone for that matter, become an infidel. Thus, he rules out rebellion against the rulers of Muslim countries which is one of the main arguments of *Farīḍah* as well as the other works of the radical Islamists and militants.[1]

John Esposito, taking notice of this assumption, refutes it in his preface to Ṭāhirul Qādrī's *fatwā* against such violent acts. He reminds the readers that, in fact, the attacks of September 11 was condemned by Yūsuf Qaraḍāwī (12 September 2001), though he is better remembered for having approved of such measures in the case of Israel. Moreover, Saudi Arabia's grand Muftī, Shaikh 'Abdul 'Azīz bin Bāz condemned the September 11 attacks on 15 September. Qaraḍāwī's monumental book on jihad, *Fiqh al-jihād*, which has been cited earlier, refutes the arguments of the radical Islamists and asserts that Muslims should live in peaceful coexistence with all those who are at peace with them.[2] Nor is this

---

1 Peters 1996: 165–66.

2 For the book, see Qaraḍāwī 2009. The fatwā is summarised as follows: Yūsuf al-Qaraḍāwī, along with Ṭāriq al-Bishrī [judge], Dr Muhammad S. al-Awā (professor of Comparative Law and Sharī'a in Egypt), Dr Haytham al-Khayyāt (Islamic scholar from Syria), Fahmi Houaydi (Islamic scholar and columnist from Egypt), and Sheikh Ṭāhā Jābir al-'Alwānī (Chairman of the North America Fiqh Council), issued a fatwā against 9/11 in response to a question by 'Abdul Rashīd, the senior most chaplain in the American armed forces. The question was as to what were the duties of Muslims in American uniform in the war on terror. The answer was that indiscriminate slaughter is forbidden (killing even one person is like killing all humanity in Q. 5: 32). Indeed, the terrorist acts in the USA were 'waging war against society' (*hirābah*), punishable by death by crucifixion, cutting off hands and feet or exile (5: 33–34). Thus Muslims in the American armed forces are duty bound to fight the terrorists. However, the fatwā goes on, Muslims are uneasy because when the US forces go out to fight Muslims in other countries, innocent people will also be killed along with the offenders. Such a predicament should cause unease in situations where people are free in their choices. But since members of the armed forces cannot choose not to fight when ordered to do so, they must fight despite 'discomfort spiritually or psychologically'. Even postings to non-combatant roles need not be requested since that too will

https://doi.org/10.1515/9783110716986-013

all: the Amman message which delegitimised the arguments of the radical Islamists in July 2005 came from figures as eminent as Shaikh Sayyid Ṭanṭāwī, Rector of Al-Azhar (1928–2010), the Shī'a Grand Ayatollah Al-Ḥusainī 'Alī al-Sīstānī(b. 1930) and, once again, Yūsuf Qaraḍāwī himself. Then came the 2007 open letter from 138 prominent Muslim leaders who reached out in friendship and understanding to other faiths. This was highly welcomed by the Archbishop of Canterbury, Rowan Williams (b. 1950 and archbishop from 2002–2012), Pope Benedict XVI (b. 1927 and pope from 2005–2013), the Orthodox Patriarch Alexei II of Russia (1928–2008 and Patriarch from 1990–2008), and Mark Hanson (b. 1946), the presiding bishop of the Lutheran World Federation from 2003–2010.[3] Afifi al-Akiti also refuted what he described as the '*fitnah*' of Islamist radicalism. In his *fatwā*, he points out that 'no Muslim authority has declared war' and any Muslim who fights in such a war 'becomes a murderer and not a martyr or a hero'.[4] He also condemns suicide bombings and the killing of non-combatants pointing out that an Israeli woman, even if militarised, cannot be killed unless 'she herself (and not someone else from her army) is engaged in direct combat'.[5] In India and Pakistan, too, a number of Muslim scholars, some at the cost of their lives, have spoken out against such acts.

The modernist tradition, as expected, interprets Islam in ways which rule out militancy. This tradition continued in Pakistan especially in the works of Khalifa Abdul Hakim (1896–1959) which are mostly in English. He was a scholar at the Institute of Islamic Culture in Lahore—the city where, as we have seen, similar ideas were also advocated by Parwēz at least as far as jihad was concerned. Hakim begins with injunctions against killing except to destroy *fitnah* and *fasād*. He defines *fitnah* as 'trial, temptation, putting a man in difficulties. It also means persecution, social tyranny, or social disorder, or forcibly keeping a man from pursuing the right path, or misleading a man into false pursuits, or into deviation from truth' and *fasād* is 'corruption and disruption and signifies social disorder and tyranny'.[6] The wars of the Prophet, he says, were against those who 'denied all liberty of conscience to human beings'.[7] However, wars need not be only defensive, so if an enemy is 'preparing to destroy your liberties

---

'harm their future careers, shed misgivings on their patriotism, or similar sentiments' (Qaraḍāwī et.al 2001: n.p).

3 Esposito 2010: xxiii-xxiv.

4 Akiti 2005: 19.

5 Ibid 32.

6 Hakim 1953: 181.

7 Ibid 182.

you must crush him before he becomes too strong for you'.[8] His ideal Islamic state will be a 'socialist republic' where everyone will have the same basic human rights—quite unlike Bannā, Quṭb, and Mawdūdī's state where non-Muslims and women will have restrictions placed over them. This state will 'secure international peace' more sincerely than the United Nations or any other institution.[9] Hakim's writing is polemical rather than scholarly. He presents an idealised version of Islam contrasting it with the actual conduct of Western powers. He uses the verses of the Qur'an and the hadith selectively without attempting to give a rigorous exegesis of the former. This was the kind of vague writing which supported the Pakistani state's use of Islam in the nineteen fifties and sixties when modernist versions of Islam were the political necessity of the ruling elite of Pakistan. But the lack of rigour resulted in his views not being much popular outside official circles.

Among those whose views did get more international fame was a Muslim of South Asian origin resident abroad by the name of Ziauddin Sardar (b. 1951). His work seems to have much appeal for the youth among the Muslim diaspora in Britain which is susceptible to radical Islamist influences. In his book *Reading the Qur'an*, he presents a thematic exegesis of the first two chapters of the Book. The verses about jihad, 2:190 – 195, are the subject of a chapter entitled 'war and Peace'.[10] Sardar uses the hermeneutical devices of using the occasions of revelation (*asbāb al-nuzūl*) to determine the historical context of the text. This is then juxtaposed to contemporary times and interpreted 'in terms of their spirit rather than as specific injunctions'.[11] This is very much in the spirit of Fazlur Rahman's 'twofold movement'—take concrete cases in the Qur'an and deduce a principle; apply this to contemporary cases—which has been mentioned earlier.[12] Sardar begins his commentary on the above mentioned verses by putting them in the historical context. The nascent Muslim community was in danger of being grievously harmed, even wiped out of existence, as the Quraysh were preparing for the Battle of Badar (624 C.E). These verses justify fighting in self defence. However, this does not allow aggression. Thus, the major battles—Badar, Uḥud, and Khandaq—were all defensive. Thus fighting is to resist *fitnah* which Sardar defines as 'persecution, suffering, slaughter, sedition and constant distress. It is synonymous with hindering people from practising their faith'.[13]

8 Ibid 188.
9 Ibid 208 and 210.
10 Sardar 2011: 135 – 141.
11 Ibid xix.
12 Rahman 1982: 20.
13 Sardar 2011: 138.

The verse 2: 193—fight till *fitnah* comes to an end and religion is all for God—means ending 'persecution and oppression' and not 'the domination of Islam and the subjugation of non-believers'. It ensures freedom of conscience for all and not only for Muslims. Here he specifically rejects Quṭb's interpretation that it means making Islam dominant and approvingly quotes Mawdūdī who believes that everybody can hold on to their beliefs. Of course, Mawdūdī makes this conditional to their being politically subservient to Muslims and never to exercise sovereignty in their own right but this Sardar does not point out here.[14]

Although Sardar's commentary of the Qur'an is only about Q. 2, he also refers to the 'sword' verse 9: 5 and 3: 149. He interprets the first by using the device of specification which is quite common among exegetes who deny that jihad necessarily means fighting against all non-Muslims for ever. Like others he says that 'it is a specific instruction to those in the thick of battle' and concludes that the breakers of treaties, the pagan Arabs of that period with whom there was an ongoing war, were 'the specific people to whom this verse refers'.[15] As for the verse of *Āl Imrān* (Q. 3)—do not follow the unbelievers who would turn you back to unbelief (3: 149)—he explains it with reference to the occasion of its revelation, the Battle of Uḥud, in which the Muslims again faced existential danger. In this context, he says, God encouraged Muslims since a battle was imminent but this does not mean that it is valid for ever. Such context-bound verses, specifically meant for the people they addressed, are not eternal or universal general commands though, laments Sardar, they have 'a strong appeal for some disillusioned Muslim youth'.[16] These are the youth who bombed the London underground system and precipitated the 21 century's greatest crisis involving Muslims so far—the attacks of September 11.

This event provoked South Asian thinkers, including some *'ulamā*, to distance themselves from the narratives adduced by radical Islamists to justify violence. In India, Mawlānā Waḥīduddīn Khān (b. 1925), whom we have met earlier in his anti-Mawdūdī role, and who was now the President of the Islamic Centre in New Delhi, took the lead in refuting radical Islam. Khān expressed his ideas about jihad in many of his publications—*The True Jihad*, *Dīn aur Sharī'at*, and accessible pamphlets. He also published a revised edition of his exegesis in English for educated South Asians and international readers.[17] But, since his exegesis in Urdu is read in South Asia, it is that which has been used in this book rather than the English version. In his brief monograph, *The True Jihad*, written in

14 Ibid 138 and 139.
15 Ibid 139 and 140.
16 Ibid 140.
17 2002; 2002 a in 2002 b.

English to disseminate his ideas outside South Asia, he sums up all he has written at various places in Urdu earlier. Beginning with the ideological assumption that all Islam's wars were defensive, he chooses the most appropriate hermeneutical devices to interpret the canonical texts. As for the commands in the Qur'an urging Muslims to 'kill them wherever you find them' 2: 191; 9: 5, he uses specification saying: 'such verses relate in a restricted sense, to those who have unilaterally attacked the Muslims' but are not permanent, general commands. He points out that the Bhagwat Gita, the holy book of the Hindus, urges Arjun to fight his kinsmen since at that time it was a duty. In the same way, Christ said 'do not think that I came to bring peace on earth. I did not come to bring peace, but a sword' (Matthew, Chapter 10). But such statements are contextual and do not make Hinduism or Christianity religions of war.[18] The implication is that Islam should not be judged on the basis of contextual statements of an aggressive kind. What is permanent is that the Prophet 'has been termed a "mercy for all mankind"' in *Al-Anbiyyā* (Q. 21)—We have sent thee as a Mercy for the worlds (21: 107).[19] He also explains 2: 193, the verse which commands fighting till *fitnah* comes to an end, using both semantic expansion as an interpretive device as well as the argument of change according to circumstances (*tataghayyar al-aḥkām bataghyyar al-zamān wal al-makān*). The term *fitnah* is defined as a 'coercive system which had reached the extremes of religious persecution'.[20] He argues that, since people can preach Islam peacefully now, the duty of ending *fitnah* by force of arms has also ceased to exist. As for the dominance of Islam, *izhār al-dīn*, it has, indeed, been prognosticated and promised in the Qur'an in *Al-Tawbah* (Q. 9)—the unbelievers want God's radiance to be extinguished but God will not allow it (9: 32); God has sent his Messenger to make his religion dominant (9: 33)—but it refers to peaceful propagation of faith, a moral revolution.[21] Since the fall of Communism, there is an intellectual vacuum and 'the place is vacant for an ideological superpower, and that, potentially belongs to Islam'.[22] So the only jihad left for Muslims is to establish peace through non-violent means.

In short, by using semantic expansion, specification, abrogation, and change of rules according to circumstances for the Quranic verses about *qitāl* and questioning the authenticity of certain *aḥādīth*, Khān abolishes aggressive wars in the name of jihad, insurrections against rulers, suicide attacks, and

18 Khān 2002: 41–42.
19 Ibid 43.
20 Ibid 61.
21 Ibid 71–75.
22 Ibid 83.

all that radical, militant Islamists stand for. He concludes that 'violence has been practically abandoned' and that it was 'an abrogated command in the language of the *shariah*'.[23] In this context, presumably because he lives in India, he gives the example of Gandhi who adopted the principle of non-violence in his struggle for Indian freedom. In his interpretation of jihad non-combatants cannot be harmed and non-violence is the norm except when actually attacked by the enemy. Here the Mawlānā gives the specific example of the September 11 attacks and suicide attacks, making it clear that neither of them is allowed in Islamic law.[24]

Waḥīduddīn Khān's interpretations were sharply refuted by critics who argued that he had abolished jihad as fighting (*qitāl*) very much like Mirzā Ghulām Aḥmad before him. One such critic was Muḥammad Rashīd, a Pakistani scholar of Islam, who wrote a trenchant critique of an article by Khān called '*Jihād kā taṣawwur Islām mẽ*' (the idea of jihad in Islam). Khān's article was published as a chapter in his book entitled *Dīn awr sharī'at* mentioned above and summed up his views about jihad spread in many of his writings. Rashīd vehemently objects to Khān's distinction between peaceful struggle (*pur amn jad-ō-jahad*) and violent struggle (*pur tashaddud jad-ō-jahad*) made in this article. In Rashīd's view such a distinctiction could not be made. Jihad was a combination of both to which the battles called Jihad in the classical period of Islam testify. And this remains a model of behaviour for Muslims forever. He also objects to Khān's use of the hermeneutical device of 'change in laws as a consequence of change of circumstances' mentioned above to justify the abolition of aggressive jihad.[25] While Khān asserts that the world has become much more peaceful than the Arab tribes of the seventh century, Rashīd argues that it has not. He points to Western colonialism, the world wars, Israel, Vietnam, Afghanistan, Bosnia, Chechnya, Kashmir, and Iraq to argue that *fasād* still exists. Moreover, the struggle of Muslims against their oppressors—the familiar list follows—is delegitimised by Khān since it comes under his definition of *fasād*.[26] Most of Rashīd's arguments are political and emotional rather than theological but his conclusion, that Khān had abolished jihad and thus facilitated the further domination of the West over the Muslim world, resonates with many Muslims and not only radical ones.

Perhaps the most powerful voice against radical Islamist interpretations is that of Jawēd Aḥmad Ghāmidī (b. 1948), a liberal Islamic scholar who has

---

23 Ibid 22.
24 Ibid 36–37.
25 Rashīd 2012: 343.
26 Ibid 357.

been forced to leave Pakistan because of the threats to his life. Ghāmidī's organisation, *Al-Mawrid*, carries out research on Islam, publishing a journal entitled *Renaissance*, which is administered by his son. *Al-Mawrid* has branches in the UK, USA, and Australia, and its main function is to keep the issue of interpretation of Islam alive in accordance with the broad principles laid down by its pioneer. It has recently published both the English translation of the Qur'an (*Al-Bayān*) and his book *Mīzān*. Ghāmidī's interpretive approach is based on an emphasis on language and the literary appreciation of the Qur'an. Asif Iftikhar places it in the hermeneutical tradition of Farāhī and Amīn Aḥsan Iṣlāḥī.[27] He points out the differences in the interpretations of Mawdūdī and Iṣlāḥī, arguing that they use discrepant hermeneutical criteria. According to Iftikhar 'contrary to the general assumption of the classical/medieval exegetes Ghāmidī believes that the Qur'ān primarily addresses the Ishmaelites, Israelites, and the Nazarites of Arabia in the Prophet's times'.[28] This makes it possible to consider its verses, especially those relating to aggressive war, as being specific rather than universal in their application.

Ghāmidī presents his theories through his essays, lectures, talks, and in his book entitled *Al-Mīzān*.[29] This book covers all aspects of Islamic thought and behaviour. The chapter on jihad[30] is especially relevant for us. He starts by stating clearly that there are two kinds of jihad. The first, which is defensive, is only permitted to resist *fitnah* which is defined as cruel persecution of Muslims and effort to alienate them from their religion. Subsumed under this is cruelty, exploitation, and antagonism. Muslims facing these conditions are permitted to fight by the orders in *Sūrah al-Ḥajj* (Q. 22)—those against whom war is going on and they are being oppressed are allowed to fight (22: 39); these are those who have been expelled from their homes, and if God does not confront such people through others, then mosques, churches and other places of worship would have become desolate (22:40). More detailed orders for this kind of defensive war are given in 2: 190 – 193 which have been quoted repeatedly. As noted earlier, the operational issue is the elimination of *fitnah*. However, two conditions should obtain: first, this is an order for the whole Muslim community, not individuals or groups acting upon their own.[31] Secondly, armed resistance should be

27 Iftikhar 2004: 70.
28 Ibid 62.
29 Ghāmidī 1990.
30 Ibid 577–607.
31 Ibid 579.

undertaken only when one's military power has reached a certain necessary level.[32]

The second type of jihad is aggressive. This is given in 9: 5 and 9: 29. Here Ghāmidī begins by determining the addressees of the Qur'an, which, as has been noted above, are the Ishmaelite polytheists, Israelites, and the Nazarites of Arabia in the seventh century. Thus, many of the actions consequent upon these people's rejection of the Prophetic message are particular to them and not relevant for later peoples. While this is the familiar use of the hermeneutical device of specification, Ghāmidī brings in the theory of God's own tradition (*sunan Ilāhiya*) in support of it. According to him, God has an unalterable law which is His own prerogative. When he sends a prophet (*rusūl*) to guide a group of people and they do not obey, God punishes them as in the case of the people of Lot and others.[33] The verse 9:5, about giving no quarter to the non-believers after four months, is divine punishment and is only reserved for the Arab polytheists but is not to be inflicted upon any other people. Similarly, the Jews and Christians who were to be subjugated after aggressive warfare and made to pay the poll tax by the orders in 9: 29 were those who had rejected the Prophet's message and this was, again, divine punishment. These orders are not valid any more so Muslims cannot fight aggressive wars, nor force people to pay *jizyah*. The only jihad they can undertake now is defensive.[34]

The gist of these arguments is that Ghāmidī uses two major interpretive devices—theories about divine punishment (ideological assumption) and restriction of aggressive war to a particular people and period (specification)—resulting in his final pronouncement that aggressive warfare in the name of jihad is completely banned. Moreover, he also refutes the arguments of radical Islamists for fighting on their own initiative despite disparity of military power compared to the enemy. Additionally, he emphasises that non-combatants should not be killed nor anyone burnt to death. For both, he cites *aḥādith* (see Annexure C). It was probably because of such clear refutation of the ideas of the radical Islamists that Ghāmidī is seen as a threat by them.

Another scholar whose interpretations were modernist and, therefore abhorred by the Islamist militants, was Fārūq Khān (d. 2010). He was a student of Ghāmidī so, in matters central to the Islamic creed, he follows the ideological rationale given by his mentor. He had been nominated as the vice chancellor of the newly established University of Swat when he was murdered by militants

32 Ibid 584.

33 Ibid 597–599.

34 Ibid 599. Explained by Asif Iftikhar 2004: 79–89; also see Nāṣir 2012: 301.

on 2 October 2010. He expressed his views in a number of speeches, accessible articles, and in a book called *Jihād ō qitāl*[35] which is his main statement concerning jihad. The book starts with the observation that the word jihad has been used twenty-nine times in the Qur'an out of which four occur in the Meccan verses when fighting had not been permitted. Then he announces seven general rules about jihad: only legitimate governments can declare war; non-state actors cannot be used to fight; suicide attacks are not permitted; non-combatants cannot be harmed; international treaties ought to be respected; the risk of fighting should be undertaken only if there is a reasonable possibility of victory; if the enemy sues for peace this should be accepted unless it is a ruse; there should be no initiation of fighting during the sacred months; and lastly, there should be reciprocity in response.[36]

In this context, Fārūq Khān mentions wars from Islamic history arguing that they were not without the permission of rulers. Sayyid Aḥmad, for instance, established a state in the tribal areas and the jihad of 1857 was under the Mughal emperor Bahādur Shāh Ẓafar (1775–1862 and r. 1837–1957).[37] In this context, he condemns Zia ul Haq's (1924–1988 and r. 1977–1988) policy of launching a covert war against the Soviet Union in Afghanistan. This was unannounced; hence, a deviation from the Islamic law of war. Zia ul Haq could have formed a government in exile as India did in the case of Bangladesh in 1971, and this government could have announced a war—but this was not done.[38] As Osama bin Laden was the hero of the radical Islamists in Pakistan in the 1990s, Fārūq Khān singles out his *fatwā* permitting the killing and robbing of non-Muslim non-combatants. He argues that bin Laden was not a ruler so he could not order jihad nor, indeed, could he violate the law of war by killing non-combatants. Bin Laden's interpretation of 9: 5, that it permitted perpetual warfare against non-Muslims, was also wrong since the verse was only applicable to the Arab polytheists of the seventh century.[39] More importantly, he denies that America has declared a war against Islam, thus refuting the radical Islamists' main argument that their attacks are defensive and that such warfare is a duty for all Muslims (*farḍul 'ayn*).

In his highly accessible writings in Urdu as well as speeches and sermons, Fārūq Khān kept refuting the ideas justifying jihad among Pakistani militants whose works we have seen in the last chapter. He gives the argument that international treaties with India were not revoked openly nor was war declared; as a

35 Khan, F. 2010.
36 Ibid 27–41.
37 Ibid 136–137.
38 Ibid 43–44.
39 Ibid 119–120.

result, the pre-requisites of waging a jihad have not been met. This, of course, was Mawdūdī's argument for the 1948 war about Kashmir. Moreover, he adds to it that this war is unlikely to be won in any case so that is further ground for considering it illegal.[40] Since Pakistani Islamists often justify aggression against India with reference to *aḥādīth* about the war with India (*ghazwah-i-hind*), he examines their authenticity. He argues that these traditions are weak since their narrators are not reliable. Moreover, he points out that the areas called Hind and Sind are not to be confused with modern India. The former included all Eastern Asia and the latter was coterminous with present-day Pakistan. Thus, to attack India on the basis of this hadith is not permissible.[41]

He also interprets verses of the Qur'an as well as traditions used to justify perpetual warfare differently from the radical Islamists. The interpretive devices he uses for 9: 5 and 9: 29 are the same as Ghāmidī's, i.e. that the first is specifically meant for the Arab polytheists since it is God's punishment. Likewise, it is not permitted to fight Jews and Christians nowadays since only those were to be fought with who were contemporaries of the Prophet and had denied his message. Subsequently, he takes up the *ahādīth* about jihad being eternal invoked by the radicals. As we have seen before, these are that jihad is for ever till everyone converts to Islam and that paradise is under the shadow of swords (for texts of the traditions, see Annexure C). Fārūq Khān interprets the first to refer to defensive wars which will be intermittent while the second, as mentioned before, stops Muslims from seeking war and exhorts them not to show cowardice if it is forced upon them.[42] Lastly, he mentions the relations of Muslims with non-Muslim states. These depend upon whether these states are friendly, indifferent, or inimical. For the first, there should be friendship; for the second, working relations should prevail; for the last category, there are no special orders but enemy attacks may be repulsed.[43] Fārūq's clear refutation of the interpretations of jihad by the Taliban and other Islamic militants finally cost him his life—he was killed on 02 October 2010. But his views are still disseminated through electronic media and websites.

Most clerics belonging to the Deobandi and Ahl-i-Hadith schools remained equivocal about the terrorist attacks of the Taliban. The problem seemed to be that they could not deviate so much from the traditional doctrines of the *'ulamā* they had guarded through the centuries, as to argue that jihad was

40 Ibid 142.
41 Ibid 121–130.
42 Ibid 50–52.
43 Ibid 83–84.

only defensive. One prominent case in point is that of Muftī Taqī 'Uthmānī (b. 1943), son of Muftī Muḥammad Shafī (1897–1976), a prominent *'ālim* of the Deobandi school. A correspondent of his, 'Abdul Shakūr Lakhnawī, had written to him that jihad was only for the oppressed, i.e. purely in self-defence. 'Uthmānī rebutted this view spiritedly, saying that it was for 'the exaltation of the word of God' and to establish the dominance of Islam.[44] When this created something of a storm,'Uthmānī replied that whatever he had said earlier was about a formal Islamic state and quoted verses enjoining peaceful co-existence with the non-believers: 8: 61 [if they incline towards peace so should you]; 2: 190 [if they desist from aggression so should you; and 60: 8 [you can live in amity with those who have not been hostile to you).[45] In short, he was torn between adhering to the interpretations of his tradition and, in response to the necessity of the time, giving a peaceful image of Islam.

But despite this dilemma, the original seminary, the Darul Ulum at Deoband in India, did give a *fatwā* against all forms of violence in the name of Islam. This was done by Muftī Habīb ur Raḥmān, the grand mufti of the seminary, with great fanfare in Delhi on 31 May 2008. Representatives from other sects with about 40,000 people were in attendance. The *fatwā* used the arguments in favour of peace presented above. The Deobandi edict was welcomed by all major parties and the public in India. Even the Bharatiya Janata Party (BJP), seen as anti-Muslim, welcomed it. Indian Muslims are said to be greatly influenced by it because of the prestige of Deoband. It is, as one author has put it, 'the first dramatic sign that Indian Muslims did not want to be branded as a community sympathetic to terrorism'.[46] In Pakistan too, nearly 150 Deobandi *'ulamā* did issue a statement against terrorism in April 2010. This statement was drafted by Taqī 'Uthmānī himself and it repeated the above arguments emphasising that suicide attacks were illegal. However, the statement was not altogether a liberal document. It did mention that suicide attacks are a result of extreme frustration and disillusionment; criticised America for its attacks on Muslims; and condemned General Musharraf's policy of joining America's war in Afghanistan.[47] However, in Pakistan, the kind of show of strength witnessed in India was not in evidence possibly because the risk of being killed was much higher.

However, a few individual clerics did muster up the courage to speak out against the Taliban. One of them was Mawlānā Ḥasan Jān (1938–2007), president of the group of Deobandi seminaries called Wifāq al-Madāris, who did

44 Uthmānī 1999: 97–109 as cited in Zaman 2012: 284.

45 In Zaman 2012: 286.

46 Dash 2008: Conclusion.

47 Zaman 2012: 289.

issue a *fatwā* against suicide bombings and was killed for it. The Mawlānā had had a brilliant clerical career having studied at the Islamic University of Medina as well as at Peshawar University from where he obtained an MA with distinction. He was also elected a member of the National Assembly of Pakistan from the Deobandi political party, the Jamī'at ul 'Ulamā of Mawlānā Faḍlur Raḥmān (spelled as Fazlur Rahman in the literature) (b.1953). The story of his assassination, as narrated in the press, is that he was requested by some men on 17 September 2007, ostensibly to solemnise a marriage. He went out with them and his dead body was found the next day in the suburbs of Peshawar.[48]

While the Taliban studied in Deobandi seminaries and were inspired by an extreme and locally modified form of the Deobandi ideology which disapproved of visiting shrines with a view to praying to the great *ṣūfī* saints who were buried there to intercede for them with God, the Barēlwīs were upholders of an interpretation of Islam in which the shrines had a central significance. The Taliban often attacked these shrines on the ground that this was a form of associating someone (the saints in this case) with God. Thus, they were more exposed to the fury of the Taliban. One *'ālim* who invited their wrath was Sarfarāz Aḥmad Na'īmī (1948–2009). He had defied the Islamist militants by condemning suicide bombings and other terrorist activities. He was the head of the *Taḥaffuz-i-Nāmūs-i-Risālat Maḥādh* (TNRM), a conglomeration of about twenty parties, whose main agenda was to prevent any disrespect to the Prophet. He was killed in his seminary in Lahore on Friday, 12 June 2009, when a youth came in and detonated his suicide jacket killing five people, one being the Mawlānā. The TTP claimed responsibility for his murder.[49]

Perhaps the most detailed *fatwā* against the radical Islamists is by Ṭāhir ul Qādrī (b. 1951), head of the Minhāj ul Qur'ān, an organisation which has offices in many countries of the world. Published in English as *Fatwa on Terrorism and Suicide Bombings* in 2010 in London, the book has seventeen chapters.[50] The first two chapters describe the basic beliefs and rituals of Islam. The subsequent chapters are about the ideas and conduct of radical Islamists. Qādrī argues that not only Muslims, but also non-Muslims, cannot be killed indiscriminately through terrorist methods. Nor, indeed, can non-combatants be harmed through suicide attacks, which are completely taboo no matter what the provocation may be. He also inveighs against rebelling against one's rulers quoting *aḥādīth* to support his point of view. For instance:

---

48 Nishapuri, A 2012.
49 *The News* (Daily), Rawalpindi, Pakistan, 12 June 2009.
50 Qadri 2010.

> On the authority of 'Ubada b. al-Ṣāmit: He (the Prophet, Peace be Upon Him) said: "do not come into conflict with the leaders that are over you unless you witness manifest disbelief for which you have proof with God".[51]

Another hadith to the same effect is as follows:
The Prophet (Peace be Upon Him) said: "Indeed, the best jihad is a just word in the presence of an unjust ruler".[52]This he interprets as the use of constitutional and legal ways of opposing rulers for grievous wrong but even then, armed resistance is not permitted. In addition to the selective use of *aḥādīth*, Qādrī also marshals an impressive list of people, both from the classical and contemporary periods, to condemn armed rebellion. Among those who are referred to are some Indian scholars such as the reformer of the Ahl-i-Hadith movement, Naẓīr Ḥusain of Delhi (1805–1902).[53] Qādrī lays down the rules of jihad which, having been covered already, need not be repeated. One point, however, deserves notice. In his discussion on the necessity of having sufficient military strength to undertake a jihad, Qādrī, in common with some others, lays down its exact proportion which, according to him, should be at least half of the strength of the enemy's army.[54]

Perhaps the most unique aspect of his book is that he equates the radicals with the Kharijites. He spends five chapters (13 to 17) to prove, through *aḥādīth* and books of history, that there are similarities between the ideas of both groups: the apparent piety, fanaticism, and cruelty. One of the *aḥadīth* he uses is as follows:

> Reported from Abū Salaman and 'Ata b. Yasār, they both went to Abu Sa' īd al-Khudrī who said that the Prophet (Peace be Upon Him) said: "There shall appear a folk in this Umma", and he did not say "from it" and you will be little in your prayers in comparison to theirs; they will read the Qur' ān but it shall not pass their throats and larynxes. They shall pass through the religion just as an arrow passes through a hunted game".[55]

He sums up his views about the radical Islamists by saying that 'their characteristics are similar to those of the Kharijites' and concludes that the judgment of the Caliph 'Alī against them 'is equally applicable to their modern counter-

---

51 *Bukhārī* in *Kitāb al-fitān* (quoted from Ibid 247).
52 *Tirmidhī* in *Kitāb al-fitān* (quoted from Ibid 247).
53 Qadri 2010: 241–247.
54 Ibid 247–248.
55 *Bukharī* in *al-Ṣaḥīḥ: Kitāb Istitāba al-Murtadīn wa 'l-Mu'ānidin was qitālihim* (the book on Demanding the Repentance of the Apostates and Reprobates, and Fighting them) 62: 2540 (Quoted from Ibid 248).

parts'.[56] In short, Qādrī is unequivocal in his view that the militants attacking civilian targets in Pakistan, India, and Afghanistan must be fought with and eliminated. In support of this view he refers to many Islamic scholars including Shāh 'Abdul 'Azīz, Shaikh 'Abdur Raḥmān Mubārakpūrī (1876–1925), who was a famous Ahl-i-Hadith scholar of India, Anwar Shāh Kashmīrī (1875–1933), who was one of Deoband's famous teachers of Hadith, and Shabbīr Aḥmad 'Uthmānī (1887–1949), the famous Deobandi scholar who supported Pakistan.[57] Qādrī's whole case rests on the alleged similarities, especially the extreme cruelty and intolerance, between the radical Islamists and the Kharijites.

In this context, it should be mentioned that the Pakistan Institute of Peace Studies (PIPS) organised a seminar on the subject of rebellion (*khurūj*) and excommunication (*takfīr*) in Islamabad. A number of scholars of Islam, both traditional *'ulamā* and academics, came together and were asked specific questions. The claims of the radical Islamists that both were permissible, indeed necessary, considering that the rulers of the Islamic world were not ruling according to the *Sharī'ah*, were examined. The consensus of opinion which emerged was that both were not permissible unless a ruler had committed an open and public confession of unbelief. But even in such cases, rebellion, especially that which had little chance of success and transition to peaceful rule, was not justified.[58] The participants, however, did not agree to call those who had indulged in what they called *khurūj* in Pakistan by the execrable name of Kharijites as Ṭāhir ul Qādrī had done.

Qādrī's charge of Kharijism is not unique having been the theme of several political commentators and clerics. Kenny tells us how the Egyptian state chose, among other things, to counter the Islamic threat by delegitimising it theologically. However, 'in its social reality, [it] was more of a loose-fitting garment of protest that could be donned or cast off as the circumstances warranted'.[59] Though the debate about Kharijism raged in Egypt, Kenny concludes in the end that modern conditions are entirely different from that of the seventh century Arabia and, therefore, the theological foundations of the phenomenon of militancy in question are not the same. Indeed, he points out that he refused to be used in a military-inspired idea to dub the Islamist militants Kharijites in order to turn public opinion against them.[60] He goes on to say that this tactic will not succeed even if it is used against Osama Bin Laden. 'There will always be questions',

56 Qadri 2010: 190.
57 Ibid 373–382.
58 PIPS 2012: 366–651.
59 Kenny 2006: 45.
60 Ibid 179–180.

he continues, 'about why he turned to violence, about the corruption of the Saudi system that produced him, about the legitimacy of the causes that he claims to defend (however cynically), and about his willingness to stand up to the West (unlike the current band of Arab leaders)'.[61]

Meanwhile, *fatwās* both for and against radical Islam keep proliferating in Pakistan and elsewhere. On 27 May 2017, at the conclusion of a seminar on the reconstruction of Pakistani society in the light of the Medina Charter which promises peace and compassion, thirty one scholars of Islam issued a unanimous *fatwā* to condemn terrorism and extremism.[62] This *fatwā* was opposed by Mawlānā Samī'ul Ḥaqq, a politician and head of the Deobandi seminary at Akora, Khattak, where a number of Taliban were trained (he is dubbed 'the father of the Taliban'). In his criticism, he said that Muslim rulers were puppets of the West and were unable to carry out jihad. Commenting on Samī'ul Ḥaqq's objections, the journalist and specialist on Islamic militancy in Pakistan Amir Rana wrote: 'perhaps what irritates Maulana Sami ul Haq is that the fatwa does not specifically exclude Afghanistan, where Taliban are killing fellow Muslims'.[63] For the radical Islamists, the crucial questions are, as Rana points out: can force be the last resort to establish an Islamic state given that democracy will not do it? Is it valid to fight rulers who follow the West? Is leaderless jihad justified? Can the non-Muslims be attacked in their own countries?

These questions remain valid all over the world and Pakistan is no exception. However, unlike Egypt, Pakistan was ambiguous about countering militant interpretations of jihad. The public was fed with so many myths that it was never clear just who the enemy was. For instance, one Pakistani discourse about the militancy before December 2014 when the militants attacked and brutally massacred the students and teachers of the Peshawar Public School, was that 'Muslims do not kill Muslims'. Thus, every attack was blamed on the proverbial 'foreign hand' which was a code word for India, though sometimes also the United States and even Israel. The US, it may be pointed out, was actually fighting the Taliban in Afghanistan, India is intermittently attacked by radical Islamists, and there is no proof that Israel is even remotely involved in such kind of militancy in Pakistan. As for India, whereas there is proof that India helps Baluch separatists, any help which India might have given to the Islamist militants could only be minimal and probably part of the perverse games which intelligence agencies play with adversaries. Any serious help of this kind could jeopardise India itself

61 Ibid 183.
62 'Editorial' 2017.
63 Rana 2017: 2.

since Islamists regard Hindus as the enemies of Islam and it would not be in India's long term interest to encourage them in a serious way. After the APS incident, however, the Chief of the Army Staff General Raheel Sharif's (b. 1956) military action against the Taliban, code named Zarb-e-Azb (Ḍarb-e-ʿAẓb)—meaning sharp strike—which began in June 2014 still continues in the form of Radd-ul-Fasād (the elimination of evil) under the present commander of the Pakistan Army, General Qamar Javed Bajwa (b. 1960). So far the militant groups which kill Shīʿas and attack India have not been targeted by the army which either still uses them as proxy fighters for Kashmir or remains sympathetic towards them for other reasons.

Possibly because of the deeply divided, even schizophrenic, responses of the Pakistani state and the public to Islamic militancy, the writings attempting to refute their narrative are not widely known. The thesis that, since being dubbed Kharijites did not succeed in Egypt it would not in Pakistan, is untenable. It is possible that in Pakistan the labels of *khārijī* and Assassins (*fidāyīn*) may have greater resonance with the public than they had elsewhere. However, a theological response would have to be considered seriously by Islamic scholars and by other stake holders to be successful.

11 Conclusion

We have traced out the history of the concept of jihad from the eighteenth century till the present time in South Asia. Basically, the trajectory of movement is from an orthodox and traditional interpretation of it to diverse ones under the pressures of modernity. Going deeper into the matter, the intellectual construction of jihad and its use is ultimately related to Muslim political power. When Islam was ascendant in India, jihad was invoked to legitimise and sacralise conquest and the political and social subjugation of the conquered people. When this power declined by the eighteenth century and some of the hitherto subjugated peoples rose in revolt to consolidate their own power, jihad was invoked to bring in foreign help or fight them in order to put them down once again and regain the lost power. Then, when a modern state became unquestionably ascendant, jihad took on diverse meanings. Those who thought power could only be gained by getting co-opted in the imperial venture of the colonial power, interpreted jihad to mean defensive warfare only. Others, who believed in anti-colonial resistance, either took to guerrilla adventurism or to mass political movements against the empire. Both responses were sacralised by fresh interpretations of jihad. In the post-colonial globalised world, a minority interprets jihad in ways which justify a global guerrilla warfare against the hegemonic 'West' or, in the case of Pakistan, a continuing conflict with India to settle territorial disputes and deny Indian hegemony in South Asia. Another minority, called progressive or modernist Muslims, interprets it as defensive warfare in keeping with the imperative of playing by international rules in order to secure maximum power in the new world order through peaceful means. Still others, possibly a majority, thinks about it in terms of Muslim history and their own understanding of the faith as both defensive and aggressive without being quite sure what is said about it in the canonical sources of religion. Interpretation is left by this last group of people to the specialists so they keep changing their opinion about the nature of Jihad according to which 'specialist' defines it. Modernity, it seems, changes the rules of the game of interpretation but the basic overall purpose of interpreting jihad in keeping with the maximisation of Muslim power remains constant.

Going by the data presented in this book, it appears that the traditional interpretations of the verses pertaining to jihad permit both aggressive and defensive war. However, many South Asian exegetes inclined towards aggressive interpretations. For instance, they used the classical exegeses, the *Jalālayn* and *Ibn Kathīr*, to support aggressive warfare. The verses which could be read to promote peaceful co-existence with non-Muslims were interpreted to be either inapplica-

https://doi.org/10.1515/9783110716986-014

ble or to have other meanings. For instance, in *Ibn Kathīr*, the permission in 60:8, to live in peace with those unbelievers who have not been hostile to Muslims, is restricted to only non-combatants. Such interpretations are typical of the reasoning Islamists give when they cite classical scholars to promote their own agenda of eternal warfare with non-Muslims. However, the Islamists borrow only selectively from the classical scholars. Moreover, they also add certain other imperatives not found in classical works. For instance, they allow jihad without there being a Muslim ruler (*imām*) to order it. They allow for attacks upon non-combatants. They permit suicide attacks and do not respect international treaties. In short, they allow terrorist attacks all over the world by non-state actors in the name of jihad. Three interpretations of the 'sword verse'—so crucial for both militants and modernist-progressive Muslims—one by a classical exegete (Ibn Kathīr), another by a South Asian revivalist (Mawdūdī), and still another by militants (Aẓhar and Sa'īd) are given below:

Table 13

	Classical and Militant Interpretations of Q. 9: 5	
Ibn Kathīr	Cancels all peace treaties and makes it necessary to fight the polytheists (*mushrikīn*) till they accept Islam. Does not restrict it to Arab *mushrikīn* only. Quotes one opinion that it has been abrogated but several that it abrogates peaceful verses (Vol. 2: 31–33).	Abrogation/ generalisation
Mawdūdī	The Arab *mushrikīn* were to be fought with till they accepted Islam. Exp 6 & 7 do not generalise the verses to all unbelievers but they do say that apostates may be fought with (Vol. 2:176–177).	Generalisation for certain groups
Mas'ūd Aẓhar	Unbelievers may be fought with wherever found. Quotes 4 swords (a) Arab polytheists (9:5) (b) People of the Book (9: 29) (c) Hypocrites (9: 73) (d) rebels (49: 9). It is general and still valid and abrogates verses of peace (Vol. 2: 380–381).	Abrogation/ generalisation
Ḥāfiẓ Sa'īd	Order to fight unbelievers. It is applicable nowadays also e.g in Kashmir, Palestine, Afghanistan and Iraq (p. 40). A local commander for jihad can be appointed just as Abū Bakr was appointed the *amīr* of Ḥajj and 'Alī was given the responsibility to announce this verse to the polytheists (pp. 38–40).	Generalisation/ ideological assumption

The modernist-progressives, as we have seen, argue that the peaceful verses are still valid and that the ones which suggest eternal conflict are no longer applicable because they were meant for a specific group of people (the Arab polytheists and *hostile* People of the Book). Let us now sum up the main points of the modernist-progressive interpretations of jihad.

Table 14

	Modernist-Progressive Interpretations of Q. 9: 5	
Azād, *Tarjumān*	Explained with reference to *asbāb al-nuzūl*—the breaking of the treaty of Ḥudaybiyyah by the Quraish—and restriction of the orders to the Arab polytheists who had initiated hostilities and broken treaties (specification). This was a special case as the Ka 'ba had to be reserved only for the worship of God (ideological assumption). This order is no longer valid (Vol. 2: 78).	Specification/ ideological assumption
Iṣlāhī, *Tadabbur*	Kill the polytheists giving no quarter. This was God's way (*Sunnāh Ilāhiah*) so these orders are specifically meant for the Arab polytheists. Thus Muslims are not to fight anyone except in defence (Vol. 3: 13–131).	Ideological assumption/ specification
Khān, *Tazkīr*	Kill the polytheists giving no quarter. This was God's way (*Sunnah Ilāhiah*) and such orders are addressed to prophets only. These orders are specifically meant for the Arab polytheists. Thus Muslims are not to fight anyone except in defence (Vol. 1: 463–464).	Ideological assumption/ specification
Parwēz, *Matālib*	Those who do not live as peaceful citizens should be fought with. Others–Muslims or non-Muslims–can live in peace. The order to 'kill wherever found' only refers to war according to rules. Nowadays there is no need for an Islamic state as one can practice Islam in peace anywhere as in India (Vol. 6: 166–169).	Generalization

As far as jihad is concerned, though not when it relates to women or slavery, the contemporary modernists-progressives stay more close to the literal meaning of the text as far as the peaceful verses are concerned. However, since they claim that jihad is only defensive—thus repudiating aggressive warfare as nineteenth century modernists did[1]—they tend to gloss over, or use ideological assumptions, to explain the removal of polytheists from Arabia and the subsequent conquests of Iranian, Byzantine and Egyptian lands during the orthodox caliphates. For the two sets of interpreters at extreme ends of the ideological divide—modernists-progressives and militants—the ideas of each other are anathema. Waḥīduddīn Khān from India and Ghāmidī from Pakistan, for instance, are special targets of, among others, Ḥāfiẓ Sa'īd's organisation[2]—as they are, indeed, of many radical Islamists.

One factor, common to all groups of interpreters, is that they all construct a belief-system which they call 'true' Islam. In so far as it deviates from traditional,

1 For the repudiation of jihad in the 19th century see Jaffar 1992.
2 Yasmeen 2017: 125.

conservative, and historical understandings of the faith, they constitute a disruption of past authority. And, as Michael Cook has observed, the trend in the modern Muslim world is to equate the injunction to 'command right and forbid wrong' as 'a praxis for spreading Islamic, not liberal, values'.[3] In the case of the interpretations of jihad, this means, at least in the hands of self-educated intellectuals getting their information from the internet and their peer group, imbibing the idea that war, rather than peace, is the norm of international relations. This is important as a trend in the intellectual history of the interpretation of Islam and is a trajectory which needs to be noted for this study.

The understanding of jihad among Indian scholars and the public changed from the medieval to the modern period. The latter period, indeed, was the one which brought about the changes which concern us the most, i.e. the anarchic, unconventional, and modernist view of jihad. This view differs from the traditional, conventional, pre-modern view of jihad in Indian Islamic thought in that it does not consider the presence of a central Muslim ruler (*imām*) as mandatory for ordering an aggressive jihad. Secondly, in this view asymmetrical warfare, even against a much more powerful antagonist, is permissible. Thirdly, it allows the use of guerrilla tactics which can, at places, cause casualties among non-combatants. And, lastly, it is undeclared. One might add that it is undertaken even in the presence of treaties, while traditional views advocated that existing peace treaties were to be ended before jihad could be declared formally by the *amīr* and not by non-state actors. This is understandable if we take the factor of Muslim political power into consideration. The medieval jurists and interpreters of jihad operated in a world in which there were powerful Muslim rulers and states which needed to defend themselves and expand and, of course, this was only possible if the central authority remained powerful. Modern interpreters of the concept operate in a world in which there are no such authorities. Moreover, those which do exist operate in the name of the nation, not a single religiously defined community. Moreover, nation-states are bound by pragmatic considerations of remaining functional parts of the world order. Those who still choose to fight know that they have to rebel not only against the nation-state and the world order but also the past interpretations of jihad undertaken in an age which is gone—hence, the diversity of interpretations of jihad.

The diversity of interpretations we have noted above is called the 'fragmentation of authority'. The interpreters use the concept of objectification defined as 'the process by which basic questions come to the fore in the consciousness of

3 Cook 2000: 515.

large numbers of believers'.[4] One consequence of this engagement with Islam as a definer of identity is that it makes an increasing number of Muslims 'take it upon themselves to interpret the textual sources, classical and modern, of Islam'.[5] Thus, there is a fragmentation of authority and the issue of who represents Islam 'becomes central to Muslim politics'.[6] There were, to be sure, different interpretations of the canonical texts during the medieval age of Islam as well. The main ones—Kharijites, Mutazilites, Murjiites, Bāṭiniyyās, etc.—are mentioned by historians, though there are many sub-sects and other small groups not mentioned specifically in any one work. However, since Abū 'l Ḥasan al-Ash'arī's (b. 873) construction of Sunni orthodoxy, the orthodox clerical establishment has been very powerful. In the words of Montgomery Watt, this Asharite thought created 'the stability of this whole Sunnite system and of the society founded on it…'.[7] Once established, this broad consensus was maintained by adhering to it (*taqlīd*) rather than charting new paths of one's own (*ijtihād*). This *taqlīd*, however, was not absolutely rigid nor was it blind adherence to conservative legal precepts. But, on the whole it favoured doctrinal stability. This stability was maintained by the informal power of the *'ulamā*. One calls it informal because Islam does not officially recognise a clergy. However, it was maintained in the same way as official clerical establishments maintain their authority: through *takfīr* (declaring someone excluded from the fold of Islam), boycott, public pressure, and state persecution. The challenge from the occasional dissenters could be contained by the 'institutions for the issuance of edicts' (*dār-al iftā's*) and the pulpit of the mosque. But such tactics could not face the modernist challenge since modernity brought into being an ubiquitous network of communication channels, a newfound emphasis upon the integrity of the individual, a rationally-oriented positivist research methodology and role models of intellectual authenticity and success of a secular kind. This resulted in a dilution and dissipation of clerical authority despite the *'ulamās'* use of *fatwās* of heresy and excommunication. Hence, some of the reformist *'ulamā* realised that 'ijtihad, not taqlid, might be the most effective means for the containment of legal anarchy'.[8] Even the critics within the clerical community, who remain committed to the authority exercised by their peers, use the space provided by

4 Eickelmann and Piscatori 1996: 38.
5 Ibid 43.
6 Ibid 43.
7 Watt 2006: 317.
8 Zaman 2012: 104.

the very fragmentation of this authority 'to reshape Islam and to enlarge the numbers of those who might be able to contribute to such processes'.[9]

But the same space, much further enlarged, is used by the Islamist radicals as well as the progressives, to give a multiplicity of meanings to the words of the canonical sources. Moreover, these opinions are disseminated by people who do not know any canonical source on their own nor would they know how to interpret one if they found it. Since virtually anyone who has access to the internet or to conventional means of dissemination of one's ideas can be an interpreter of the faith, or at least a conduit of other peoples' ideas, such plurality of interpretations can no longer be under clerical control. This is a form of democratisation of interpretation. But, since this implies that there is no coherent body of axioms (apart from the *shahādā:* 'there is no deity except Allah and Muḥammad (PBUH) is His prophet') which can be called as the faith system of Islam, it can also be called, for want of a better word, 'anarchisation'. This benefits the progressive Muslims of the contemporary world who want to interpret Islam as a religion of peace, gender equality, and freedom; equally, it also benefits the radical Islamists who, as we have seen, want to interpret it to mean perpetual warfare, including the use of terrorist tactics, against all non-Muslims including non-combatant civilians.

This brings us to a highly significant issue: what constitutes religious authority? In a very insightful discussion on the subject, Qasim Zaman says that the 'the 'ulama have long recognized the contextual and relational aspects of authority'. Elaborating upon this, he continues:

> religious authority is a matter of unrelenting contestation. Claims to it involve contesting other claims to it, dislodging or otherwise unsettling rivals, showing the inadequacy of views, and defending one own.[10]

In short, one can see why the Syrian born Hugarian academic 'Azīz al-'Azmeh (b. 1947) speaks of both Islam and democracy in the plural forms when he studies the relationships between the two,i.e. 'there are as many Islams as there are situations that sustain it'.[11] In this context Shahab Ahmed's recent book *What is Islam?* (2016) may be useful. Ahmed begins with such disparate, even problematic (for orthodoxy) phenomena as amorous poetry, figural art, celebration of wine-drinking, mysticism, all practices which the strictly textual interpretations of Islam frown upon in the Balkan to Bengal complex i.e traditional Persianate

9 Ibid 73.
10 Ibid 33.
11 Azmeh 1993: 1.

Muslim societies. Unlike others he does not marginalise them as cultural aberrations nor does he slot them as being unIslamic, secular or mundane. Instead he finds a new language to include them into a holistic human phenomenon he calls 'being Islamic'– hence the sub-title of the book: *The Importance of Being Islamic*. His project is to create a language comprising the terms: Pre-Text, Text and Con-Text. The Pre-Text is the world of the Unseen and reason as well as mystical intuition are ways of engaging with it. The Text is revelation and the Con-Text includes the phenomena mentioned above. It also includes all the interpretations, modes of saying and doing, existential explorations and meaning-making which Muslims practically indulge in. Gven this language the term 'Islamic' is defined as 'meaning-making for the Self in terms of Pre-Text, Text and Con-Text' and this 'enables us to recognize that *all* acts and statements of meaning-making for the Self by Muslims, that are carried out in terms of Islam–that is, in terms of any of Pre-Text, Text or Con-Text–should properly be understood as *Islamic*' (emphasis in the original).[12] What light does this shed upon violence in the name of Islam? Shahab Ahmed gives his answer to this question in two paragraphs. The crucial one is as follows:

> As long as the Muslim actor is making his act of violence meaningful to himself in terms of Islam – In terms of Pre-Text, Text, or Con-Text of Revelation – then it is appropriate and meaningful to speak of that act of violence as Islamic violence. The point of designation is *not* that Islam *causes* violence; rather it is that the violence is made meaningful by the actor in terms of Islam – just as the prodigious violence undertaken by soldiers of democratic nation-states is made *meaningful* for them and by them in terms of nation-state, and may, therefore, meaningfully be called "democratic violence" (or may meaningfully be designated in terms of the particular nation-state as "American-violence" or "Israeli violence" (emphasis in the original).[13]

This implies that the violent actions of Islamist militants are one way of being Islamic. But this merely extends the issue of legitimacy of authority both chronologically and spatially without providing any way to delegitimise militancy. For those who want peace, then, the only solution is to valorise and legitimate those interpretations which one finds necessary as an existential choice of surviving in a dangerous world.

One issue, which could be a subject of further research, is to what extent any interpretation actually influences human behaviour. A tentative answer could be that there are conditions to which one response is resistance. This is legitimised through certain interpretations which, then, take on a momentum of their own,

12 Ahmed 2016: 544.
13 Ibid 452.

influencing behaviour. Modernity, one could argue, was such a condition. But it did not come to Muslim lands merely as rational, empirical, positivist knowledge, new ways of thinking about human beings (individualism versus the collectivism of Muslim societies), new mantras about grand narratives like progress, egalitarianism, human rights, democracy, and so on. Instead, it came in the wake of Western conquests of Muslim lands and reforms so radical and disorienting that it created a schizophrenic, confused, and alienated society uncertain of its values and unsure about its direction. Those who were impressed by the intellectual imperative of rationality—people like Shaikh ʻAbdūh in Egypt and Sir Sayyid, Chirāgh ʻAlī, and Ameer Ali in India—accepted this and attempted to interpret Islam as being compatible with it. But acceptance of modernity did not mean indifference to Western critiques of Islam. Indeed, it was this critique which created the enormous intellectual ferment of the nineteenth century in India which is called modernist Islam. This work, now called progressive Islam, is going on in the Muslim diaspora and jihad is perhaps the most important theme which is being addressed in it since it is Islamist radicalism which is the most pressing problem for Western countries. Another response was what Emmanuel Sivan calls 'total rejection of modernity' in the case of Sayyid Quṭb and the radical Islamists.[14] However, this response was never total as the technology of the West was taken over and used effectively, and, in any case, radicalism itself was also a reaction to modernity. Despite the radicals' use of some medieval thinkers, like Ibn Taymiyyah and Ibn Kathīr, it is modern in its selection of this material, modern in its interpretation of it, and contemporary in its use of it against conditions which are found today (such as the Israeli-Palestinian conflict, the American occupation of Afghanistan, the rise of al-Qaeda and ISIS, etc.). In this context, the insight offered into this issue by Fazlur Rahman is instructive. At a mundane level, he calls fundamentalism one kind of response to modernity, another being modernist Islam. But 'while the modernist was engaged by the West through attraction, the neo-revivalist is equally haunted by the West through repulsion'.[15] In concrete terms, while the modernists wanted to interpret jihad as a purely defensive doctrine such as the UN considers legitimate for all states; the radical Islamist interprets it as the duty to spread Islam by force as well as offensive-defence against Western domination and persecution of Muslims (perceived or actual). Both, as mentioned above, are responses to the overwhelming power of Western societies. The modernist-progressive desires to reconcile with the state of affairs and carve out one's own share of power peace-

14 Sivan 1985: 27.
15 Rahman 1982: 136.

fully by playing with the rules; the radical Islamist wants to change the rules by force.

But in order to change the rules, i.e. to end Western domination, a state is required—hence the recurring theme of the Islamist narrative for the creation and consolidation of an Islamic state. Such a state was created in Iran in 1979 though, ironically for the Sunnis, it was a Shīʿa one. It is in this context that Daniel Pipes asserted that the Iranian revolution was the first political movement *away* from Western political ideals and that the secularisation theory of the West causes 'the press and scholarship too often to ignore Islam's role in politics'.[16] To correct Pipes, the Iranian revolution was the first *major* and successful movement to set up an Islamic state in the twentieth century but hardly the first as it was preceded by many minor and transitory ones (such as that of Sayyid Aḥmad Barēlwī). And, more importantly, it is precisely because imperialism, especially American neo-imperialism, actually moves away from the political ideals ostensibly considered sacrosanct verities (human rights, freedom, absence of exploitation in international relations, non-aggression under the charter of the UN, etc.), that Islam becomes a rallying cry for revolutionaries in the Muslim world.

While the theoreticians respond to modernity at the deeper, philosophical level (rejection of individualism, the democratic ideas of sovereignty belonging to the people, the secular assumptions of modern education, and so on), they join their rank and file by reserving their jeremiads for the forms of entertainment and the new behavioural norms for women they see in Muslim countries. Thus, the Islamic political parties and their student offshoots, such as the Jamʿiyyat-e-Ṭulabā', which is the student wing of the Jamāʿat-e-Islāmī of Pakistan, delivered jeremiads against romantic film songs, the tight-fitting clothes of 'teddy girls' in the sixties in the big cities of Pakistan, and the mixing of men and women on the campuses. This, indeed, became more important than human life and resulted in attacks on people whose lifestyles were not considered Islamic enough. That is why the works of Bannā, Quṭb, and Mawdūdī are so full of references to create an Islamic state in which the lifestyle would be made to conform to Islam.

But the objective conditions of Muslim societies were not a matter of knowledge-production and lifestyle only. This, indeed, represented one aspect of power. The real issue, at least from the radical perspective, was that political and economic power was held by a Westernised elite in Pakistan while in the Arab world it was monopolised by dictators. In Egypt, this led to the invocation

16 Pipes 1983.

of the idea of revolt against rulers like Nasir —'the Pharaoh' as the blind Shaikh 'Umar 'Abd al-Raḥmān, who was the mastermind of the bomb explosions under the Twin Towers in 1993, used to refer to him in his fiery anti-regime sermons[17]— whose promise of Arab nationalism and progress had turned into a nightmare for the Islamists who were being tortured in his jails.

In the Arab world, the defeat in the 1967 war against Israel also led to radicalisation. But, since both Arab nationalism and Marxism had not succeeded, this radicalisation was Islamic. Sivan points to the growth of the production of religious literature in Egypt (from 8–9 to 19 percent in the 1970s), stories of young people turning to religion and finding answers denied to them both by their parents' generation and the conservative *'ulamā* with their respect for authority and taboo on rebellion against the government.[18] In Pakistan, the Arab-Israel wars did have a resonance but not to the extent it had on Arab countries which were directly involved. However, the Kashmir issue, the Afghan war against the Soviet Union and later the United States, as well as the ongoing battle of Pakistani troops against militant groups under the Taliban umbrella, did. These events did disseminate radical interpretations, making them ineluctable for vulnerable groups (Pashtun tribesmen, angry youth, etc.). The educated youth of Egypt did not turn to the traditional *'ulamā* for guidance,[19] but in Pakistan Deobandi madrasahs supplied much of the anti-unbeliever fervour already part of their worldview. This worldview was basically religious. It became more so since Islamisation, especially during the Zia ul Haq era (1977–1988), increased it and turned it towards the hardline direction. Thus, the invocation of jihad during the First Afghan war against the Soviet Union (1979–89) brought the concept of jihad into currency among the youth. The example of the Iranian revolution had already given confidence to religious forces which were now trained on the battle fields of Afghanistan.

Even more importantly, the idea of religion being a very powerful force was used in support of Pakistan's own national interest, specifically obtaining Kashmir, which was supported at some level by the most powerful institution in Pakistan—the army. As an indicator of the growing Islamic orientation of the officer cadre of the army, there is increase in the writings on jihad in army publications.[20] There is also a corresponding lack of confidence in the civilian leadership as a study of writings from the National Defence University in Islamabad

17 Euben and Zaman 2009: 345.
18 Sivan 1985: 131–134.
19 Ibid 56.
20 Fair 2014: 66–102.

where the senior ranks of the armed forces are trained, suggests.[21] This implies that, in Pakistan, control over militants, as instruments of policy, is in the hands of decision-makers who might have absorbed at least some of the ideas of the militants to begin with.

The present situation, both among radical Islamists and the states which fight them, is best defined as anti-politics. This concept was used by Mikel Thorup for the reaction of Western powers towards radical Islam but it is also true for the reaction of Islamists towards others. Thorup's definition of anti-politics is as follows:

> That democratic debate must cease, ordinary rule-bound practice must be suspended or altered, because we are in a situation of imminent and catastrophic threat; that this is the only option available and that any problematization thereof is not an insistence on debate but an amoral weakening of the defence. There can be no discussion but only action.[22]

This concept can also be applied to Islamist militants. One has only to substitute concepts like the 'rule-bound practice' of jihad (not killing non-combatants, order by the *amīr*, non-violation of treaties, etc.) instead of 'democratic debate' to understand the ideological assumptions of the Islamists, i.e. worldwide victimisation of Muslims. Of course, the response of those who fight them (as in Afghanistan, Iraq, etc.), as Thorup indicates, deviate from classical liberal-humanist norms of political conduct too just as the Islamist militants deviate from the norms of traditional understanding of the rules of jihad.

This study has concerned itself only with ideas about jihad. Perhaps a crucial question, not addressed here, is whether people are really influenced by these ideas? In short, is it because there are radical interpretations in circulation on the internet, among role models of the peer group, among friends and relatives, that people get radicalised? Or is it that they join for other reasons such as poverty, lack of education, mental illness, sexual frustration, or money? This gap in the present study can be filled by future researchers. Of course, there are studies providing tentative answers which are mentioned briefly below.

We have seen that the narrative of the Islamists is that of the victimhood of Muslims, and Islam itself, at the hands of Western governments and societies. Not everybody who believes in the whole or part of this narrative necessarily believes in violence. Jason Burke identified three groups of Islamists in 2002. The first were leaders, often intellectuals, who had come from the educated lower-middle class—a class which had supplied leaders for all political movements

---

21 Shah 2014: 237–253.
22 Thorup 2010: 192.

such as anti-colonialism, Marxism, Anarchism, and so on. They felt frustrated and angry and blamed the system for their problems. The second group rose to prominence in the 1980s. They were less educated and narrower in their approach. They already existed on the fringes of society and took to jihadist teachings to get some meaning out of their lives and possibly a way of feeling powerful. Then there were the ordinary young people who came from migrant backgrounds—from the village to the city or from Muslim countries to the West—and had unresolved identity crises.[23] Perhaps they would have reacted to perceived injustice around them or, indeed, stories of such injustice, by joining the Communist Party in the 1930s. But now they read militant interpretations of Islam around them and joined the radical Islamist groups. Not all of them actually performed violent acts, of course, but they approved of them in theory at least.

Marc Sageman conducted studies on the profiles of jihadis.[24] The 2004 study was based on a sample of 172 fighters. He divided them further into clusters. The first was the central staff of Al-Qaeda. They were, as it were, theoreticians and leaders who joined the initial movement during the 1980s. The second cluster came from core Arab states (Egypt, Saudi Arabia, Yemen, and Kuwait). The third cluster was from North Africa (Algeria, Tunisia, and Morocco), including people from these countries residing in France. And the last cluster was from South East Asia.[25] Sageman found that militants were not among the poorest nor the least educated people among their cohorts. They had not been brainwashed into extremist beliefs since childhood nor were they desperate people with no economic opportunity. They were mostly married, though some had contracted marriage before their militant actions. Psychological explanations were also controversial and not convincing. They normally joined jihadist activities from the ages of 29 to 35 years and not as children; and they were not forced nor, indeed, actively recruited. However, they had joined generally (70 per cent) in a country 'where they had not grown up'.[26] They could, for instance, be workers or the children of immigrants or students in European countries. At the time of joining, they had become very religious following a fundamentalist (*salafī*) version of Islam.[27]

In his second study, Sageman repeated some of the same findings adding that the hypothesis that militants are sexually frustrated people are just

23 Burke 2003: 301–307.
24 Sageman 2004 and 2008.
25 Ibid 2004: 70 and 137–138.
26 Ibid 92.
27 Ibid 93.

myths. More crucially, he added that globalisation creates the kind of 'radicalization that generates small, local, self-organized groups in a hostile habitat but linked through the Internet also leads to a disconnected global network, the leaderless jihad'.[28] In these networks, there need not be active recruitment. Indeed, 'participation is often through friendship and kinship networks, which grow according to the forum of participation, whether it is a physical protest demonstration against some foreign Western intervention or chatting on the Internet'.[29] This virtual jihad community, or would-be community, cannot be controlled. It is, in a sense, headless.

Edwin Bakker, studying jihadis in Europe from 2001 till 2009, identified 65 jihadi terrorist incidents and found a sample of 304 individuals responsible for them. Out of them, socioeconomic data were available for only 93 persons of whom 'only five can be regarded as upper class, 36 middle class and 52 lower class'.[30] A majority finished secondary education—not in itself an achievement in Europe—and 22 finished college or university. They were generally not raised in highly religious homes and were mostly married. They actively started pursuing a jihadist course of action at the average age of 27.7 years and were recruited mostly in Europe where they had their homes. The final conclusion is that 'there is no standard Jihadi terrorist in Europe'.[31] What can be generalised, however, is that most are Arabs, from immigrant families, and from the lower strata of the society. In Egypt, at least, the Islamists were 'young, science students and reject the ulema because the latter accept secular governments'.[32] In Western countries, they were self-recruited through networks of friendship and kinship. According to Rik Coolsaet, 'individuals do not adhere to extremist groups as a direct consequence of their extremist ideas. It is not the narrative that lures individuals into terrorism—if even at the end it can acquire its own momentum'.[33] But at what moment do ideas take over? And why does the narrative bring about 'conversions'— and biographies do suggest it does. These questions remain largely unanswered.

As for the profiles of the people who do pursue jihad in Pakistan, here we are on surer grounds. In common with other countries, in Pakistan, too, the jihadis do not belong to the poorest of the poor. According to Christine Fair, who has analysed the biographies of LeT/ JUD fighters, 89 percent came from the Punjab

---

28 Sageman 2008: 143.
29 Sageman 2011: 121.
30 Bakker 2011: 140.
31 Ibid 142.
32 Roy 1999: 36–38.
33 Coolsaet 2011: 261.

and not the poorest and most peripheral areas. Moreover, their educational attainment was actually higher than the average person in their cohort.[34] Ajmal 'Āmir Kasāb (1987–2012), the LeT fighter from Okara who was captured and executed in India after the Mumbai attack of November 2008, was from the lower middle class. So was 'Umar Kundī (d. 2010), who was shot by Pakistan army commandos after he had attacked an ISI office in Lahore in May 2009. More evidence from Pakistan may be adduced. Sohail Abbas, a Pakistani psychologist, interviewed 517 men in jail for having attempted to go to Afghanistan to fight US troops. He found that 'they were recruited largely from the mainstream of the Pakistani population'. Having attended government Urdu-medium schools, 'their literacy level is above the average of general population' though, suggests Abbas, their 'intelligence level' was 'assessed to be barely average in most cases'.[35] They were not from extremist madrasahs nor were they particularly devout to begin with. Being a psychologist, Abbas also carried out personality tests on the group and concluded that 'a slightly higher degree of psychological morbidity was observable among the *jihadi* groups'.[36] But it is not quite clear what one is to make of this finding. What is common between this group and others studied by researchers is that it too felt victimised and outraged. As Abbas tells us, they were angry with the US, and with the Pakistani government which they accused of being a stooge in the hands of the Americans. They were also against the exploitative society which frustrated and humiliated them and 'has kept them deprived for ages'.[37] Fair too has similar findings to offer. She tells us that, in the case of those fighting in Kashmir—and 98.9 percent fighters of the Let/ JUD fought there—there was heightened religiosity and, more importantly, a sense of outrage upon hearing India's violation of Kashmiri Muslims' human rights.[38] Amir Rana, who has been mentioned earlier, has collected biographies of militants and has classified them in three cohorts (or generations). The first generation came from moderate, Barēlwī families and got inspired by the ongoing battle in Kashmir. The second generation emerged after the 1990s and took a definite form after the attacks of September 11. They were hardliners and much more violent than their predecessors. The third generation was highly committed and more educated than the previous ones. Their biographies suggest that 'the element of adventure' rather than lack of ed-

34 Fair. Forthcoming: 195–198.
35 Abbas 2004: 189.
36 Ibid 190.
37 Ibid 192.
38 Fair. forthcoming: 207–209.

ucation, poverty, or religiosity made them take part in jihadi activities.[39] They belonged to the lower-middle or the middle classes but were not necessarily in abject poverty.[40] Nor, at least to begin with, were they very religious, though they did have connections, or found them later, with very religious people. However, at least in the first generation, the Barēlwīs forced their parents and siblings to veer towards the stricter Deobandi and Ahl-i-Hadith orientations as they got radicalised.[41] Indeed, these surveys from Pakistan point to the same conclusion that one finds in Western surveys, i.e. there is no determining cause for the inclination to join the jihad though there are trends which can be identified. These are: a perception of victimisation, education—but not the liberal arts subjects at an advanced level—and peer group pressure.

While it is conceded that people do not fight only because they are inspired by theory—indeed, they fight for various complicated reasons—this is no reason for not trying to understand the intellectual history of such theories. Whatever the reason they initially come to join militant groups, they do come in contact with some radical ideas which acquire a niche in their worldview, and they use them to justify their deeds to themselves and others. The adherence to these ideas gives them a sense of belonging to a community, even if it is a virtual one, which they might lack otherwise. This book has attempted to put together a historical narrative of an idea which people ostensibly cite to justify their actions without going into the question of their deeper, covert psychological motivations.

Whether this history of the idea of jihad is of any practical use is a point in which the present researcher has interest insofar as it refers to the presentation of ideas. If this book has successfully described how interpretative devices are used to privilege one kind of interpretation of jihad rather than another in South Asia, it would be a very satisfactory outcome. If, however, someone uses interpretations promoting domestic and international peace and ensuring amicable co-existence of Muslim countries with others, it will be an added bonus. However, considering that such pro-peace narratives already exist—some pertaining to South Asia being discussed in chapter 10 on refuting the militants—it is highly unlikely that this book will provide them where others have failed. Indeed, it seems that the problem is not with the narrative but with who presents it and in what circumstances it is presented. If the authorities of Egypt call Islamists Kharijites and the *'ulamā* of al-Azhar present learned disqui-

39 Rana 2015:56.
40 Ibid 57–59.
41 Ibid 60.

sitions in support of such a stance, people being tortured by the state's military machine and those who are still smarting after the defeat at the hands of the Israelis and the elite's perceived corruption, will not pay any heed to it. Likewise, in Pakistan, the state, which has itself used Islamic militants, will not be believed if it presents counter-narratives now emphasising peace. To be credible to the ordinary people, the Pakistani state will have to abandon its double-faced, often obfuscating, and contradictory policy towards religious militancy. This, at least, is possible, though after having brain-washed the people into believing that it is necessary to fight for Kashmir, even at the risk of nuclear annihilation, it is a job which only a really stable and popular government can do. Other things which make the radical interpretations persuasive may not be in any Arab or Pakistani government's control. For instance, nobody from these countries is likely to be able to persuade Israel to create a viable, really independent Palestinian state possibly by withdrawing to pre-1967 boundaries. Instead, the advice coming from the right wing writers about Islam, like Daniel Pipes, is that this conflict will 'wind down only after the Palestinians accept the existence of Israel'.[42] This advice can also be given to Israel which, in fact, has more agency in the conflict than the Palestinians owing to its status as the occupier.

However, peace is possible at least in theory. For instance, if Israel itself or the United States think it will serve their national interest—by ensuring peace for their citizens—they can take initiatives in this direction. Similarly, some satisfactory solution to Kashmir, in consonance with the wishes of the Kashmiri people, may be found if India and Pakistan are sincere about it. But there are certainly no signs of any of these changes yet. In short, the changes which can privilege peaceful interpretations of jihad are beyond the domain of interpreters or historians. This, as mentioned before, is no reason for not studying the history of the idea of jihad and if the reader has derived intellectual gratification from this book, as the author certainly has, it would have served its purpose.

42 Pipes 2004: 5.

Annexure A: War–related Verses in the Qur'an

The column on the right does is not a translation nor a summary of the whole verse. It is a brief abstract of that part of the verse which deals directly or indirectly to war. The words used for jihad (effort) and war or killing (*qitāl*) or war (*ḥarb*) are given.

Sr. No.	Verse	Abstract
		Admonition
1	*Āl-i-'Imrān* 3: 156	Do not become like these unbelievers who say when their brothers go out for a journey or war that had they been with them they would not have died **or been killed** (*maā qutilū*).
2	*Al-Nisā* 4: 72	Among you are people who if disaster strikes you will declare that God was kind to him as he did not go with the others [for those who avoided war].
3	*Al-Tawbah* 9: 94	They [hypocrites] will give excuses when you (Prophet) return but God has exposed their reality [those who avoided going for Tabuk].
4	*Al-Tawbah* 9: 95	They [hypocrites] will take oaths to exonerate themselves but you (O Prophet) should shun them [as above].
5	*Al-Tawbah* 9: 96	They [hypocrites] will take oaths so that you excuse them but though you (Prophet) do so yet God will never forgive them [as above].
6	*Al-Muḥammad* 47: 20	Now that orders have come for **war** (*qitāl*), those with disease in their hearts, are looking at you (Prophet) as if fainting with death.
7	*Al-Muḥammad* 47: 21	They declared loyalty and said good things yet when the above order came they turned away. It is better for them if they are loyal to God (and do not lag behind in war).
8	*Al-Tawbah* 9: 25	When you (Muslims) were proud of your large numbers, you had to retreat but God helped you [in the battle of Ḥunayn].

		History
1	*Al-Baqarah* 2: 246	The Jews asked for a ruler to **'make us fight in the way of God'** (*nuqātil fī sabīlillahi*). When their prophet asked will it not happen that **'if ordered to fight you would not fight'** (*kutiba 'alaikumul qitālu allā tuqātilū*). They said it is not possible that **we do not fight in the way of God** (*allā nuqātila fī sabīlillāh i*) people who had forced us out of our homes etc. Yet, when **ordered to fight** (*falammā kutiba 'alaihim qitāl*) most refused to do so.

https://doi.org/10.1515/9783110716986-015

Continued

		History
2	*Āl-i-'Imrān* 3: 154	They said **'we would not have been killed'** (*maā qutilnā*) (in a war). Tell them they would have died had **'they been fated to die'** (*kutiba 'alaihimul qatlu*) even if they had not come out of their houses.
3	*Al-Māidah* 5: 24	The Jews said to Moses that **'you and your God should fight'** (*anta wa rabbuka faqātilaā*) (the formidable enemy) while they sat waiting.
4	*Al-Anfāl* 8: 7	Remember when you (Muslims) wanted to get the weaker group [caravan of the Quraish] but God wanted you to defeat the larger one [the army of the Quraish] to prove His order correct [Badar]
5	*Al-Anfāl* 8: 9	And you were pleading with God and He promised to send a thousand angels to help you [Badar]
6	*Al-Anfāl* 8: 12	God told the angels that He is with the Believers and puts fear in the hearts of the infidels. You strike the necks of the enemies and their joints.
7	*Al-Anfāl* 8: 42	When you (O Prophet) stood on a mount and the caravan was below and had you decided (differently) a delay would have occurred. God helped Muslims [Badar].
8	*Al-Naṣr* 110: 1	When God's helps comes; and victory is achieved and people enter into Islam in large numbers.
9	*Al-Tawbah* 9.:47	Even if they (hypocrites) accompanied you (Prophet), they would have created problems [Tabūk]
10	*Āl-i-'Imrān* 3: 166	When the two hosts met in battle you were harmed by your own mistakes [Uḥud]
11	*Āl-i-'Imrān* 3: 167	The hypocrites were told to **fight in the way of God** (*qātilū fī sabīlillāhi*) or at least defend Medina they said if they knew there will be **a war** (*qitālan*) they would participate but in saying this they were nearer unbelief than belief [Uḥud].
12	*Āl-i-'Imrān* 3: 168	The hypocrites said their relatives who went to war **would not have died** (*mā qatilū*) had they listened to them but they cannot avoid their own deaths.
13	*Al-Tawbah* 9: 42	The hypocrites did go to war with you (Prophet) since the journey war long and there were difficulties but now they are making excuses [Tabūk]
14	*Al-Tawbah* 9: 43	God pardon you, why did you (Prophet) allow them (hypocrites) to remain behind? Had you not, you would have known who are shirkers (of war) and liars [Tabūk].
15	*Al-Tawbah* 9: 46	Had they (hypocrites) wanted to go to war they would have made ready for it but they did not and God did not facilitate them [Tabūk].

Continued

		History
16	*Al-Tawbah* 9: 49	Among them (hypocrites) are those who give the excuse for avoiding war that they do not want to be tested or put under stress. But they have put themselves in greater trouble [Tabūk].
17	*Al-Tawbah* 9: 81	There who remained behind pleading hot weather were content that they did not have to **struggle with life and wealth** (*yujāhidū biam-wālihim wa anfisihim fī sabīlillāhi*) but hell is hotter [Tabūk].
18	*Al-Tawbah* 9: 83	If a group of them (the shirkers) come back and offers to go to war, tell them they can never join you since they deliberately remained behind [Tabūk].
19	*Al-Tawbah* 9: 86	When a verse is revealed telling them (the hypocrites) to believe and **struggle** (*jāhidū*) with His Prophet, they ask you (Prophet) to excuse them so that they may remain behind [Tabūk].
20	*Al-Tawbah* 9: 90	Among the Bedouin there were those who made excuses to stay back and they made false promises and adopted the ways of unbelief [Tabūk].
21	*Al-Tawbah* 9: 93	Only those are blamed who could afford to go to war but took your (the Prophet's) permission to avoid it. [Tabūk].
22	*Al-Aḥzāb* 33: 15	They (Jews) had promised not to run away from the battle and such promises must be answered to God [Battle of Aḥzāb and Banī Qarīḍa]
23	*Al-Aḥzāb* 33: 16	Running away (from battle) will not save them from death [as above].
24	*Al-Aḥzāb* 33:17	Ask them who can save them from God? Who can stop his favours if he wants? There is no helper but Him [as above]
25	*Al-Aḥzāb* 33: 18	God knows those who stop their compatriots from aiding in war and they hardly join battle [as above].
26	*Al-Aḥzāb* 33: 19	The hypocrites do not spend their wealth on struggle for God and they are your critics not believers [as above].
27	*Al-Aḥzāb* 33: 20	They (hypocrites) think the enemy army has not withdrawn and if they reappear they (hypocrites) will not fight them [as above].
28	*Āl-i-'Imrān* 3: 123	God had helped you in Badar so you should be grateful to Him [Uḥud].
29	*Al-Anfāl* 8: 43	God showed less number of the enemy to you (Prophet) to encourage you [in Badar].
30	*Al-Ḥashr* 59: 2	He it is who brought the unbelievers out of their homes in the first attack. You did not think they would go out. They also thought their forts would save them. But God came from a direction they did not

Continued

		History
		think of and they got afraid and they destroyed their homes themselves [the expulsion of the Jewish tribe of Banī Naḍīr from their forts in Medina].
31	*Al-Ḥashr* 59: 4	They resisted (combated) God and His Prophet and whoever does that God is strict in punishment [as above].
32	*Āl-i-'Imrān* 3: 140	You were hurt like your adversaries but there are ups and down of life. God wants to test you as who is a sincere Muslim [Uḥud in which Muslims were hurt like the Quraish were in Badar].
33	*Āl-i-'Imrān* 3: 152	God made good His promise but you succumbed to the temptation of wealth so God made you taste defeat but even so he pardoned you [Uḥud].
34	*Āl-i-'Imrān* 3: 153	Remember when you ran away and God's Prophet kept calling you so you suffered but you got a lesson and God know your deeds [Uḥud].
35	*Al-Anfāl* 8: 48	The devil misled the enemies of Muslims (the Quraish) but ran away himself when the two armies faced each other [Badar].
36	*Al-Tawbah* 9: 26	Then God sent invisible hosts to help you and punished the deniers of the Truth [Ḥunain in which Muslims were hard pressed in the beginning].
37	*Al-Aḥzāb* 33: 9	God send wind and unseen forces when an army came against you [Battle of Aḥzāb].
38	*Al-Aḥzāb* 33: 10	The infidels closed in on you (Muslims) from all sides and hearts were afraid and you formed (negative) opinions about God [as above] [as above].
39	*Al-Aḥzāb* 33: 11	The true Muslims faced a stringent trial [as above].
40	*Al-Aḥzāb* 33: 12	The hypocrites and those with illness in their hearts (skeptics) said God's promise to us was false [as above].
41	*Al-Aḥzāb* 33: 13	A group of them told the people of Medina to abandon the battlefield and some took permission from the Prophet on the pretext that their houses were unattended [as above].
42	*Al-Aḥzāb* 33: 14	If the enemy had attacked and asked them (hypocrites) to create trouble they would have [as above].
43	*Al-Aḥzāb* 33: 25	God made enemy retreat without success. He is the Muslims' supporter [as above].
44	*Al-Aḥzāb* 33: 26	The Jews who helped your enemies, you expelled from their forts, killed some and imprisoned others [the expulsion of Banī Quraydah].

Continued

		History
45	*Al-Fatḥ* 48: 22	If the infidels had **fought you** (*qātalakum*) they would have been defeated [refers to the treaty of Ḥudaybiyyah instead of a war at that time].
46	*Al-Fatḥ* 48: 24	God prevented you (Muslims) from striking the enemies and them from striking you in the valley of Mecca and made you victorious [as above referring to the conquest of Mecca].
47	*Al-Anfāl* 8: 17	God fought with the Muslims (in Badar) when the prophet threw dust at the enemies.
48	*Āl-i-'Imrān* 3: 121	O Prophet! Tell Muslims of the morning you arranged fighters for War (Uḥud].
49	*Āl-i-'Imrān* 3: 122	Remember how two groups were ready to show cowardice but God was there to help and Muslims should trust Him [as above].
50	*Āl-i-'Imrān* 3: 124	Remember you told Muslim God sent 3000 angels to help [Uḥud with reference to Badar].
51	*Al-Tawbah* 9: 118	The three Muslims who delayed preparation and did not go for battle were punished till God accepted their repentance and pardoned them [Tabūk in which three Muslims repented their not joining the war].
52	*Al-Aḥzāb* 33: 22	True Muslims when they saw the enemy army they said this is what was promised by God and the Prophet [Aḥzāb].
53	*Al-Ḥashr* 59: 13	They (the hypocrites who urged the Jews to resist the Muslims) have your fear in their hearts rather than God's and they have no sense [in the context of the expulsion of Banī Qurayḍah].
54	*Āl-i-'Imrān* 3: 13	In the battle you (Muslims) saw half of your opponents (which raised your morale) and God helped you [Badar].
55	*Al-Anfāl* 8: 44	God had decided to give Muslims a victory so he did not show the whole strength of their opponents to Muslims [Badar].

		Orders
1	*Al-Baqarah* 2: 191	**Fight them** (*waqtulūhum*) and expel them who expelled you. **Persecution or evil is worse than fighting** (*walfitnatu ashaddu min al-qatl*). **Do not fight them** (*la tuqātilūhum*) near the Ka'bah unless **they fight you** (*yuqātilūkum*) there. If they **fight you** (*qātalūkum*) fight them (*faqtulūhum*).
2	*Al-Baqarah* 2: 193	**Fight them** (*qātilūhum*) till **persecution or evil** (*fitnatun*) is eradicated and religion is for God only.

Continued

		Orders
3	*Al-Baqarah* 2: 194	Give a befitting reply even in the sacred month if attacked.
4	*Al-Baqarah* 2: 216	You (Muslims) have **been ordered to fight** (*kutiba 'alaikumul qitāl*) which you do not like.
5	*Al-Baqarah* 2: 217	They ask about **fighting** (*qitāl*) in the holy month. Say **it** (*qitāl*) is bad but preventing people from following their religion and expelling them from their homes i.e **persecution** (*fitnatun*) is **worse than fighting** (*akbarū min al-qatl*).
6	*Al-Baqarah* 2: 244	**Fight in the way of God** (*qātilu fī sabīlillāhi*).
7	*Al-Nisā* 4: 89	The hypocrites want you to be like them so if they do not migrate do not make friends with them. And if they betray you, **kill them** (*waqtulūhum*) wherever you find them.
8	*Al-Nisā* 4: 104	Keep chasing them and Muslims will prevail.
9	*Al-Māidah* 5: 35	Believers should be moral and **struggle in the path of God** (*jāhidū fī sabīlillāhi*).
10	*Al-Anfāl* 8: 57	If the enemies break their oaths with you (Muslims) and you find them **in war** (*fil ḥarb*) then disperse them to deter others.
11	*Al-Tawbah* 9: 5	When the sacred months pass, you (Muslims) **kill the polytheists** (*faqtulul mushrikīna*) wherever you find them... [part left out as it is in Annexure B].
12	*Al-Tawbah* 9: 12	If they break their oaths and condemn your faith **fight** (*faqātilū*) the unbelievers.
13	*Al-Tawbah* 9: 13	Will you not **fight** (*tuqātilūna*) those who expelled your Prophet, broke their oaths and began this conflict?
14	*Al-Tawbah* 9: 14	**Fight them** (*qātilūhum*) and God will punish them through you.
15	*Al-Tawbah* 9: 29	**Fight** (*qātilū*) those of the people of the Book who do not follow the true faith till they are vanquished (*ṣāghirūna*) and pay the poll tax (*jizyah*) [see Annexure B for the full translation].
16	*Al-Tawbah* 9: 36	**Fight the polytheists** (*qātilul mushrikīna*) together as they fight you (*yuqātilūnakum*) [left out on both sides].
17	*Al-Tawbah* 9: 41	Go to war whether light or heavy and **struggle in God's path with lives and wealth** (*jāhidū bi amwālikum wa anfusikum fī sabīlillāhi*).
18	*Al-Tawbah* 9: 73	O Prophet! **Fight** (*jāhid*) the infidels and hypocrites and be strict with them.

Continued

		Orders
19	*Al-Tawbah* 9: 123	**fight** (*qātilū*) the infidels in your vicinity and they should find you strict.
20	*Al-Ḥajj* 22: 78	**Struggle for God as is His right** (*jāhidū fllāhi ḥaqqa jihādihī*). He gave you the name of 'Muslim' [end left out].
21	*Al-Mumtaḥina* 60: 1	(O Muslims) who have left their homes to **struggle for My path** (*jihādun fī sabīlī*) do not make friends with the enemies of God and yours who expel your Prophet.
22	*Al-Ṣaff* 61: 11	Believe in God and His Prophet and **struggle in His path with your lives and property** (*tujāhidūna fī sabīlillāhi biamwālikum wa anfusikum*).
23	*Al-Taḥrīm* 66: 9	(O Prophet) **fight** (*jāhid*) the infidels and the hypocrites and be hard with them.
24	*Al-Tawbah* 9: 38	Why do you not go out to fight in the path of God when ordered to do so? Do you prefer worldly life to eternal life?
25	*Al-Muḥammad* 47: 4	When you meet the infidels cut their necks in battle till you dominate them. You can take ransom or release your captives till **war** (*ḥarb*) lays down its instruments.
26	*Al-Nisā* 4: 75	Why do you **not fight in the way of God** (*lā tuqātilūna fī sabīlillāhī*) to help oppressed Muslims who could not emigrate and are ruled by cruel people and who pray to be released from this abode of cruelty.
27	*Al-Ḥajj* 22: 39	Those who are **being fought with** (*yuqātilūna*) are oppressed and are allowed to fight back.
28	*Al-Anfāl* 8: 45	When you (Muslims) meet the infidels in battle be steadfast and remember God.
29	*Al-Anfāl* 8: 60	Maintain your military strength to make the enemy afraid and deterred.
30	*Al-Māidah* 5: 33	Those who **make war** against God and the Prophet (*yuḥāribūna*) and spread disorder will be **killed** (*yuqattalū*) or crucified or have their hands and feet cut off on alternate sides or exiled.
31	*Al-Baqarah* 2: 192	Stop fighting when your opponents seek peace.
32	*Al-Māidah* 5: 34	Unless they repent before you defeat them as God pardons people.
33	*Al-Furqān* 25: 52	You (Prophet) do not believe in the infidels and begin a **great struggle against them** (*Jāhidhum bihī jihāddan kabīran*) [with this Qur'an].

Continued

		Orders
34	*Al-Anfāl* 8: 65	(O Prophet) inspire Muslim to fight and if steadfast they will dominate two hundred if they are twenty and if a hundred, two hundred.
35	*Al-Anfāl* 8: 66	Seeing the Muslims' weakness if there are hundred they can fight two hundred and if a thousand, two thousand.
36	*Al-Anfāl* 8: 39	And **fight them** (*waqātilūhum*) till **persecution or evil** (*fitnatun*) comes to an end and religion is only for God. However, if they stop, you also stop.
37	*Al-Nisā* 4: 91	As for those who pretend to be with you but join your enemies whenever they get a chance. Find them and **kill them** (*waqtulūhum*) whenever found unless they sue for peace and hold their hands [from fighting you].
38	*Al-Nisā* 4: 76	The believers **fight in the way of God** (*yuqātilūna fī sabīlillahi*) and the infidels **fight in the way of idols** (*yuqātilūna fī sabīli al-ṭāghūti*) (i.e evil).
39	*Al-Ḥujarāt* 49: 9	If Muslims **fight** (*qatalū*) with each other make peace between them and **fight those** (*faqātilu allatī*) who are the transgressors among them.
40	*Al-Mumtaḥina* 60: 9	God only stops you from making friends with those who threw you out of your homes and **fought you** (*qātilūkum*) in religious matters.
41	*Al-Nisā* 4: 84	(O Prophet) fight in the way of God (*faqātil fī sabīlillāhi*) and you are not responsible for anyone except yourself but urge Muslims to do the same and God can break the opponents' power.
42	*Al-Baqarah* 2: 190	**Fight in the path of God** (*wa qātilū fī sabīlillāhi)* if **they fight you** (*yuqātilūnakum*) but do not exceed [limits].
43	*Al-Ḥujarāt* 49: 10	Muslims are brothers so make peace between warring factions (of them)
44	*Al-Baqarah* 2: 218	To escape persecution You can emigrate to a land of peace and **struggle in God's path** (*jāhidu fī sabīlillāhi*).
45	*Al-Mumtaḥina* 60: 8	God does not stop you from doing good and being just towards **those who have not fought you** (*lam yuqātilūkum*) nor thrown you out of their homes.

		Prognostication
1	*Āl-i-'Imrān* 3: 195	God will not waste the good deeds of anyone man or woman. Those who left their homes and **fought for Him and were killed** (*qātalū wa*

Continued

		Prognostication
		qutilū) will be rewarded and will enter gardens with flowing streams below.
2	*Al-Māidah* 5: 54	O Believers! If someone turns away from his faith, God will bring a people who will love him and they will be soft to Muslims and hard to infidels and will **struggle in the way of God** (*yujāhidūna fī sabīlillāhi*).
3	*Al-Tawbah* 9: 39	If you (Muslims) do not go out you will be replaced by other people.
4	*Al-Ḥashr* 59: 11	The hypocrites tell the Jews they will help you **if you are attacked** (*qūtiltum*) but they are lying.
5	*Al-Ḥashr* 59: 12	If the Jews are expelled or **attacked** (*qūtilū*) the hypocrites will not help them and even if they do they will run away.
6	*Al-Aḥzāb* 33: 27	You (Muslims) will inherit the wealth and land of your enemies which is not yet known to you.
7	*Al-Fatḥ* 48: 1	God has opened the door for a **clear victory** (*fatḥan mubīnan*) for you (Muslims)
8	*Al-Fatḥ* 48: 16	Tell (O Prophet) the Bedouin left behind that you will be called upon to fight very determined fighters and you **will fight them** (*tuqātilunahum*). But if you turn back you will be punished.
9	*Al-Fatḥ* 48: 19	The [Muslims] will win a large amount of booty in war.
10	*Al-Fatḥ* 48: 20	God has promised you more booty in future battles and prevents your tormentors from troubling you.
11	*Al-Fatḥ* 48: 21	God will give you (Muslims) further victories which you cannot achieve without His help.
12	*Al-Ḥashr* 59: 14	[The Jews] will not **fight you** (*yuqātilūnakum*) as a united force. They will fight from safe locations and will remain disunited.
13	*Al-Anfāl* 8: 18	God will weaken the infidels' power.
14	*Al-Anfāl* 8: 19	God's verdict has arrived and it is better if the infidels to stop fighting otherwise they will be punished.
15	*Al-Anfāl* 8: 59	The infidels should not think they can dominate Islam.
16	*Al-Anfāl* 8: 62	If the enemies intend to deceive you (Muslim), God will help you [this comes after 8: 61 i.e if he inclines to peace so should you].

Continued

		Prognostication
17	*Al-Fatḥ* 48: 27	You (Muslims) will enter the Kā 'ba with shorn hair and God gives you a **victory soon** (*fatḥan qarīban*).
18	*Al-Fatḥ* 48: 18	When the believers were making covenant with you under a tree we gave them contentment and gave them prediction of **victory which is near** (*fatḥan qarīban*).
19	*Āl-i-'Imrān* 3: 111	They cannot harm you and if they **fight you** (*yuqātilukum*) they will be defeated.
20	*Āl-i-'Imrān* 3: 125	If you fear and obey God, five thousand angels will help you when the enemy attacks you suddenly.
21	*Āl-i-'Imrān* 3: 139	Do not be sad you will dominate if you are true Muslims.

		Regulations
1	*Al-Nisā* 4: 94	O Believers when you go out distinguish between friend and enemy. If someone says *salām* do not say he is an infidel [only relevant part summarised].
2	*Al-Nisā* 4: 102	Even when praying during war be careful about your weapons unless you are sick or caught in rain. But the enemy wants to attack you so be careful.
3	*Al-Anfal* 8: 15	Do not turn your backs (Muslims) in battles with infidels.
4	*Al-Anfāl* 8: 46	Obey God and His Prophet and maintain your strength by not quarreling with each other.
5	*Al-Anfāl* 8: 58	If you (Muslim) fear betrayal from your opponents, break your treaties with them.
6	*Al-Anfāl* 8: 67	A prophet should not have prisoners until he dominates in a war.
7	*Al-Anfāl* 8: 41	One fifth of the booty in war is for the Prophet, his near ones, orphans, the poor, the wayfarers [only relevant part summarised].
8	*Al-Nisā* 4: 71	Arm yourselves and go out separately or all together.
9	*Al-Anfāl* 8: 61	If the enemy inclines for peace, you (Muslims) should also agree to peace.
10	*Al-Nisā* 4: 90	If they join people with whom you have a peace treaty or if they neither want to **fight you** (*yuqātilūkum*) nor **fight their own people** (*yuqātilū qaumahum*) do not fight them. God could have made them dominant

Continued

	Regulations
	over you and they would have fought you (*faqātalukum*). Thus if they **do not fight you** (*fa lam yuqātilūkum*) leave them in peace.
11 *Al-Anfāl* 8:16	God will be angry at those who turn their backs except in a **battle** (*qitāl*) for tactical reasons.
12 *Al-Ḥashr* 59: 5	The date trees you cut down and those you left standing is by God's will. God gave this permission to humiliate the evil doers [used to determine which tactical actions are permissible in war).
13 *Al-Ḥashr* 59: 6	And that wealth which God took out of their possession and gave you is not that on which you ran your camels and horses. God gives domination to his Prophet and controls all.
14 *Al-Muḥammad* 47: 35	Do not sue for peace when you can win and you will prevail.
15 *Al-Ḥashr* 59: 7	Whatever is obtained [in *fae*] from their villages [those vanquished] is for the Prophet, his relatives, orphans, the poor and the wayfarers. Take what is given and stop when stopped.
16 *Al-Ḥashr* 59: 8	And the above is also for those who have been driven out of their homes and their belongings have been taken away from them.
17 *Al-Fatḥ* 48: 17	There is no compulsion for going into battle for the blind, lame or sick.
18 *Al-Baqarah* 2: 154	Do not call those **killed in the way of God** (*yuqtalū fī sabīlillāhi*) dead.
19 *Al-Tawbah* 9: 122	All of you need not go out for (*Jihad*) some should stay to preach and teach good deeds.
20 *Al-Tawbah* 9: 91	There is no sin for the sick, the poor and the weak if they do not go to war.
21 *Al-Tawbah* 9: 92	There is no sin on those who asked you (O Prophet) for transport but it could not be provided.

	Values
1 *Āl-i-'Imrān* 3: 142	You think you will enter paradise without God judging **who out of you struggles** (*jāhadū minkum*) for Him.
2 *Āl-i-'Imrān* 3: 157	And if you are **killed in God's way** (*qutlitum fī sabīlillāhi*) your reward is greater than the wealth they collect.
3 *Āl-i-'Imrān* 3: 158	And if you are **killed or die** (*qutiltum*) you will be brought to God.

Continued

		Values
4	*Al-Nisā* 4: 74	**Those who fight for God** (*yuqātilu fī sabīlillāhi*) have sold this life for eternal life and **he who fights for God** (*yuqātil fī sabīlillāhi*) and **is killed** (*yuqtal*) or triumphs will get a great reward.
5	*Al-Anfāl* 8: 47	Do not go out in full battle dress only to impress others nor obstruct people from the path of God.
6	*Al-Anfāl* 8: 74	Those who **migrated and struggled in God's way** (*hājarū wa jāhadū fī sabīlillāhi*) are the true Muslims.
7	*Al-Anfāl* 8: 75	Those who believed and later **migrated and struggled with you** (*hājarū wa jāhadū ma 'kum*) for God are from you (Muslim community)
8	*Al-Tawbah* 9: 16	Do not think they [new converts] will not be tested. They too will have to **struggle** (*jāhadū*).
9	*Al-Tawbah* 9: 19	**Struggling in the path of God** (*jāhida fī sabīlillāhi*) is superior to giving water to pilgrims (services) or going to the grand mosque.
10	*Al-Tawbah* 9: 20	Those who believe, migrate and **struggle in God's path with their lives and wealth** (*jāhadū fī sabīlillāhi bi amwālihim wa anfusehim*) have a high reward and status in God's eyes.
11	*Al-Tawbah* 9: 24	Those who prefer families and worldly goods to **struggle for God** (*wa jihādan fī sabīlehī*) and His Prophet should wait for His verdict against them.
12	*Al-Tawbah* 9: 44	True believers would not ask you (Prophet) to be left behind. They **struggle** in God's path **with lives and wealth** (*jāhadū bi amwālihim wa anfusehim*).
13	*Al-Tawbah* 9: 88	There who fight with the Prophet and the Prophet himself, who **struggle** in the path of God **with their lives and wealth** (*jāhadū bi amwālihim wa anfusehim*) are the successful ones.
14	*Al-Tawbah* 9: 111	God has purchased the lives of true believers who **fight in His path** (*yuqātilūna fī sabīl illāh*) and **kill** (*fayaqtulūna*) and **are killed** (*yuqtalūn*) in it.
15	*Al-'Ankabūt* 29: 6	Anyone who **struggles** (*jāhada*), **struggles for himself** (*yujāhidu*).
16	*Al-Muḥammad* 47: 31	God will test you Mulims to know who **struggles** (*mujahidīna*) for God.
17	*Al-Ḥujarāt* 49: 15	True Muslims believe in and **struggle for God through their wealth and lives** (*jāhadū bi amwālihim wa anfusihim fī sabīlillāh*).

Continued

		Values
18	*Al-Ḥadīd* 57: 10	Those who spent their wealth **and fought** (*wa qātala*) before the victory are lower in rank to those who spent on the cause and **fought** (*qātalū*) after it.
19	*Al-Ṣaff* 61: 4	God loves those who **fight in His path** (*yuqātilūna fī sabīlihī*) in ranks like a fortified wall.
20	*Al-Ḥajj* 22: 58	And those who migrated in God's way and then were **killed** (*qutilū*) God will give them good sustenance.
21	*Āl-i-'Imrān* 3: 160	If God helps you, you will dominate and if He leaves you nobody can help you. So trust Him.
22	*Āl-i-'Imrān* 3: 175	The devil makes men fear his partisans; do not fear him; fear only God [in the context of those who returned from a war].
23	*Al-Nisā* 4: 95	Those who **struggle in the way of God with lives and wealth** (*wal mu-jāhidūna fī sabīlillāhi bi amwālihim wa anfusihim*) are superior to those who keep sitting [even when jihad is going on].
24	*Al-Anfāl* 8: 72	Those who migrated and **with their wealth and lives struggled in God's path** (*jāhadū bi amwālihim wa anfusihim fī sabīlillahī*) and those who gave refuge to them are friends. Those who did not migrate have no right of friendship but can be helped in purely religious matters.
25	*Āl-i-'Imrān* 3: 169	Do you think **being killed in the path of God is death** (*qutilū fī sabīlillāhi amwātan*)? But it is life and God gives them sustenance.
26	*Al-Nisā* 4: 77	The hypocrites are afraid (of death) when the **order for them to fight** (*kutiba 'alaihum ul qitāl*) was received. They are more afraid of men than God.
27	*Āl-i-'Imrān* 3: 172	Those who obeyed God and the Prophet though wounded will have a great reward.
28	*Āl-i-'Imrān* 3: 173	When they (the above) were told that the infidels have a great army for you they said God is for us.
29	*Āl-i-'Imrān* 3: 174	Resultantly they returned without any harm and with God's blessing [refers to an expedition towards Badar after Uḥud for which the Quraish did not appear].
30	*Al-Tawbah* 9: 120	The inhabitants if Medina and the Bedouin living around it should not remain behind the Prophet and love their lives more than his [Tabuk].
31	*Al-Tawbah* 9: 121	Whatever they spend and whichever place they pass through, all of it is credited to them so that God should reward them [while travelling to-wards Tabuk for jihad].

Continued

		Values
32	*Al-Muzzammil* 73: 20	You (Prophet) worship God at night. God knows who are with you and are sick or travel for His sake. He values those who fight for His sake.

Annexure B

Al-Baqarah 2 (The Cow)

2: 190 Fight in the way of Allah against those who fight you, but begin not hostilities. Lo! Allah loveth not aggressors.

2: 191 And slay them wherever ye find them and drive them out of the places whence they drove you out, for persecution (*fitnah*) is worse than slaughter. And fight not with them at the inviolable place of worship until they first attack you there, but if they attack you (there) then slay them. Such is the reward of disbelievers'

2: 193 And fight them until persecution is no more and religion is for Allah. But if they desist, then let there be no hostility except against wrongdoers.

Al-Anfāl 8 (Spoils of War)

8: 39 And fight them until persecution is no more, and religion is all for Allah. But if they cease, then Lo! Allah is Seer of what they do.

8: 61 And if the incline to peace incline thou also to it, and trust in Allah...(part left out).

Al-Tawbah 9

9: 5 Then, when the sacred months have passed, slay the idolaters wherever ye find them, and take them (captive), and besiege them, and prepare for them each ambush. But if they repent and establish worship and pay the poor due, then leave their way free. Lo! Allah is Forgiving, Merciful.

9: 29 Fight against such of those who have been given the Scripture as believe not in the Allah nor the Last Day, and forbid not that which Allah has forbidden by His messenger, and follow not the Religion of Truth, until they pay the tribute readily, being brought low.

Al-Mumtaḥina 60 (She that is to be examined)

60: 8 Allah forbiddeth you not those who warred not against you on account of religion and drove you not out from your homes, that ye show them kindness and deal justly with them. Lo! Allah loveth the just dealers.

(Pickthall 1930).

Annexure C

Aḥādīth

As mentioned in chapter 3, the *aḥādīth* on jihad fall into the following categories according to subject. Here a sample of at least one hadith is being given for each of them.

1. Extolling the virtues of jihad and the high merit of those who sacrifice their lives. For instance, they get a place in the highest level of paradise.

> Yāhyā bin Ṣaleh etc. etc. narrate on the authority of Abū Hurayrah that the Prophet (Peace be Upon Him) said: ...paradise has hundred levels and those are created by Allah for those who do jihad for His sake. Any two levels are as much distant from each other as the heavens and the earth. So if you pray, then pray for Firdaus which is the highest level of paradise. I think he also added that only God's throne is above it and the streams of paradise flow from here (*Bukhārī* Vol. 2: item 58 '*Kitāb al-jihād wa al-siyār*'; *Ibn Mājah* Vol. 2, item 2753 '*Abwāb al-jihād*').

2. That the martyr will desire to go back to be killed again and again.

> Anas (May God be Pleased with Him) narrates that the Prophet (Peace be Upon Him) said: Anyone who enters paradise never wants to come back to the world even if he is given all earthly goods. But the martyr will want to come back and be killed ten times since he will understand the status of martyrdom (*Muslim* Vol. 5: item 4868 'Kitāb al-Imāra' ; *Ibn Mājah* vol. 2, item 2802; *Nasā'ī* Vol. 2, Items 3153, 3154, 3162).

3. That the martyr's body will smell of musk.

> 'Abdullāh bin Yūsuf....[other names] narrate on the authority of Haḍrat Abū Hurayrah that the Prophet [Upon Whom be Peace] said: 'I swear by Him in whose hand is my life he who is wounded in the path of God, and God knows such a one, he will be lifted on the day of Judgment in the same state. His blood will be of the colour of fresh blood and it will smell of musk (*Bukhārī* item 69; *Ibn Mājah* Item 2795; *Muslim* Item 4862 *'Kitāb al-Imāra'; Abū Dāwūd* Vol. 4, Item 2541; *Nasā'ī* Vol. 2, Items 3049, 3150;).

4. That jihad will go on for ever or till everyone accepts Islam.

> [list of names]...narrate on the authority of Haḍrat Abū Hurayra that the Prophet (On whom be Peace) said I have been ordered that I do jihad with the people till they say "there is no diety except God". Then whoso says "there is no deity except God" his life and wealth will be protected in exchange for the Truth. His salvation is then with God. This has also been reported by Haḍrat 'Umar and Ibn 'Umar' (*Bukhārī* Item 204; *Abū Dāwūd* Vol. 4, item 2484,

'Kitab al-jihad',he says it will go on till the war with the Dajjal (*Ṣaḥīḥ*); Item 2532 to the same effect is classified *ḍaīf*; *Nisaī* Vol. 2 Items 3092, 3093, 3094, 3095 and 3097).

5. That non-combatants such as women, children old men, hermits and those who cannot fight will not be killed.

Ishāq bin Ibrahīm, Abū 'Usāmah, 'Ubaidullāh, Nāfe' narrate on the authority of Haḍrat Ibn 'Umar (May God be pleased with Him) that the Prophet (Peace be Upon Him) saw a woman killed in a jihad and forbade the killing of women and children (*Bukhārī* item 267; also item 266; *Ibn Mājah* Items 2841 and 2842; *Muslim* Item 4047 Vol. 5 *'Kitāb al-jihād was Sīr'*; *Tirmidhī* Item 1569, Vol. 3 *'Abwab us Siyār'*).

The militant Islamists quote another *hadith* to counter this one which is :

[List of names]...narrate on the authority of Sa'b bin Jithāma that in the place called Abwa' or Wadwān the Prophet (Peace be Upon Him) passed by and was asked about the the polytheists who were hostile. The question was that when they were raided at night their [the polytheists'] women and children are also killed, so he replied "they are of them also" (*Bukhārī* Item 265; *Ibn Mājah* Item 2839; *Muslim* Item 4049 adds that it should be in a nocturnal raid and not deliberate; *Tirmidhī* Item 1570).

A *hadith* often quoted in militant circles especially in Pakistan is about attacking India (*Ghazwah-e-Hind*):

Abū Hurayrah (May God be Pleased with him) said that the Prophet (Upon whom be Peace) promised us Muslims that India would be attacked by us. If it happened in my lifetime [Abū Hurayrah's] then I will join it with my life and wealth. If I die I will be among the best of martyrs. If I come back I will be the SAVED (*Nisaī* Vol. 2 Items 3174 & 3176 both *ḍaīf*).

Another version is:

Thaubān (May God be Pleased with him) reported that the Prophet (Peace be Upon Him) said: In my Ummah there are two groups whom God has saved from fire. One which attacks Hind and the other which will be with 'Isā Ibn Maryam' (*Nisaī* Vol. 2 Item 3177, *Ṣaḥīḥ*).

The *hadith* often quoted by those who consider jihad primarily as moral improvement is as follows:

When returning from a war the Prophet (Upon whom be Peace) said: 'we are returning from the smaller jihad (*al-jihād al-sughrā*) and going towards the greater one (*al-jihād al-akbar*). The Companions asked: 'which is the greater Jihad?'. He (PBUH) replied 'the jihad of the heart' (*qāla jihād al-qalb*) (*Mashara' al-ashwaq*).

Glossary

'Ālim	(Pl. *'ulamā*) One possessing knowledge. Usually used for people who graduate from a madrasah and have learned how to process religious knowledge.
Aḥmadī(s)	Followers of Mirzā Ghulām Aḥmad of Qadian (East Punjab), who believe that he was the Messiah. The sect based in Lahore takes him to be a reformer but not the Messiah.
Bāghī	Rebel.
Faqīr	A holy man who has taken a vow of poverty; beggar; religious mystic.
Ghāzī	One who is successful in jihad.
Ḥāfiẓ	Used as a title for one who has memorized the entire Qur'ān
Mawlānā	Islamic scholars; prayer-leaders.
Maulwī	Prayer-leaders; Muslim clergymen.
Muḥarram	The first month of the Islamic calendar. Also, a month of mourning, especially for the Shī'ī community, because of the martyrdom of Ḥusain Ibn 'Alī in the Battle of Karbalah.
Mullā	Prayer-leaders; Muslim clergymen.
Madrasah (Pl. *madāris)*	Islamic centre of learning; follows, among other things, a religious curriculum.
Muftī	A scholar (*'ālim*) who issues a non-binding religious opinion (*fatwā*).
Naskh	Abrogation. A doctrine in the Qur'anic sciences pertaining to the abrogation of certain verses. A hermeneutical device for interpreting the meaning of the fundamental texts of Islam.
Pīr (Lit. old in Persian)	It is used in India and Pakistan for mystic guides and teachers.
Sunni	The majority sect of Muslims. Also called *Ahl-i-Sunnah wa 'l Jamā'ah* (the followers of the Prophetic Traditions and the Majority).
Shī'a	A minority sect of Muslims believing in the spiritual succession of 'Alī Ibn Abī Ṭālib and his children through Fāṭimah to the leadership and governance of Muslims.
Shahīd	*Martyr.* One who gives his life in jihad. In addition to that, however, other men and women who die in various ways are also assigned to this category.
Tafsīr	Exegesis. Commentary. Explanation. A genre pertaining to the commentary on the Qur'an.
Ta'wīl	An explanation deviating from the literal or conventional meaning given to a text. An esoteric or metaphorical exegesis of the Qur'an.
Thānā	Police station.
Zakāt	Urdu pronunciation of *Zakāh* which is a poll-tax on wealthy Muslims.

https://doi.org/10.1515/9783110716986-016

Bibliography

The date following the name of the author is the date of writing or first publication. Where another date is also given in the end, it is the date of the edition used in this study.

1 Primary Sources

1.1. The Qur'an and its Exegeses

Ali, Mohammad. 1917. *The Holy Qur'ān: Arabic Text, English Translation and Commentary.* Lahore: Ahmadiyyah Anjuman Isha'at Islam, 1973.

Bayḍāwī. c. 13 C. *Anwar ut tanzīl wa isrār ut tāwīl* (Arabic: Lights of Revelation and Secrets of Explanation) by Nāṣir al-Dīn bin 'Umar bin Muḥammad al-Bayḍāwī. Trans. into Urdu. 2 vols. Nuri 2005.

Fatḥ. 2007. *Fatḥ al-jawwād: fī ma'ārif āyāt al-jihād* (Arabic/Urdu: The Victory of the Generous One: In the Exposition of the Verses about Jihad). 4 Vols. By Mas'ūd Aẓhar. Vols 2, 3 & 4, 2008. Lahore: Maktaba Irfan.

Ghāmidī, Jawēd Aḥmad.2009–2014. *Al-Bayān: an Annotated Qur'ān Translation.* Translated from Urdu to English by Shehzad Saleem 5 vols. Lahore: Al-Mawrid, 2016.

Hilali, Taqi Ud Din and Khan, Muhsin.1999. *Translation of the Meanings of the Noble Qur'ān in the English Language.* Madinah: King Fahd Complex for the Printing of the Holy Qur'an.

Ibn Kathīr. c. 14th C. *Tafsīr Ibn Kathīr* [Arabic] by Imāduddīn Ibn Kathīr. Urdu translation. By 'Abdul Rashīd Nu'mānī. 5 vols. Karachi: Nur Mohammad Karkhana-e-Tijarat, n.d.

Jalālayn. 2008. *Tafsīr al-Jalālayn: Great Commentaries on the Holy Qur'ān.* Trans. into English. Feras Hamza. Louiseville, USA: Fons Vitae & Royal Aalal-Bayt Institute for Islamic Thought, Amman, Jordan.

*Maṭālib.*1975–1991. *Maṭālib al-Furqān: Qur'ān majīd kī tafsīr khud Qur'ān sē* [Urdu: The meanings of the Quran: An exegesis of the Qur'an from the Qur'an Itself] by Ghulām Aḥmad Parwēz. 7 vols. Lahore: Tulu-e-Islam, 2011.

Murādiyah. 1868. *Khudā kī nē 'mat al-mā'rūf tafsīr-ē-Murādiyah* [Urdu: God's Gift Known as the Exegesis of Murad) by Murādullah Ansārī. Bombay: Matba 'a Haideri.

Na'īm, Muḥammad. 2012. *Kamālayn: Sharḥ Urdū tafsīr Jalālayn* [Urdu: Miracles: Commentary on the Exegesis of the two Jalals) Jalāluddīn al-Maḥlī and Jalāluddīn al-Suyūṭī. Trans. into Urdu and explained. Karachi: Darul Isha'at 2 vols., 2012.

Nūrī, Muḥammad Khān .2005. *Anwār al-Bayḍāwī* [Urdu: The Radiance of Bayḍāwī). Urdu translation of *Bayḍāwī's* exegesis of the Qur'an up to *Sūrah al-Baqarah.* Lahore: Zia ul Qur'an Publications.

Pickthall, Marmaduke.1930. *The Holy Qur'ān: Arabic Texts with Transliteration in Roman and English Translation.* Revised. ed. based on the Hyderabad, 1938 edition. Karachi: Iqbal Book Depot, 1989.

Qādir, Shāh 'Abdul. 1792. *Qur'ān-e-Majīd: khushnumā mutarjim ma' tarjumā o tafsīr muwaḍḍaḥ al-Qur'ān Ḥaḍrat Shāh 'Abdul Qādir Ṣaḥib Dehlawī* [Urdu: The exalted

https://doi.org/10.1515/9783110716986-017

Qur'an: Beautiful translation with exegesis of Shāh 'Abdul Qādir's translation called 'the Explicator of the Qur'an'). Lahore: Urdu Bazar, n.d.

Rafī'uddīn, Shāh. 1840. *al-Qur'ān al-Karīm: tarjumah Mawlānā Shāh Rafī'uddīn Dehlawī Tafsīr Shāh 'Abdul Qādir* [Urdu: The Exalted Qur'an: Shāh Rafī'uddīn's Translation and Exegesis by Shāh 'Abdul Qādir). Lahore: Pak Company, n.d.

Sindhī, 'Ubaydullāh. 2009. *Qur'ānī sha'ūr-e-inqilāb* [Urdu: the Quranic consciousness of revolution). Ed. and comp. Mawlānā Bashīr Aḥmad Ludhiānawī. Lahore: Rahimiya Matbu'at.

Ṭabarī. c. 10 C. *Jāmi' al-bayān wa tā'wīl āy al-Qur'ān* (Arabic/English: Comprehensive Narrative and Explanation of the Qur'an). Trans. into English by J. Cooper. Vol. 1. Oxford: Oxford University Press and Hakim Investment Holdings Ltd, 1987.

Tadabbur. 1958–1976. *Tadabbur al-Qur'ān* [Urdu: Thoughtfulness about the Qur'an). 8 vols. by Amīn Aḥsan Iṣlāḥī. Lahore: Khuddam al-Qur'an. Repr. Faran repr. 2006.

*Tafhīm.*1942–1972. *Tafhīm al-Qur'ān* 6 vols. (Arabic/Urdu: Understanding of the Quran) by Mawdūdī. S. Lahore: Jamā 'at-e-Islāmī.

Tafsīr-e-'Azīzī. c. 18 C a. (Persian). Edition used. *Jawāhar-e-'Azīzī* (Persian: the Pearls of Azīz) by Shāh 'Abdul 'Azīz.4 vols. Trans. in Urdu by Saeed Muhammad Mahfuz ul Haq. Lahore: Maktaba Nooria Rizvia, 2011.

Tafsīr-e-Sayyid. c. 19 C. *Tafsīr al-Qur'ān wa huwa al-hudā wa'l furqān* [Urdu: Exegesis of the Qur'an and Guidance for understanding the Criterion) by Sayyid Ahmad Khan. 2 vols. Lahore: Matbua Falah Aam Steam Press.

Tarjumān . 1931& 1936. *Tarjumān al-Qur'ān* [Urdu: the Explicator of the Quran). 2 vols. Vol. 1 (1931) and Vol. 2 (1936) by Abū'l Kalām Āzād. Lahore: Islami Akadmi, 1976.

Tawbah . 2006. *Tafsīr Sūrah Tawbah* [Urdu: The Exegesis of the Chapter Tawbah] by Ḥāfiẓ Muḥammad Sa'īd. Lahore: Darul Andalus.

Tazkīr. 1985. *Tazkīr al-Qur'ān* Vol. 2 vols. [Urdu: Reminder of the Qur' an] by Wahīduddīn Khān. New Delhi: Maktaba al-Risala. 2nd ed. 1987.

Uthmānī. 1931. *Tafsīr-e-'Uthmānī* [Urdu: Exegesis of Uthmani) in one volume. By Shabbīr Aḥmad 'Uthmānī. Translation of the Qur'an in Urdu by Maḥmud al-Ḥasan (1917). Lahore: Pak Company, n.d.

Walīullāh, Shāh.*Tarjumah. Fatḥ al-Raḥmān batarjumatul Qur'ān* (Persian/Arabic: Insights by the Compassionate One in the Translation of the Qur'an). Digital copy.

Yūsuf. 2009. *Tafsīr Sūrah Yūsuf* [Urdu: Exegesis of Chapter Yūsuf) by Ḥāfiẓ Sa'īd. Lahore: Darul Andalus.

Ẓilāl. 1999–2004. *Fī Ẓilāl al-Qur' ān: In the Shade of the Qur' ān* (Arabic/English) by Sayyid Quṭb. Trans. into English & ed. 9 vols. Leicester: The Islamic Foundation. Vol. 1 Trans. M.A. Salahi and A.A. Shamis, 1999. Vol. 7 Trans. Adil Salahi, 2003; Vol. 8 Trans. Adil Salahi, 2003.

1.2 The Hadith

Abū Dāwūd. c. 9 C. *Sunan Abū Dāwūd* Comp. Abū Dāwūd bin Ash'ath. 4 vols. Translated into English. Nasiruddin al-Khattab. Riyadh: Darussalam, 2008.

Bukhārī. c. 9 C. *Bukhārī Sharīf* Vol. 2. Bukhārī, Abū 'Abdullāh Muḥammad bin Ismā 'īl al-. 256/869. Trans. from Arabic to Urdu by Amjad al-'Ali, Subhān Maḥmūd, Abul Fatḥ and Qarī. Aḥmad Karachi: Idara Islamiyat, 2003.

Ibn Mājah. c. 9 C. *Sunan Ibn Mājah* Vol. 2 By Abū 'Abdullāh Muḥammad bin Yazīd Ibn Mājah. Trans. into Urdu by Sayyid Mujtabah Sa'īdī. Lahore: Maktaba Islamia, 2012.

Mashāriq. c. 11 C. *Mashāriq al-anwār* by Ḥasan Saghānī. Trans. From Arabic to Urdu by Khurram Ali. Lucknow: Nawal Kishor, 1874.

Mishkāt .c. 12 C. *Mishkāt al-Masābih* (a niche for lamps) by Abū Muḥammad al-Ḥusain al-Farrā al-Baghawī. Expanded version of *Masābih al-Sunnāh* by Muḥammad ibn 'Abdullāh al-Tabrēzī. Trans. From Arabic to English. 4 vols. by James Robson. Lahore: Sheikh Muhammad Ashraf, 1964.

Muslim. c. 9 C. *Ṣaḥīḥ Muslim* Vol. 3. By Muslim ibn al-Ḥajjāj 203/817–18. Trans. into Urdu by Waheed uz Zaman. Lahore: Maktaba Islamia, 2014.

Muwaṭṭā. c. 8 C. by Imām Mālik. Trans from Arabic to English by Muḥammad Raḥīmuddīn. Lahore: Sheikh Mohammad Ashraf. 1985.

Nisā'ī. c. 10 C. *Sunan al-Nisā'ī* 3 Vols. by Abū 'Abd al-Raḥmān Aḥmad bin Shu'aib al-Nisā' ī Trans. from the Arabic into Urdu. 'Abd al-Raḥmān bin 'Abd al-Jabbār Al-Faraewī. New Delhi: Majlis 'Ilmi Dar al-Da'wa.

Tirmidhī. c. 9 C. *Jāmi' al-Tirmidhī* by Tirmidhī, Abū 'Isā Muḥammad Ibn 'Isā. Trans. into English by Abu Khaliyl Vol. 3. Riyadh: Islamic Research Section.

1.3 Edicts (fatāwā)

'Ālamgīrī. c. 17 C. *Fatāwa-e-Hindiyā* or *Fatāwa-e -'Ālamgīrī* . 10 vols. Trans. from Persian to Urdu. Sayyid 'Amīr 'Alī. Lahore: Maktaba-e-Rahmania, n.d.

Deoband. n.d. *Fatāwā Darul 'Ulūm Deoband* [Urdu] 14 vols. (comp.) Zafeer al-Din. Multan: Maktaba-e-Haqqania, n.d.

Fatāwā. 1962. *Parwēz kē bārē mē 'ulamā kā mutafiqqah fayṣalah ma' iḍāfāt-i jadīdah* [Urdu: The Consensual Edict of the Islamic Scholars about Parwēz] Karachi.

Fatāwā-e-'Azīzī .c 18C. *Jawāhir-e-'Azīzī* (Trans. From Persian to Urdu). 4 vols. By Shāh 'Abdul 'Azīz. Karachi: Sa 'id Coy, 1967.

Ḥayy, 'Abdul .1892. *Majmū'a fatāwā-e-'Abdul Ḥayy* Vol. 1 (Persian and Urdu: The Collection of the Edicts of Abdul Hayy). Lucknow: Farangi Mahall.

Hidāyah. c. 12 C. *Aḥsan al-hidāyah* (Arabic and Urdu: The Best of Guidance) 16 vols. By Abū'l Ḥasan 'Alī ibn Abī Bakr al-Marghinānī.Trans. from Arabic Abdul Haleem Qasmi. Lahore: Maktaba-e- Rahmania.

*Rashīdiyyah.*c. 19 C. *Fatāwā-e-Rashīdiyah kāmil* [Urdu: The Complete Edicts of Rashīd) by Rashīd Aḥmad Gangohī. Karachi: Saeed Company.

Riḍwiyyah. 1919–1920. *Fatāwā-e-Riḍwiyyah* 11 vols. By Aḥmad Raḍā Khān. Karachi: Darul Ulum Amjadia, Maktab Rizwiyya, 1985.

1.4 Manuscripts and Recordings (all these sources are from the Oriental and India Office Collection, the British Library, unless otherwise indicated)

Board. 1833. Board's Collections 1832–1833 54184–54222 Vol. 1361 Shelf mark F.4.1361.
Ipi. Int. 1948–9. 'Activities of the Faqir of Ipi, Intelligence reports, NWFP, Waziristan, Karachi'.
Ipi. Int.1930s 'Secret Weekly Intelligence Reports, Waziristan'. In IOR/PS/12/3236.
Ipi. pol.1930s. 'Weekly Reports by the Political agent , Waziristan'. In Mss. Eur D 923.
Ipi.Burrows .1949. 'Brigadier Burrow's Request for Early History of the faqir of Ipi'. IOR/L/PS/12/1393
Montgomery. 'Interview of Lt. Col Montgomery by Coward Wood'. In 'memoirs of the British in India'. IOLR Int. No. 10 T 6106 WR Spool.
Parsons, Lt Col E.H.H 'Interview'. In 'Memoirs of the British in India'. Mss. Eur.R.141/1 Two cassettes.
Shareef. 'Interview of Col. Mohammad Shareef Khan'. In 'memoirs of the British in India'. Mss Eur R 179/1 Two cassettes.
Silk 1917 b. *Who is Who in the Silk Letter Case: Punjab* Lahore: Printed at the Govt. Printing Press.
Silk. 1916 a. First Note on the Silk Letters. 14 Sep.
Silk. 1916 b. Second Note on the Silk Letters. 20 Sep.
Silk. 1916 C. Third Note on the Silk Letters. 28 Sep.
Silk. 1917 a. Momorandum by C.I.D on the Silk Letters, 17 Jun.
Wahabi Trials. 1860s. 'Papers Connected with the trial of Moulvie Ahmedoollah, of Patna and Others, for Conspiracy and Treason'. IOR Neg. 344404.

2 Other Sources

Abbas, Sohail. 2007. *Probing the Jihadi Mindset.* Islamabad: National Book Foundation.
Abid, Qutbuddin (ed). 2003. *Khuṭbāt-e-Shāmazaī* [Urdu: The Sermons of Shāmazaī]. 2 Vols. Karachi: Mufti Mehmood Academy.
Adams, Charles J. 1988. 'Abū' l- A'lā Mawdūdī's Tafhīm al-Qur' ān'. In Rippin 1988: 307–323.
Adams, Charles J. 1983. 'Mawdudi and the Islamic State'. In Esposito 1983: 99–133.
Adel, Gholamali Haddad; M. Jafar Elmi and Hassan Taromi (eds.) 2012. *Qur'anic Exegeses: Selected Entries from Encyclopaedia of the World of Islam.* London: EWI Press Ltd.
Adm. NWFP. 1938. *Administrative Report of the North West Frontier Province 1936–37.* Peshawar: Printed by the Manager, Government Stationery and Printing, North-West Frontier Province.
Adm. NWFP. 1940. *Administrative Report of the North West Frontier Province 1937–38.* Peshawar: Printed by the Manager, Government Stationery and Printing, North-West Frontier Province.
Adm. NWFP. 1941. *Administrative Report of the North West Frontier Province 1938–39.* Peshawar: Printed by the Manager, Government Stationery and Printing, North-West Frontier Province.
Afsaruddin, Asma. 2013. *Striving in the Path of God: Jihād and Martyrdom in Islamic Thought.* New York: Oxford University Press.

Ahmad, Aziz and Grunebaum, Gustav Edmund von. 1970. *Muslim Self-Statement in India and Pakistan 1857 to 1968.* Lahore: Suhail Academy, 2004.
Ahmad, Aziz. 1967. *Islamic Modernism in India and Pakistan 1857–1964.* London: Oxford University Press.
Aḥmad, Mirzā Ghulām. 1880. *Barahīn-e-Aḥmadiyyah* [Urdu: the arguments of Ahmad]. Parts 1 & 2 Amritsar: Safir-e-Hind Press.
Aḥmad, Mirzā Ghulām. 1900. 'The British Government and Jehad' [First published in Urdu in 1900]. *The Review of Religions* November, 1911: 448–470.
Ahmad, Qeyamuddin. 1994. *The Wahabi Movement in India.* Delhi: Manohar.
Ahmed, Ishtiaq. 1991. *The Concept of an Islamic State in Pakistan: an Analysis of Ideological Controversies.* Lahore: Vanguard Press (Pvt) Ltd.
Ahmed, Khalid. 2016. *Sleepwalking to Surrender: Dealing with Terrorism in Pakistan.* Gurgaon: Penguin Viking (India).
Ahmed, Safdar. 2013. *Reform and Modernity in Islam: the Philosophical, Cultural and Political Discourses among Muslim Reformers.* London: I.B.Tauris.
Ahmed, Shahab.2016. *What is Islam? The Importance of Being Islamic.* Princeton, N.J: Princeton University Press.
Ahmed, Waleed. 2011. 'Lot's Daughters in the Qur'ān: an Investigation Through the Lens of intertextuality'. In *New Perspectives on the Qur'ān: the Qur'ān in its Historical Context* 2 (ed.). Reynolds, Gabriel Said. London & New York: Routledge. 411–424.
Aibak, Ẓafar Ḥassan. n.d. *Khātirāt: Āp Bītī* Lahore. Edition used. Tooba-elibrary.blogspot.com
Akasoy, Anna. 2010. 'Convivencia and Its Discontents: Interfaith Life in al-Andalus', *International Journal of Middle East Studies* 42: 489–499.
Akiti, Muhammad Afifi al-. 2005. *Defending the Transgressed by Censuring the Reckless against the Killing of Civilians.* U.K.: Aqsa Press; Germany: Warda Publications.
Alam, Muzaffar. 2009. 'Guiding the Ruler and Prince'. In Metcalf 2009: 271–292.
'Alī, Chirāgh. 1885. *A Critical exposition of the Popular "Jihád".* Calcutta: Thacker, Spink and Co. Urdu translation: *Taḥqīq al-jihād* (1913). Trans. by Ghulam ul Husain. Repr. Karachi: Nafees Academy, 1967 [the name is spelled as Cherágh Ali in this edition].
'Alī, Chirāgh. 1910. *A'ẓam al-kalām fī irtiqā al-Islām. Proposed Political, Legal and Social Reforms under Muslim Rule.* (1882) Trans. into Urdu by Abdul Haq. Hyderabad: Kutab Khana Asifiya.
'Alī, Chirāgh. 1918. *Tahdhīb al-kalām fī ḥaqīqat al-Islām.* Published from the manuscripts of the author by Maulvī 'Abdullah Khān. Hyderabad, Deccan: Kutab Khana Asifiya.
Ali, Mohammad.1920s. 'Tuzuk-i-Moḥammad 'Alī'. In Jafri 1965: 29–94.
Ali, Syed Ameer. 1891. *The Spirit of Islam: a History of the Evolution and ideals of Islam and a life of the Prophet.* Karachi: Pakistan Publishing House, 1969.
Ali, Syed Ameer. 1891 a. 'The Real Status of Women in Islam', *TheNineteenth Century* 30: 175 (Sept), 387–399. In Wasti 1968a: 1–15.
Ali, Syed Ameer. 1895. 'Islam and Canon Mac Coll', *Fortnightly Review* (October). In Wasti 1968a: 40–49.
Ali, Syed Ameer. 1896. *A Short History of the Saracens: Being a Concise Account of the Rise and Decline of the Saracenic Power and of the Economic, Social and Intellectual Development of the Arab Nation.* London: Macmillan and Co., Ltd., 1916.
Ali, Syed Ameer. 1906. 'Spain Under the Saracens', *The Nineteenth Century.* 59: 352 (Jun), 933–943. In Wasti 1968 b: 90–102.

Ali, Syed Ameer. 1927. 'The Modernity of Islam', *Islamic Culture* (January), 1–5. In Aziz 1968: 450–456.

Ali, Syed Ameer. n.d. 'Memoirs'. In Wasti 1968 b: 5–129.

Anderson, Benedict. 1983. *Imagined Communities: Reflections on the Origin and Spread of Nationalism.* London: Verso (revised ed.), 1990.

Ansari, Ishrat Husain and Qureshi, Hamid Afaq . 2008. *1857: Urdu Sources (Translation).* Lucknow: New Royal Book Company.

Arnold, Thomas Walker. 1896. *The Preaching of Islam: a History of the Propagation of the Muslim Faith.* London: Constable & Company Ltd. 2nd ed., 1913.

Asad, Talal. 2003. *Formations of the Secular: Christianity, Islam, Modernity.* Stanford: Stanford University Press.

Ashraf, Mujeeb. 2005. 'Madrasa-i-Rahimiah Growth and Pattern of Educational Curriculum Origin and Character of Islamic Education'. In Husain, S.M. Azizuddin. 2005. *Madrasa Education in India: Eleventh to Twenty First Century.* New Delhi: Kanishka Publishers.

Averroes (Ibn Rushd). 1977. *Bidāyat al-mudjtahid.* Trans. from Arabic by Peters 1977: 9–25.

Āzād, Abū'l Kalām. 1920. *Mas' alah-e-khilāfat* [Urdu: The Issue of the Caliphate]. Lahore: Maktaba Jamal, 2006.

Āzād, Abū'l Kalām. 1920s. *Khuṭbāt-e-Āzād* [Urdu: the Addresses of Azad]. Lahore: Maktaba-e-Jamal, 2013.

Āzād, Abū'l Kalām. 1959. *India Wins Freedom.* Delhi: Orient Longmans. Complete Version, 1988.

Aẓhar, Mas 'ūd. 2000. *Khuṭbāt-e-jihād* [Urdu: The Addresses of Jihad]. Vols. 1 & 2 Bahawalpur: Maktaba Hasan.

Aẓhar, Mas 'ūd. 1999. *Faḍā'il-e-jihād* [Urdu: the Blessings of Jihad]. Karachi: Jaish-e-Mohammad.

Aziz, Khursheed Kamal. (ed.). 1968. *Ameer Ali: His Life and Work.* Lahore: Publishers United Ltd.

Azmeh, Aziz al-. 1993. *Islams and Modernities.* London: Verso. 3rd ed. 2009.

Azmi, Muhammad Mustafa. 2001. *Studies in Early Hadith Literature.* Lahore: Suhail Academy. 2nd ed., 2011.

'Azzām, 'Abdullāh. 2002. *Defence Of The Muslim Lands The First Obligation After Iman.* 2nd Revised English Edition. religioscope.http://www.religioscope.com/info/doc/Jihād/azzam_defence_2_html. Retrieved 21 April 2016.

Bābar, Ẓahīruddīn. c. 16 C. *Babur-Nāmā: Memoirs of Babur.* Trans. from Turkish by Annette S. Beveridge, 1921. Lahore: Sang-e-Meel.

Baker, Deborah. 2011. *The Convert: A Tale of Exile and Extremism.* Delhi: Penguin Books.

Bakker, Edwin. 2011. 'Characteristics of Jihādi Terrorists in Europe (2001–2009)'. In Coolsaet 2011: 131–144.

Baljon, Johannes M. S. 1977. A Comparison Between the Qur' ānic Views of 'Ubayd Allāh Sindhī and Shāh Walī Allāh', *Islamic Studies* 16:2 (Summer), 179–188.

Baljon, Johannes M. S. 1986. *Religion and Thought of Shāh Walī Allāh Dihlawī 1703–1762.* Leiden: E.J. Brill.

Baljon, Johannes M. S. 1949. *The Reforms and Religious Ideas of Sir Sayyid Aḥmad Khān.* Leiden: E.J. Brill.

Baljon, Johannes M. S. 1961. *Modern Muslim Koran Interpretations (1880–1960)*. Leiden: E.J. Brill.
Bar, Shmuel. 2006. *Warrant for Terror: Fatwas of Radical Islam and the Duty of Jihād*. New York: Rowman & Littlefield Publishers with the Hoover Institution.
Bārānī, Ḍiauddīn. c. 14 C. *Ta'rīkh-e-Fīrōz Shāhī* [Urdu: The History of Feroz Shah]. Trans. From the Persian by Syed Moinul Haq. Lahore: Markazi Urdu Board, 1969.
Bārānī, Ḍiauddīn. 1358–59. *'Fatāwā-i-Jahāndārī'*. In Habib, Muhammad and Afsar Umar Salim Khan (Eds. Trans. from the Persian). n.d. *The political Theory of the Delhi Sultanate (including a translation of the Fatwa-i-Jahandari)*. Allahabad: Kitab Mahal.
Bari, Mohammad Abdul. 1954. 'A Comparative Study of the Early Wahabi Doctrines and Contemporary Reform Movements in Indian Islam'. Unpublished D.Phil. thesis, University of Oxford.
Bayly, Christopher. 2004. *The Birth of the Modern World 1780–1914: Global Connections and Comparisons*. Oxford: Blackwell Publishing Ltd.
Bergen, Peter. 2001. *Holy War, Inc.: Inside the Secret World of Osama bin Laden*. London: Weidenfeld & Nicolson.
Bergen, Peter. 2006. *The Osama bin Laden I Knew: an Oral History of al Qaeda's Leader*. New York& London: Free Press.
Bhatti, M. Ishaq. 2013. *Fuqahā-e Hind* [Urdu: The jurists of India]. 3 Vols. Lahore: M. Ishaq Bhatti Research Institute with Darul Nawadir.
Bonner, Michael. 2006. *Jihād in Islamic History: Doctrines and Practice*. Princeton: Princeton University Press.
Bonney, Richard. 2004. *Jihād: From Qur'ān to Bin Laden*. London: Palgrave Macmillan.
Bostom, Andrew G. (ed.). 2005. *The Legacy of Jihad: Islamic Holy War and the Fate of Non-Muslims*. New York: Prometheus Books.
Bouhdiba, Abdelwahab. 1998. 'The Protection of Minorities'. In *The Different aspects of Islamic Culture: the Individual and Society in Islam*. eds. A. Bouhdiba and M. Ma 'rūf al-Dawālībi Paris: UNESCO. pp. 331–346.
Bowen, Innes. 2014. *Medina in Birmingham, Najaf in Brent: Inside British Islam*. Hurst: London.
Boyle, John Andrew. 1958. *The History of the World-conqueror by 'Ala-ad-Din 'Ata Malik Juvainī*. Manchester: Manchester University Press.
Brass, Paul. 1974. *Language, Religion and Politics in North India*. Cambridge: Cambridge University Press.
Breckenridge, Carol A. and Appadurai, Arjun. 1996. 'Public Modernity in India'. In Breckenridge, C (ed.). 1996. *Consuming Modernity: Public Culture in Contemporary India*. Delhi: Oxford University Press. pp. 1–16.
Brisard, Jean-Charles and Martinez, Damien .2005. *Zarqawi: the New Face of Al-Qaeda*. Trans. from the French. Cambridge: Polity Press.
Brown, Daniel W. 1996. *Rethinking Tradition in Modern Islamic thought*. Cambridge: Cambridge University Press.
Brown, Jonathan A.C. 2009. *Hadith: Muhammad's Legacy in the Medieval and the Modern World*. Oxford: Oneworld.
Burgat, François. 2011. 'From National Struggle to the Disillusionments of "Recolonization": the Triple temporality of Islamism'. In Volpi 2011: 29–43.

Burge, Stephen R. (ed.). 2015. *The Meaning of the Word: Lexicology and the Qur'anic Exegesis.* New York and London: Oxford University Press in association with The Institute of Ismaili Studies.

Burge, Stephen.R. 2015 b. 'Introduction: Words, Hermeneutics, and the Construction of Meaning'. In Burge 2015: 1–39.

Burke, Jason. 2003. *Al Qaeda: The True Story of Radical Islam.* Revised ed. London: Penguin, 2007.

Burton, John. 1990. *The Sources of Islamic Law: Islamic Theories of Abrogation.* Edinburgh: Edinburgh University Press.

Burton, John. 1994. *An Introduction to Hadith.* Edinburgh: Edinburgh University Press.

Burton, John. 1977. *The Collection of the Qur'an.* Cambridge: Cambridge University Press.

Campanini, Massimo. 2008. *The Qur'an: Modern Muslim Interpretations.* Trans. from the Italian by Caroline Higgitt. London: Routledge, 2011.

Chandra, Satish. 1969. 'Jiziya and the State in India during Seventeenth Century', *Journal of the Economic and Social History ofthe Orient.* 12. Part 3 (Sept), 322–340. Quoted from Eaton 2003: 133–149.

Chatterjee, Partha. 1997. *Our Modernity*, lecture published by Kuala Lumpur: Rotterdam/ Dakar South-South Exchange Programme for Research on the History of Development & the Council for the Development of Social Science research in Africa.

Christie, Niall. 2015. *The Book of the Jihad of 'Ali ibn Tahir al-Sulami (d. 1106): Text, Translation and Commentary.* Surrey, Farnham: Ashgate Publishing.

Chughtai, M. Ikram (ed.). 2007. *1857 Roznāmchē, Ma'asir Taeḥrīrē, Yad' dāshtē* [Urdu: 1857 Diaries, Contemporary writings and Memoirs]. Lahore: Sang-e-Meel.

Commins, David. 2009. *The Wahhabi Mission and Saudi Arabia.* London: I.B. Tauris.

Cook, David. 2012. 'Fighting to Create the Just State: apocalypse in radical Muslim discourse'. In Hashmi 2012: 364–381.

Cook, David. 2007. *Martyrdom in Islam.* Cambridge: Cambridge University Press.

Cook, David. 2005. *Understanding Jihad.* Oakland, CA: University of California Press. Second ed., 2015.

Cook, Michael. 2000. *Commanding Right and Forbidding Wrong in Islamic Thought.* Cambridge: Cambridge University Press.

Coolsaet, Rik (ed.). 2011. *Jihadi Terrorism and the Radicalisation Challenge: European and American Experiences.* Farnham, Surrey & Burlington, USA: Ashgate Publishing.

Crone, P. 2004. *Medieval Islamic Political Thought.* Edinburgh: Edinburgh University Press.

Crone, Patricia. 2009. '"No Compulsion in Religion" Q.2: 256 in Mediaeval and Modern Interpretation', *Le Shī'isme Imāmite Quarante Ans Après hommage À Etan Kohlberg.* Sous la direction de Amir-Moezzi, Mohammad; Meir M. Bar-Asher and Simon Hopkins. Belgium: Brepols Publishers, 2009: 131–178.

Crone, Patricia and Zimmermann, Friedrich. 2001. *The Epistle of Sālim Ibn Dhakwan.* Oxford and New York: Oxford University Press.

Cörke, Andreas and Pink, Johanna (eds.). 2014. *Tafsīr and Islamic Intellectual History: exploring the Boundaries of a Genre.* New York: Oxford University Press in association with the Institute of Ismaili Studies.

Daftary, Farhad. 1994. *The Assassin Legends: Myths of the Isma'ilis.* London: I.B. Tauris, paperback ed. 1995.

Darling, Linda T. (2000). 'Contested Territory: Ottoman Holy War in Comparative Context', *Studia Islamica* 91: 133–163.
Dash, Kamala Kanta. 2008. 'The Fatwa against Terrorism: Indian Deobandis Renounce Violence but Policing Remains Unchanged'. International Conference on Radicalisation Crossing Borders, Global Terrorism Research Centre (GTReC), Monash University, 26–27 November 2008. http://artsonline.monash.edu.au/gtrec/files/2012/08/gtrec-proceedings-2008–10-kamala-dash.pdf. Retrieved on 11 October 2017.
Davies, Eryl W. 2013. *Biblical Criticism: a Guide for the Perplexed.* London: Bloomsbury.
Denoux, Guilain. 2011. 'The Forgotten Swamp: Navigating Political Islam'. In Volpi 2011: 55–80.
Devji, Faisal. 2005. *Landscapes of the Jihād: Militancy, Morality and Modernity.* Ithaca, NY: Cornell University Press.
Devji, Faisal. 2011. 'Accounting for Al-Qaeda'. In Volpi 2011: 317–325.
Donner, Fred M. 1991. 'The Sources of Islamic Conceptions of War'. In Kelsay and Johnson 1991: 31–69.
Douglas, Ian Henderson.1993. *Abul Kalam Azad: an Intellectual and Religious Biography.* (eds.) Gail Minault and Christian W. Troll Delhi: Oxford University Press.
Duderija, Adis.2011. *Constructing a Religiously Ideal 'Believer' and 'Woman' in Islam: Neo-Traditional Salafi and Progressive Muslims' Methods of Interpretation* London: Palgrave Macmillan.
Eaton, Richard M. 2017. 'Reconsidering "Conversion to Islam" in Indian History'. In Peacock, A.C.S. (ed.).2017. *Islamisation Comparative Perspectives from History.* Edinburgh: Edinburgh University Press.
Eaton, Richard M. 2003. *India's Islamic traditions, 711–1750.* New Delhi: Oxford University Press. Paperback edition, 2008.
Editorial. 2017. 'Fatwa Against Terrorism'. In *Dawn* [Karachi Daily] (01 June).
Eickelman Dale F. and Piscatori, James.1996. *Muslim Politics.* Princeton: Princeton University Press.
Eisenstadt, Shmuel.N. 1999. 'Multiple Modernities in an age of Globalization', *The Canadian Journal of Sociology* 24:2 (Spring): 283–295.
Eisenstadt, Shmuel.N. 2000. 'Multiple Modernities', *Daedalus* 129:1 (Winter): 1–29.
El-Rouayheb, Khaled. 2015. *Islamic Intellectual History in the Seventeenth Century: Scholarly Currents in the Ottoman Empire and the Maghreb.* Cambridge: Cambridge University Press.
Emon, Anver M. 2012. *Religious Pluralism and Islamic Law: Dhimmis and Others in the Empire of Law.* Oxford: Oxford University Press.
Esposito, John. (ed). 1983. *Voices of Resurgent Islam.* Oxford and New York: Oxford University Press.
Esposito, John. (ed.). 1997. *Political Islam: Revolution, Radicalism, or Reforms.* Colorado and London: Lynne Riennner Publishers.
Esposito, John. 1998. *Islam and Politics.* Syracuse, NY: Syracuse University Press.
Esposito, John. 2002. *Unholy War: Terror in the Name of Islam.* New York: Oxford University Press.
Esposito, John. 2010. 'Foreword'. In Qadri 2010: xxiii-xxviii.
Esposito, John. 1983. 'Muhammad Iqbal and the Islamic State'. In Esposito 1983: 175–190.

Euben, Roxanne and Zaman, M. Qasim (eds.). 2009. *Princeton Readings in Islamist thought: Texts and Contexts from al-Banna to Bin Laden*. Princeton and Oxford: Princeton University Press.

Fair, Christine. 2014. *Fighting to the End: the Pakistan Army's Way of War.* Karachi: Oxford University Press.

Fair, Christine. 2018. *In Their Own Words: Understanding Lashkar-e-Tayyaba.* London: Hurst & Company.

Faisal, M. Ahsanullah. 2010. *Haji Shariatullah's Faraizi Movement: History, Da'wah and Political Ideology.* Dhaka: Shariatia Library.

Faruqi, Ismail R. 1980. 'The rights of non-Muslims under Islam: Social and Cultural Aspects', in *Muslim Communities in non-Muslim States.* London: Islamic council of Europe. pp. 43–66.

Faruqi, Shamsur Rahman. 2003. 'A Long History of Urdu Literary Culture, Part 1'. In Pollock, Sheldon. 2003. *Literary Cultures in History: Reconstructions from South Asia.* Berkeley and Los Angeles: University of California Press. pp. 805–863.

Fatoohi, Louay. 2013. *Abrogation in the Qur'an and Islamic Law: a Critical Study of the Concept of "Naskh" and its Impact.* London: Routledge. First ed. Delhi. Repr. Karachi: Darul Isha'at.

Firestone, Reuven. 1999. *Jihād: the Origin of Holy War in Islam.* New York: Oxford University Press.

Fish, Stanley E. 1980. *Is there a Text in this Class? The Authority of Interpretive Communities.* London and Cambridge, MA: Harvard University Press.

Forward, Martin. 1999. *The Failure of Islamic Modernism: Syed Ameer Ali's Interpretation of Islam.* Bern: Peter Lang.

Friedmann, Yohanan. 1971. *Shaykh Ahmad Sirhindi: an Outline of His thought and a Study of His Image in the Eyes of Posterity.* Montreal and London: McGill University Institute of Islamic Studies.

Friedmann, Yohanan. 1989. *Prophecy Continuous: Aspects of Ahmadi Religious Thought and Its Medieval Background.* New Delhi: Oxford University Press, 2003.

Gadamer, Hans-Georg. 1927. *Truth and Method.* trans. from the German. William Glen-Doepel. London: Sheed and Ward, 1975.

Germain, Eric. 2015. '"Jihadists of the Pen" in Victorian England'. In Kendall and Stein 2015: 297–311.

Ghāmidī, Jawēd Aḥmad. 1990. *Mīzān* [Urdu: Balance]. Lahore: al-Mawrid, 2010.

Ghannouchi-al, Sheikh Rachid. 2015. 'What is New about al-Qardawi's Jihād'. In Kendall and Stein 2015: 334–350. Also see http://zulfkiflihasan-files.wordpress.com/2008/06/jihad-in-islam-by-qaradawi.pdf. Retrieved on 13 September 2017.

Ghazali, Muhammad. 2001. *The Socio-Political thought of Shāh Walī Allāh.* Islamabad: International Institute of Islamic Thought.

Gīlānī, Manāẓir Aḥsan. 1953. *Sawāniḥ Qāsimī* [Urdu: the biography of Mawlānā Qāsim Nānawtwī]. 2 Vols. Lahore: Maktaba Rahmania.

Gilliot, Claude. 1999. 'The Beginnings of Qur' anic Exegesis'. In Rippin 1999: 1–27.

Goldziher, Ignaz. 1890. *Muslim Studies* (ed.) S.M. Stern. Trans. from the German by C.R. Barber and S.M. Stern. Vol. 2. London: George Allen & Unwin Ltd, 1971.

Guenther, Alan M. 2003. 'Hanafi *Fiqh* in Mughal India: the Fatāwá-i 'Alamgīrī'. In Eaton 2003: 209–229.

Guenther, Alan M. 1997. 'The *ḥadīth* in Christian-Muslim Discourse in British India, 1857–1888', Unpublished M.A. Thesis, Institute of Islamic Studies, McGill University, Montreal.
Guezzou, Mokrane. Trans. 2008. *Al-Wāḥidī's Asbāb al-Nuzūl: Great Commentaries on the Holy Qur'an*. Louiseville, KY: Fons Vitae and Royal Aal al-Bayt Institute for Islamic Thought, Amman.
Gwynne, Rosalind Ward. 2016. 'Reasoning in the Qur'an'. In *The Routledge Companion to Islamic Philosophy*. (eds.) Richard C. Taylor and Luis Xavier López-Farjeat. New York: Routledge.
Haddad, Yvonne Y. 1983. 'Sayyid Qutb: Ideologue of the Islamic Revival'. In Esposito 1983: 67–98.
Hakim, Khalifa Abdul. 1953. *Islamic Ideology: the Fundamental Beliefs and Principles of Islam and Their Application to practical Life*. Lahore: Institute of Islamic Culture.
Ḥālī, Alṭāf Ḥusain. 1879. *'Al dīn yāsar'*, *Tahdhīb al-ikhlāq* [Urdu: the Refinement of Manners]. Reprinted in Pānīpatī 1967. Vol. 1: 3–39.
Ḥālī, Alṭāf Ḥusain.1899. *'Qurān majīd mẽ ab nayī tafsīr kī gunjāesh bāqī hae yā nahī?'*, [Urdu: Is there room for writing a new exegesis of the Quran?]. *Ma 'ārif* (Aligarh). Reprinted in Pānīpatī 1967, Vol. 1: 70–97.
Ḥālī, Alṭāf Ḥusain. 1898. *'Sir Sayyid kī Islāmī aur mazhabī khidmāt'*, [Urdu: Sir Sayyid's Services to Islam] *Mohammadan Anglo-Oriental College Magazine* (May), 115–162. Reprinted in Pānīpatī 1967, Vol. 1: 358–384.
Ḥālī, Alṭāf Ḥusain.1901. *Hayāt-i-Jāwēd (A Biography of Sir Sayyid)*. Trans. from Urdu to English by David J. Matthews Delhi: Rupa & Co, 1994.
Hallaq, Wael. 1999. 'The Authenticity of the Prophetic Ḥadīth: a Pseudo-Problem', *Studia Islamica* 89: 75–90.
Ḥaqq, 'Abdul. 1911. *'Muqaddamah az mutarajjim'* [Urdu: Preface by the Translator]. In 'Alī 1911, part 2: 1–88.
Haq, Mushirul. 1995. *Shah 'Abdul 'Aziz: His Life and Time: a Study of Muslims' Attitude to the British in the early 19th Century*. Lahore: Institute of Islamic Culture.
Hardy, Peter. 1972. *The Muslims of British India*. Cambridge: Cambridge University Press. Pakistan edition, Karachi, 1973.
Haroon, Sana. 2007. *Frontier of Faith: a History of Religious Mobilisation in the Pakhtun Tribal Areas c. 1890–1950*. Karachi: Oxford University Press, 2011.
Hasan, Mushirul. 2005. *A Moral Reckoning: Muslim Intellectuals in Nineteenth-Century Delhi*. New Delhi: Oxford University Press.
Hasan, Tariq. 2015. *Colonialism and the Call to Jihad in British India*. New Delhi: Sage.
Hashmi, Sohail H. (ed.). 2012. *Just wars, Holy Wars, and Jihāds: Christian, Jewish, and Muslim Encounters and Exchange*. New York: Oxford University Press.
Hauner, Milan. 1981. 'One Man against the Empire: The Faqir of Ipi and the British in Central Asia on the Eve of the Second World War', *Journal of Contemporary History* 16: 1: Part 1 (Jan), 183–212.
Hefner, Robert W. 1998. 'Multiple Modernities: Christianity, Islam, and Hinduism in a Globalizing Age', *Annual Review of Anthropology* 27: 83–104.
Hirsch, Eric.D. 1967. *Validity in Interpretation*. New Haven & London: Yale University Press.

Hodgson, Marshall G.S. 1955. *The Secret Order of the Assassins: the Struggle of the Early Nizari Isma'ilis Against the Islamic World.* Philadelphia: University of Pennsylvania Press, 2005.

Hooker, M.Barry. 1997. '*Shari'a*'. *Encyclopaedia of Islam.* New ed. Vol. 9 Leiden: E.J. Brill.

Hughes, Thomas Patrick. 1875. *Notes on Mohammadanism: Being Outlines of the Religious System of Islam.* 2nd ed. Revised and enlarged London: Wm. H. Allen & Co., 1877.

Hughes, Thomas Patrick. 1885. *A Dictionary of Islam.* 2nd ed. London: W.H. Allen & Co. 1935.

Hunter, William Wilson. 1871. *The Indian Muslims: Are they Bound in Conscience to Rebel against the Queen?* Repr. Lahore: Premier Book House, 1974.

Husain, Khwaja Manzur. 1978. *Taḥrīk-e-jadd-o-jahd bataor mawḍū'-e-sukhan* [Urdu: The movement for struggle and resistance as a poetic theme]. Lahore: National Book Foundation.

Husain, M. Hidayat. 1912. 'The Persian Autobiography of Shāh Walīullah bin 'Abd al-Rahīm al-Dihlavī: its English Translation and a List of His Works', *Journal of the Asiatic Society of Bengal* Vol. 8 (April), 161–175.

Hussain, Mujahid. 2012. *Punjabi Taliban: Driving Extremism in Pakistan.* Trans. from Urdu. New Delhi: Pentagon Security International.

Hussain, Sheikh Showkat. 1993. 'Status of Non-Muslims in Islamic State', *Hamdard Islamicus* 16: 1: 67–79.

Hussain, Syed Shabbir. 1991. *Al-Mashriqi: the Disowned Genius.* Lahore: Jang Publishers.

Hussain, Zahid. 2008. *Frontline Pakistan: the Struggle with Militant Islam.* New York: Columbia University Press.

Ibn Taymiyyah, Taqī al-Dīn. c. 13 C. *Al-siyāsa al-shar'iyyah al-rai wa al-ra'iyya* (Arabic: Governance according to God's Law in Reforming both the Ruler and His Flock). Excerpts in English in Peters 1996: 44–54.

Iftikhar, Asif. 2004. 'Jihād and the Establishment of Islamic Global Order: a Comparative Study of the Worldviews and Interpretative Approaches of Abū al-A'lā Mawdūdī and Jāved Ahmad Ghāmidī', unpublished M.A. thesis, McGill University, Canada.

Ikram, Sheikh Muhammad. 2015. *Yādgār-e-Shiblī* [Urdu: Memoir of Shibli]. Lahore: Yadgar Saqafat-e-Islamia.

Ingram, Haroro J. 2013. *The Charismatic Phenomenon in Radical Militant Islamism.* Farnham, Surrey: Ashgate Publishing Ltd.

Iqbāl, Muḥammad. 1911. '*Shikwah*', *Bāng-e-Darā* [Originally in Urdu] (ed. & trans. from Persian and explained). Mahar, Ghulām Rasūl. n.d. *Maṭālib kalām-e-Iqbāl: Urdū* [Urdu: Meanings of the Poetry of Iqbāl in Urdu]. Lahore: Sang-e-Meel.

Iqbal, Muhammad. 1934. *The Reconstruction of Religious Thought in Islam* (ed. and annotated). Saeed Sheikh Lahore: Institute of Islamic Culture, 1986.

Ishaq, Muhammad. 1955. *India's Contribution to the Study of Hadith Literature.* Dacca: University of Dacca.

Jackson, Paul. 1982. 'Sheikh Sharfuddin Maneri's Use of the Quran in His Maktubat-i Sadi'. In Troll 1982: 33–42.

Jackson, Sherman. 2015. 'The Appeal of Yusuf al-Qaradawi's Interpretations of Jihād'. In Kendall and Stein 2015: 312–333.

Jaffar, Ghulam Mohammad. 1992. 'The Repudiation of Jihad by the Indian Scholars in the Nineteenth Century', *Hamdard Islamicus* 15:3 (Autumn), 93–100.

Jafri, S. Rais Ahmad. 1965. *Selections from Maulana Mohammad Ali's Comrade*. Lahore: Mohammad Ali Academy.

Jalal, Ayesha. 2008. *Partisans of Allah*. Lahore: Sang-e-Meel Publications.

Jansen, Johannes. 1986. *The Neglected Duty: the Creed of Sadat's Assassins and Islamic Resurgence in the Middle East*. Trans. from The Arabic. 'Abd al-Salam, Faraj. c. 1970s. *Al Jihād: al-Farīḍah al-Ghaibah*. New York: Macmillan Publishing Company. 159 – 234.

Jarrar, Maher. 2004. 'The Martyrdom of Passionate Lovers: Holy War as a Sacred Wedding'. In Motzki 2004: 317 – 337.

Jeffery, Arthur. 1998. 'Abu 'Ubaid on the Verses Missing from the Koran'. In Warraq, Ibn 1998: 150 – 153.

Johnson, James Turner. 1991. *Holy War Idea in Western and Islamic Traditions*. Philadelphia: Pennsylvania State Press.

Jones, Kenneth W. 1994. *Socio-religious Reform Movements in British India*. Cambridge: Cambridge University Press.

Joshi, Sanjay. 2001. *Fractured Modernity: Making of a Middle Class in Colonial India*. New Delhi: Oxford University Press.

Joshi, Sohan Singh. 1977. *Hindustan Gadar Party: a Short History*. New Delhi: People's Publishing House.

J.R.C. 1832. 'Notice of the Peculiar Tenets held by the followers of Syed Ahmad, taken chiefly from the "Sirat-ul-Mustaqim" a principal treatise of that Sect, written by Maulvi Muhammad Ismail', *Journal of the Asiatic Society* No.11 (November), 479 – 498.

Juynboll, Gautier. 1983. *Muslim Tradition: Studies in Chronology, Provenance and Authorship of Early Hadith*. Cambridge: Cambridge University Press.

Kamran, Tahir. 2016. 'The Genesis, Evolution and Impact of Deobandi Islam on the Punjab: an Overview'. In Syed, Jawad, Edward Pio, Tahir Kamran and Abbas Zaidi (eds.) *Faith-Based Violence and Deobandi Militancy in Pakistan*. London: Palgrave Macmillan. pp. 65 – 92.

Karīmīnīyā, Murtaḍa. 2012 a. 'Tafsīr al-Jalālayn'. in Adel 2012: 35 – 39.

Karīmīnīyā, Murtaḍa. 2012 b. 'Al-Bayḍāwi's Exegesis'. In Adel 2012: 121 – 129.

Kaye, Cecil (Comp.). 1919. Report by the Director, CID, Sir Cecil Kaye. Published as *Communism in India with Unpublished Documents from the National Archives of India* (1919 – 1924). (Comp. and ed.) Subodh Ray Calcutta: Editions Indian, 1971.

Keddie, Nikki R. 1972. *Sayyid Jamāl ad-Dīn "al-Afghānī": a Political Biography*. Los Angeles & Berkeley: Near Eastern Center, University of California Press.

Kelly, Donald R. 2002. *The Descent of ideas: The History of Intellectual History*. Aldershot: Ashgate.

Kelly, Saul. 2013. 'Crazy in the Extreme'? The Silk Letters Conspiracy', *Middle Eastern Studies* 49:2: 162 – 178.

Kelsay, John and Johnson, James Turner (ed). 1991. *Just War and Jihād: Historical and Theoretical Perspectives on War and Peace in Western and Islamic Traditions*. New York: Greenwood Press.

Kelsay, John. 2007. *Arguing the Just War in Islam*. Cambridge, MA: Harvard University Press.

Kendall, Elisabeth and Stein, Ewan (eds.). 2015. *Twenty-First Century Jihād: Law, Society and Military Action*. London and New York: I.B. Tauris.

Kenny, Jeffrey T. 2006. *Muslim Rebels: Kharijites and the Politics of Extremism in Egypt*. New York: Oxford University Press.

Kepel, Gilles. 2000. *Jihad: the Trail of Political Islam.* Trans. from the French by Anthony F. Roberts. London: I.B. Tauris, 2006. Repr. 2011.

Khaddūrī, Majīd. 1955. 'Introduction' and 'The Doctrine of Jihad'. In *War and Peace in the Law of Islam. Book 2: the Law of War: the Jihad.* Baltimore: John Hopkins University Press. Quoted from Bostom 2005: 305–319.

Khairābādī, Faḍl-i-Ḥaqq. 1860s. Account of 1857. Trans. from Arabic into English by Moinul Haq, 'The Story of the War of Independence 1857–58', *Journal of the Pakistan Historical Society* 5:1 (Jan 1957), 23–57.

Khalid, Saleem M. 2000. *Shāh 'Abdul Qādir kē Urdū tarjumah-e-Qur'ān kā lisānī-o adabī muṭāla'ah* [Urdu: The linguistic and literary study of Shah Abdul Qadir's translation of the Qur' an], unpublished M.Phil. thesis, Allama Iqbal Open University, Islamabad.

Khan, Iqtidar. 1968. 'The Nobility Under Akbar and the Development of His Religious Policy, 1560–80'. In Eaton 2003: 121–132.

Khān, Khafī.c. 17 C. *Khafi Khan's History of 'Alamgir Being an English Translation of the Relevant Portions of Muntakhab al-Lubāb with Notes and Introduction.* Trans. From Persian to English by Haq, Moinul. Karachi: Pakistan Historical Society.

Khan, Moinuddin Ahmad. 1965. *History of the Fara'iḍī Movement in Bengal, 1818–1906.* Karachi: Asiatic Society of Pakistan.

Khan, Moinuddin Ahmad.1959. 'Shah Waliullah's Conception of Ijtihād', *Journal of the Pakistan Historical Society* VII, Part III (July), 173–179.

Khan, Muhammad Afzal. 2016. 'The Taliban Becoming', Unpublished Ph.D dissertation, University of Erfurt.

Khān, Muḥammad Fārūq. 2010. *Jihād aur qitāl: chānd aham mabāhith* [Urdu: Striving and Fighting: Some important Debates]. Mardan: Agahi Barae Aitidal.

Khān, Nawwāb Muḥammad Wazīr. n.d. *Wāqi'ā-e Sayyid Aḥmad Shahīd* [Urdu: Events of the Life of Sayyid Aḥmad]. Typescript.

Khān, Sayyid Ahmad. 1844. *Tōḥfah ḥasan* (The Good Gift: Urdu translation of parts of Shah Abdul Aziz'z *Tōḥfah ithnā 'asharī'a* i.e. Gift to the Twelver Shi'ā). In Pānīpatī, Vol. 16, 1965: 785–863.

Khān, Sayyid Ahmad. 1872. *Review of Dr Hunter's Indian Musalmans: Are they Bound in Conscience to Rebel Against the Queen?* Benares: Printed in the Medical Hall Press.

Khān, Sayyid Ahmad. 1847. 'Shāhjahān Ābad kē lōgō ka bayān'. In Pānīpatī Vol. 16, 1965: 312–321.

Khān, Sayyid Ahmad. 1859. '*Tārīkh-e-sarkashī ḍil'a Bijnaor*' [Urdu: History of the Rebellion of Bijnour]. In Pānīpatī 1990: 272–425.

Khān, Sayyid Ahmad. 1871. 'Letter to the Editor', *The Pioneer* (04 April).

Khān, S.A. 1898. *Akhrī maḍāmīn* [Urdu: Last Essays]. Comp. Mohammad Imam Uddin Lahore: Rifah-e-'Am Press.

Khān, Sayyid Ahmad. 1887. *Khuṭbāt-e-Aḥmadiyyah* [Urdu: Addresses of Sayyid Aḥmad]. Present title *Maqālāt-e-Sir Sayyid:* Pānīpatī, Ismā'īl (ed. and comp.) Vol. 11. Lahore: Majlis e-Taraqqi-e-Adab, n.d.

Khān, Waḥīduddīn. 2002 a. *'Jihād kā taṣawwur Islām mē'* [Urdu: the concept of Jihad in Islam]. In Khān 2002 b: 251–261.

Khān, Waḥīduddīn. 2002. *The True Jihād: the Concepts of Peace, Tolerance and Non-Violence in Islam.* Delhi: Goodward Giftbook.

Khān, Waḥīduddīn. 2002 b. *Dīn aur sharī'at: Dīn-ē-Islām kā ēk fikrī mutāla'ā* [Urdu: Religion and the Law]. New Delhi: Goodward Books Pvt. Ltd, 2004.
Khān, Waḥīduddīn. 1963. *Ta'bīr kī ghalaṭī* [Urdu: Mistake of Interpretation]. Lahore: Malik and Company, 2nd ed. 1986.
Koselleck, Reinhart. 2002. *The Practice of Conceptual History: Timing History, Spacing Concepts*. Trans. from the German by Todd Samuel Presner and others. Stanford: Stanford University Press.
Krämer, Gudrun. 2010. *Hasan al-Banna* Oxford: Oneworld.
Laghārī, 'Abdallāh. 1980. *Mawlānā 'Ubaydullāh Sindhī kī sarguzasht-e-Kābul* [Urdu: Sindhi's Story of Kabul]. Islamabad: National Institute of Historical and Cultural Research.
Landa-Tassecron, Ella. 2003. 'Jihād'. In *Encyclopaedia of the Qur'an* Vol. 3: 35–42.
Lawrence, Bruce. 1991. 'Holy war (Jihād) in Islamic Religion and Nation-State Ideologies'. In Kelsay and Johnson 1991: 141–160.
Leithart, Peter J. 2014. *Gratitude: An Intellectual History*. Waco. TX: Baylor University Press.
Levy, Ran .A.2014. 'The Idea of *Jihād* and its Evolution: Ḥasan al-Bannā and the Society of Muslim Brothers', *Die Welt Des Islams* 54: 139–159.
Lewis, Bernard. 2003. *The Crisis of Islam: Holy War and Unholy Terror*. London: Weidenfeld & Nicolson.
Lloyd, Steffen. 2007. *Holy War, Just War: Exploring the Moral Meaning of Religious Violence*. New York: Rowman & Littlefield.
Maclean, Derryl N. 2000. 'The Sociology of Political Engagement: the Mahdiwiyah and the State', *Revue des mondes musulmans et de la mediterranee*, 91–92: 243–60. In Eaton 2003: 150–166.
Madanī, Hussain Aḥmad. 1953. *Naqsh-e-Ḥayāt* [Urdu: Mark of Life] 2 parts in one. Karachi: Darul Isha'at.
Madanī, Hussain Aḥmad. 1933. Untitled Essay on 'Ubaydullāh Sindhī. In Sindhī 1933: 41–50.
Madanī, Hussain Aḥmad. 2005. *Ta'ārruf wa ḥaqā'ieq* [Urdu: Introduction and Realities–Selected Urdu letters of Mawlānā Madanī]. Comp. and ed. Syed Raziuddin. Karachi: Banuri Town.
Madanī, Hussain Aḥmad. 1921. *Safar nāmah athīr-i-Mālṯā wa ḥayāt-i-Maḥmūd: sawāniḥ Shaikh al-Hind* [Urdu: Travelogue of the Captive of Malta and Life of Shaikh al-Hind]. Deoband: Darul Isha'at wa'l Tijarat.
Mahar, Ghulām Rasūl. 1952. *Sayyid Aḥmad Shahīd* [Urdu: The Biography of Sayyid Aḥmad the Martyr]. Lahore: Sheikh Ghulam Ali.
Malik, Iftikhar H. 2005. *Jihad, Hindutva and the Taliban: South Asia at the Crossroads*. Karachi: Oxford University Press.
Malik, Jamal. 2009. 'Maudūdī's *al-jihād fī' l-Islām:* a Neglected Document'. In *Zeitschrift für Religionswissenschaft* (17. Jahrgang): 61–69.
Malik, Jamal. 2006. 'Letters, Prison Sketches and Autobiographical Literature: the Case of Faḍl-i-Haqq Khairabadi in the AndamanPenal Colony', *The Indian Economic and Social History Review* 43:1: 77–100.
Malik, Tajammal Hussain .1991. *The Story of My Struggle* Lahore: Jang Publishers.
Mansfield, Laura. 2006. *His Own Words: A Translation of the Writings of Dr. Ayman al Zawahiri*. TLG Publishers.
Mashriqī, 'Ināyatullāh Khān.1924. *Tadhkirah with iftitāḥiyya*. Amritsar: Idarat ul Isha'at.

Masud, Khalid. 2016. 'Islamic Modernism'. In Masud, Khalid; Armando Salvatore and Martin van Bruinessen. 2016. *Islam and Modernity: Key Issues and Debates.* Edinburgh: Edinburgh University Press. pp. 237–260.

Mawdūdī, Sayyid Abū'l A'lā. 1930. *al-Jihād fī al-Islām* [Urdu: Jihād in Islam]. Lahore: Islamic Publications. Repr. 1971.

Mawdūdī, Sayyid Abū'l A'lā. 1939. *Pardah* [Urdu: Veil]. Lahore: Islamic Publications, 2003. English version. *Purdah and the Status of Women in Islam.* http://www.khalifahbooks.com/wp-content/ebook-download/english/khalifa.

Mawdūdī, Sayyid Abū'l A'lā. 1940. *Tafhīmāt* [Urdu: Understandings]. Vol. 1 Lahore: Islamic Publications, Repr. 1986.

Mawdūdī, Sayyid Abū'l A'lā. 1942. 'Islām aur iqtidār', [Urdu: Islam and Political Power]. *Tarjumān al-Qur'ān* (Sept-Nov). In Mawdūdī 1962: 58–74.

Mawdūdī, Sayyid Abū'l A'lā. 1948. '*Kashmīr kā jihād az ruē Qur'ān jā'iz nahī*', [Urdu: The jihad in Kashmir is not permissible according to the Qur'an]. Interview of Maulana Mawdūdī in *Kauthar* (17 Aug 1948). Repr. *Al-Ikhwā.* [Lahore] (July 1998), 9–13.

Mawdūdī, Sayyid Abū'l A'lā. 1953. *Qur'ān kī chār bunyādī istilāhē.* Karachi: Islamic Publications Ltd., 1968.

Mawdūdī, Sayyid Abū'l A'lā. 1958. '*Sunnat-ē-Rasūl bahaythiyat ma'ākhiz-e-qānūn*' [Urdu: the Prophet's Example as Sources for Law], *Tarjumān al-Qur'ān* (December). In Mawdūdī 1962: 297–307.

Mawdūdī, Sayyid Abū'l A'lā. 1962. *Islāmī riyāsat* [Urdu: The Islamic State]. Comp. Khurshīd Aḥmad Lahore: Islamic Publications, 1977.

Mawdūdī, Sayyid Abū'l A'lā. 1966. *Khilāfat aur mulūkiyyat.* Lahore: Islamic Publications.

McAuliffe, Jane Dammen. 1988. 'Quranic Hermeneutics: the views of al-Ṭabarī and Ibn Kathīr'. In Rippin 1988: 46–62.

McDonough, Sheila. 1963. 'An Ideology for Pakistan: a Study of the Works of Ghulām Aḥmad Parwēz'. Unpublished Ph.D. thesis, Department of Islamic Studies, Mc Gill University.

Metcalf, Barbara D. 2009 a. *Husain Ahmad Madani: the Jihad for Islam and India's Freedom.* Oxford: Oneworld.

Metcalf, Barbara D. (ed.). 2009. *Islam in South Asia in Practice.* Princeton and Oxford: Princeton University Press.

Metcalf, Barbara D. 2004. 'The Past in the Present: Instruction, Pleasure, and Blessing in Maulana Muhammad Zakariyya's *Aap biti*'. In Metcalf, B. 2004 a. *Islamic Contestations: Essays on Muslims in India and Pakistan.* New Delhi: Oxford University Press. pp. 67–95.

Metcalf, Barbara D.. 1982. *Islamic Revival in British India: Deoband, 1860–1900.* Karachi: Royal Book Company, 1989.

Miān, Sayyid Muḥammad. 1999. *Asīrān-e-Mālṭā* [Urdu: the Prisoners of Malta]. Lahore: Ishtiaq A. Mushtaq Press.

Miān, Sayyid Muḥammad. 1999a. *Taḥrīk-e-rēshmī rumāl* [Urdu: the Silk Letters Movement]. Lahore: Ishtiaq A. Mushtaq Press.

Michell, Richard Paul. 1969. *The Society of the Muslim Brothers.* New York & Oxford: Oxford University Press.

Mir, Amir. 2008. *Fluttering Flag of Jihād.* Lahore, Pakistan: Mashal Books.

Mīr, Taqī Mīr. 1808. *Dhikr-e-Mīr* [Persian: The Memoir of Mir]. Digital copy.

Motzki, Harald (ed.). 2004. *Hadith: Origins and Developments.* Farnham, Surrey: Ashgate Publishing Ltd.
Muhammad, Ghazi bin; Ibrahim Kalin and Kamali, M. Hashmi (eds.). 2013. *War and Peace in Islam: the Uses and Abuses of Jihad.* Amman & Kuala Lumpur: The Royal Islamic Strategic Studies Centre, Jordan & the International Institute of Advanced Islamic Studies, Malaysia.
Muḥammad, Nūr. 1978. *Jihād-e-Afghānistān* [Urdu: The Jihad of Afghanistan]. Wana, North Waziristan: Darul 'Ulum Markazi Jami' Masjid.
Murad, Mehr Afroz .1976. *Intellectual Modernism of Shibli Nu'mānī: an Exposition of His Religious and Political Ideas.* Lahore: Institute of Islamic Culture.
Mutiny. 1911. *Mutiny Records: Correspondence (2 parts in 1).* Lahore: Printed at the Punjab Government Press. Repr. Lahore: Sang-e-Meel, 2005.
Nadwī, Abū'l Ḥasan 'Alī.1939& 1969. *Ta'rīkh-e-dā'wat-o-'Aẓmiyyat: Sīrat-e-Sayyid Aḥmad Shahīd* [Urdu: History of the Call for Reform and the Greatness of Sayyid Aḥmad the Martyr]. Vol. 1, 1939; Vol. 2 1969. Karachi: Nashriat-e-Islam, 2011.
Nadwī, Abū'l Ḥasan 'Alī. 1978. *'Aṣr-i ḥāḍir mē dīn kī tafhīm-o-tashrīḥ* [Urdu: The Understanding and Explanation of the Faith During the Present Time]. Lucknow: Dar-i 'Arafat.
Nadwī, Abū'l Ḥasan 'Alī.1984. *'Tarjumān ul Qur'ān'.* In Shāhjahānpūrī 1984: 19–23.
Nadwī, Sayyid Sulaiman.1943. *Hayāt-e-Shiblī* [Urdu: the life of Shibli] Azamgarh: Dar ul Musannifin.
Nadwī, Sayyid Sulaimān.1968. *Maqālāt-e-Sulaimān* [Urdu: The Dissertations of Sulaiman]. Karachi: Kaleem Press. Repr. Revised edition, 1951.
Nafisi, Shadi .2012. 'Sir Sayyid Ahmad Khan's Exegesis'. In Adel et al.: 75–85.
Nānawtwī, Muḥammad Qāsim .1890. *Tasfiyāt al-'aqā'id* [Urdu: Reconciliation of Beliefs]. Delhi. In Ahmad and Grunebaum 1970: 60–76.
Nāṣir, 'Ammār Khān. 2012. *'Jihād: ēk muṭāla'ah'* [Urdu: Jihad: a Study]. *Al-Sharī'ah* 23: 3 (March), 109–340.
Nasr,S.Vali Reza. 1996. *Mawdudi and the Making of Islamic Revivalism.* New York: Oxford University Press.
Nasr, S.Vali Reza. 2000. "The Rise of Sunni Militancy in Pakistan: The Changing Role of Islamism and the Ulama in Society and Politics". *Modern Asian Studies* 34 :1: 139–80.
Nasr, S.Vali Reza. 2004. *The Vanguard of the Islamic Revolution: the Jama'at-i-Islami of Pakistan.* London: I.B. Tauris.
Nīshāpūrī, A. 2012. 'Maulana Hasan Jan: An Unsung Hero'. https://worldshiaforum.wordpress.com/2012/07131/maulana-hasan-jan-an-unsung-hero-by-abdul-nishapuri/.Retrieved on 11 Oct 2017.
Nizami, Khaliq Ahmad (ed.). 1950. *Shāh Walīullāh kē siyāsī maktūbāt* [Urdu: the Political Letters of Shāh Walīullāh]. Aligarh: n.p.
Nizami, Khaliq Ahmad. 1961. *Religion and Politics in India During the Thirteenth Century.* New Delhi: Oxford University Press, 2002.
Nu'mānī, Shiblī. 1893. *Sīrat al-Nu'mān* [Urdu: The Life of Abū Ḥanīfah]. Lahore: Maktaba Rahmania, n.d.
Nu'mānī, Shiblī. 1898. *Al-Fārūq: sawāniḥ 'umarī Haḍrat 'Umar Fārūq* [Urdu: The Life of the Exalted Umar Faruq]. Lahore: al-Waqar Press, 2011.

Nu'mānī, Shiblī. 1938. *Maqālāt-e-Shiblī* [Urdu: Dissertations of Shiblī]. Vol. 8 'Azam Garh: Matba'a Ma'arif.

Nu'mānī, Shiblī and Nadwī, Sulaimān. 1918. *Sīrat un nabī* [Urdu: Life of the Prophet]. Vol. 7 Lahore: Al-Faisal, 1991.

Nu'mānī, M. Yaḥya. 2012. *'Maḥarbah 'Illat al-qitāl hai na kē kufr yā shawkat-e-kufr'* [Urdu: The cause of war is aggression not disbelief nor the Power of the Unbelievers]. *Al-Sharī'ah* [monthly from Gujranwala] Vol. 23: No. 3 (March), 15–105.

Pānīpatī, Ismā'īl (ed. and comp.). 1965. *Maqālat-e-Sir Sayyid* [Urdu: The Dissertations of Sir Sayyid]. Vol. 16. Lahore: Majlis-e-Taraqqi-e-Adab, 1965.

Pānīpatī, Ismā'īl (ed. and comp.) 1967. *Kulliyāt nasr-e-Ḥālī* [Urdu: The Collected Prose of *Ḥālī*]. Vol. 1 (ed.) Pānīpatī, Ismā'īl Lahore: Majlis Taraqqi Adab.

Pānīpatī, Ismā'īl (ed.). 1990. *Maqālāt-e-Sir Sayyid: ta'rīkhī maḍāmīn* [Urdu: Historical Essays]. Vol. 6 Lahore: Majlis-e-Taraqqi-e-Adab.

Parwēz, Ghulām Aḥmad.1950s. *Mizāj shinās-e-Rasūl* [Urdu: One who Understands the Prophet's Mind]. Lahore: Tuluh-e-Islam Trust, 2nd ed. 1996.

Parwēz, Ghulām Aḥmad. 1953. *Muqām-e-hadīth* [Urdu: The Status of Hadith]. Lahore: Tulu-e-Islam Trust.

Parwēz, Ghulām Aḥmad. 1960. *Lughat al-Qur'ān* [Urdu: the Vocabulary of the Qur' an]. Vol. 1 Lahore: Tuluh-e-Islam Trust.

Parwēz, Ghulām Aḥmad. 1967. *Jihād: ṣaḥiḥ mafhūm Qur'ān karīm kī roshanī mē̃* [Urdu: Jihad: the True Meaning in the Light of the Beneficent Qur'an]. Lahore: Tulu-e-Islam, 1996.

Peervani, Latimah-Parvin. Trans. 2004. *On the Hermeneutics of the Light Verse of the Qur'ān (Tafsīr Āyat al-Nūr)* from the Persian of Mullā Ṣadrā Shirāzī. London: Islamic College for Advanced Studies.

Peters, Rudolph. 1977. *Jihad in Mediaeval and Modern Islam.* Trans. from the Arabic and annotated. Leiden: E.J. Brill.

Peters, Rudolph. (comp.). 1996. *Jihad: a History in Documents.* Princeton: Markus Weiner Publishers, Third updated ed. 2016.

Pipes, Daniel. 1983. *In the Path of God: Islam and Political Power.* New York: Basic Books Inc.

Pipes, Daniel. 2004. *Miniatures: Views of Islamic and Middle Eastern Politics.* New Brunswick and London: Transaction Publishers.

PIPS. 2012. *'Mu'aṣir muslim riyasatō kē khilāf khurūj kā mas'alah* [Urdu: The Problem of Rebellion against Contemporary Muslim States]. PIPS Seminar, Proceedings. In *Al-Sharī'ah* 23:3 (March), 366–651.

Powers, David S. 1988. 'The Exegetical Genre *nāsikh al-Qur'ān wa mansūkhuhu'*. In Rippin 1988: 117–138.

Poythress, Sheridan V. 1988. *Science and Hermeneutics: Implications of Scientific Method for Biblical Interpretation.* Leicester, England: Academe Books.

Pratāp, Mahendra. 1947. *My Life Story of Fifty-five Years* .This edition, (ed.) Vir Singh. Delhi: Books for All, 2004.

Qadir, Altaf .2006. 'Ḥājī Ṣāhib of Turangza'i and His Reform Movement in the North West Frontier Province', *Journal of the Pakistan Historical Society*, 54:3: 85–95.

Qadir, Altaf. 2008. 'Anti-colonial Movement: the Struggle of Ḥājī Ṣāhib Turangza'i to do away with the Authority of the British Rāj', *Journal of the Pakistan Historical Society*, 56:2: 111–123.

Qadir, Altaf. 2015. *Sayyid Ahmad Barailvi: His Movement and Legacy From the Pakhtūn Perspective.* Delhi: Sage Publications.
Qādri, Ṭahirul. 2010. *Fatwā on Terrorism and Suicide Bombings.* London: Minhaj-ul-Quran International.
Qamaruddin, M. 1985. *The Mahdawi Movement in India.* Delhi: Idara-i-Adabiyat-i-Dilli.
Qaraḍāwī, Yūsuf al- et. al. 2001. 'Qaradawi et. al. Fatwa Against 9/11'. http//www. fatwa. qardawi. Retrieved on 21 March 2017.
Qaraḍāwī. 2009. *Fiqh al-jihād* [Arabic: The Law of Jihad]. Cairo. Used English summary in Ghannouchi 2015.
Qasmi, Ali Usman. 2011. *Questioning the Authority of the Past: the Ahl al-Qur'an Movements in the Punjab.* Karachi: Oxford University Press.
Qazi, Shehzad S. 2011. 'Rebels of the Frontier: Origins, Organization, and Recruitment of the Pakistani Taliban', *Small Wars & Insurgencies* 22:4: 574–602.
Qureshi, Ishtiaq Husain. 1977. *The Muslim Community of the Indo-Pakistan Subcontinent (610–1947).* Karachi: University of Karachi, 2003.
Qureshi, Naeem. 1999. *Pan Islam in British Indian Politics: a Study of the Khilafat Movement, 1918–1924.* Leiden: E.J. Brill.
Qureshi, Naeem. 2014. *Ottoman Turkey, Ataturk, and Muslim South Asia: Perspectives, Perceptions, and Responses.* Karachi: Oxford University Press.
Quṭb, Sayyid. 1964. *Milestones.* Egypt: Kazi Publications.
Rahman, Fazlur. 1964. *Islamic Methodology in History.* Islamabad: Islamic Research Institute.
Rahman, Fazlur. 1980. *Major Themes of the Qur'an.* Chicago: University of Chicago Press.
Rahman, Fazlur. 1982. *Islam and Modernity: Transformation of an Intellectual Tradition.* Chicago: University of Chicago Press.
Rahman, Fazlur. 1986. 'Non-Muslim Minorities in an Islamic State', *Journal Institute of Muslim Minority Affairs* 7: 13–24.
Rahman, Fazlur. 2000. *Revival and Reform In Islam: a Study of Islamic Fundamentalism* (ed. and with an introduction by Ebrahim Moosa). Oxford: One world.
Rahman, Tariq. 2008. 'The Events of 1857 in Contemporary Writings in Urdu', *South Asia* 32:2 (August), 212–229.
Rahman, Tariq. 2011. *From Hindi to Urdu: a Social and Political History.* Karachi: Oxford University Press.
Rahman, Wahidur. 1982. 'The Religious Thought of Moulvi Chiragh 'Ali', Unpublished M.A. Dissertation, Institute of Islamic Studies, McGill University.
Rana, Amir. 2015. *The Militant: Development of a Jihādi Character in Pakistan.* Islamabad: Narratives.
Rana, Amir. 2017. 'Going Beyond Edicts', *Dawn* (06 June).
Rashīd, Mohammad. 2012. '"*Pur amn tarīqa-e kār" ba muqābalah "pur tashaddud tarīqa-e kār*"' [Urdu: Peaceful Ways Contrasted with Violent Ways]. *Al-Sharī'ah* 23: 3 (March), 341–359.
Reetz, Deitrich. 2006. *Islam in the Public Sphere: Religious Groups in India 1900–1947.* New Delhi: Oxford University Press.
Riedel, Bruce. 2009. *The Search for al-Qaeda: its Leadership, Ideology and Future.* Lahore: Vanguard.
Rippin, Andrew. (ed.). 1988. *Approaches to the History of the Interpretation of the Qur'ān.* Oxford: the Clarendon Press.

Rippin, Andrew. 1997. '*Tafsīr*'. *Encyclopaedia of Islam*. Vol. 10 Leiden: E.J. Brill.
Rippin, Andrew. (ed.). 1999. *The Qur'an: Formative Interpretation*. Aldershot: Ashgate Variorum.
Rippin, Andrew. 2001 a. *The Qur'an and its Interpretative Tradition*. Aldershot, Hampshire: Ashgate Variorum.
Rippin, Andrew. 2001 b. 'The Exegetical Genre Asbab al-Nuzul: a Bibliographical and Terminological Survey'. In Rippin 2001 a: 1–15.
Rippin, Andrew. (ed.). 2006. *The Blackwell Companion to the Qur'an*. Oxford: Blackwell Publishing.
Rizvi, Saiyid Athar Abbas .1980. *Shāh Walī Allāh and his Times: a study of Eighteenth Century Islam, Politics and Society in India*. Canberra, Australia: Ma'rifat Publishing House.
Rizvi, Saiyid Athar Abbas. 1982. *Shāh 'Abd al-'Azīz: Puritanism, Sectarianism, Polemics and Jihād*. Canberra: Ma'rifat Publishing House.
Robinson, Francis. 1974. *Separatism Among Indian Muslims: the Politics of the United Provinces' Muslims 1860–1923*. Cambridge: Cambridge University Press.
Robinson, Francis. 1996. 'Islam and the Impact of Print in South Asia'. In Nigel Crook (ed.). 1996. *The Transmission of Knowledge in South Asia*. Delhi: Oxford University Press, 62–97.
Robinson, Francis. 2002. *The 'Ulama of Farangi Mahall and Islamic Culture in South Asia*. Lahore: Ferozsons.
Robson, James. c. 19 C. 'Introduction' to the English Translation of *Mishkāt ul Masābih*. Vol. 1, pp. xi-xv. Repr. Lahore: Sheikh Mohammad Ashraf, n.d.
Roy, Olivier. 1999. *The Failure of Political Islam*. Trans. from the French. Carol Volk. London: I.B. Tauris.
Roy, Olivier. 2004. *Globalized Islam: the Search for a New Umma. The CERI Series in Comparative Politics and International Studies*. New York: Columbia University Press.
Saeed, Abdullah. 2006. *Interpreting the Qur'an: Towards a Contemporary Approach*. London and New York: Routledge, Taylor and Francis.
Sageman, Mark. 2004. *Understanding Terror Networks*. Philadelphia: University of Pennsylvania Press.
Sageman, Mark. 2008. *Leaderless Jihād: Terror Networks in the Twenty-First Century*. Philadelphia: University of Pennsylvania Press.
Sageman, Mark. 2011. 'The Turn to Political Violence in the West'. In Coolsaet 2011: 117–129.
Salem, Elie Adib .1956. *Political Theory and Institutions of the Khawarij*. Baltimore, MD: John Hopkins University Press.
Sallām, Abū 'Ubayd al-Qāsim ibn. 839. *The Abrogating and Abrogated in the Koran: Al-Naskh wa'l-mansukh fi'l-Qur'an* . (ed.) Fuat Sezgin. Cambridge: E.J.W. Gibb Memorial with Book Production Consultants.
Sanyal, Usha. 1996. *Devotional Islam and Politics in British India: Ahmad Riza Khan Barelvi and His Movement, 1870–1920*. New Delhi: Oxford University Press.
Sardar, Ziauddin. 2011. *Reading the Qur'an: the Contemporary Relevance of the Sacred Text of Islam*. London: Hurst & Company.
Sauer, Rebecca. 2014. '*Tafsīr* between Law and Exegesis: the case of Q. 49: 9 (the Rebellion Verse/ *āyat al-baghy*)'. In Cörke, Andreas and Pink, Johanna 2014: 223–250.
Schacht, Joseph F. 1950. *Origins of Muhammadan Jurisprudence*. Oxford: Clarendon Press.

Sell, Edward. 1880. *The Faith of Islam*. London: Kegan Paul, Trench, Trubner & Co Ltd. 2nd ed. 1896.

Shāfi'ī, Muḥammad bin Idrīs al-. c. 9 C. *Ash-Shafi'i's risālah: Basic Ideas with English Translation of the Chapters on an-nāsikh wa-al-mansūkh*. Trans. Khalil I. Semaan. Lahore: Sheikh Muhammad Ashraf, 1961. Repr. 1974.

Shah, Aqil. 2014. *The Army and Democracy: Military Politics in Pakistan*. Cambridge, MA: Harvard University Press.

Shāhjahānpūrī, Abū Salmān.1984. *Abū'l Kalām Āzād: Ba haithiyyat mufassir-o muḥaddith* [Urdu: Azad as exegete and hadith scholar]. Karachi: Idara Tasnif-o-Tahqiq Pakistan.

Shāhjahānpūrī, Abū Salmān 2008. *Barr-e a'ẓam Hind-o-Pākistān kī shar'ī ḥaithiyyat* [Urdu: the Status of the Indo-Pakistan Subcontinent in Islamic Legal Theory]. Lahore: Ishtiaq A. Mushtaq.

Shahzad, Syed Saleem. 2011. *Inside al-Qaeda and the Taliban: Beyond Bin Laden and 9/11*. London: Pluto Press.

Shaikh, Muhammad Hajjan. 1986. *Maulana Ubaid Allah Sindhi: a Revolutionary Scholar*. Islamabad: National Institute of Historical and Cultural Research.

Shaltūt, Maḥmud. 1948. *al-Qur'ān wa 'l qitāl* [Arabic: Translated as 'Koran and Fighting']. In Peters 1996: 60–101.

Shamazaī, Niẓāmuddīn. 2012. *'Aqīdah Ẓahūr-e-Mahdī* [Urdu: the Belief in the Emergence of the Mehdi]. Karachi: Maktaba Shamazai and Maktaba Imam Mohammad.

Sharify-Funk, Meena. 2008. *Encountering the Transnational: Women, Islam and the Politics of Interpretation*. Hampshire: Ashgate.

Sheikh, Mona Kanwal. 2016. *Guardian of God: Inside the Religious Mind of the Taliban*. New Delhi: Oxford University Press.

Shepard, William E. 1987. 'Islam and Ideology: Towards a Typology', *International Journal of Middle Eastern Studies* 19: 307–336.

Sindhī, 'Ubaydullāh. 1933. *Dhātī Diary* [Urdu: Personal Diary]. Lahore: Adabistan, 1946.

Sindhī, 'Ubaydullāh. 1941. *Shāh Walīullāh aur unkī siyāsī taḥrīk* [Urdu: Walīullāh and his Political Movement]. Lahore: Sind Sagar Academy.

Sivan, Emmanuel. 1985. *Radical Islam: Medieval Theology and Modern Politics*. New Haven: Yale University Press.

Skinner, Quentin. 1969. 'Meaning and Understanding in the History of Ideas', *History and Theory* 8:1: 3–53.

Smith, Wilfred Cantwell. 1981. 'The'*Ulama* in Indian Politics'. In *On Understanding Islam: Selected Studies*. The Hague: Mouton.

Sprenger, A. 1856. 'On the Origin and Progress of Writing Down Historical Facts Among the Musalmans', *Journal of the Asiatic Society* 4: 303–329 & 5: 375–381.

Stark, Ulrike. 2008. *An Empire of Books: the Naval Kishore Press and the Diffusion of the Printed Word in Colonial India*. Delhi: Permanent Black.

Stephens, Julia. 2013. 'The Phantom Wahabi: Liberalism and the Muslim fanatic in Mid-Victorian India', *Modern Asian Studies* 47:1 (Jan): 22–52.

Sufi, Ghulām.M.D. 1941. *Al-Minhāj: Being the Evolution of Curriculum in the Muslim Educational Instutions of India*. Delhi: Idarah-i Adabiyat-i Dilli, 1977.

Sulaiman, Mahmud bin. 2013. *Ẓahūr-e-Mahdī: kab? kahā̃? aur kis ṭarah* [Urdu: The Emergence of the Mahdi: When? Where? And How?]. Karachi: Maktaba ul Hafeez.

Sulamī (al), 'Ali Ibn Ṭāhir.1105. *Kitāb ul jihād* in Christie 2015: 1–365.

Suyūṭī, Jalāl al-Dīn. c. 15 C. *Al-Itqān fī 'ulūm al-Qur'ān* (the Perfect Guide to the Sciences of the Qur'an). Trans. into English by Muneer Fareed. http//:rahnuma.org/religion/Quran/Aliqtanfiulumalqurn-Suyuti English.pdf Retrieved on 19 October 2017.

Ṭabarī (al), Ja'far bin Muḥammad bin Jarīr. c. 10 C. a. *Kitāb ul jihād* Trans. from Arabic by Ibrahim, Yasir S. 2007. *Al Tabari's Book of Jihad: a translation from the Original Arabic.* Canada, Queenston, Ontario: The Edwin Mellen Press.

Ṭabarī, al-. c. 10 C b. *Ta'rīkh-e-Ṭabarī: Ta'rīkh al-umam wa'l mulūk* [Arabic: History of the Nations and Kings]. Trans. From Arabic to Urdu. By Syed Mohammad Ibrahim and Habib ur Rahman Siddiqui Karachi: Nafees Academy, 1977.

Taimūr, Amīr. c. 14 C.*Tuzk-e-taimūri* [Memoirs of Taimur] Trans. from the Persian into Urdu by Abū Hāshim Nadwī. Lahore: Sang-e-Meel, 1985.

Talbot, Ian and Kamran, Tahir. 2016. *Lahore in the Time of the Raj.* Gurgaon, Haryana: Viking Penguin.

Tarjumān. 1948. *Tarjumān al- Qur'ān.* 31:2 (June). Lahore: Jamā'at-i-Islāmī.

T͟hānēsārī, Ja'far. 1879. *Kālā pānī (Tawarīkh 'Ajīb)* [Urdu: Black Waters: A Strange History]. Lahore: Sang-e-Meel, 1981.

Thapar, Romila. 2013. 'Somnatha'. In *Readings in Early Indian History.* New Delhi: Oxford University Press. pp. 454–476.

Therborn, Goran. 2003. 'Entangled Modernities', *European Journal of Social Theory* 6:3: 293–305.

Thorup, Mikkel. 2010. *An Intellectual History of Terror: War, Violence and the State.* London: Routledge.

Tritton, Arthur Stanley. 1930. *The Caliphs and their Non-Muslim Subjects: a Critical Study of the Covenant of 'Umar.* London: Frank Cass & Co. Ltd., 1970.

Troll, Christian. 1978. *Sayyid Aḥmad Khān: a Reinterpretation of Muslim Theology.* Karachi: Oxford University Press, 1979.

Troll, Christian. (ed.). 1982. *Islam in India: Studies and Commentaries.* Vol. 1. New Delhi: Vikas Publishing House, Pvt. Ltd.

Uthmānī, Taqī. 1999. *'Iqdāmī aor difā 'ī jihād: ēk maktūb aor uskā jawāb'.* [Urdu: Aggressive and Defensive Jihad: a Letter and its Reply] In *Islām aur jiddat pasandī* [Islam and Modernity]. Karachi: Maktaba-I Dar al-'ulum' in http://www.muftitaqiusmani.com/News Events.aspx?ID=14. Retreived on 11 October 2017.

Veer, Peter van der. 2001. *Imperial Encounters: Religion and Modernity in India and Britain.* Princeton and Oxford: Princeton University Press.

Vishanoff, David R. 2011. *The Formation of Islamic Hermeneutics: How Sunni Legal Theorists Imagined a Revealed Law.* New Haven, Connecticut: American Oriental Society.

Volpi, Frédéric (ed.). 2011. *Political Islam: a Critical Reader.* London: Routledge.

Volpi, Frédéric. 2011 a. 'Introduction: Critically Studying Political Islam'. In Volpi 2011: 1–11.

Waardenburg, Jacques. 2002. *Islam: Historical, Social, and Political Perspectives.* Berlin: Walter de Gruyter.

Wadud, Amina. 1992. *Qur'an and Woman: Rereading the Sacred Text from a Woman's Perspective.* New York: Oxford University Press, 1999.

Walīullāh, Shāh. *Fauz. al-Fauz al-kabīr fī uṣul al-tafsīr* [Persian: The Great Success in the Principles of Exegesis] trans. from Persian to Urdu by Rashīd Aḥmad Anṣārī Delhi: Maktaba Burhan, Urdu Bazar, 1955.

Walīullāh, Shāh. *Budūr. Al-Budūr al-Bāzighah* [Arabic: The Full Moon] trans. into English by G.N. Jalbani. Islamabad: National Hijra Council, 1985.
Walīullāh, Shāh. c. 18 C. *Maktūbāt* [Persian: letters]. In Niẓāmī 1950.
Walīullāh, Shāh. *Waṣīyyat. 'Waṣīyyat Nāmah* [Persian: Will of Shāh Walīullāh]. Trans. M. Ayub Qadri. In *Majmu'ā Waṣāyā' Arba' 'ā*. Hyderabad: Shah Waliullah Academy, n.d.
Walīullāh, Shāh. 1996. *Hujjat. Hujjat Allāh al-Bāligha*. Trans. from the Arabic as *The Conclusive Argument from God* by Hermansen, Marcia K. Leiden: E.J. Brill.
Warraq, Ibn. 1998. *The Origins of the Koran: Classic Essays on Islam's Holy Book*. Amherst, New York: Prometheus Books.
Warren Alan. 2000. *Waziristan: the Faqir of Ipi, and the Indian Army: the North West Frontier Revolts of 1936–37*. Karachi: Oxford University Press.
Wasti, Syed Razi. (ed.).1968 a. *Syed Ameer Ali on Islamic History and Culture*. Karachi: People's Publishing House.
Wasti, Syed Razi (ed.). 1968 b. *Memoirs and Other Writings of Syed Ameer Ali*. Karachi: People's Publishing House.
Wasti, Syed Tanwir. 2006. 'The Political Aspirations of Indian Muslims and the Ottoman Nexus', *Middle Eastern Studies* 42: 5 (Sep): 709–722.
Watt, W. Montgomery. 2006. *The Formative Period of Islamic Thought*. Oxford: Oneworld. First South Asian edition.
Wendell, Charles. 1978. *Five Tracts of Hasan al-Banna (1906–1949)*. Trans. from the Arabic and annotated. Berkeley and Los Angeles: University of California Press.
Westphal, Merold. 2009. *Whose Community? Which Interpretation?: Philosophical Hermeneutics for the Church*. Michigan, Grand Rapids: Baker Academics.
Wiktorowicz, Quintan. 2011. 'A Genealogy of Radical Islam'. In Volpi 2011: 271–295.
Wilson, John. 2011. *Caliphate's Soldiers: the Lashkar-e-Tayyaba's Long War*. Delhi: Amyrillis.
Yasmeen, Samina. 2017. *Jihad and Dawah*. London: Hurst.
Yavari, Neguin. 2014. '*Tafsīr* and the Mythology of Islamic fundamentalism'. In Cörke, Andreas and Johanna Pink 2014: 289–319.
Ye'or, Bat. 1980. *The Dhimmi: Jews and Christians Under Islam* trans. from the French. David Maisel, Paul Fenton and David Littman. Cranbury, N.J.: Associated University Presses, 1985.
Yūsufza'ī, Faḍl Muḥammad. 1999. *Da'wat-e-Jihād: faḍā'il, Masā'il, Wāqi'āt* [Urdu: The Invitation for Jihad: Blessings, Problems and Events]. Karachi: Walī Ullāh 'Uthmānī.
Yusufzai, Rahimullah .2008. 'A Who is Who of the Insurgency in Pakistan's NWFP: Part-1 North and South Waziristan', *Terrorism Monitor* 6 (18) http://www.jamestown.org/single/?tx_ttnews[tt_news]=5169&no_cache=1#.U3tC6bFR-bo (20 May 2014).
Yusufzai, R .2009. 'A Who's Who of the Insurgency in Pakistan's North-West Frontier Province: Part Two – FATA excluding North and South Waziristan' *Terrorism Monitor* 7 (4) http://www.jamestown.org/single/?no_cache=1&tx_ttnews[tt_news]=34574#.U3tAtbFR-bo (20 May 2014).
Zadeh, Travis .2015. 'The Fātiḥa of Salmān al-Fārisī and the Modern Controversy over Translating the Qur'an'. In Burge 2015: 375–375–420.
Zaheeruddin, Munshi. 1788. '*Muqaddimah*' [Urdu: Preface] to *Tarjumah-e-Qur'ān* by Shāh 'Abdul Qādir. Kānpur: Nawal Kishor.
Zakariyya, Muḥammad. 1975. *Fitnah-e-Mawdūdiyyat* [Urdu: The Evil of Mawdūdīsm]. Lahore: Makataba ul Qasim.

Zakariyya, Muḥammad.1987. *Āp Bītī* [Urdu: Biography] .2 Vols. Karachi: Maktabat ul Shaikh.

Zaman, M. Qasim. 2002. *The Ulema in Contemporary Islam: Custodians of Change.* Princeton: Princeton University Press.

Zaman, M. Qasim. 2009. 'Studying Hadith in a madrasa in the Early Twentieth Century'. In Metcalf 2009: 225–239.

Zaman, M. Qasim. 2012. *Modern Islamic Thought in a Radical Age: Religious Authority and Internal Criticism.* Cambridge: Cambridge University Press.

Ẓawāhirī, Ayman al-.2008. *Tala'a annaharo faṭfi ul qindīlā* (The Morning has Dawned so Put off the Torches) trans. into Urdu by Maulana Abdus Samad as *Supaēdā-e-Saḥer aor Ṯimṯimātā Chirāgh.* Idara Hittin.

Zelin, Aaron Y. 2012. '*al-Farida al Ggha'iba* and al-Sadat's Asssassination, a 30 Year Retrospective', *International Journal for Arab Studies* 3:2 (July): 1–34.

Zilli, Ishtiyaq Ahmad (ed.). 2007. *The Mughal State and Culture 1556–1598: Selected Letters and Documents from Manshaat-i-Namakin.* New Delhi: Manohar.

Zubayri, M. Amin. 1934. *Ḥayāt-i Muḥsin* [Urdu: The Life of Muhsin]. Aligarh: Aligarh Muslim University.

Index

The most well-known versions of the names of people have been used. In some cases, it may not be the last name of the person (e.g., Sayyid Aḥmad Khān is known as Sir Sayyid rather than Khan).

Abbasides 17
Abdālī, Aḥmad Shāh 94–97, 166
Abdūh, Muḥammad 29, 46, 119, 255
'Abdul 'Azīz, Shāh 22f., 51, 73, 77, 89f., 99–103, 109, 111, 141, 232, 245
'Abdul Bārī Farangī Maḥallī 77f., 121, 137, 146
'Abdul Ḥayy 89, 102, 109, 121, 147
'Abdul Qādir, Shāh 36, 39f., 89, 104f., 145
'Abdul Raḥīm, Shāh 86, 90, 94
'Abdullāh Yūsuf 'Alī 38
Abrogation (see *naskh*) 40, 78–81, 197, 224, 249, 282
Abū Ḥanīfah (also spelled Hanifa) 54, 59, 66f., 86, 88, 125, 128
Abū Hurayrah 54, 75, 187, 280f.
Abu'l Fazl *(Faḍl)* 63
Afghānī, Jamāl al-Dīn 30, 141
Afghanistan 1, 5, 7, 13, 24, 94, 106, 110, 141, 144, 147f., 150, 178, 191, 193f., 200, 205–208, 211–213, 217, 220f., 226–231, 237, 240, 242, 245f., 249, 255, 257f., 261
Aḥmad Uddīn Amritsarī 56
Ahmadi (s) 143, 155, 159, 237
Akbar, Jalāluddīn 63, 76, 138
Al-Azhar 9, 233
al-Zarqāwī, Abū Muṣ'ab 208
al-Ẓawāhirī, Ayman 16, 22, 24, 206–209
'Alī Ibn Abī Ṭālib 17, 282
America (see United States)
Apologist (s) 6, 16, 51, 65, 106f., 113, 131
– Apologia 9. 169
Arabic 8, 22, 29, 32f., 39f., 52, 70, 72, 76f., 94f., 105, 119, 122, 126, 137, 155, 165, 196, 222
Army (of Pakistan) 137, 247
Ash'arī, Abū 'l Ḥasan al- 38, 75, 128, 252
Aslam Jayrājpurī 56
Assassin 17, 247
Aurangzēb 'Ālamgīr 63, 68
Authority:
– fragmentation of 16, 18, 141, 151, 251f.
– state/political 89, 93, 96, 132, 141, 146, 153, 186, 204, 209, 251, 257, 301
– traditional 28, 75, 85, 153, 232, 244, 280f., 292
Ayūb Khān (President) 175
Āzād, Abū 'l Kalām 11, 22f., 30, 32, 36, 138, 143, 147–149, 152, 155–161, 187, 250, 284, 288, 303
'Azzām, 'Abdullāh 7, 22, 24, 200, 206f., 214, 227

Bābar, Ẓahīruddīn 62f., 288
Balakot 105, 138
Bannā, Ḥasan al- 194–196, 204, 234, 256
Barēlwī, Sayyid Aḥmad 13, 23, 89, 100, 105–111, 114, 121, 134, 138, 150, 166, 231, 243, 256, 261f.
Bible 26f., 171, 199
Bosnia 7, 193, 205, 226, 237
Britain (UK) ix, 18, 157, 201, 234

Caliph 42, 54, 57, 65, 129, 162, 244
Caliphate 92f., 146, 154–157, 190, 201, 212, 250
Chakṛālawī, 'Abdullāh 56
Chirāgh 'Alī 11, 23, 31, 34, 46, 53–55, 114f., 122–127, 130, 153, 255
Christianity/Christians 25, 31, 35, 43f., 52, 67, 79, 82, 84, 136, 159, 228, 236
– Church 26
– Missionaries 125
Collateral damage 7

https://doi.org/10.1515/9783110716986-018

Colonial 16, 21, 23, 78, 89, 100, 112 f., 146, 151 f., 157, 160 – 166, 192, 228
- anti-colonial vi, 16, 23, 89, 110, 113 – 115, 133 – 192, 195 f., 231, 248, 259, 301
- colonialism 13, 103, 115, 130, 141, 157, 193, 237, 259
- post-colonial 26 f., 100, 112, 248
- powers 71, 78, 113, 152, 156 f., 248
- rulers 55, 112, 142, 146, 151, 158, 166, 222

Commentary (see exegesis) 78 – 81, 116 f., 159 f., 176, 179 f., 182, 188 f., 197, 203, 217, 223 f., 282

Companions (*ashab*) 8, 34, 41, 49 f., 81, 202, 281

Crusade (s) (er) 5, 7, 84

Curriculum 70, 77, 79, 90, 237

Dārul Ḥarb 16, 23, 61, 83, 99 f., 102, 125, 135, 140, 145

Dārul Aymān (*Aman, 'Ahd*) 83, 125, 147, 174,

Dārul Islām 16, 23, 61, 83, 99 f., 102, 125, 135, 140, 145

Dārul Ṣulh 83

Delhi 69, 71 f., 78, 90, 95 – 97, 99, 101, 115, 136 f., 142, 166, 168, 212, 235, 242, 244

Democracy 176

Deoband (i) 23, 54, 69, 72 f., 77, 98, 119, 134, 138, 142 f., 145 f., 148 – 150, 155, 159, 161, 211, 219, 241 – 246, 257, 262

Dhimmī (s) 65 – 67, 81, 87 f., 97, 99, 105, 117, 130, 178, 224

Diaspora 10, 234, 255

Dūdū Miyā 134

Education
- British colonial/modern 18 – 2, 30, 78, 112, 115, 120, 144, 155, 168
- Madrasa 27, 75, 77, 79 f., 86, 257
- prominent Muslims' experience of 78, 167 f., 176, 186, 191, 196, 219, 258, 260 – 262
- Ottoman 71
- Safavid 71

Egypt 39, 119, 157, 186, 194, 201 f., 207, 210, 219, 232, 245 – 247, 255 – 257, 259 f., 262 f.

Enlightenment 20, 29

Exegeses (italics are for books)
- Azād (*Tarjumān*) 22, 156 – 160, 251
- *Bayḍāwī* 17, 28 f., 77, 79 f.
- Ghāmidī 237 – 239
- Ḥāfiẓ Sa'īd (*Tawbah*) 12, 22, 211, 216 – 219, 249
- *Ibn Kathīr* 28 f., 80 – 82, 158, 202 f., 205
- Iṣlāḥī (*Tadabbur*) 45, 178 – 181, 250
- *Jalālayn* 28, 77 – 79, 248
- Kashhāf 77
- *Madārik* 77
- Mas'ūd Aẓhar (*Fatḥ*) 12, 22, 211, 222 – 226, 249
- Mawdūdī (*Tafhīm*) 22 f., 168, 172, 176 f., 181, 191, 198, 249
- Murād Ullāh (*Murādiyah*) 139, 283
- opinion (*bi'l rāy*) 28, 31
- Parwēz (*Maṭālib*) 22, 31, 186 f.,189, 250
- Quṭb (*Ẓilāl*) 22, 22, 191, 196, 198 – 200, 255 f.
- Rāzi (*Kabīr*) 28 f., 78
- Science of exegesis 42, 44, 90 f., 203, 305
- Scientific 30
- Shāh 'Abdul 'Azīz 21 f., 51, 73, 77, 89 f., 99 – 103, 109, 111, 232, 245
- Shāh 'Abdul Qādir 36, 39 f., 89, 104 f., 110, 145, 150
- Sindhī 142 f., 145, 152 – 156
- Sir Sayyid 22, 30 f., 35, 42, 52 – 55, 72, 106, 109, 114 – 121
- *Ṭabarī* 28 f., 37, 52, 55, 65, 83 f.
- teaching of 28, 71, 77 – 80
- traditional (*bi'il ma 'thūr*) 28 f.
- Uthmānī 145, 284
- Waheeduddin Khan 22, 31, 181 – 183, 235, 250
- *Zamakshari* 28

Faḍā'il-e-jihād 60, 220 f., 228

Faqīr (s) 106, 151, 282

Faqīr of Ipī 14, 151 f.

Farāhī, Ḥamīduddīn 45, 168, 238

Farāj, 'Abd-al Salām 16, 201 – 204, 206 f., 227, 232

Farangī Maḥall 72, 147 f.

Fārūq Khān 239 – 241

FATA 106, 139, 231
Fatwās (Fatāwā)
- 'Abdul 'Azīz 89, 99–102, 111
- 'Abdul Ḥayy 147
- Aḥmad Raḍa Khān 149
- *'Alamgīrī* 66–68, 86–88, 90, 140
- anti-terrorism 232 f., 242
- Azzām 206 f.
- Bin Laden 21, 240
- Deoband 54, 69, 72 f., 77, 119, 134, 138, 142 f., 148–150, 155, 159, 161, 242, 245
- Gangohī 146 f.
- *Hidāyah* 65–67, 86, 140
- Khilafat Movement 99, 146–148
- Mutiny 135–137, 138
- Ottoman 162
- Shamazaī 209
- Ṭahīr ul Qadrī 243,
Fazlur Rahman 4, 16, 28, 43, 47, 57, 76, 129, 165, 202, 234, 243, 255
Feminist criticism 26 f., 33
Fitnah 4, 8, 20, 31, 36, 48, 78–81, 104 f., 116, 137, 145, 169 f., 176 f., 179, 181 f., 188, 223 f.

Gadamer, Hans-Georg 25–27, 29, 38
Gandhi, M.K. 143, 155, 159, 237
Gangohī, Rashīd Aḥmad 73, 138, 142, 146 f.
Ghāmidī, Jāwēd Aḥmad 33, 35, 57 f., 181, 237–239, 241, 250

Hadith 6 f., 28, 40–43, 45, 61, 103, 118, 124, 130,149, 152, 158, 173 f., 244 f., 262, 280–282
- deniers/doubters of 43, 49–60, 125, 186–188, 301
- in South Asia 50–60, 69–73, 90, 230
- interpretation of vi, 11, 14, 23, 25, 29, 49–60
- jihad in vi, 8, 10, 73–76, 85, 109, 127, 157, 170, 174, 194 f., 201
- Western scholars 49–52, 55, 292, 303
Ḥafiz Sa'id 11 f., 22, 24, 211–219, 225, 249 f.
Ḥājjī Turangzai 14, 150
Ḥālī, Altāf Ḥussain 54, 72, 116, 119, 121, 129, 136, 164, 293
Ḥasan Jān 242

Hermeneutic (s) 5, 14, 25 f., 31 f., 37, 47 f., 60 f., 152, 154, 158, 238, 290, 298, 300, 304 f.,
Hermeneutical devices vi, 11 f., 23 f., 26, 32, 35, 40, 44–48, 51, 59 f., 76, 78–82, 85, 90, 105, 116–119, 124, 132, 159 f., 171, 176–189, 197–204, 217, 222–225, 234, 236–241, 262
- *asbābul nuzūl* (causes of revelation) 44 f., 48, 79–81, 119, 145, 160, 174, 183, 234, 250, 293, 302
- emphasis 60
- ideological imperative/assumptions 25, 27, 33, 48, 60, 76, 80 f., 117, 160 f., 176–183, 188–190, 198, 203, 215, 217, 223–225, 231, 236, 239, 249 f., 258
- *naskh* (abrogation) vi, 9, 40–46, 54, 78–81, 85, 91, 132, 154 f., 184, 203, 217, 224, 236, 249, 282
- semantic expansion 35 f., 48, 78, 79–81, 91, 119, 154, 159, 169 f., 172, 176 f., 182, 184, 187 f., 197–199, 222–226, 236
- *takhṣīṣ* (specification) 21, 45 f., 48, 59, 82, 117
Hindu (s) 64, 66–69, 86 f., 95–97, 112, 115, 118, 128, 136, 144, 146, 157–159, 161–165, 170, 199, 214–216, 236, 247
Hinduism 19, 39, 158 f., 168, 189, 236
Ḥudaybiyyah 21, 75, 78, 80, 85, 160, 174, 218, 227, 250
Humanist (-ism) 57, 103, 128, 133, 258
Hunter, William 109, 120 f., 125, 140 f.

Ibn Rushd (Averroes) 84 f.
Ibn Taymiyyah 9, 163, 202 f., 209 f., 213, 255
Ideas, history of (see intellectual history)
Identity
- change of 2, 112, 138, 259
- other 42, 65, 140, 178
- Muslim 2, 20, 40, 65, 138, 192, 252
- national(ist) 138
Ideology 6, 19–21, 27, 29, 36, 39, 103, 109, 163, 169, 176, 190, 209, 214, 222, 243
- ideological 2, 5 f., 16, 19 f., 29, 39, 140, 163, 169, 189, 213, 236, 239
- criticism 275 f.

– ideological assumptions (see hermeneutical devices)
Işlāḥī, Amīn Aḥsan 45, 168, 178–181
India (also see South Asia/Subcontinent) 1–5, 12 f., 18 f., 21–23, 29 f., 32, 39 f., 51 f., 55, 62–67, 69–73, 76–78, 86, 90, 94–100, 102–105, 107–116, 118, 120 f., 124 f., 129, 133, 135–141, 143–152, 154, 156–158, 162, 164–166, 171–173, 175, 181, 184, 186, 193, 196, 199, 205, 209–216, 218–221, 226, 230, 233, 235, 237, 240–242, 245–248, 250, 255, 261, 263, 281 f.
Intellectual history 2, 11, 14–17, 22, 204, 251, 262
Internet 250, 252, 257, 259
Interpretation (s) (also see hermeneutical)
– Bible 26 f., 171, 199
– communities of 26
– Hadith vii, 23, 25, 49–60
– ideological 27, 33, 47
– Jihad 6 f., 10–16, 20, 22, 24, 46, 60, 74 f., 79–82, 103, 108, 111, 126, 131 f., 152, 156 f., 166, 168, 178, 186, 190, 194, 196, 204, 237, 241, 246–252, 262
– miscellaneous 2–5, 14, 18, 20–22, 25–32, 38, 44–51, 60 f., 72, 77, 80, 98, 102, 105, 113, 115 f., 119 f., 125, 134, 155, 159, 161, 164, 166, 167, 170 f., 174, 178, 181, 186 f., 189 f., 195, 205, 213, 215, 219, 225, 235, 238–240, 242 f., 248–259, 263
– mystical 38, 194
– Qur'an 3, 8, 10, 12, 20, 22–25, 27 f., 30–33, 35–40, 42 f., 45–47, 57 f., 76 f., 85, 89 f., 102–104, 116, 119, 139, 145, 152, 154, 158, 166, 170–172, 176, 178, 181, 186, 190 f., 196, 199, 203 f., 211, 213, 216, 219, 222, 225, 234 f., 238 f., 241, 282
– validity of 25
Iqbāl, Muḥammad 38, 56, 163–165, 186, 190
ISI 12, 212, 220, 261
Islam (see also Muslim)
– fundamentalist 2, 6, 19, 29, 103, 155, 255, 260
– political 1, 6 f., 124, 176, 194
– revivalist 8, 19, 29, 69, 78, 103, 156, 190, 192, 209, 249, 255
– Shī'a 1, 8, 71, 97 f., 110, 131, 141, 208, 211, 233, 247, 256
– *Sufī* (mystical) 70, 76 f., 193, 243
– Sunnī 5–7, 16, 32, 48–52, 57, 62, 69, 76, 79, 86, 90, 98, 125, 131, 149, 209, 232, 252, 256
Islamic State (IS)/Daesh xv, 7, 166, 178, 214
Islamism 1 f., 7, 149
Islamist 1–3, 5–9, 11 f., 15–21, 23 f., 33, 36, 48, 59, 74–76, 82 f., 96, 98, 103, 108, 120, 133, 141, 145, 156, 166, 167 f., 172, 184, 190 f., 193–196, 200–206, 208 f., 211–214, 218, 225 f., 228, 231–235, 237, 239–241, 243–247, 249, 251, 253–260, 263, 281
Ismā'īl, Muḥammad 89, 108 f., 121 f., 154
Ismā'īlī (s) 17, 28
Israel 18, 193, 196, 201, 204 f., 208, 218 f., 232, 237, 246, 257, 263

Jamā't-i-Islāmī 168, 175, 177 f., 256
Jamā't ud Dā 'wah (JUD) 13
Jew (s) 5, 35, 43 f., 70, 79, 82, 85, 123, 145, 157, 215, 217, 228, 230, 239, 241, 264–268, 272
Jihad (see also *Qitāl*)
– aggressive (*jihād-e-iqdāmī*) 1, 5–10, 13, 21, 36, 48, 51, 62, 68, 75, 79–82, 84, 93, 98–100, 104, 106, 126, 140, 169,175 190, 194, 196 f., 204, 213, 216, 219 f., 225 f., 228, 231, 239, 251
– books on 5, 83–85
– fighting 4, 8, 10, 21, 88, 91, 96, 102, 156, 189, 203, 248, 280
– instructions 5, 61, 70, 84, 86–88, 106, 125, 137 f., 145–148, 156, 168, 170, 178, 206 f., 209, 214, 217, 221, 226, 231, 237, 240 f., 249, 251, 258
– meaning of 3 f., 10 f., 23, 37 f., 46, 59 f., 76, 102, 123, 140, 169, 171, 184, 222 f., 240, 248
– moral improvement 11, 31, 36, 75 f., 96, 110, 113, 127, 131, 195, 198, 204, 220, 237, 244, 281

- self-defence 8–10, 45, 60, 110, 114–118, 122–126, 130, 132, 160, 180, 183, 189, 236, 238 f., 242, 250, 255
Judaism 42, 159, 189
jizyah 5, 16, 21, 48, 66–68, 81, 86 f., 117 f., 124, 127, 160 f., 173, 177, 180, 182 f., 189, 216 f., 224, 229, 239, 269

Kashmir 7, 12 f., 24, 149, 167, 173 f., 205 f., 212 f., 215–220, 226, 230, 237, 241, 247, 249, 257, 261–263
Khaddūrī, Majīd 9
Khairābādī, Faḍl ul Ḥaq 136 f.
Khalīfa 'Abdūl Ḥakīm 233
Kharijites 17, 184, 193, 244 f., 247, 252, 263
Khilafat Movement 100, 103, 115, 146, 157, 159
Khusraw, Amīr 62
KP (also see NWFP) 13, 23, 107
Kurd(ish) 7

Lahore 30, 69, 112, 114, 143, 165, 167, 171, 196, 214, 233, 243, 261, 282
Lashkar-e-Ṭayyabah (LeT) 6, 12, 62, 151, 214, 219
Lexis/semantics vi, 28, 32–38
Liberal
- intellectuals 167
- Muslims 237
- values 103, 251, 258
- Liberalism 228
London xiv, 1, 7, 52, 129, 235, 243
Lot (the Prophet) 36 f., 169, 239
Lughā (see lexis)

Ma'anā (also see lexis) 28 f., 32
Madanī Ḥusain Aḥmad 111, 141, 144 f., 149, 152, 155
Madrasah xvi, 28, 72–80, 86, 90, 126, 138, 142 f., 145, 168, 228, 242 f., 246, 257, 261
Mahdī 131, 213, 229 f.
Mahdī 'Alī Khān 54, 120, 196
Maḥmūd al Ḥasan 141–144, 150, 153, 155, 161
Manāẓir Aḥsan Gīlānī 72, 142
Marhattās 63, 94–97, 101, 111
Mashriqī, Ināyatullah Khān 32, 163, 165
Mas'ūd Aẓhar 12, 22, 24, 211–213, 219, 225, 228, 249
Mawdūdī, Sayyid Abū'l A'lā 8, 10 f., 13, 16, 22 f., 31, 35, 48, 58 f., 69, 156, 167–179, 181–192, 194, 196, 199 f., 234 f., 238, 241, 249, 256
Mecca 4, 78, 80, 90, 131, 139 f., 145, 155, 173, 197, 227, 240, 268
Medīna 4, 48, 52, 131, 227, 243, 246, 265, 267, 276
Militant (s)/militancy x, 1, 5 f., 7, 10, 12 f., 16 f., 21, 23 f., 36, 44, 60, 75 f., 79, 81, 83, 85, 92, 102, 105 f., 108, 127, 134 f., 141, 145, 153 f., 157, 165 f., 170, 184, 190 f., 203, 206–215, 218 f., 221 f., 228, 331 f., 237–250, 254, 257–263, 281
Mirzā, Ghulām Aḥmad 114, 131 f., 136, 151, 170, 189, 228–230, 237, 282
Modernity 2, 6, 14, 17–20, 23, 26, 29, 78, 103, 112 f., 132–134, 165, 190, 195, 248, 252, 255 f.
Mohamed Ali (of Comrade fame) 103 f., 143, 162
Momin, Momin Khān 109
Mubārakpūrī, Shaikh 'Abdul Raḥmān 245
Mughal 62 f., 68, 72, 78, 93 f., 97, 135, 138, 146, 229, 240
Muḥammad 'Alī (Lahori) 103 f., 143, 162 f.
Muir, Sir William 30, 52 f., 115
Mullā Ṣadrā 37
Mullah (s) 13, 150 f., 226
Musharraf, Pervez 73, 149, 208 f., 211, 213, 228, 242
Muslim (s)
- Brotherhood 193 f., 196, 201
- early (Salafi) 2, 9 f., 29 f., 45, 47, 57, 73 f., 89, 124, 152, 234
- Modernist 20, 23, 34, 48, 51, 56, 65, 93, 112–133, 198, 248
- progressive ix, 2, 16, 21, 19–34, 47, 51, 112, 120, 141, 170, 248–256
- rulers of 7, 10, 17, 23 f., 62 f., 66–69, 86 f., 93, 111, 130, 135, 198, 202, 204, 214, 218, 225, 233, 246, 249, 251
- societies 3, 15, 132, 157, 165, 254 f., 257
- world 6, 8, 17, 30, 57, 76, 113

Mutiny (1857) 135 f.
Mystic (-ism) 2, 37 f., 70, 73, 76, 90, 94, 98, 102 f., 110, 113, 121, 137 m, 148, 164, 193, 229, 254

Nādir Shāh 95
Nadwī, Abū 'l Ḥasan 'Alī 13, 29, 54 f., 106, 108, 126 – 128, 181, 199
Nadwī, Sayyid Sulaimān 28, 54 f., 126 – 128
Nānawtwī, Muḥammad Qāsim 72, 119 f., 142 f., 153, 155
Naṣīḥat al muslimīn 110
Non-Muslims 1, 5, 11, 21, 24, 35 f., 44, 48, 59 f., 64 – 70, 75, 85, 95, 100, 105, 110 f., 117 f., 121, 123 – 128, 147, 154 – 157, 161, 168, 173 f., 175, 177
NWFP (North West Frontier Province) xiv. 13, 23, 107, 134, 151
Nūr Muḥammad 13, 213, 226, 228

Orient (al) 29, 113, 123 ,170
Osama bin Laden 7, 21, 143, 206 f., 209, 214, 240, 245
Ottoman 14, 44, 63 f., 71, 114, 125, 146, 149, 156, 159, 162

Pakistan 1 – 3, 5, 9, 13, 19, 23, 40, 58, 105 f., 110, 137 f., 141, 145, 148 – 151, 166, 167, 170, 172 – 175, 178, 180 f., 184, 186 f., 190 f., 193 f., 199, 205 – 209, 211 – 215, 219 – 221, 226, 228, 230, 233 f., 238, 240 – 243, 245 – 248, 250, 256 – 258, 261 – 263, 281 f.
Palestine 7, 157, 205 f., 217, 226, 249, 263
– Palestinians 193, 204, 206, 218, 255, 263
Parwēz, Ghulām Aḥmad 10, 22, 30 – 34, 36, 43, 45, 56, 59, 186 – 190, 233, 250
Pashtūn/Paṯhān 62, 110, 121, 150, 257
People of the Book (see Christians and Jews)
Persian language 22, 33, 38, 63 f., 89 f., 94 f., 97, 102, 104, 122, 126, 129, 139, 141, 147, 154, 162 f., 200, 282
Phulwārī, Jā'far Shāh 56
Poll tax (see *jizyah*)
Post-colonial (-ism) (see colonial)
Power
– miscellaneous 16, 18, 21, 25, 65, 67, 80 f., 91, 95, 97, 115, 132, 141, 145 f., 151, 159. 164 f., 166, 170 – 182, 187, 193, 196, 200, 205, 209, 214, 217, 222 – 224, 226 – 231, 252, 257
– Muslim 2, 8, 23, 68 f., 78, 83 f., 87 f., 93 – 101, 108, 111, 124, 145, 150, 153 f., 156 f., 163, 169 – 173, 177, 182, 197 f., 203 f., 222, 224, 228 f., 239, 248, 251
– Western/colonial 1, 29, 99, 111, 120, 148, 152, 156 f., 160, 190, 199, 209, 222, 226, 234, 256, 258
Printing 71 f., 77, 112
Prophet (Muhammad, PBUH) 8, 30, 35 f., 41 f., 49, 51, 53 – 59, 62, 73 – 75, 80, 82, 88, 92, 102, 117 f., 120, 122, 127, 129, 131, 139, 152, 157 f., 160, 173 f., 176, 179 f., 203, 205, 207, 217 – 219, 222, 225, 227, 233, 236, 238 f., 241, 243 f., 264 – 277, 280 f.
Punjab 106 f., 113 f., 122, 148 f., 213, 219, 230, 261, 282

Qādrī, Ṭāhirul 232, 243 – 245
Qaeda (al) 7, 16 f., 207, 255, 259
Qaraḍāwī, Yūsuf 8 f., 44, 59, 203 – 206, 218, 232 f.
Qitāl (see also Jihad) 3 f., 86, 103, 140, 169, 209, 212, 223, 236 f., 240, 244, 264, 269, 274, 276
Quṭb, Sayyid 8, 16, 20, 22, 31, 176, 178, 185 f., 190 f., 194, 196, 198 – 200, 202, 256
Qur'an
– Jihad 3 f., 8, 12, 20, 24, 44, 62, 79 – 82, 85, 90, 118, 123, 127, 130, 139, 145, 153 f., 160, 176, 180, 184, 195, 198, 215, 217, 227, 235 f., 239, 250, 264 – 281
– polygamy 32, 51, 113 f., 125, 130
– slavery 17, 32, 112 – 114, 123, 125, 130, 250
– translation of ix, 3, 20, 22, 24, 28 f., 35 – 40, 44, 60, 70 f., 77 f., 89 f., 103 – 105, 145, 158, 171, 197, 222, 227, 238, 264, 269, 283 f.

- women 19, 32–36, 42, 46 f., 70, 74, 80, 84, 87 f., 105, 112, 115, 117, 128, 153 f., 177 f., 197, 208, 220 f., 226 f., 234, 250, 256, 281 f.
Qurān, Ahl-i (movement) 55 f.

Radical (-ization) vi, 1–4, 8–10, 16 f., 19–24, 29, 33, 36, 59, 73 f., 96, 98, 103, 120, 133 f.,154, 156, 161, 172, 184, 190 f., 193–196, 200, 202, 205–213, 218–225, 231–246, 250–262
Radio 112, 167, 212
Rafī'uddīn, Shāh (Rafī' al-Dīn) 34, 39 f., 89, 104 f.
Raheel Sharif, General 247
Rājā Mahindra Pratāp 144, 154
Rānā Sangrām Singh 62
Ranjīt Singh 106
Rashīd Riḍā 29, 38, 46
Rational (-ity) 20 f., 28–30, 53–59, 71, 78, 116, 120, 125, 127 f., 164 f., 189, 252, 255

Sabbāh, Ḥasan Ibn 17
Saudi (Sa'ūdī) 6 f., 36, 38, 44, 178, 191, 200, 207, 214, 232, 246, 259
Sayyāf, 'Abdul Rabb Rasūl 207
Sayyid Aḥmad Khān (see Sir Sayyid)
Schacht, Joseph 49–51
Secular (-ism) 2, 11, 19, 58, 77, 112, 144, 162, 170, 195, 199, 209, 212, 228, 252
Semantics (see lexis)
September 11, 2001 (attacks of) 1, 183, 211, 216, 228, 232, 235, 237, 262
Shāfi'ī, Imām 40–42, 51, 84, 86, 124
Shaltūt, Mehmoud (Maḥmūd) 9, 228
Sharī'ah 17, 35, 66, 97, 103, 108, 147, 171, 179, 184, 198, 200, 212 f., 222, 232, 245
Shī'a 5, 8, 71, 97 f., 110, 131, 141, 208, 211, 233, 247, 256, 282
Shiblī, Nu'mānī 47, 54 f., 59, 65 f., 88, 114, 126–128, 183
Siffīn, Battle of 17
Sikh (s) 68, 89, 96, 101, 105–109, 111, 114, 121 f., 137, 144, 150, 163, 199, 231
Silk Letters Conspiracy 89, 134, 141, 143
Sindhī, 'Ubaydullāh 14, 22 f., 77 f., 89, 95 f., 98 f., 104, 143, 152–155
Sir Sayyid 30 f., 35, 42, 52–55, 72, 106, 109 f., 114–122, 126 f., 129 f., 132, 136, 155, 161, 186, 190, 228, 255
Somnath 64, 128
South Africa 31
South Asia (see also India) 3, 9–13, 16 f., 19–24, 28–32, 34, 36, 39, 43, 45, 61 f., 73 f., 79 f., 89, 94, 98, 105, 112 f., 134, 167, 193 f., 208, 221, 231, 234–236, 248 f., 262 f.
Specification (see hermeneutical devices)
Sprenger, Aloys 51 f.
Suicide attacks 7, 15, 17, 83, 96, 168, 204 f., 209, 212, 226, 231–233, 236 f., 240–243, 249
Sunnah 41, 183, 250, 282
Suyūṭī, Jalāl al-Dīn al- 42, 46, 77
Swat 106, 151, 212, 228, 239

Tafsīr (see exegesis)
Tāghūt 7, 16, 105, 172 f., 179, 184, 187 f., 199 f., 222
Taimūr, Amīr 62 f.
Takfīr 12, 17, 217, 225, 229, 245, 252
Taliban 10, 13, 16 f., 106, 150, 166, 178, 193, 205, 211 f., 220, 226, 228–230, 241–243, 246 f., 257
Tamannā 'Imādī 56
Taqwiyyat al Īmān 109
Ta'wīl 28, 77, 119, 155, 225
Terror 15, 216, 232
Terrorism 6, 110, 243
Terrorist 12, 17, 44, 65, 191, 201, 214, 232, 241, 243, 249, 253, 260
Thānawī, Ashraf 'Alī 149
Thānesāry, Ja'far 106 f., 109, 139
Theology 14, 22, 31 f., 71, 158, 169
Tribal Areas (see FATA)
Turkey 125, 141, 144, 146, 148, 155–157, 159, 162
Turks (-ish) 10, 62, 64, 143, 156, 164

'Umar Ibn al-Khaṭṭāb (Caliph) 52, 54, 57, 65, 81, 127, 129, 226, 257, 261, 280 f.
Umayyads 31, 49, 59, 76
United Kingdom (see Britain)
United Nations (UN) 214, 225, 234

United States (see also America) 196, 207, 212, 222, 246, 257, 263
Urdu 3, 20–22, 24, 28, 34, 36, 38–40, 52, 59, 70 f., 77–79, 86, 89, 101, 104, 107, 109, 114–116, 122, 124, 127, 129, 131, 136, 139, 141, 147 f., 155, 163–165, 168, 171, 176, 186, 208, 212, 221, 223, 226–228, 235 f., 240, 261, 282
'Uthman Ibn 'Affān (Caliph) 54
'Uthmānī, Shabbīr Aḥmad 145, 149, 242, 245
'Uthmānī, Tāqī 149, 242

Wadud, Amina 33 f., 47
Wahhāb, Ibn 'Abd al- 2, 134, 213
Wahhābīs (-ism) 2, 120 f., 134 f., 138 f., 150, 166
Waḥīduddīn Khān 10, 31, 34, 36, 110, 181–183, 185, 235, 237, 250
Walīullāh, Shāh 38, 42, 47, 53 f., 69, 71, 73, 77, 86, 88–100, 103–105, 109–111, 153, 155, 163
West (ern) 1, 7 f., 11, 18–20, 29 f., 55, 109, 115, 133 f., 137, 165, 190, 192, 196, 237, 246, 248, 255 f., 259

Yāghistān (see FATA)
Yūsufza'ī, Faḍl Muḥammad 13, 213, 227 f.

Zakariyya, Muḥammad 59, 69, 73, 220
Ziauddin Sardar 35, 38, 46 f., 234
Ziaul Haq 240, 257
Zoroastrian (s) 38 f., 85 f.

www.ingramcontent.com/pod-product-compliance
Lightning Source LLC
Chambersburg PA
CBHW030731230426
43667CB00007B/672
* 9 7 8 3 1 1 0 5 5 0 3 9 9 *